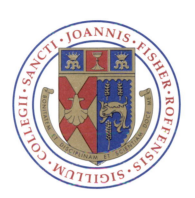

Lavery Library

St. John Fisher College
Rochester, New York

Latin America Writes Back

Hispanic Issues

HISPANIC ISSUES
VOLUME 28

Latin America Writes Back
Postmodernity in the Periphery
(An Interdisciplinary Perspective)

EMIL VOLEK

◆

EDITOR

HEIDI ANN GARCÍA AND BARBARA D. RIESS
COLLABORATORS

Routledge
Taylor & Francis Group

NEW YORK AND LONDON

The editors gratefully acknowledge assistance from the College of Liberal Arts and the Department of Spanish and Portuguese Studies at the University of Minnesota.

Published in 2002 by
Routledge
29 West 35th Street
New York, NY 10001
www.routledge-ny.com

Published in Great Britain by
Routledge
11 New Fetter Lane
London EC4P 4EE
www.routledge.co.uk

Printed on acid-free, 250-year life-paper.
Manufactured in the United States of America.

1 0 9 8 7 6 5 4 3 2 1

Library of Congress Cataloging-in-Publication Data

Latin America Writes Back. Postmodernity in the Periphery (An Interdisciplinary Perspective) / edited by Emil Volek.
p. cm.— (Hispanic Issues, v. 28)
Includes bibliographical references and index.
ISBN 0-8153-3256-4 (Hb: acid-free, 250-year-life paper)
Latin America. Volek, Emil. II Reference library of humanities. III. Reference library of humanities. Hispanic Issues; v. 28.

HT145.S6I24   2001
307.76'0946—dc21   00-065302

Hispanic Issues

Nicholas Spadaccini
Editor in Chief

Antonio Ramos-Gascón
Jenaro Talens
General Editors

Luis A. Ramos-García
Gwendolyn Barnes-Karol
Nelsy Echávez-Solano
Associate Editors

Contents

◆ Acknowledgments

In the first place, my thanks go to Jean Graham-Jones (Florida State University, Tallahassee), to Cynthia M. Tompkins (Arizona State), and to the group of doctoral students in Spanish at Arizona State and recent graduates who undertook the daunting task of translation: Mary Louise Babineau, Kristina Ríos de Lumbreras, Shara Moseley, Daniel Smith, Eva L. Ramírez (California Lutheran University), Barbara Riess (Allegheny College), and Sukhada Kilambi (Prairie View A&M University). My special thanks go to Cynthia Tompkins who was always there in time for rescue, and never complained. Barbara Riess used her acumen in translation spending countless hours polishing the texts and salvaging many dubious passages from obscurity; Heidi García worked the technical part, putting the pieces together from countless different programs and personal styles, keeping track of different versions, introducing corrections, and managing the flow of information with *Hispanic Issues*. Barbara and Heidi were my research assistants at different times of the project, and heroically decided to continue beyond the call of duty. Only they know how much the volume owes them. Last but not least, without the encouragement and patience of Nick Spadaccini, editor of the *Hispanic Issues* series, this volume would never see the light of the day.

Looking farther back, I recall the first batch of students with whom we explored, at the end of the 1980s, the issues of postmodern cultural changes that only then were coming to the fore in Latin America: Daniel Altamiranda, Claudia Ferman, Carmen Urioste, and later Rose Costantino. All of them are now on to distinguished careers in the profession. Their inspiration lingers on.

I would like to thank Joe Segura for the gracious permission to use Claudia Bernardi's "Minúsculo intento de alcanzar el azul" (2001) for the cover. Claudia Bernardi has drawn inspiration from her work with the Argentine forensic archaeologic team in El Salvador.

I would also like to thank to the University of California Press for the permission to quote copyrighted material from Pablo Neruda's *Canto General. Fiftieth Anniversary Edition* (translated/edited by Jack Schmitt, 1991).

◆ Introduction

Changing Reality, Changing Paradigm: Who Is Afraid of Postmodernity?

Emil Volek

Since the second half of the twentieth century, Latin America has been going through a new wave of momentous changes that have been termed by some "the second modernization." These changes have been delayed by military dictatorships that marked the end of the protracted failing of the most diverse autarkic nationalistic economic projects relying on the State as the agency of modernization (mainly between the 1930s and 1950s). Today, chronic underdevelopment and resilient premodern realities meet sweeping postmodern global trends. In the U.S., some of these changes have been registered since the late 1980s but have been discussed almost exclusively from the peculiar local context, imposing U.S. hegemonic and cultural perspectives. The result has been a serious distortion in the interpretation of the new hybrid realities emerging in Latin America which could not fit their preordained "slots" in the U.S. imaginary. Regrettably, this situation did not change much in the 1990s.

As a result of the new wave of modernization, Latin America is not what it used to be. In many countries, some consisting of many different countries within, modern technology has helped overcome the lack of traditional infrastructure in communications (from which the drug lords seem to have profited most). The mythical folkloric nineteenth-century dictators, those hapless comic heads of "banana republics" and endearing scoundrels, perpetuated in the literature of "magic realism" well into the second half of the twentieth century, were replaced in the 1970s and 1980s by ordinary affable intelligent and cold-blooded military assassins, who were replaced in their turn by the faded crop of ordinary, democratically elected politicians (with a couple of more or less colorful exceptions). Fortunately for Mexico, the Zapatista guerrillas in Chiapas have preferred to wage a love war in cyberspace and *subcomandante* Marcos has kept himself busy penning stories for children. It is definitely preferable to cope with an unending soap-opera than with civil war. On the other front, the Sandinistas, who surprised the world by accepting their stunning electoral defeat in 1990, pledged, after the recent close loss in November, to "work for the free-market economy from within the National Assembly." The lack of viable economic project for the Left has seriously undermined its credibility and aspirations. Democracy now seems to be an accepted goal and not just a tactical maneuver to seize power. Fledgling civil societies have been developing in Mexico, especially after the devastating earthquake of September 19, 1985. The self-appointed *ombudsman* "Superbarrio," clad in superman-like outfit, descends from films and comics to help solve local problems. Fundamentalist Protestant Churches sweep Central American communities, changing attitudes and values with their strict anti-alcoholism, upward mobility, and work ethics. Slowly but surely, the dependence on the State, *caudillo*, or Party for jobs is eroding. Even the scandalously skewed privatizations may have helped this process.

Large migrations have produced new cultural, political and economic phenomena. While the avant-garde U.S. academic criticism has continued to spin out serial fables about the "Third World," "dependency," "subalternity," and other typically modern intellectual constructs, the illiterate and barefoot *wetbacks*, undocumented "aliens," and exiles running from the mayhem in their countries have effected a sort of "reverse conquest" of significant bits of the "empire" and, in the process, have changed it as well as their original countries, though not always for the better (Take, for example, the Los Angeles-style gang activity brought to Central America by deported émigré youths). In many countries, the indigenous population has swamped the middle-class Creole or Europeanized metropolises, and Latin Americans at large have established numerous beachheads in the North. Due basically to the initial Cuban influx after the Revolution of 1959, Florida has been reconquered for Latin America and Miami has become the offshore international banking, entertainment and economic capital of that continent. While failing almost in everything else, and at great cost for its people, this has been one stunning, albeit unwitting, lasting contribution of the Cuban Revolution.

Similarly, the strength of Puerto Rican culture today cannot be understood without its close ties to New York. The intellectual mindset of the island has come a long way from the curse put on exiles in the early decades to the current love affair with "our" New York. The Mexican cultural mainstream (the Mexican North being eons ahead) has only just begun to feel and to recognize with pride the influence and importance of the border (spearheaded by the Tijuana phenomenon) and of U.S. *chicano* literature and culture. Miami and Havana are still two hostile territories of one Cuban body and soul. These symbiotic, yet not necessarily harmonious, relationships with the "significant other" have added to the already rich processes of cultural diversification going on within. Take, for example, contemporary Mexico's important revival of traditional regional cultural centers (Guadalajara, Xalapa, Mérida), the creation of new centers in the North, the ever stronger writing by women, and the emergent diverse marginal cultural production (for example, the remarkable indigenous revival, or Jewish and gay/lesbian writing).

Even the Indian population that has stayed put has changed. Not only do the surviving Indian tribes dare to request their land back (sometimes asking for the whole country, as in Guatemala), but they modernize and go on to establish an international political and economic base without bothering to join the mainstream national cultures (the heralded *mestizaje* requirement). In the Amazon jungles, remote tribes exchange and compare their rituals on video with their distant kin to see what they may have changed or forgotten while their communities have been separated. The Ecuadorian Otávalo Indians have created what is actually the first transnational tribal corporation. To the dismay of the representatives of the Mexican Indigenista Institute, the Otomí Indians could care less about being good Mexicans and prefer playing rock music for their tribal reunions rather than *rancheras* or other kosher Mexican tunes. In contradistinction, the Guatemalan Indians are glued to Mexican soap operas viewed on cable-TV and listen to Mexican country music on the radio all day long. Zapotec art dealers, with the same naturalness, speak in their own language with their *comadres* and *compadres*, in fluent Spanish with their visitors from Mexico City, and in impeccable English through satellite phones with their business contacts all over the world. Yes, the world has changed, and perhaps where it would be least expected. Since international aid has become widely accessible to the right people, even Maya sorcerers have lined up and have created their own NGO (Non-Governmental Organization) with all the appropriate lingo for the willing benefactors' ears—and there is nothing wrong with that: Survival is survival. If somebody gives, why not ask for more or for me. It is only wrong when somebody naïvely takes this cunning globalization of right posturing for "resistance to globalization."

The *picardía* of the sorcerers takes us to the resilient magical streak in Latin America. The recent Peronista dalliance with the Middle Eastern sultanate, the Peruvian adventure with shogun democracy, or the Cuban Revolution's refuge in *Santería* (the Afro-Cuban syncretic ritual and religion)—which would appear to be the appropriate terminal stage of the notorious *machismo-leninismo*—are just a few cases of the "magic real" (*lo real maravilloso*, as Alejo Carpentier called it in the preface to *The Kingdom of this World*, in 1949).

While magic has its charms, many other transformations have tended to the ugly. If the peace process in Colombia continues, there will be soon nothing left of the country. Unfortunately, war is not resulting in other outcomes either. Other long-term trends have been wreaking havoc all over. Even Nature (that long-standing romantic icon of Latin American identity) has not resisted man. (Or has man failed to resist his nature?) The so much prophesied "continent of the future" now lies greatly amidst an ecological disaster. This disaster is aggravated by the continuing population explosion, followed by relentless deforestation, which provokes climatic changes, which require more deforestation or hasten the flight to cities, subsequent rampant urbanization and urban decay, followed by an uncontrollable wave of social violence. The *maquiladoras* plague adds to the devastation of border regions. And drugs are all over the place. Not so long ago (back in the mid-1980s), one could hear frequently from the South: "Drugs? That's the Yankees' problem." Not any longer. It certainly continues to be a problem in the North, but it has now turned into a large-scale tornado in Latin America. It is a cancer eating up the little healthy social fiber remaining. There is no solution in sight. Legalization is out of the question for shortsighted local political reasons in the North, and the "war on drugs" North *and* South has led nowhere. Actually there is an interesting twist to all this: in the nineteenth century, imperial Britain waged the Opium War on the Chinese in the name of free trade. Obviously, the concept of "free trade" must have changed (yes, many things change magically with power).

In the process of these changes, many old securities have been lost: the position of the cultural elites as guardians of the national project, the very project of national culture as something homogeneous and unique, the State as benefactor, and the nation itself as it emerged from the nineteenth-century imaginary. Concomitantly, old insecurities have been aggravated: the long anguish around Latin American "identity" regarding the past, present and future. In the midst of ongoing transformations, these societies, cultures, and deliberations on them make their way tentatively outside of their well-trodden paths (*hacen su camino al andar*, says Antonio Machado's verse), outside or, many times, against the prescriptions laid down by the "avant-garde" intellectuals who have lagged behind, set in old, already antiquated, molds.

Globalization has many surprising points of entry, of appropriation and of transformation: it does not come from one center only and, besides all its flaws, it has different flows. Latin American countries and cultures have been negotiating these changes in many unexpected ways.

Habent sua fata libelli

In the mid-1990s, I proposed to the editors of *Escritos,* published by the Center of Language Sciences at the Autonomous University of Puebla, a special issue exploring the Postmodernism debate "from the Latin American perspective(s)." I felt that U.S. Latin Americanism was too tributary to its own local—although hegemonic—political and ideological contexts and that it did not respond to the new Latin American realities. Meanwhile in Latin America itself, after an initial wave mimetic of the international scene, a number of impressive works began to appear that not only incisively tackled those new realities, but also promised to be a significant contribution to the international debate itself. In view of a certain sterility that I perceived in strictly literary approaches (after all, literature had not been at the forefront of postmodern changes), the second aim of the project was to strive for an interdisciplinary focus, under the umbrella of the study of culture (not to be confused with its distant relative, the so-called Cultural Studies which, following good modern tradition, seems to have little to do with culture per se). In sum, the purpose of the issue was, according to the proposal, "to investigate important cultural aspects of this new, postmodern, transition of Latin America that has produced, since the 1960s, a striking series of hybrid cultural phenomena in which, side by side with already postmodern features, modern and premodern aspects continue to occupy an important place."

In my search for the Latin American perspective(s) I recognized the nomadic nature of intellectual work today, and although I felt that it might be preferable if the contributors actually *lived* in Latin America, this wish did not seem to me to be the determining factor. Many live there and write happily mimicking the North or Europe. What mattered, then, was whether the new Latin American problematic was in the forefront and was illuminated in some new meaningful way. Since the purpose of the project was to focus on and diagnose recent societal and cultural changes, the specific macrocultural terms employed to conceptualize them—such as "modernization," "Modernity," "Postmodernism" or "Postmodernity," though not at all synonymous—seemed of lesser importance. Of course, each of these concepts, when used, helps frame—or even "frame-up"—a certain *vision* of the phenomena studied, but for me it was much more important to point out the new emerging realities and their impact on those still lingering on from the older existing cultural strata.

My working concept of the postmodern does not imply any fixed qualitative determination: It refers simply to our contemporary historical period unveiling before our eyes massively and on global scale since about the 1960s and marking important milestones such as 1968, 1989, right up to September 11, 2001. While I would reserve Postmodernism for aesthetics and criticism, Postmodernity is not primarily something coming *after* or going *against*, but rather a historical period characterized by many continuities and discontinuities, and as complex, heterogeneous and contradictory as Modernity was, as was any historical time before and certainly after. In this sense, to try to limit "hybridity" to postmodern phenomena would be naïve. Historical processes in a living civilization appear to be rather cumulative: adding, reshuffling, and putting in/out of sight temporarily.

The call for contributions was launched in November of 1996. I knew some contributors socially, from conferences, others I met more personally, and yet others, in the library. Luck helped. In 1985, I was in Bogotá with a group of U.S. academics; the present cycle of violence in Colombia was barely beginning at that time. Fulbright sensed danger and packed us off to the Americanistas conference: There I listened to a presentation by Jesús Martín Barbero and became aware of the pioneering work he was doing. The Fulbright grant in 1987 helped me to put foothold in Argentina, for which David Lagmanovich was instrumental. In 1992, I met Fernando Ainsa in Prague, of all places. And I was impressed by Larraín's *Ideology and Cultural Identity* (1994). When I subsequently read Ainsa's and Larraín's contributions, I was puzzled by their complementarity. Later I learned that both of them had participated at one conference, developed their papers from that encounter, only to meet again by chance in my project. Travel was of paramount importance: Mexico, Colombia, Costa Rica, Argentina, and Chile. In San José, I was introduced to an affable philosopher; in a short while, he came back and gave me an offprint of an article. Back in the hotel I looked into it casually: It was in Czech. I read it in one gulp and I knew immediately that the author was my man. That was how I met Rafael Angel Herra. In Chile, I coincided with a miniseminar given by Néstor García Canclini in the program of Cultural Critique directed by Nelly Richard. García Canclini could not contribute, but I was able to secure the essay by Richard. And I walked off with some precious issues of her journal *Revista de crítica cultural*. At that time, I was already intrigued by the work of José Joaquín Brunner; in Chile, I was lucky to get hold of his magnificent *Cartografías de la modernidad* (1994) that, since then, has not left my *cabecera*. Larraín was helpful in making the contact. There would be similar stories behind all the other essays included. One cannot do anything serious on Latin America without going there. The result of this first effort was published in 1998 as issue 13-14 of *Escritos* (1996).

When the idea emerged to present a selection from *Escritos* in English, I was aware that the project had to be reworked from scratch for the new context. The original volume was slimmed down, reconfigured, some new contributions were commissioned, though not all of them came in time.

A Tale of Two Academies

In its English metamorphosis, the project acquired yet another mission: that of bridging the growing gap between the Latin American and the North American academies. There may be a lot of apparent interaction, even mimicry, between the two, and, as always, a good number of Latin American intellectuals of the first order work full- or part-time in the U.S. But this only covers up the fact that the two academies are on different tracks. Those Latin Americans who are not mimicking current fashions in the North seem oddly out of place here, are ostracized or find themselves in the category of provincial "subalterns" who really *don't or cannot* speak for themselves, and need the right interpreters. Some Latin Americans have preferred to return home, in spite of their economies being in shambles. Others, such as Nelson Osorio, a good friend from my Prague years, say openly that they work and write for the Latin American context and don't bother about what is going on in the North.

In this tale of two academies, the North is pretty much narcissistically self-centered. In literature, the outer limit of the universe of knowledge is usually the MLA Bibliography. How many empires were built on recycling its gaping gaps! Theoretical models that have little or nothing to do with the specific Latin American context are "applied" with blind faith. When reality does not conform, it is "adjusted" or omitted. Too much U.S. research on Latin America moves in circles and is written for local consumption. For others, for whom theory has fallen in postmodern disrepute, methodological frameworks tend to be substituted by feel-good politics. The whole industry created around the "subaltern" and the need to interpret for him/her (of course, many volunteer) testifies to this. While political activism may be justified on moral grounds and is commendable precisely as civic activism, the problem arises when good will (or perhaps "bad conscience" for being part of the "First World") may begin to interfere with critical thinking, and shapes or even substitutes the reality to be studied and interpreted critically in the first place. The hoopla around *Testimonio* is a good case in point. When we read what the academic imagination perpetrated around this genre, we can see why the appearance of David Stoll's book *Rigoberta Menchú and the Story of All Poor Guatemalans* (1999) repeats a similar lesson given to the Postmodernist *establishment* in the social sciences (grouped around *Social Text*, from Duke) by Alan Sokal: In the case of Rigoberta Menchú's *Testimonio*, an apprentice of anthropology that was David Stoll a decade ago when he began his research in Guatemala, went to the archives and talked to people in some faraway places of that relatively small Central American country, and all those academic constructs fell crushingly on their faces. Of course, the academics did not take this affront by reality lightly. Touching somebody's erotic fetish would likely produce less uproar. In the same corner of the academy, Postcolonial Studies would appear to mix feel-good politics with theory into some more or less fiery concoctions. It seems to import happily Southeast Asia and its own import of Antonio Gramsci to Latin America, so completing the circle and Columbus' journey in reverse: Clearly, the self-imposed task to reject Occidentalism is not that easy (Unless one thinks that Gramsci comes to Latin America somewhat improved by his Southeast-Asian mutation). If Gramsci is introduced indirectly, through "second elaboration," Foucault, Lacan, and Derrida come "unreconstructed" and give postcolonial discourse its compelling opacity. Yet Asia and Latin America definitely are not the same thing. Not even by a long stretch of the imagination. On the other hand, does the feel-good side not tend to churn up excuses for postcolonials' own mistakes and ineptitudes? The "New World," born out of Columbus' miscalculation and equivocation and defined through the Western imagination, seems to continuously call for more equivocations. Finally, take cultural studies: The version coming from Latin America, closer to the Birmingham School (oriented towards social sciences), is innovative and promising (after all, many essays in this volume were selected for being part of this trend). What is worrisome is rather that the U.S. version, coming from the Humanities and from "culture wars," appears to be focused exclusively on identity politics. Furthermore, as a study venturing into nonliterary fields, it is greatly threatened by dilettantism, ignorance, or both.

The gap between the most productive trends in the Latin American academy and the academic studies in the U.S. has long been recognized; but efforts to bridge it have fallen short. "Views from South" written rigorously from the North have not helped in spite of their stated purpose. The comparison between two recent journals, *Nepantla* (from Duke) and *Hermes criollo* (published in Montevideo) may be instructive: *Nepantla* takes its symbol from Nahuatl (the word means "cut in two" and refers to the break in tradition and culture brought about by the Conquest; in the Chicano culture, it refers to the "in between" positon of that culture), yet it highlights North American discourse on Latin America; *Hermes criollo* appropriates an Occidental symbol, yet it critically examines texts that continue to be considered sacrosanct in the North (such as the Bible of postcolonial criticism in the U.S., the *Caliban*, by Roberto Fernández Retamar, penned to save his skin in the Stalinist turn of the Cuban culture in 1971; actually, *Caliban* and the infamous "confessions" by the poet Heberto Padilla are two sides of the same coin). The two journals would seem to be typical for the opposing trends in the two academies: one is self-centered and/or apologetic of attitudes past their prime, the other is uncompromisingly critical. The brutal breakdown of "dreams of reason" in Latin America, in all their forms, and the apparently unstoppable slide into the dystopic "Macondo" demand this critical and unapologetic stance: a thorough revision of Latin American thinking, imagination, and values.

Some will argue that I have drawn a caricature; fortunately there are always exceptions. However, caricatures have the advantage of putting things in sharper focus. In spite of all the postcolonial, solidarity and PC rhetoric, North American Latin Americanism acts more and more clearly as an *imperial academy,* indulging in an imaginary Disney World ride through the Third World, designating "the rest" benevolently—always benevolently—as subalterns and "dissing" the realities that are beyond its imaginary.

Yet it is naïve sophistry to dismiss facts, because sooner or later "reality bites back." Of course, Postmodernism comes to the rescue here, declaring that reality is only our construction and that facts and truths are obsolete in our age (Many things seemed to be obsolete for the "new economy" until it fell apart in the old-fashioned way). This postmodern axiom, so readily accepted by popular mass culture, relies on Nietzsche's dictum that "there are no facts, only interpretations," without noticing that this is also only an interpretation and not necessarily the most lucid one. And yes, reality is our construction, to a point. The old U.S. semiotics was more ambitious: Change the word, change the perception, and change the world, it promised. Today's therapy is more modest: If you cannot change reality, change your perception of it (and live happily ever after). This type of therapy or naïve sophistry works in a worriless postmodern world (preferably in video games). Unfortunately, reality "bit back" and September 11 has changed that world. Not some hapless "subalterns" but very sophisticated "others" attacked "us." If Baudrillard could have joked that the Gulf War did not take place, the destruction of the Twin Towers among other things was certainly not a Nintendo game, nor mere interpretation (the necessary "misreading"), nor some social construction that could be "deconstructed" by sleight of hand, nor was it any myopic textual accident that could be restored by pushing some button. What was buried under the rubble of the Twin Towers was precisely the frivolous, relativistic, and scholastic Postmodernism, together with many other *postisms*, all seduced into a blind alley of ever-expanding textuality by the playful yet so many times indecipherable Lacanian and Derridean deconstructions (a physicist had to come out and tell that to us to rid us of our fascination with the emperor's clothes). Postmodernism may be dead, yet Postmodernity has barely begun.

The volume that the reader may now be contemplating brings the new Latin American realities into the focus in the North. They simply cannot be ignored any longer. And as far as the Latin American intellectuals participating in this adventure are concerned, they are no subalterns of anybody. They can speak for themselves and make their case loud and clear. If they also reveal the scant clothing on the imperial academy, that is just a bonus for those who are willing to mature and evolve. And it may also be an act of poetic justice.

Focus of the Volume

Drawing on the international debate about the ongoing global postmodern changes in cultures and societies, a group of distinguished Latin American intellectuals focuses, from an interdisciplinary cultural perspective, on the new realities emerging in Latin America at the close of the twentieth century. In light of these new realities, the essays reexamine the chronic Latin American misencounters with Modernity, open new vistas on the vexing problems of Latin American cultural identity, discuss postmodern changes in society, politics and arts as well as strategies of resistance to the sweeping global trends, and set a cultural agenda for the new century. In the process, they question a number of diehard assumptions regarding Latin America perpetuated both by the right and the left U.S. Latin Americanism, transfixed as both still are in the imaginary of the 1960s.

In Latin America itself, the first round of the debate on Postmodernism, in the mid-1980s, was not very felicitous. The mindset then was still indebted to the 1960s, and the social upheavals of the 1970s and early 1980s (the infamous military dictatorships, "dirty wars," bloody insurrections, crushing external debt crisis) overshadowed the processes of modernization taking place as if beneath that agitated surface. However, the sheer volume of changes, framed and dramatized by the technology-driven transformations on the one hand, and by the demise of the Soviet empire on the other, created both a new reality at home and a new global context that made facing up to this new situation unavoidable. The usual heuristic models (coming mainly from Marxism and its derivatives) lost credibility and explanatory power. Fresh thinking was on the agenda of the day. Towards the beginning of the 1990s, some leading Latin American sociologists, thinkers, and intellectuals began producing highly original works not only analyzing insightfully the new realities emerging in their home countries, but also works that had the potential to become important contributions to the international debate. A few of these earlier works were translated into English: Roberto Schwarz' *Misplaced Ideas* (1992) and Jesús Martín Barbero's *Communication, Culture and Hegemony; From the Media to Mediations* (1993), published in England; and in the U.S., Néstor García Canclini's *Hybrid Cultures; Strategies for Entering and Leaving Modernity* (1995); other signal contributions have remained untranslated and their potential unrecognized.

The essays in this volume fall into four broad and in many instances overlapping categories: The first group (José Joaquín Brunner, Jesús Martín Barbero) deals mainly with Latin American Modernity and modernizations; the second group (Fernando Ainsa, Jorge Larraín, and José Joaquín Brunner) focuses on the cultural identity problem in Latin America in the global age; the third (Mario Roberto Morales, Armando Silva, Osvaldo Pelletieri, Raúl Bueno, and Abelardo Castillo) offers a cross-section view of some of the postmodern phenomena emerging in societies, politics, and arts, and gives a glimpse of local appropriations of and resistances to the waves of globalization; the fourth group (Mempo Giardinelli, Nelly Richard, Rafael Angel Herra, Daniel Altamiranda and Hernán Thomas) takes up various specific issues on the cultural agenda in Latin America today.

The Saga of Latin American Modernizations

In Spanish Latin America, modernization was always an unsettling proposition. As a colony of a peripheral European nation that emerged unexpectedly to glory, but squandered the opportunity and was getting deeper and deeper in trouble, Spanish America was a periphery of the periphery. Since the mid-sixteenth century, Spain barricaded herself against Europe behind the Pyrenees and the Counter Reformation. Religion was everything, the rest mattered only in function of religion or did not, because, after all, this was just the temporary world. Modern ideas were coming always from outside and were carefully screened for infection. The Tribunal of the Inquisition worked diligently and relentlessly. Any modernization had to be implemented against enormous social and administrative inertia. This mindset of the colony conditioned attitudes for a long time to come.

One of the strong motives for independence was actually the Creole elite's resistance to the halfhearted modernization the Spanish kingdom attempted to impose on its colonies in the eighteenth century. After independence was accomplished on the mainland, if modernization could have been avoided, it was. The rest of the nineteenth century was lost to the struggle between the conservatives who wanted to maintain the proven colonial order in the republics and the liberals who pursued the windmills of modernization on paper (how else to modernize against the bulk of the society?). The culprits for the inertia were expediently found: the Church and the Indians. The war on the Church destroyed a good part of the colonial cultural heritage. The elites shared the spoils of the property confiscated from the Church and through land "reform." The latter was just a progressive legalistic term for the expropriation of the Indian land that still belonged to their communities. These events were the first big "privatization" after Independence. The reapportion done on the grand scale did not bring any of the intended positive results, rather the Indians lost further ground.

In his Chilean exile and inspired by Tocqueville, Domingo Faustino Sarmiento dreamt up a development program for Argentina. In his early pamphlet, parading as an analysis of the conditions of his country, *Civilización y barbarie* (1845), Sarmiento opposed the city as incarnation of the Enlightenment ideal to the country as icon of the backwardness and barbarism in Argentina (and in Latin America at large). The city appeared to him as the closest thing to Europe, harbinger of the enlightened ideals. However, Sarmiento must have been thinking rather of Santiago de Chile, because in his Buenos Aires (the city he did not know firsthand until much later), the majority of the people were actually staunch supporters of the dictator Rosas, precisely the embodiment of what Sarmiento found wrong with his country. This pattern of support for the "strong hand" will be repeated up to the *Peronismo* of today. On the other hand, when he expanded on the topic of the *gaucho* (the Argentine "cowboy"), who should emerge precisely as the negative symbol of the "bad" country, his Romanticism got the better of him and the gaucho came out with flying colors. The all too apparent conflict between Enlightenment and Romanticism did not bother Sarmiento or his readers.

This is what we find all too frequently in the Latin American essay: What pretends to be a serious analysis of reality, at a closer look ends up being more wishful thinking or worse. The "federalist" general, who united the country under his iron fist, countered that he was the defender of the "American cause" (whatever that might be), while Sarmiento and his *Unitarian* allies (their religion was centralized government) were "europhile traitors" (whatever that might be). The general lost in the end, and Sarmiento's views were anointed officially as *the* Argentine reality of that time. During his stint as Argentine ambassador in the U.S., he got more ideas. Some were good, for example, later as the president he imported to Argentina a host of schoolteachers from Boston (although how they communicated with their pupils remains a mystery). Other ideas did not work out that well. For example, he favored the drive to open the West that implied destruction of the nomadic Indian tribes who lived there and from their camps harassed the nearby white settlements. However, what was opened for development was not anything like the fertile U.S. West, but some uninviting uninhabitable barren semi-desert. In the same way, the idea to develop Argentina by bringing in European immigrants seemed excellent on the surface, but the poor illiterate peasants from the South of Italy who volunteered most could not do the trick. Anyway, Argentina changed, becoming half-Italian in a couple of decades.

Interestingly, Sarmiento imagines Rosas as the Sphinx that blocks the road to the future utopia that will be reached once the riddle of that country's organization has been correctly answered. Considering Argentina's ongoing travails in this regard (for example, the unsuccessful proposal by president Alfonsín in the 1980s to move the capital), this mystery has not been solved yet (At the beginning of the most recent crisis in Argentina, in December 2001, the editorial of the respected journal *Punto de vista*, published by Beatriz Sarlo, still speaks about "the great Argentine mystery to be deciphered").

Monsters blocking the road to progress, rational proposals that work in surprisingly unintended ways—generally backwards—or do not work at all, give us a glimpse of Latin America as "Macondo." This symbol was coined in Gabriel García Márquez's celebrated novel *One Hundred Years of Solitude* (1967), which may be read as a grand allegory of Latin American history, and soon became valued as a heuristic instrument for the interpretation of Latin American reality (as a way of "understanding" without understanding, as José Joaquín Brunner convincingly shows).

If the enlightened Sarmiento has a good claim to be counted among the founding fathers of the Latin American Macondo, José Martí has even stronger credentials. In his celebrated essay *Nuestra América* (Our America, 1891), he takes up the "American cause," but with a twist: Latin America needs to be modernized, but modern ideas have to be "grafted" onto a "trunk of our Republics." What that "trunk" might be or where to look for it, he does not say. If we take as illustration of his art of grafting his proposal to make wine from bananas (he must have been reading *Bouvard et Pécuchet* at that time), we land directly in Macondo. As of this day, Martí's riddle has not been solved since all the candidates for that trunk proposed so far have failed miserably. *Nuestra América* is a well-meaning concoction that calls for solidarity against the emerging menace of the U.S. (one point he was right about), and abounds in contradictions and wishful thinking, but since this was meant as a pep talk, nobody bothered to look into his ideas more carefully. In one other respect Martí significantly advances the cause for Macondo: For him, Latin American reality is *so* original and *so* different, that "neither the European book, nor the Yankee book could offer a clue to the Spanish American enigma." In sum, "nobody understands us," implying "neither do we." While Sarmiento tilts to Enlightenment, yet clings to Romanticism, Martí is more openly romantic (see his "natural man" as the solution to all problems), yet maintains Enlightenment as a broad framework for his visions. As far as his utopia of the natural man is concerned, again, he does not reveal where to look for him (maybe in Chateaubriand?). Yet even Ernesto Che Guevara's call for the "new man" in the early 1960s can be easily "grafted" into the "trunk" of Martí's "natural man" (whatever that might be in the end). For many, Sarmiento and Martí appear to be antipodes, yet they both end up advancing the same cause.

At the turn of the twentieth century, the curse of Macondo entered a new stage. A host of semiliterate dictators emerged from Mexico to Central America whose alleged purpose was to modernize their countries by command. All of them tried out some grandiose project, more or less ridiculous, and heroically failed in their main objective. Their only modernizing accomplishment was to be that their composite figures would later people modernist narratives of "magic realism." The warped mirror of the genre leads us to forget under what well-intentioned banner they took power. Once this context is restored, the striking similarity to some later specimens becomes painfully clear (of course, while the banners have changed according to the times, the results, less so). The persistence of the phenomenon is striking: I think that not only the strong surviving feudal *caudillo* tradition, but also the tradition of voluntarism, rooted in religion ("I wish therefore it will be"), and the deteriorating context may have contributed to the perseverance of desire over reality principles.

Once the paradigm of the "progressive dictator" had been exhausted, it became clear that it was all but impossible to stir any modernizing movement when the only capital available was in the hands of the land oligarchy that had no interest in change. To build capitalism without capital has always been a daunting proposition. In the 1930s, the State came to the rescue and enlisted itself as the modernizing agency. Lázaro Cárdenas' bold nationalization of Mexican oil is one of the highlights of those times. Of course, the previous dictators always behaved as if they were the owners of the State, but their legitimacy was limited. Now the State has been retooled for the new mission but the old crew has remained on board. Neither chaos (Latin America in general or the early revolutionary Cuba and the "Bolivarian Revolution" in Venezuela today) nor planning (the later revolutionary Cuba following in the footsteps of late Soviet Union) has produced the desired results. The State-driven modernization fizzled in the 1950s amidst corruption and bureaucracy. It had been a "mission impossible," anyway. Yet that is precisely when Fidel decided that this State-lead bourgeois revolution had gotten bogged down because it had not been radical enough and that, if he had a chance, he would drive the process to its last consequences, which still endures in his "Socialism or Death" slogan. While this may have sounded as a disjunction at the beginning, it looks more and more like identification now. However, in either version, it affirms surreptitiously that nothing else exists out there.

Since the late 1980s, the State has been abandoned wholesale. In this remarkable lose/lose operation, the State has distributed its best assets among friends, and has kept the losers and the debts. The crooked privatization parading as neoliberalism (we are still in the phase of capitalism without capital, just the debts have grown bigger) has not brought the desired results either.

The saga of Latin American modernizations "from above," though hilarious in literature, is indeed tremendously sad in reality. The reality of *Macondoamérica* has surpassed fiction. However, this is not the whole story. While failed "from above," there has been a lot going on "from below." Written each from a different perspective, the contributions to this volume take up the Latin American struggle for Modernity (now called Postmodernity) roughly from here.

Macondo or Death: Imagining Latin American Modernity

One essay especially deserves a more detailed commentary before we turn this volume over to the perhaps already impatient reader. José Joaquín Brunner's "Traditionalism and Modernity in Latin American Culture" is a brilliant, almost heretic, tour de force and an indispensable clue for the interpretation of present-day Latin America. In it, the Chilean sociologist deconstructs and demolishes the most current and prestigious assumptions about contemporary Latin American culture and Modernity, supported by the names of Angel Rama, Octavio Paz, and all the followers of *Macondismo*. Again, we find out that antipodes end up working for the same cause.

Brunner breaks with the tradition of looking at things through the lens of high culture (which still haunts Rama, Paz, and many others). His search for Modernity takes into account the whole "operative context of the culture"—not only its production but also its modes of transmission, circulation and consumption. In that perspective, what was "modern" for Rama, is actually just a limited—elite-bound—modernization within the firm framework of traditional culture. Besides, for Brunner, there is no one culture in Latin America but, instead, an unfinished *collage* of cultures in construction.

In Latin America, the discontent with the perceived state of Modernity has lead to two apparently opposed attitudes. Those who see the "half-full" accomplished Modernity, as Octavio Paz does, look through the lens of high culture and go to History for reasons of the present debacles. The lack of a strong Enlightenment period that would have created the decisive break with Tradition stands out as one powerful motive for the present "deficiencies." This perceived weakness is made to look worse by measuring Latin America's present against an idealized West. Latin Americans are put into an awkward position of striving to become what the others already were. Since Modernity comes from outside, this leads to the assertion that "to become modern, we had to sacrifice being ourselves," from which comes the conclusion that Latin America's half-accomplished Modernity is just a mask, a falsification, a superficial varnish over some hidden soul which must resurface or be recovered eventually to become wholesome. The quest for an authentic Modernity thus turns into a quest for the lost self. This myth-turned-history-turned-myth underlies Paz's vision of Mexican history since his early essay *The Labyrinth of Solitude* (1950). The frustrated search for the self and for identity with the Other, two quests at cross-purpose, leave little space for optimism for the future. Because Latin America missed out on the eighteenth century, it seems forever condemned, like the dead souls of Juan Rulfo, to the Purgatory of incomplete or pseudo-Modernity.

Those who despair over the half-empty glass, or see it as irretrievably broken, look for reasons in the very constitution of the Latin American. In this vision, Latin American "difference" acquires features of "radical Otherness." What was the troubling end-result of the failed identity quest in Paz, is postulated upfront here: Western Modernity has not worked in Latin America because it *cannot* work there. Nature and the non-Western origin of the native population, among others, have created an absolutely different reality (the *marvelous real*) that does not respond to the enticements of modern instrumental reason. The quest for Modernity is hopeless and it might be better to celebrate the resulting disfunctionality in a carnival *fiesta*. According to some Macondians, Latin American culture is condemned to be a carnivalesque parody of the West. The image of Macondo crystallized and made this interpretation of Latin American culture and reality more palatable. The lens of traditional popular Creole culture enhanced by fantasy made the Macondo reality gracious, even hilarious, and fascinated foreign audiences who asked for more. Macondo *was* Latin America. Due to the mediation and diligence of Isabel Allende, *magic realism* became full-fledged industry. Through the concept of hybridization the *magic real* turned *postmodern* and, in spite of García Canclini's protestations, became an apology for Macondo. For some, Latin America was *always* postmodern (they must have been counting from the first *chingada*, I guess).

These two attitudes only appear as opposed; actually they are "communicating vessels," being complementary and even frequently echoing each other. It is not by chance that the title of Paz's essay resonates in García Márquez's novel. While the theory of "deficiencies" may be true as History, it does not fully explain the present. And similarly, while gracious *Macondismo* may be good for literature, it fails as a heuristic prism for interpretation of the complex Latin American realities of today and, worse, it covers up the ugly underside of these realities.

In his search for Latin American Modernity, Brunner does not look for identity with Western Modernity, just for structural homology. According to him, modern Latin American culture "is not an offspring of ideologies" but rather of "the expansion of universal schooling, of the means of electronic communication, and of the constitution of industrial mass culture." It is established moreover as an urban experience. And television not only produces the social imaginary of the masses, but it brings critique of all forms of traditionalism (To see TV as agency of modernization is a far cry from the "Critical Theory" of the Frankfurt School and its followers). And he concludes: "Modernity in Latin America was not born out of the heads of modernizers . . . but rather through the operation of the cultural apparatuses that produce it, even behind the backs of our intellectuals." "We are not 'different' but equal to the societies that preceded us." In sum, between 1950 and 1990, a cycle of incorporation into cultural modernity opened up, resulting in "the incorporation into a shared experience of differences, but within a common matrix provided by schooling, televised communication, continuous consumption of information, and the necessity of living connected communicatively in the 'city of signs.'" Latin American culture is now in full process of incorporation into Modernity, which is *yet another constellation of Western Modernity.*

Postmodern discourse in Latin America, according to Brunner, has not been born from the exhaustion of "master narratives," "because these never fully arrived to our shores." Postmodern discourse, that emerged in Europe as a coalescence of fragments of modern idealist philosophy, in Latin America, paradoxically "serves to question the previous forms of local idealism: the propensity to think the future as if it were a mental product of ideological utopias."

Now that the air has been cleared of traditional debris, be it impressive intellectual fabrications or great artistic creations, good for literature but bad if taken for reality, the critical work can begin.

Envoi

We need not be afraid of Postmodernity. Jorge Luis Borges would say that our consolation is that it will not be much worse or much better than any other time, just different. In the end, after all those alleged "crises" that the superficial Modernity imposed on us (the crisis of language, of representation, of the subject—as if any time before the struggle to speak, to represent and to be was any different), can't the allegedly superficial Postmodernity perhaps be some return to sanity? And maybe, just maybe, even Latin America will find its path to a better future. The sobering yet inspiring account of contemporary realities offered in this volume, including new and old follies, may show the way in that direction.

Part I   **Macondo or Death, But Not Exactly:
The Case of Unrequited Modernity
That Does Not Go Away**

1.

Traditionalism and Modernity in Latin American Culture

José Joaquín Brunner

(*translated by Shara Moseley*)

> *Culture may be described as that which makes life worth living.*
> T. S. Eliot
> *Notes Towards the Definition of Culture*, 1949.

The Traditionally Based Culture

Order

Any study of Latin American culture runs the risk of becoming a genuine Tower of Babel. There is an excess of historical, theoretical, and even political references that come into play each time that the "soul of the continent" and its expressions in the varied languages of culture are disputed. Such expressions include museums and poems, monuments and religious images, daily habits and school, television and analphabetism, fashion and editorial industry, Sunday sermons and opera, ideologies and sexual ethics, beliefs and values, architecture and folklore; in other words, they include all the forms of living, working, loving, and dying in this part of the world.

Perhaps we are condemned, then, to speak fragmentarily of the culture of our time—as an unfinished collage in construction, where each part, piece or remnant refers to others, all moving in a continuous dance of signs. Does the above mean that our culture, which we now need to recognize as plural, fails to produce an order—whatever its form may be—capable of systemizing itself in a narrative of any given genre?

Of course our initial hypothesis assumes this radical impossibility. We postulate that in its contemporary development, the cultures of Latin America do not express an order, be it of nation, of class, of religion, of State, of interest, of tradition, nor of any other type. Rather, they reflect in their organization the contradictory and heterogeneous processes of constitution of a late Modernity, produced in the conditions of an accelerated internationalization of symbolic markets on a worldwide scale.

The cultural analysis of the great conglomerates (nations or states, regions, historical periods) customarily implies the idea of an order. The history of culture following Alfred Weber, for example, has been written with that interpretive imperative in mind. A civilizing principle, omnipresent and omnipotent, parades before us like an army or like a large machine unfolding its organizing energies from the center of culture to the periphery and from the beginning of time into the future. The idea of "progress" like so many others elaborated in the Age of Enlightenment, gives us an organized vision of cultural history. Each time that it is incarnated in a relatively coherent concept we have a "master narrative," whose clues reveal to us our singular position in History.

Perhaps we do not have the faith necessary to adhere to any philosophy of our own cultural history. Moreover, today we lack these "master narratives," whose end we live out as a tragedy in the embalming of Marx and relive, with the end of History banalized by Fukuyama, as a tragicomedy. Slowly, the "narratives" that would interpret for us our history begin to disappear; but History continues and we find ourselves, in the end, destined to take it up and deal with it from our own vantage point and on our terms.

Cultural analysis as an academic discipline supposes that culture is a replica of the natural order, a "microcosm of meanings" integrated around a more general meaning that endows the whole with an immanent rationality. As Pitrim Sorokin has taught, what is interesting from such an approach is the discovery of the central principle (Reason), that penetrates all the components, gives sense and meaning to each one of them and, in this way, manages to convert the chaos of multiple dispersed fragments into a cosmos (18).

Later, while the Social Sciences abandoned their ingenuous but powerful imitation of the "positive sciences" and completed the cycle of acquiring hermeneutic techniques, the cultural analysis retained, however, its radical attachment to the idea or principle of order, only now internalized as an inclination of individual consciousness (Berger and Luckman) or as a balance born out of short-distance interactions (Goffman).

Is it possible then to escape the determinants of the very field of cultural analysis? And in so doing, to offer a narrative (any whatsoever) that would assume, on the contrary, the independence of the fragments, the absence of identities, the lack of a principle of totality, and the necessity of an organizing synthesis in our cultures?

More radically, could one attempt to look at culture without starting from a common sense of order and without reading empirical processes as if they were directed towards it? And, further, do it without aligning oneself, at least initially, with any philosophical bloc inspired by the gesture that, from Saint Augustin to Hegel and Marx, has offered to construct the meaning of History as unfolding of a singular organizing principle? We do not know if this is possible. But we must conclude that any attempt at prematurely systematizing the processes of reasoning results in a pseudo-methodological banality or, even worse, in a radical misunderstanding.

For the moment we cannot speak systematically about Latin American culture. Even the best contemporary analyses of it very often avoid any sort of traditional formalization. This is clearly the case of Carlos Monsiváis and also of Octavio Paz whose essays are contradictory because of their vitality. We move then with and within the dance of signs. We listen to their music, participating in it, we see bodies twirling, dancing, and yet not following any style, nor denoting any pattern. The figures break as they pause and resume their posture as they begin again. There is a hall of mirrors where the dancers' movements become a twisted reflection. The intermittent light disfigures their faces; at times they seem to be masks and nothing more. Perhaps this is a folk festival. Perhaps they are celebrating in this ceremony the fall of a dictator or the death of a sister, we can never be completely certain. Perhaps what we have before us is a religious ceremony. Some mirrors are smashed, as if we were in an old hotel. At times someone opens a window and a sea breeze fills the salon. More likely, it is just nothing more than a big city whose noise pierces the onlooker's ears while neon lights illuminate the streets. Someone points out to us that perhaps we are in Hong Kong. From afar we can hear a siren. A piercing noise like that of a gunshot is confused with the applause from the salon. Almost all the TV sets are on. The people are chattering. A parade carrying flags and banners passes by. A couple pauses at the entrance of a cinema. At the next table everyone is yelling. And they are arguing about Latin American cultural identity.

Context

The fact that Latin American culture, that is, the sum of cultures that compose the *collage*, is usually analyzed based on its products, has led to the use of exaggerated types of periodization that, ultimately, refer to its producers' (intellectual) style or to their ideological orientation. On the other hand, these analyses mainly lack contextual references, however fragmentary they may be, in a continent where we are still struggling to obtain the most elementary statistics. Much confusion results from there: We tend to suppose that the waves of modernization, or rather the modernizers and their movements or groups, be it in the realm of ideas, letters or politics, could have inaugurated the Modernity of our culture before this Modernity could have ever existed. In sum, we commit the error of analyzing our culture's "texts" outside their context of production, circulation and reception.

A partial substitute for this contextual void is the introduction of some deficits considered to be specifically Latin American which, by absence, would act as indicators of an incomplete History, mutilated or, if you wish, only potential. Octavio Paz has been the guru of this current that analyzes culture through its omissions. For example, when he writes,

> the great difference between France and England, on the one hand, and Spain and Spanish America, on the other, is that we never had an 18th Century. We never had a Kant, a Voltaire, a Diderot, or a Hume. (*El ogro* 34-5)[1]

Following a similar line of thought we arrive at the conclusion that we would have lacked almost everything that was supposedly necessary for us to reach Modernity: a religious reform headed by a Luther-type leader, a French Revolution, a De Tocqueville-style civil society like the one in the United States, a liberal universal ideology that could have permitted the individual citizen to develop himself, as well as Protestant work ethic to inspire savings and investment as well as work.

With respect to the Western model, the interpretation of our cultural history through its omissions reflects not only the consecrated hegemony of this model, but also the old gesture of perplexity in the face of these specific Latin American differences when this new territory is analyzed by the discoverer's mental categories. Remember that for Hegel, even if the birds in the Northern Hemisphere, the nightingale and the lark for example, could not compete with the colorful plumage of those from the tropical South, they sing better than those in the tropics. Moreover, such a specific American deficit, Hegel tells us, could very well transform itself into a future possibility. Perhaps the inferior harmonic quality of our birds is not due so much to the tropical heat as to the shrill voices of the jungle inhabitants so that, "the day when the almost inarticulate sounds of degenerate men are no longer heard in the tropical forests of Brazil is when many feathered singers[2] will also produce more refined melodies" (Gerbi 542-43 n. 492).[3]

What meaning can we attribute to such comparative readings of cultural history when they inevitably will conclude, as always, that all of the subordinate or peripheral cultures—with respect to a predominant model—lack the qualities of a singing voice or a

Voltaire while possessing an overabundance of feathers and dictators? Could it not be that such an analytical path seeks to confer an (absent) meaning on the one that has not been sufficiently contextualized? Thus Hegel, surprised comparatively, reacts by applying his contextual categories to the new territories. Octavio Paz, on the other hand, reacts by denouncing to some extent what we lack in order to become what others were. In both cases, however, we are left without a context. We merely substitute it with a want of ideas or with a surplus of feathers.

Modernizations

Such a contextual substitution results from the very notion of culture that comes into play there. If culture were understood to be solely symbolic products and, consequentially, pertaining exclusively to the superior realm of ideas, then the spontaneous context of that culture would reside in the symbolic domains of an age, materialized in esthetic schools, modes of thought, or philosophical currents.

We have known for some time now, however, that culture is a universe of meanings that does not communicate nor exist independently of its mode of production, circulation, reception, consumption, or recognition. The McLuhanian dictum, the medium is the message, does not apply only to electronic images but was also valid long before in spreading the religious sermon as a configurative medium for the bourgeois culture (Groethuysen), or in conceiving the locally circulating incipient press as a market medium and as an agency to objectify communicated discussions while liberating them from the personal authority of the speaker (Gouldner).

Cultural analysis would also need to begin in Latin America with the means of production and circulation and with the forms and conditions of reception in order to endow itself (from within) with the contexts in which a culture can be interpreted. It would have to begin, for example, with the understanding of the operative context of the culture that is often referred to as traditional (and in some countries, oligarchic), in order to undertake, if so desired, the analysis of ruptures and of continuities implied by the emergence of Latin American Modernity.

There is no doubt that long before the advent of the twentieth century, diverse movements in culture occurred in the region and gave shape to the course of Modernity from various perspectives. For example, Angel Rama situates the "Latin American literary modernization" in the period between 1870 and 1910.[4] To which contextual elements does Rama resort to in order to validate this assertion? He refers to the incipient conquest of literary and artistic specialization, the first sign of a future professionalization of the cultural domain; the concomitant formation of an educated public thanks to an initial urban impulse; the foreign influences which promote an initial integration of local producers to the international market on a literary scale; the artistic autonomy reached then in the region in respect to its historical progenitors; and, finally, what Rama calls democratization of artistic forms consistent with the idea of "modernized forms." For the first time, these forms would permit the integration of others, such as traditional and popular ones, resulting in languages that he considers appropriate for the social sectors that brought about that socioeconomic transformation (83).

While it is true that Latin American traditional culture experienced early modernization processes in different countries and in diverse scope,[5] this does not mean that its modes of production, communication and consumption were incorporated into a structure that could be called modern.[6]

Another process that is a significant illustration of this point is the university reform started in 1918 in the Argentine city of Cordoba. Begun as a reaction against a profoundly traditional, conservative and authoritarian order, the reform soon turned into a stirring Latin American movement. Through it, the students expressed themselves as an ascending intellectual class of the time. They reclaimed for themselves not only a space and formative processes "oriented in the direction of modern currents of ideas" but, also, claimed their generational politico-intellectual participation in the new cultural world in formation. In fact, such a movement began as the Great War ended and the Bolsheviks launched their Revolution. This was an inaugural time for culture. Only in this atmosphere can one understand the exalted lyricism opening the *Liminar Manifesto*:

> Men of a free republic, we have just broken the last chain that in the midst of the 20th Century has bound us to ancient monarchic and monastic domination. We have resolved to call all things by their names. Cordoba is redeemed. From this day on we count one less shame and one more liberty for the country. The pains that are still left are the liberties that are lacking. We believe that we are not wrong, our hearts tell us: we are beginning a revolution, we are living an American hour.[7]

This "American hour," however, was only singing its praises for the tiniest minority among the continent's inhabitants, since the rest were still submerged in the old dependencies. The university students were only a handful in every country and their ideas of progress and liberation had barely resonated outside the principal cities, even though there they may have produced a "holy fear" among the members of the educated class.

Underdevelopment

Antonio Cándido has suggested that up to about 1930 and, perhaps, we may even add the Great Depression, in Latin America the notion of "new countries" was predominant, meaning these were countries whose history had not yet been able to unfold and were, therefore, full of possibilities. After that, however, as Cándido shows, the notion of "underdevelopment" began imposing itself on the Latin American conscience (335). For cultural analysis that state of consciousness is of major importance. In fact, it is the context marked by underdevelopment that, until the middle of the twentieth century, maintains the continuity of the traditional culture in force.

Indeed, even around 1950 we were talking about a continent where sixty-one percent of the population was rural and where no more than twenty-six percent resided in areas of more than 20,000 inhabitants. For the entire region, the rate of illiteracy for those fifteen years of age and older reached almost a rate of fifty percent. On the other hand, the gross rate of schooling at the primary level scarcely reached on average fifty-seven percent, and that at the secondary level, seven percent. About this same year, or three decades after the Cordoba movement, only 250 thousand students studied at an advanced level in Latin America, representing less than two percent of their corresponding age group. Considering the national population of the respective countries, in none of them did the percentage of individuals with thirteen years or more of education reach three percent, but generally it was figured at below one percent.[8]

Within such an underdeveloped context, what modern constitution of culture could be expected in the region? Rather, there existed a high culture of scarce patrons, an incipient culture of ascending middle classes, and a varied and heterogeneous culture of the popular majorities—urban and rural—that, until 1950, continued living in territories of illiteracy.

It is not, therefore, a lack of movements of ideas, such as religious reform or liberal ideology, that characterizes (by absence) traditional Latin American culture. Rather, it is a deficient productive infrastructure, a scarcity of long distance communication and a reduced number of patrons dedicated to following the development of ideas. It is these deficits of development, those of the material, technical and cultural productive forces, that generate and reproduce traditionalism in the culture.

In the enlightened upper class, culture is connected to the outside and is fed from there, while among lower classes, culture is lived by the majority as oral and local communication, bound to the routine of daily life, to parishes, and to the organic transmission of narratives, beliefs, and values of the community group.

Masks

Antonio Cándido has already suggested that a traditionally structured culture, where extensive illiteracy and social refinement of the educated yet provincial elites coexist side by side, propels these elites not to Modernity, but to a kind of inevitable alienation. *Beautiful, refined or educated* thinking and writing cannot refer to a local public of consumers, but needs to relate itself to a European market, even if only as a mere imitation or artifice. For example, Brazilian symbolists, as well as the Chilean poet Vicente Huidobro, would choose to write directly in French, as would Claudio Manuel da Costa in Italian.

If the masks operate for Modernity as another form of a bottomless revelation, lacking the last real face behind the mask, then, for traditional culture, instead, the question of masks appears culturally as the question of deceptive mediation of European culture. It is for this reason that some contemporary analysts of our culture affirm that Latin America must have been conceived in falsehood and unauthenticity. Octavio Paz is categorical in this respect:

> Masked realities: the beginning of unauthenticity and lies, the endemic ailments of Latin American countries. At the beginning of the 20th Century we were already established in a complete pseudo-Modernity: with railroads and latifundia, with democratic constitution and a *caudillo* in the best Hispano-Arabic tradition, with positivist philosophers and pre-Columbian *caciques*, with symbolist poetry and illiteracy. (*El ogro* 64)

Long before Paz, the Argentine essayist Ezequiel Martínez Estrada explored the same topic in his *Radiografía de la pampa* (1933). In this work, as in many later Latin American intellectual and literary manifestations, the contradiction between a Nature, which is real and authentic, and a culture, transplanted from Europe, that is merely a mask of civilization acquires a foundational value. According to Beatriz Sarlo,

> For Martínez Estrada, the Argentine way of life is a mask, a mimetic fiction: as if it were Europe (but is not), as if it belonged to History (but it belongs to ethnography), as if relationships between groups and individuals had been established when we know that these fictional bonds are part of a representation, a *mise en scène* of a society that, in reality, is not so. (227-28)

In sum, instead of analyzing culture as an expression of society and of its conditions of development, we have seen that culture is opposed to Nature—the supposed depository of our authenticity and primigenial truth.

In point of fact, traditional culture finds itself in tension not only between Europe, represented or imitated by the local elites, and rural parochialism, which continues to reflect the condition of the cultural life of the majorities, but also between the poles of authenticity, provided by Nature (and those who remain closest to her), and the pole of words and of culture (of a class dominant in the political, economic, social, cognitive and communicative aspects) that distorts traditional culture by naming it, yet without submitting it to the modern gesture par excellence: that of a Faustian technocrat, planner and organizer of the masses, and impresario.[9]

Nature

The glorification of Nature plays a reverse role in Latin American traditional culture in comparison with the Europeans' misunderstanding it in previous centuries. If for Hegel the birds of the Amazon sing badly and off-key, like the shrill Indian that inhabits the tropical forest, for many writers of the region, American Nature provides, instead, the mirror that reflects a true American History. It furnishes the analyst with powerful myths upon which he can establish his interpretation and from whence he can contest the artifices of Modernity.

In the first part of *Canto General,* Pablo Neruda exalts the Nature of the continent "From the peace of the buffalo / to the pummeled sands / of the land's end, in the accumulated / spray of the Antarctic light" (14). In the beginning the Earth was at peace: "In fertility time grew" while "All was flight in our land" (14, 17). Native men were a prolongation of Nature: "The mineral race was / like a cup of clay, man / made of stone and atmosphere" (24). And "Like dazzling pheasants / the priests descended / the Aztec steps" (24). All of this, before America had a name or measure.

Martyrdom begins with the conquistadors: "The butchers razed the islands," writes Neruda, "Then there was blood and ash" (43). When Cortés passes by he leaves behind "a quiet murmuring of grief" (47). "In Panama the demons convened. / There the ferrets' pact was sealed" (54).

Almagros and Pizarros and Valverdes,
Castillos and Uriases and Beltranes
stabbed one another in the back, sowing
among themselves the betrayals acquired,
stealing one another's women and god,
disputing the dynasty.
They lynched one another in the corrals,

> stripped one another in the plaza,
> hanged one another in the Councils.
> The tree of plunder fell
> among stabbings and gangrene. (58)

Then the poet exclaims: "Alone, in the wilderness, / I want to weep like the rivers, I want / to grow dark, to sleep / like an ancient mineral night" (57).

Nature is the refuge where traditional culture is reunited with a primigenial America, from whose quarry it unearths the blood's and the land's secrets. Even the nation is thought of as a marriage between the race and Nature, to the point that in Chile a whole myth has been constructed out of the seismic conditions of the national territory and its alleged influences on the Chilean character. The cycle of traditional oppositions between Nature and History—where the first is the embracing and fertilizing mother and the second is the law of the father consecrating his domination—will come to a close in Latin America with the advent of the themes of Modernity. From then on, Nature (and society as well) will be object of man's action, yielding to the movements of the market and serving, at most, to condemn a culture that makes headway tearing down gods and forests.

Controversies

Let us ask once again, are modernizers sufficient to make Modernity? According to a widely held view, Latin American intellectuals and politicians, regardless of their ideological attitudes or political affiliations, would have propelled the same project from the beginning of the twentieth century: that of the modernization of their societies. "Beyond their differences," writes Paz, "there is a common idea that inspires liberals, positivists and socialists: the project of modernizing Mexico" (56).

However, the term "modernization," as we understand it today, has only lately come to be a part of our modern vocabulary: This has happened when modernization was related to the United States as a model and to Sociology and to the Social Sciences as the semantic context in which it acquires its full meaning. This is why, we insist, we should not confuse Modernity with the modernizations that take place at the heart of traditional culture. These modernizations are nothing more than eruptions of the new, novelties that are opposed to the old in the scheme of ideas or in the symbolic works in general.

Latin American culture in its modern constitution is not the offspring of ideologies, although this objective was pursued by liberals, positivists and socialists; rather, it is the offspring of the expansion of universal schooling, of the means of electronic communication, and of the constitution of industrial mass culture.

Even today, cultural Modernity in the region is only just surfacing and cannot be confused with the disputes between the old and the modern at the heart of traditional culture. Let us say that the Córdoba University reform of 1918, certain elements of the Mexican Revolution, as well as the ideas of Mariátegui and Martí, represent moments—always seen as ambiguous from a cultural standpoint—of irruption of new elements in traditional cultures. However, these moments alone do not bring about Modernity; its advent will have to wait until a favorable ground—social, technological, and professional—is found on which it may be sustained.

To the contrary, while it exists only in the heads of the elites, or is manifested exclusively as ideological cracks within traditional culture, the arrival of Modernity remains latent, counterbalanced in its potentiality by the hegemony of rural life, the segmented organization of cultures, the predominant of distinction of aristocracy or oligarchy, the influence of parochialism, extended illiteracy, and the symbolic glorification of Nature.

This is why the modernization in the domain of letters, to which we have referred above citing Angel Rama, can be better understood as an intellectual movement than as a constellation of a modern culture proper. The *Modernismo*, although analyzed through its sociological antecedents by Rama, is merely a new expression—of doctrines, esthetics, and work conditions—at the heart of an enlightened culture which continues, and is limited, by its operational context, to the traditions and modes of communication of a single class. There is no relationship, on the other hand, between this "literary modernism"—from the point of view of its cultural productivity—with the social groups marginalized from the official power and from the means of communication, groups which continue to be largely linked to Nature and to oral communication.

Still, intellectual modernizations without modern cultural context do not produce masks or falsifications, as certain current of Latin American thought would have it. On the contrary, through their own dynamic they lead to more intense communicative processes with the outside. Because of this, these are moments or canals for the local elites to access the international market of ideas and symbols—the European market in the beginning and, later on, that of the United States.

It is not that this orientation of enlightened natives would respond to an effect of fascination for the North, but, rather, it constitutes a first indication of what would later be an essential element of Modernity: the deterritorialization of cultures or, in other words, the creation of communicative spaces or networks integrated around topics, styles, perceptions, or values. In fact, culture has always operated around two poles: one at the local level of communication and another around communication at a distance, through structures that are not concerned with political boundaries, but constitute their own communicative geography (the empires as a cultural manifestation, the markets since their origin, religions, and so on).

Clashes with Modernity

Macondo I

Perhaps the biggest question for contemporary culture at the world level consists in establishing whether we are still modern or if we have already fully entered an age which, like the America of long ago, still lacks a name but is named in reference to its point of origin: New Spain, or, in this case, Postmodernity. For us, the question is, instead, whether present Latin American societies are modern, or at least considered as such according to the conformation of their cultures.

There is a way to respond negatively to this question, one that is associated with the supposed explanatory value of Latin American literature, value which, be it as it may, would always be greater than that of the Social Sciences. Said response may be identified with the symbol of *Macondo*, not so much derived from an analysis of García Márquez's *One Hundred Years of Solitude* (1967), but rather from the way that this novel has been received and is used in certain intellectual circles.

What does *Macondism* consist of? First of all, it means interpreting Latin America through literature or, more exactly, as a product of the narratives that we tell to ourselves in order to mark out our identity. Second, it conveys a belief that these narratives, especially those acclaimed by foreign critics, constitute the Latin American reality—producing it as a text in which we would be called upon to recognize ourselves. Third, *Macondism* prolongs and proposes once again the traditional predominance of Nature over culture, but now in more complex ways. Indeed, it is as in certain myths where Nature accompanies and transforms culture, in the sense that culture is seen as completed and revitalized by the movements of a Nature that acts through signs and wonders. In other words, *Macondo* would be a metaphor for the mysterious or the Magic Real of Latin America—its essence ever unnamable by the categories of Reason and by the political, commercial and scientific cartography of the moderns. Fourth, *Macondism* covers with its magically expanding wings the totality of the present-day realities of our societies, blurring in a single process the maladjustments of this reality with the true wonders originated by this unattainable and unnamable essence of America. If before our feathered friends sang poorly and off-key, now in *Macondo,* the rain can fall uninterruptedly for years without end, and it can even rain from the ground up. Fifth and last, *Macondo* has become a catchword, alluding to all that we do not understand or do not know or that surprises us by its novelty. Moreover, a catchword that helps us to remember what we want to continue dreaming when "we are no longer what we wanted to be" (Calderón 229).

Thus, *Macondism* is nostalgic without being conservative; it is a wall of defense before the future, but only in the way that someone waits to see the results before assuming a formal commitment. From there, *Macondism* has extended, together with the *Boom*, among a sector of Latin American intelligentsia that does not want to renounce making America a land of promised wonders. The land of dreams and utopias; the new world out of which an alternative rationality will emerge for the West, divested of the instrumental, Protestant and Faustian character of the rationality axis of Modernity.[10]

Differences I

There exists yet another response to the question concerning our Modernity. It consists in showing simultaneously its partial presence and, in contrast to the North, its deficits and fundamental differences. For example, Octavio Paz has insisted on "numerous and, above all, decisive differences" that spring into view when Europe is considered side by side with its farthest overseas extensions, North America and Latin America (*México* 462).

First, "the presence (in our America) of non-European elements"—Indians of varied ethnic origin and blacks. Both, but especially the former, "have attuned the sensibility and excited the fantasy of our peoples"; different characteristics of their cultures, mixed with the Hispanic ones, would be present "in our beliefs, institutions, and customs" (462). Second, the peculiar version of European culture incarnated in Spain and Portugal as opposed to the rest of Europe. Most importantly, the fact that both peoples were dominated for centuries by Islam, which gave rise to a culture fusing Hispanic and Arabic elements. Third, Spain and Portugal, after inaugurating the modern world with their overseas discoveries, became closed, and, "closed off in themselves, they negated the emerging Modernity" (463). The Counter-Reformation would be the symbol of this closure. As a consequence, "the North Americans were born with the Reformation and the Enlightenment, this is, with the modern world; we were born with the Counter-Reformation and Neo-Scholasticism, in other words, against the modern world. We had neither intellectual revolution nor a bourgeois democratic revolution" (465).

In this way, we get quickly to the notion that Modernity has been rising in Latin America with muddy feet and wearing masks misrepresenting our most profound historical and cultural filiation. Paz concludes that, "In the beginning of the 19th Century we decided that we would be what the United States already was: a modern nation. The entry into Modernity demanded a sacrifice: that of ourselves. The result of this sacrifice is well known: we are still not modern but since then we go about in search of ourselves" (419).

As we can see, this analysis sustains itself on the continuous confusion of the time and conditions of Modernity with modernizing movements. Thus, for example, it could be maintained with the same, yet contrary, force that the Independence leaders did not indeed look for a modern society; and when some did, they were merely enlightened reformers—an incipient intellectual movement—in the midst of a traditional cultural context.

In short, while the "magic-real" response of the *Macondians* continues to negate the Modernity which the contemporary intellectuals cannot fail to glimpse around them, the answer in line with Octavio Paz, recurring to "different origins" and to "intellectual deficits" impairing the generation of an authentic Modernity, supplies an account of alleged flaws, mutilations, and masked lies of a supposed Latin American Modernity. Both sides converge in their questioning of Latin America's access to modern culture. They do it, on the one hand, through the exaltation of Latin America's wonders and mysteries, in other words, through the exaltation of what is unmistakably Latin American, persisting in the metaphor of *Macondo*; and, on the other hand, by calling attention to the specific intellectual deficits that are supposed to reduce the continent's capacity to follow the European and North American models towards Modernity.

Negations

We are proposing here, piece by piece, a different vision in regard to Modernity in culture—or the sum of cultures that is Latin America. We are moving in uncharted waters. Yet, we are doing it forewarned by tentative reports of explorations and mappings.[11] In order to advance we need to settle the accounts with these supposed "clashes with Modernity" proclaimed by the *Macondian* intellectuals and by those belonging to the current of "specific differences."

Macondo II

We can say now that *Macondo* is not only used as a metaphor for the incongruities perceived culturally in the (recent) modernization of Latin America but, more profoundly, as a representation of the continent's "contested soul"; as a type of multiple sign, adaptable to the contortions and fractures of the collective conscience of our societies unsettled by their access to Modernity.

In other words, Latin American culture is looked at and is "read" through *Macondo,* as a reverberating unfolding of contradictions, of anomalies, of fusions between the old and the new, of the inlayings and simultaneousness of diverse historical times, of the contemporary presence of elements of very diverse social or cultural origin. *Macondo* means: "they will not be able to understand us (the Latin Americans) easily." To whom is this admonition directed? Basically, to those local intellectuals who form no part of our own circle but use a competing code of interpretation; also, to certain foreigners: academics, intellectuals, informed readers, politicians, international bureaucrats, and agents in cooperation.

On an extremely banal level, *Macondo* speaks of the "exotic" nature of our continent and repeats the gesture, only now with an inverted sign, of the Europeans contemplating, a few centuries ago, our flora, fauna, oceans, and natives. On a more refined level, *Macondo* speaks of the mystery of being Latin American at the end of the twentieth century. "It is not easy to understand us" is, in this case, either a clamoring for the identity we lack or for that which has vanished. But *Macondo* is also a move on the chessboard of development. This move signifies that "they will not be able to impose upon us a pattern of modernization that does not suit our mystery." While others come to buy and sell, we respond with a noble gesture that exalts our spirit. We speak of morality, religion, and literature, all mixed together, through the ineffable *Macondian* metaphor. It is the same old gesture, made by the impoverished aristocrat, in the face of the merchant or banker shaking his purse beneath our noses. With Flaubert, we continue to believe that the bourgeois is an animal that does not understand the human soul. *Macondo,* it is said to us, is not Europe (and will not be) because it does not share the same rationality, nor is it the United States because it is not a market. But, moreover, *Macondoamérica* is subtly superior to anything else because it has "poetry," reveals "passion," communicates "mystery," speaks in tongues, and manifests the full powers of a Nature sheltering men under its mantle. *Macondo* is the final aristocratic gesture of a semideveloped continent that finally is obliged to recognize itself in Modernity.

Differences II

The thesis of specific differences or deficits is used, on the other hand, to reveal our lost identity in yet another way. Hidden beneath the masks imposed by successive and premature modernizations there would apparently lie the untouched or, in any case, misunderstood foundation of our soul, shaped by the historical sedimentations of the Baroque, processes of *mestizaje* (crossbreeding), and Christian heritage.

Contrary to this, the history of creole modernizations would have been made without regard for this soul, the true Latin American cultural synthesis which, however, manages to resurface, with enduring constancy, in spite of everything. For example, it appears in popular religious cultures, through rites more ancient than writing,[12] or in our dictators-*caudillos*, these ever-fascinating figures in the literature of the continent.[13] For those defending the thesis of deficits, the modernization of Latin America would appear, moreover, to be a necessarily imperfect or insufficient synthesis, incapable in any way of expressing preceding cultural syntheses that supposedly would have been more successful and authentic.

Thus, the lost identity of Latin America would not be fragmented just in the present, in which case at best it would be nothing more than an epiphenomenon of its pseudo-modernization, but it would also be broken in regard to the past. Concerning Mexican society, Octavio Paz remarked:

> In reality, we are standing before three distinct societies. The first is the pre-Columbian . . . Here the deep cut represented by the Conquest is found. It is the line of separation. In the 17th Century a new society is born: the Creole society, dependent upon Spain but ever more autonomous . . . But the Independence—which is simultaneously the dismemberment of the Spanish Empire and the birth of another society—is the end of the Creole society. The agony of New Spain was long and ended only in the second half of the 19th Century with the restored Republic. Thus, in the 19th Century the imperial project of the 18th Century was aborted. Out of the ruins of this project a third society was born, the one that we are living now, and which is still not completely formed. (*El ogro* 33)

The idea that within a society there exist distinct societies, times that are discontinuous yet simultaneously present, beliefs and principles organizing culture which coexist in open or hidden conflict, has been a relatively enduring key for reading and interpreting Latin American culture, shared by *Macondians* and by the critics of pseudo-modernization. Moreover, this was also a landmark idea in the region's sociology, but this time as an analysis of the dualism of Latin American societies or, for the Marxists, as a coexistence of diverse modes of production.

The social use of the above idea by the intellectuals of the region has brought a way of thinking about the cultural history of Latin America as something special, something that has never existed in the history of societies in the world. Although in many historical periods and places there have coexisted different conflicting modes of production and diverse societies within the same society, certain gods replacing other idols in the collective consciousness, and even though practically everywhere the advance is made through ruptures with continuity and the new lives mixing together with the old until novelty is produced (or aborted), all this seems to be forgotten when the cultural history of Latin America is analyzed in that way. It is as if only in this land we have experienced History as an imposition, mixture, and overcoming of previous economic, political, social, and cultural arrangements.

Likewise, the privilege conceded to the first in History as the primigenial in the concept, so that whatever may follow would be unauthentic in relation to the precedent, constitutes a gesture supported more by belief than by any factual base. But, of course, who has said that History need be constructed with scientific rigor, if it is possible, instead, to use the much stronger and solid cement of belief?

Latin America's Cultural Modernity

Revolution

Our next step will be to describe the new cultural topography of Latin America, in order to now justify the hypothesis that the region's culture has recently ended up establishing itself *as yet another constellation of Western Modernity.*

We have already seen that there are those who maintain that Latin America has been pursuing its own modernization like a false dream, or one emerging contrary to its more profound nature. We have only very partially accepted this thesis. Indeed, what we have had in our countries have been but modernizing movements at the heart of traditional culture, like new ideas, attitudes, and values which emerge amid what is established, striving for recognition.

According to our thesis, on the contrary, there has not existed, nor could there exist a modern cultural configuration—the Modernity that interests us here—until after the 1950s; in other words, since the beginning of the transformation of traditional modes of production, transmission, and reception of culture.

What happened with these modes of how culture is organized between 1950 and today? Let us consider some facts. Schooling has extended all over Latin America. Not completely, nor homogeneously, nor equally, nor offering an education of similar quality to all, but the advance made after 1950 has been, in any case, spectacular. Today, the gross numbers of those schooled in the region reach one hundred percent at the primary level; more than half at the secondary and seventeen of every one hundred young people in their respective age groups at the post-secondary or university level. More than seven million students account for this third level, and each year students graduating with higher education degrees comprise more than five hundred thousand. In the principal countries, the proportion of the population older than twenty-five years of age with a post-secondary education is reaching between five percent and seven percent which is a comparable number to that of Austria, Hungary and Italy. In Latin America there presently exist more than 100 million students at all levels and nearly five million teachers and professors, of which a half million are employed at the post-secondary level.

In 1987 the governments spent nearly thirty-three billion U.S. dollars on education, which accounted for 4.1% of the regional GNP for that year. Likewise, between 1950 and 1987 the number of published titles per one million inhabitants doubled in the region; and in 1987 the estimated editions of daily periodicals reached thirty-six million, while the total number of radio broadcasting stations surpassed six thousand. Radio receivers, in turn, increased to nearly 140 million in 1987, with 332 for every 1,000 inhabitants, a proportion which easily doubles the average in developed countries. On the other hand, the number of television stations, which in 1965 numbered 250, reached 1,590 in 1987, while the number of television receivers had grown to eight million in 1965. This number reached sixty million in 1987, thus raising the participation from thirty-two per thousand inhabitants to one hundred forty-seven per thousand, while in Asia it was forty nine per thousand and in Africa fourteen per thousand in 1987.

From the perspective of the production and communication infrastructure of culture one may say, then, that after 1950 a true revolution has been under way which has implied at least the following simultaneous and convergent phenomena:

a) *Education* has become a massive enterprise, reaching an ever wider sector of the younger population. In fact, one may say unequivocally that the schooling of the population has become the axis for the constitution of contemporary Latin American societies. School is the most extensive and intensive factor of socialization, notwithstanding its multiple and well-known deficiencies.

b) The educated or semi-educated *public* has consequently ended up imposing its particular tastes, sensibilities, and values on mass culture, which is no longer that of margins, popular or folkloric, but, increasingly, a culture of consumers of symbolic commodities produced and communicated industrially.[14]

c) To this end, *television* provides, together with schooling, the other extensive and intensive network for articulation of this mass culture, imposing on it its preferred genres, its commercial and advertising esthetic mixture, its internationalism, and its patterns of consumption, projection and identification. The new Latin American *social imaginary of the masses* is produced by television in the same way that schools and cities intervene in its formation.

d) For all that has been said, the rapidly emerging modern culture is established moreover as an *urban experience*, understanding the urban not only as identification with the city but, principally, as a particular sensibility and communicative experience which develops around the very idea of "longing to be modern."

In sum, we may affirm that in Latin America between 1950 and 1990 a cycle of incorporation into cultural Modernity opened up, at the same time that its economic, political, and social structures were being transformed under the pressure of a growing continental integration into international markets.[15] It would be superfluous to say that this incorporation has been contradictory, has been realized under very dissimilar political and economic conditions, and has advanced in irregular ways in different countries. But, as a global tendency it has operated everywhere, from Mexico in the North to Chile in the South.

The traditional cultural configuration which Angel Rama once called *lettered city*,[16] that bastion of scarce intellectuals, professors, writers, artists, and bureaucrats serving power and high culture, has been definitely overwhelmed by the masses, insofar as they had access to schooling, television and urban communication.

Autonomy

We assert that Latin American cultural Modernity has arrived hand in hand with profound transformations in the modes of producing, transmitting, and consuming culture. Therein solely resides the peculiarity of our Modernity and there its specific differences in regard to the European project of Modernity should be found.

We are not different but equal to the societies that preceded us in the construction of Modernity: we are a product of the social, economic, and technical transformation of the cultural domain. Culture becomes modern when it achieves its autonomy from the other social domains and differentiates within itself a whole range of specialized subfields. This is the old and well-known theorem of sociology and history of culture, analyzed by Max Weber in his work and later studied in greater depth by others.

From that moment, as it is occurring in Latin America today, the *domain of culture* acquires its own structure and divides into a variety of relatively differentiated and specialized apparatuses and circuits. Along with the Church which maintains control over the administration of the goods of salvation, unfolds a sphere of *morality*, the disputed region between a variety of actors and agencies. Further, *law* is affirming and projecting itself more and more like a second Nature around the interests and tensions of a society that has become complex and is searching to self-regulate its conflicts. Something similar is occurring with *art* and with each of its specialized branches; with *education,* which ends up institutionalizing itself in a hierarchy of levels and reaching massive proportions in all of them; with *mass communication* which goes on to organize itself industrially; and with the domain of *knowledge* which becomes fragmented into a multiplicity of relatively autonomous disciplines oriented toward their utilization by society.

Autonomy of the cultural spheres and their internal ramification leads, likewise, to more professional producers and transmitters, if not to more professional consumers or receivers. Culture, generically considered, will continue to be the "people's way of life," the tribal language, but its more dynamic internal structure will tend to professionalization, specialization, and institutionalization.

Beginning with Modernity, cultural roles diversify beyond the hybridizations that continue or the new forms of interconnection that are generated. But, to begin with the most obvious, producers and consumers now form two fronts within a polarized field. Likewise, the producers multiply, specialize, and classify themselves, in successive steps, constituting a dense network of positions within an ever-finer division and organization of production and symbolic transmission.

From the consumers' side, instead of uniting around a homogenous and standardized demand, their preferences also carry them to increasing levels of specialization, whether as readers of certain magazines, or as televiewers specialized in certain programs, or as listeners of one among a thousand various types of music.

Once culture accesses Modernity, its circuits proliferate continually. Analytical simplifications that distinguish between high culture, middle culture and low culture, are not borne out by the new facts. Instead, we see everywhere specialized circuits of production, transmission, and consumption. Some of these circuits are technologically more complex, others are closer to the body and voice; some locally structured, others highly internationalized; some esoteric to the point that they live off of their own translation and vulgarization, and others oriented toward the masses and characterized by a lesser degree of specialized codification.

Masses

Culture then finally becomes a mass social formation tending to the international, with a progressively industrial, highly differentiated base that cannot be controlled from any center. It is a decentered and deterritorialized culture which no longer reflects the people's soul, but the desires, sensibility, and work of a new class—that of the symbolic producers and mediators—and, at the same time, the generative work of millions of receivers-consumers who process, interpret, appropriate and live this mass of produced and transmitted signs in their own way, individually or, at times, collectively.

This is precisely why modern culture cannot be understood outside of market operations that are the specifically modern institutional mechanisms that coordinate this multifaceted business, which, however, without ceasing to be an "adventure of the spirit," is now organized as a planetary, regional, national, and local arena where producers and their diverse public exchange signs and even signs about signs.

The market of symbols—signs that dance: knowledge, artistic goods, messages, idols, well-packaged religions, texts, information—has single-handedly become one of the most powerful tools of contemporary economy. Its territories, creating a new political economy of the production and consumption of symbolic commodities, are the true determinants of inclusion and exclusion, of centrality and periphery, of civilization and barbarism, of the dynamic and the stagnant, and so on.

Latin America in its entirety invests annually as much in research and development as a handful of large North American businesses. Its active researchers barely account for two percent of the worldwide total; and among the 263 thousand scientific articles registered internationally each year, the region contributes a modest three thousand.

The Modernity of the culture operates and takes place in international markets of symbols, and its conflicts and innovations are produced and resolved there, at the heart of societies that find themselves forced to join such an organization in order to keep the march of History going.

Conversely, the State retreats to its fundamental functions. It can no longer mobilize nor imprint its order upon the cultural sphere. It may, for a time, subject it to the administration through its bureaucratic means or the police, but with no lasting effects. In the final analysis, the State can only control efficiently and directly that which it can submit to an administrative or repressive network. How could it do this with the international market's movement of symbolic commodities? How could it produce and communicate at the same time the full sense of life in societies ever more differentiated and complex that need to produce and transmit knowledge, information, therapies, sources of production, topics of conversation, sacraments, stories, myths, advertisement, entertainment, rituals, ideologies and images that would be sufficient for itself and for the world?

For this reason, the very role of the State is in the process of redefinition in Latin America vis-à-vis the new modern cultural constellation emerging from the 1950s. No longer is the State requested to administer culture or create a national cultural system but, more modestly, to assure the autonomy of the domain and its subsectors, the freedom for actors and agencies, and the uninterrupted circulation of signs. Next, to multiply the opportunities for access to culture providing to all at least the minimal cultural cognitive base through public education, and to distribute more equitably—where it can do that—the means of participating in culture, especially at the local level. Thirdly, the State is asked to subsidize certain cultural activities, preferably those of most interest to the heirs of the *lettered city*: good reading, serious theater and music, ballet and opera, national cinema.[17]

Once modern culture becomes autonomous, institutionalized, industrialized, massified, and professionalized, it can lay the groundwork for the emergence of what Gouldner called a "new class" of symbolic operators. The present day literati have become relatively independent of the power and the court, even though they often serve as the Prince's assessors. Their very variety renders them now unrecognizable in midst of society: They are teachers, journalists, scientists, essayists, photographers, movie producers, publicists, actors, priests, translators, technocrats, sound mixers, singers, ideologists, each one acting in different places, but according to their specialized roles. The "great intellectuals" tend to disappear in this process, giving way to intellectuals-specialists whose prestige is associated with the positions that they occupy and with the visibility they acquire in an increasingly saturated cultural domain.

Labyrinths

Be that as it may, and wherever the balance established in different countries between the market and the State may fall, Latin American culture is in the full process of incorporation into Modernity, precisely from the moment when it left behind the exclusive and excluding characteristics of the *lettered city,* to transform itself into the multiform vehicle of a growing integration of the masses.

This integration must not be understood as incorporation into a given cultural nucleus or single circuit, nor any specific and unique modality of symbolic consumption. The integration which comes from Modernity is the incorporation into a shared experience of differences, but within a common matrix provided by schooling, televised communication, continuous consumption of information, and the necessity of living connected communicatively in the "city of signs."

Such a "city of signs," Italo Calvino calls Tamara:[18]

> You penetrate it along streets thick with signboards jutting from the walls. The eye does not see things but images of things that mean other things . . . Your gaze scans the streets as if they were written pages: the city says everything you must think, makes you repeat her discourse, and while you believe you are visiting Tamara you are only recording the names with which she defines herself and all her parts. However the city may really be, beneath this thick coating of signs, whatever it may contain or conceal, you leave Tamara without having discovered it. (13-14)

Inside Tamara, "city of signs," individuals continue to be different, and to group and classify themselves in diverse cultural strata. They do not possess the same education nor do they come from similar families. They have been socialized in culture, in the way of those who enter it through many diverse doors, accessing positions and spaces that are only interconnected as they would be in a labyrinth. There, the mirroring signified (and generator of mirages) is the single red thread that allows one to orient himself, among voices, music, texts, sculptures and traces left by the culture that dances in its signs.

In contrast to what occurs in cities of ancient Modernity (those in which, as Walter Benjamin says, "the modern always cites proto-history") (185), the labyrinth of a recently modern culture lacks historical channels—memory, architecture, national myths, and established language—to help the inhabitants of *Tamaramérica* to walk neatly and with acquired sureness, as a young British woman would certainly do in the narrow streets of Oxford or as a Frenchman would use the walkways of the Metro in Paris, to reconstruct their social and personal history.[19] This lack of historical normalization has nothing to do with America's age nor with its indigenous and later arriving populations, but with the novelty of the modern in its culture. Forty years of Modernity is barely a beginning.[20]

If we understand the integration of masses of individuals to the same modern cultural labyrinth, it is clear that it does not presently suppose either a better integrative equity, or erasing of educational differences or knowledge, or the fusion of (evident) contradictions through some social democratic version of our Modernity. It means, instead, that men and women of the continent, in spite of all their flagrant differences, begin to share similar experiences, made possible by the present-day organization of cultural production, communication, and consumption. They begin then to access the same labyrinth-city, the same forms of signifiers, even though they access meanings, the value of which is very dissimilar with respect to recognition and change. That is, they begin to be submerged in the same mode of cultural production and consumption, even though they occupy diverse and disparate positions within it.

Due to this, the Latin American consciousness is starting to reproduce manifestations of this modern culture, like an internal labyrinth of meanings that do not cease to generate multiple dissonances and echoes of other things. It is a social consciousness connected communicatively, where illiteracy may be fused with television, the most remote rural localism with the stream of international images, or the history of the universities of Paris and Bologna may be taught at a remote elementary school in Patagonia.

The new stratifications of this consciousness are motivated by the continuous consumption of media overloaded with meaning. Ancient gods rule only over a part of this consciousness and barely succeed in conferring upon it an internal order. They are in competition with idols produced by cultural industry, and with manifold new knowledge related to a possibility of a better job, within an urban geography that reverberates with signs and projects itself beyond the national horizon.

The Mexican Carlos Monsiváis writes:

> The classic form in which society registers its moral temperament and testifies to its intimate convictions continues to be the melodrama, a direct path to expression and fixation of socially valid feelings . . . In the melodrama, the dominant morale is weakened and strengthened, ruled by the convulsive, trembling faith in the values of ·poetry. The message is transparent: melodrama is the midpoint between social realization and absolute pessimism; one cannot understand Mexico if one does not comprehend why Sara García cries in silence, if one does not accept that social life is a martyrdom which each family must traverse before arriving at a happy ending. Without knowing it or without pointing it out to them, what bourgeois, proletariat, middle class, and lumpen all search for throughout cultural industry and find is the systematic understanding of reality, unified in and transfigured by the melodrama. (38-39)

According to Martín Barbero, in the Latin American *telenovela* soap opera), the "drama of recognition" is at play (225). Its images are part of the labyrinth of signs of our city, and in its consumption, as if before a smashed mirror, the desire materializes to see things as images of things that signify other things. "And while you believe you are visiting Tamara, you are only recording the names with which she defines herself and all her parts."

Transfigurations

The intellectual modernizations bequeathed upon us by our ancestors did not bring us Modernity. When it finally arrived, it came without the modernization presupposed by the (European) project of the modern thinkers. Out of this comes the transfiguration that this project experiences as it emerges in Latin American conditions.

In their moment, Modern Times—Hegel's *neue Zeit*—served to mark a break with the previous age, the Middle Ages. The dividing line between the ages brought together the founding events of Modernity in a single nucleus: the discovery of the New World, the Renaissance, and the Reformation. The discourse of Modernity, propelled by the necessity of ascertaining and explaining itself without reference to the past, gave rise to the philosophical foundation of Modern Times.[21] Hegel writes: "The principle governing the recent world is, in general, freedom enjoyed by subjectivity, the fact that this subjectivity can develop and that its right to all the essential aspects which are present in a spiritual totality be recognized." In this context, as Habermas has shown, the notion of *subjectivity* comprises four essential aspects: individualism, the right to critique, the autonomy of action, and idealist philosophy. These are the principles realized through the Reformation, the Enlightenment and the French Revolution—in other words, all that we lacked and that remained absent from New Spain's intellectual history.

However, in Europe as well, the materialization of the modern project occurs first on the organizational plane of the economic, social, political, and cultural processes, rather than in the pure unfolding of abstract Reason. In its most productive conceptual nucleus, Marx's criticism of capitalist development points precisely toward the separation between Reason and History. In Latin America, as we have said, Modernity is born out of this same project but not out of its discourse, which is barely appropriated by small groups of enlightened intellectuals.

Individualism imposes itself, even in the absence of a liberal ideology, when the market begins to finally break the political, corporative, and populist pact of the Latin American benefactor State, destroying its supports, including its ideological and ethical bases.

The right to critique, on the contrary, suffers the same ups and downs as democracy, and appears buried, during [too] long intervals, under tyranny and military authoritarianism. When it finally begins to become recognized, its most solid bases in the public domain had long since disappeared. Now, the right to critique must be constructed in an environment saturated with publicity and private control over the principal apparatuses of mass communication.

Idealist philosophy, a product of modern Reason founded on itself and capable of understanding itself, was shattered long ago into a thousand fragments and variants to now turn into what is now the discourse which calls itself postmodern. Paradoxically, in Latin America, this discourse serves to question the previous forms of local idealism: the propensity to think the future as if it were a mental product of ideological utopias. To the contrary, postmodern discourse is not born here from the exhaustion of master narratives, because these never fully arrived to our shores. Rather, today, these narratives lose even the conditions for their local reception, or flounder in the midst of a pragmatism that is converting us by force to Protestant ethics due to our need to produce and compete in international markets.

Apparatuses

In other words, Modernity in Latin America was not born out of the heads of modernizers and of the radiation of their ideas in the minds of their contemporaries, but rather through the operation of the cultural apparatuses that produce it, even behind the backs of our intellectuals.

The Enlightenment with its lights comes to us hand in hand with underfunded schools, full of underpaid teachers who are at times inadequately prepared, but schools strong in their expansive capacity and their ability to penetrate the remote corners of Latin American consciousness. In spite of its multiple limitations and shortcomings, this is a massive, civilizing enlightenment. Discipline through schooling—far from preparing for industry or replicating its gesture—assumes here the role of a latter day Kant. The school becomes the Kant of the poor.

Television, in turn, brings us a critique of tradition and of all forms of traditionalism: religion, taste, ethics, parochialism, including religion and aristocratic culture. Seen as a critical matrix provided by Latin American Modernity, television is barely a metaphor for its internationalization, for the new configuration of mass culture, or for the emergence of a social imaginary precisely around images that are ever more quickly substituting tradition. All that is solid melts into television.

The city of signs, *Tamaramérica* five hundred years after its Discovery, provides the fusion of all the experiences constituting our Modernity, a dance in which no sign may stand on its feet for long under the pressure of technological and cultural changes that nowadays rain on *Macondo* every night.

The poverty that attends night schools, far from the intellectual salon; the expectations that move away from experience, which once Walter Benjamin considered as the generating nucleus of Modernity; the slow degradation of the autochthonous, ethnically based cultures, infiltrated by the lethal germ of the market and radio broadcasting;

the drugs that shape a new world map where, for once, the center of production is in the South and its receiving pole in the North, consuming crack on the street corners of New York; the utopian violence that runs along its last shining path, already a relic of the past even if its flag still often waves over the highest mast of the University of San Marcos in Lima; the TV melodrama where we are invited to recognize ourselves . . . All these are signs that dance without interruption, in the midst of which identities are made and unmade, establishing us as the changing subjects of Modernity.

"The eye does not see things but images of things that mean other things." Only the intellectual sloth makes us think that History is fixated on the "images of things." Behind them or wrapped up in them, instead, these images "mean other things." The modern city speaks through signs, and we can no longer know "whatever it may contain or conceal" and one day we must leave "without having discovered it."

Naive consciousness, as well as the glorious nature of *Macondoamérica,* are traditions that no longer exist; they are buried beneath the signs that dance in the consciousness of *Tamaramérica* (like minimal, repetitive music), communicating from one shore to another—and even beyond the edge of the Earth—the discovery of its own Modernity.

Notes

1. Also certain Europeans have fallen victim to this type of deficit analysis. For example, Bernice Hamilton points out that Spain "remained almost untouched by the Protestant Reformation or the Renaissance in its Italian form; it did not have a scientific revolution that could be cited, nor an equivalent of Hobbes or Locke; no political insurgences, none of this Social Contract Theory, no Industrial Revolution." See *Political Thought in the Sixteenth-Century Spain* (Oxford, 1963), 3. For further discussion on this topic consult Richard Morse, *El espejo de Próspero* (Mexico: Siglo XXI, 1982).

2. The author uses "plumíferos," a term that in Spanish may refer to the plumage of birds and also to poor writers. [Translator's Note].

3. Concerning the theme of the off-key American birds consult in the same book the paragraphs from the English naturalist, Goldsmith, pp. 23-26.

4. This period is referred to traditionally, in Hispanic context, as *Modernismo,* in contradistinction to the Anglo-American *Modernism* and the Brazilian *Modernismo,* spanning between 1920s and 1950s. Hispanic *Modernismo* is, then, related to the continental *Moderne* of the 1890s (this would be the time of "high" *Modernismo*) and not to the Avant-Garde, as Brazilian and Anglo-American *Modernisms* are. [Editor's Note].

5. Such phenomena have begun to be systematically analyzed in recent years. Consider, for example, the case of Argentina in Beatriz Sarlo, *Una modernidad periférica* (Buenos Aires: Ediciones Nueva Visión, 1988); Peru, in Julio Ortega, *Cultura y modernización en la Lima del 900* (Lima: CEDEP, 1986); or Chile, in

Bernardo Subercaseaux, *Fin de Siglo, La época de Balmaceda. Modernización y cultura en Chile* (Santiago: CENECA Editorial Aconagua, 1988).

6. In reality, modernization processes can be found also further back in the cultural history of Latin America, as far back as the late colonial period. But, as Richard Morse astutely shows us, "a continent and a half with a population of more than twenty million at the end of the colonial period, when four out of five people were slaves, dependent workers, farmers and shepherds living at subsistence level or occupying precarious positions in between, who often even did not speak the language of the conquistadors, was an unlikely stage for carrying out grandiose European plans of participatory integration" (95-96).

7. *Manifiesto Liminar* directed "To the free men of South America." Published in Cordoba, on June 21, 1918, in and extraordinary edition of *La Gaceta Universitaria*. The text is reproduced in Juan Carlos Portantiero, *Estudiantes y política en América Latina* (Mexico: Siglo XXI, 1978), 131-36.

8. See Centro Latinoamericano de Investigaciones en Ciencias Sociales, *Situación social de América Latina* (Buenos Aires: Solar Hachette, 1969); and Germán Rama, comp., *Educación y sociedad en América Latina y el Caribe* (UNESCO-CEPAL-PNUD, Santiago: UNICEF, 1980), 7-33.

9. Concerning the figure of Faust, see the well-known analysis of Marshall Berman, *All That is Solid Melts into Air* (New York: Simon and Schuster, 1982), especially part one, 6ff.

10. Concerning the American potentiality to produce an alternative rationality, see Aníbal Quijano, "Modernidad, identidad y utopía en América Latina," in F. Calderón, comp. *Imágenes desconocidas . . .* 17-24.

11. I refer, among others, to various of my earlier works, such as *El espejo trizado. Ensayos sobre cultura y políticas culturales* (Santiago: FLACSO, 1989); "¿Existe o no la modernidad en América Latina?" in F. Calderón, comp. *Imágenes desconocidas . . .* 95-99; "Cultura y crisis de hegemonías," introductory study in J. J. Brunner and C. Catalán, *Cinco estudios sobre cultura y sociedad* (Santiago: FLACSO, 1985); "Modernidad, democracia y cultura," in Gonzalo Martner, coord., *Chile hacia el 2000* (Caracas: Editorial Nueva Sociedad/PROFAL, 1988); and also J. J. Brunner, A. Barrios, and C. Catalán, *Transformaciones culturales y modernidad* (Santiago: FLACSO, 1989).

12. For a development of this thesis see Pedro Morandé, *Cultura y modernización en América Latina* (Santiago: Pontificia Universidad Católica de Chile, 1984).

13. See Angel Rama, "El dictador letrado de la revolución americana," in his *La crítica . . .*; and Tulio Halperin Donghi, *El espejo de la Historia* (Buenos Aires: Editorial Sudamericana, 1987), 15-39.

14. Consult Néstor García Canclini and Rafael Roncagliolo, eds., *Cultura transnacional y culturas populares* (Lima: IPAL, 1988). Also, Néstor García Canclini, *Las culturas populares en el capitalismo* (Mexico: Nueva Imagen, 1982).

15. See CEPAL, *Transformación productiva con equidad* (Santiago: CEPAL, 1990).

16. See Angel Rama, *La ciudad letrada* (Hanover, N.H.: Ediciones del Norte, 1984; *The Lettered City*. Trans. John Ch. Chasteen. Durham and London: Duke UP, 1996).

17. With respect to this point, see Sergio Miceli, "Teoría e práctica da política cultural no Brasil," in his book, *Estado e cultura no Brasil* (São Paolo: DIFEL, 1984).

18. See Italo Calvino, *Invisible Cities* (trans. William Weaver, New York: Harcourt Brace & Co., 1974).

19. I refer to Marc Augé, *El viajero subterráneo. Un etnólogo en el metro* (Buenos Aires: Gedisa, 1987).

20. Concerning the relation between Modernity and new cities see Richard Morse, "Ciudades periféricas como arenas culturales (Rusia, Austria, América Latina)," in Richard Morse and Jorge Enrique Hardoy, eds., *Cultura urbana latinoamericana* (Buenos Aires: CLACSO, 1985). Also Marshall Berman, *All That is Solid Melts Into Air* (New York: Simon and Schuster, 1982), cap. IV.

21. I follow Jürgen Habermas, *El discurso filosófico de la Modernidad* (Buenos Aires: Taurus, 1989), chapters 1 and 2.

Works Cited

Benjamin, Walter. *Iluminaciones*. Madrid: Taurus, 1980. Vol. I.

Berger, Peter L. and Thomas Luckman. *The Social Construction of Reality*. Penguin University Books, 1971.

Calderón, Fernando, comp. *Imágenes desconocidas. La modernidad en la encrucijada postmoderna*. Buenos Aires: CLACSO, 1989.

_____. "Identidad y tiempos mixtos o cómo pensar la modernidad sin dejar de ser boliviano." In his *Imágenes desconocidas . . .* 225-29.

Cándido, Antonio. "Literatura y subdesarrollo." In César Fernández Moreno, coord. *América Latina en su literatura*. Mexico: Siglo XXI-UNESCO, 1977.

Gerbi, Antonello. *La disputa del nuevo mundo*. Mexico: FCE, 1982.

Goffman, Erving. *Frame Analysis*. New York: Harper & Row, 1974.

Gouldner, Alwin. *The Dialectic of Ideology and Technology*. London: The Macmillan Press, 1976.

Groethuysen, Bernhard. *La formación de la conciencia burguesa en Francia durante el siglo XVIII*. Mexico: F.C.E., 1943.

Martín Barbero, Jesús. *De los medios a las mediaciones*. Barcelona: Gustavo Gili, 1987. Quoted after *Communication, Culture, and Hegemony: From Media to Mediations*. Trans. Elizabeth Fox and Robert A. White. London: SAGE Publications, 1993.

Monsiváis, Carlos. *Amor perdido*. Mexico: Era, 1982.

Morse, Richard. *El espejo de Próspero*. Mexico: Siglo XXI, 1982.

Neruda, Pablo. *Canto General*. Trans. Jack Schmitt. Berkeley: California UP, 1991.

Paz, Octavio. *El ogro filantrópico*. Mexico: Joaquín Mortiz, 1979.

_____. *México en la obra de Octavio Paz, I: El peregrino en su patria*. Mexico: F.C.E., 1987.

Sarlo, Beatriz. *Una modernidad periférica*. Buenos Aires: Ediciones Nueva Visión, 1988.

Rama, Angel. *La crítica de la cultura en América Latina*. Caracas: Biblioteca Ayacucho, 1985.

Sorokin, Pitrim. *Dinámica social y cultural*, Madrid: Instituto de Estudios Políticos, Vol. I.

2.

Modernity and Postmodernity in the Periphery

Jesús Martín Barbero

(*translated by Kristina Ríos de Lumbreras*)

A plural Modernity or rather modernities: We have here a statement that introduces into the debate an irresistible twist and a dislocation that is unacceptable even to the most radical of postmoderns. This is because the crisis of Reason and of the subject, the end of metaphysics, and the deconstruction of logocentrism all have as their horizon the Modernity shared by defenders and critics alike. Nevertheless, the primary condition for conceptualizing this crisis *from a Latin American perspective* is our wresting away from the logic according to which our societies are irreparably extraneous to the process of Modernity and that our Modernity can only be a deformation and degradation of the true one.

To break with that logic implies asking if the incapacity of Modernity to recognize itself in the alterities that resist that process from within, does not actually form part of the crisis: of the crisis not thought of from the center and, in fact, only thinkable from the periphery as a breakdown of the universal project, and as a difference that can be neither dissolved nor pushed aside. Which is what specifies Latin America's heterogeneity most profoundly: its decentered mode, prevented from the inclusion in, and appropriation of, Modernity. To think of this crisis in a Latin American way thus translates into the task of explaining our particular *uneasiness with/in Modernity* (Brunner, *Los debates* 36ff.).[1] This uneasiness is thinkable neither from the unfinished European modern project reflected upon by Jürgen

Habermas—since there, the inheritence left by the Enlightenment is restricted to its quality of emancipation yet leaves out that part of the project that rationalizes domination and expansion—nor from the recognition of difference that postmodern reflection were to trace since in this reflection diversity tends to become confused with fragmentation, which is the opposite of the interaction in which plurality is woven and sustained.

The uneasiness with Modernity refers primarily to the fact that Latin Americans have been constructing optimized images of the European modernizing project. The origin of this attitude can be found in the tendency to define the *Latin American difference* in terms of the parodical displacement of a European model characterized by a high degree of purity and homogeneity, and the difference is seen, then, as an "effect of the parody of a certain plenitude" (Ramos 82). The new vision of the modernizing process that European historians themselves are developing will play a decisive role in overcoming these images. According to this new vision, Modernity in Europe was not at all a unitary, integrated, and coherent process but rather a hybrid and uneven one, produced—as Perry Anderson has written—in

> the space between a still usable classical past, a still indeterminate technical present, and a still unpredictable political future. Or put another way, it arose at the intersection between a semi-aristocratic ruling order, a semi-industrialized capitalist economy, and a semi-emergent or -insurgent labour movement. (105)

This places us squarely before the need to understand "the sinuous Latin American Modernity by rethinking the different modernisms as attempts to intervene in the intersection of a semi-oligarchic dominant order, a semi-industrialized capitalist economy, and semitransformative social movements" (García Canclini 54).

Two consequences result from this new vision of the modern project. First, Modernity is not a linear and inescapable result in the socioeconomic modernization's culture but rather the interweaving of multiple temporalities and social, technical, political, and cultural mediations. Second, this vision deals an injurious blow to the development and complementary imaginaries that, since the beginning of the twentieth century have irreconcilably opposed Tradition and Modernity, whether opting for modernization as a means for a definitive "overcoming backwardness" or pleading for a "return to our roots and denouncing Modernity as a simulacrum." In an illuminating text, the Brazilian Roberto Schwarz examines the misunderstanding that leads to summarily labeling the liberal ideas in countries that still practiced slavery as "false." According to him, since liberal ideas could neither be practiced nor discarded, the important thing to understand was the "practical constellation" within which these ideas are inscribed, that is, the dislocations and deviations, the system of ambiguities and operations, that endow the "extraneous ideas" with meaning by permitting this system to appropriate them in an improper sense, improper in the relation to the movement that originated them but proper as a "social mechanism that makes of them an internal and active element of culture" (Schwarz 24). This is a line of reflection followed by Renato Ortiz in a book that from its very title, *A moderna tradição brasileira*, traces the movement of a Modernity that, by not operating as an explicit rupture with, could become part of, the traditional—that is, of the ensemble of institutions and values that, like nationalism or cultural industry, form the irreversible cultural space of several generations.

It is not surprising that one of the most contradictory dimensions of Latin American Modernity should be found in the projects of and imbalances vis-à-vis *the national* considering that the constitution of those nations took place to the rhythm of their transformation into "modern countries." In the twenties, when the national was proposed as a synthesis of cultural particularity and political generality that would transform "the multiplicity of desires of different cultures into a single desire to participate in (be a part of) the national sentiment" (Noves 10); in the fifties, when nationalism turned into populisms and developmental policies that consecrated the protagonism of the State to the detriment of civil society—a protagonism rationalized as modernizing within both leftist ideology and rightist politics (Garretón); and the eighties, when the affirmation of Modernity identified the substitution of the State by the market as the constructive agent of hegemony, will end up producing a profound devaluation of the national (Schwarz, "Nacional por sustracción"). But the political contradiction does not exhaust the relationship between Modernity and nation. In fact, this relation's most frequent and explicit thematization refers to culture, to *Modernismo* as a foreign influence and as transplanted extraneous forms and models.[2] Each country wanted to be a nation so as to finally achieve an identity, securing a recognizable identity happened through their incorporation into the modern discourse, since only in terms of this discourse would efforts and successes be validated as such: "We could only attain our Modernity through the translation of our raw materials into an expression that could be recognized abroad" (Squeffa 55). This is a contradiction that marks Latin American *Modernismo* but does not reduce it to a mere importation or imitation because—as cultural history and sociology of art and literature demonstrate—this *Modernismo* is also the secularization of language (Gutiérrez Girardot, Sarlo, Subercaseaux), the professionalization of cultural work (Franco), the overcoming of the colonial inferiority complex, and the liberation of a cannibalizing capacity that proposes to "devour the European father-totem, assimilating its virtues and taking its place" (Zilio). *Modernismo* in Latin America has thus not only been a Modernity compensating for the inequalities caused by the underdevelopment of other dimensions of social life, but also an inauguration of a new cultural project: the introduction of the national into the modern aesthetic development through reelaborations that in many cases were linked to the search for a social transformation. Far from being irreparably denationalizing, *Modernismo* in Latin America was in quite a few cases the milieu and inspiration for the recreation of the national.

The most extensive and dense process of modernization in Latin America will take place beginning with the fifties and sixties and will be linked decisively to the development of the culture industries. These are the years of diversification and reinforcement of economic growth, consolidation of urban expansion, unprecedented increase of schooling and reduction of illiteracy. This process of development will be accompanied and shaped by the expansion of mass media and the establishment of the cultural market. According to José Joaquín Brunner, it is only after the intersection of these processes that we can speak of Modernity in these countries. This is so because Latin American Modernity is more than an intellectual experience related to the principles of the Enlightenment (Brunner, "Existe o no la modernidad" 3ff.).[3] Rather, it emerges the *decentering* of the sources of cultural production from the community to the specialized "apparatuses," from the *substitution* of the traditional ways of life by the lifestyles configured through consumption, from the *secularization and internationalization* of the symbolic worlds, and from the *fragmentation* of communities and their conversion into audiences segmented by the market. All these are processes that, if in some respects began at the turn of the century nevertheless did not gain real social visibility until education became widespread and until culture attained its differentiation and autonomy from other social domains through the general professionalization of its producers and the segmentation of its consumers. And this in turn happens when the State can no longer order or mobilize the cultural sphere and must limit itself to assuring its autonomy, freedom of its actors, and opportunities for access to different social groups, leaving the coordination and energizing of the area to the market. Modernity among us turns out to be a result of "a shared experience of differences, but within a common matrix provided by schooling, televised communication, continuous consumption of information, and the necessity of living connected communicatively in the city of signs" (Brunner, *Tradicionalismo y modernidad*).

Cultural politics, dedicated to searching out roots and preserving authenticities or denouncing the decadence of art and cultural confusion, appear not to have either heard of nor engaged with this Modernity. And this is not surprising, since the Latin American majorities' experience of Modernity is as far from the traditionalists' conservative preoccupations as it is from the avant-garde's experimentalisms. Postmodern in its own way, that Modernity is created by strong shifts in the compartments and exclusions that the traditionalists had instituted for more than a century, thereby generating hybridizations between the autochthonous and the extraneous, the popular and high culture, the traditional and the modern. All these categories and demarcations have become incapable of elucidating the beat that energizes the world of culture and moves the integration and differentiation experienced by our societies. Modernization, Néstor García Canclini has written:

> relocates art and folklore, academic knowledge and industrialized culture, under relatively similar conditions. The work of the artist and that of the artisan approximate each other when each one feels that the specific symbolic order in which it is nourished is redefined by the logic of the market. Less and less can they remove themselves from modern information and iconography, from the disenchantment of their self-centered worlds and from the reenchantment that is favored by the spectacularization of the media. (5)

Cultural experiences have stopped corresponding linearly or exclusively to the milieus and repertoires of ethnicities or social classes. There is a traditionalism of the high culture elites that has nothing to do with the popular sectors, and a modernism in which a large part of the upper and middle classes meet with the majority of the popular classes, convened by tastes molded by culture industries.

Heavily burdened with premodern components, Latin American Modernity becomes a collective experience of the majorities only through postmodern social dislocations and perceptions. This is a Postmodernity that instead of coming to replace comes to reorganize the relationship between Modernity and tradition. This is the space in which our "differences" are played out—differences, as Alejandro Piscitelli alerts us, that are neither formed by regressions to the premodern nor fall into irrationality by not being part of the unfinished European modern project. In "Un desencanto llamado posmodernidad," Norbert Lechner writes: "Postmodernity consists in assuming social heterogeneity as a value and in interrogating ourselves about its articulation as a collective order." And he proposes a reading of the most radical aspects of postmodern disenchantment *from a Latin American perspective*: while in the central countries the praise of difference tends to signify dissolution of any idea of community, in our countries, as he affirms, heterogeneity will only produce a social dynamic linked to a some notion of community. Not to an idea of community rescued from the past, but rather one reconstructed using as its base the postmodern political experience. In other words, it will be linked to a *crisis* which brings us, on the one hand, a "cooling of politics"—its *dedramatization* through the desacralization of its principles, the detotalization of its ideologies, and the reduction of the distance between political programs and people's everyday experiences; and, on the other hand, a *formalization* of the public sphere, that is the predominance of its contractual dimension over its capacity to create collective identity, with the subsequent weakening of moral commitment and affective ties, and the differentiation and specialization of its space, with the consequential predominance of instrumental rationality (Lechner, "La democratización" 253ff.).

Postmodernity in Latin America is less a question of style than one of culture and politics. It is a question of dismantling the *separation* that attributes a modern profile to the elites while at the same time it confines the colonial to the popular sectors, the separation that places the massification of cultural goods in opposition to cultural development, proposes that the State dedicate itself to the conservation of tradition, leaving to private initiatives the task of renovating and innovating, that permits many to adhere fascinatedly to technological modernization while professing fear and distaste for the industrialization of creativity and the democratization of audiences. It is also a question of recreating the forms of coexistence and deliberation in civic life without reassuming of moralized principles, absolutized ideologies, or substancialized social subjects. It is further a question of reconstituting identities without fundamentalisms, recreating, instead, the modes of symbolizing conflicts and pacts from the opacity of hybridizations, dispossesions, and reappropriations.

Notes

1. For the update of this debate, see José Joaquín Brunner, "¿Existe o no la modernidad en América Latina?"

2. See note 4 to José Joaquín Brunner, "Traditionalism and Modernity in Latin American Culture." [Editor's Note]

3. See also José Joaquín Brunner, Carlos Catalán, and Alicia Barrios, *Chile: Transformaciones culturales y conflictos de la modernidad* (Santiago, 1989).

Works Cited

Anderson, Perry. "Modernity and Revolution." *New Left Review* 144 (1984): 96-113.
Brunner, José Joaquín. *Los debates sobre la modernidad y el futuro de América Latina.*
   Santiago de Chile: FLACSO, 1986.
_____. "¿Existe o no la modernidad en América Latina?" *Punto de vista* 31 (1987):
   1-5. Also in F. Calderón, comp. *Imágenes desconocidas* . . . 95-99.
_____. *Tradicionalismo y modernidad en la cultura latinoamericana.* Satiago de
   Chile: FLACSO, 1990.
Calderón, Fernando, comp. *Imágenes desconocidas: La modernidad en la encrucijada
   posmoderna.* Buenos Aires: CLACSO, 1989.
Franco, Jean. *The Modern Culture of Latin America.* New York: 1967.
García Canclini, Néstor. *Hybrid Cultures: Strategies for Entering and Leaving
   Modernity.* Trans. Christopher L. Chiappari and Silvia López. Minneapolis: U
   of Minnesota P, 1995.
Gutiérrez Girardot, Rafael. *Modernismo: Supuestos históricos y culturales.* México,
   1987.
Lechner, Norbert. "Un desencanto llamado posmodernidad." *Punto de vista* 33 (1988):
   25-31.
_____. "La democratización en el contexto de una cultura posmoderna." *Cultura,
   política y democratización.* Santiago: FLACSO, 1987. 253.
Noves, A. *O nacional e o popular na cultura popular.* São Paulo: Brasilense, 1983.
Ortiz, Renato. *A moderna tradição brasileira.* São Paulo: Brasilense, 1988.
Piscitelli, Alejandro. "Sur, post-modernidad y después." In F. Calderón, comp.
   Imágenes desconocidas. . . 69-83. ·
Ramos, Julio. *Desencuentros de la modernidad en América Latina.* Mexico: Fondo de
   Cultura Económica, 1989.
Sarlo, Beatriz. *Una modernidad periférica: Buenos Aires 1920 y 1930.* Buenos Aires,
   1988.
Schwarz, Roberto. *Misplaced Ideas: Essays on Brazilian Culture.* Trans. John
   Gledson. New York: Verso, 1992.
_____. "Nacional por sustracción." *Punto de vista* 28 (1987): 15-22.
Squeffa, Enio. *O nacional e o popular na cultura brasileira: Música.* São Paulo:
   Brasilense, 1983.
Subercaseaux, Benjamín. *Modernización y cultura en Chile.* Santiago de Chile, 1988.
Zilio, C. "Da antropofágia a tropicália." *O nacional e o popular na cultura brasileira:
   Artes plásticas.* São Paulo: Brasilense, 1982.

◆ 3.

Communications: Decentering Modernity

Jesús Martín Barbero

(*translated by Kristina Ríos de Lumbreras*)

To abstract modernization from its original context is but a recognition that modernization needs to be thought "theoretically," as Habermas would say, and that its constitutive processes have lost their center (origin) as they were extending themselves all over the world following the rhythms of capital formation, internationalization of markets, diffusion of knowledge and technology, globalization of the mass media, continuous migrations and flows of people, advances of urbanization, democratization of political forms, extension of schooling, vertiginous circulation of fashions, and the universalization of certain patterns of consumption.
José Joaquín Brunner, *Cartografías de la modernidad, 1994*

Even though the crisis in our Modernity seems more tied to *debt*—and thus to the contradictions in a modernization designed by entrepreneurs and politicians—than to *doubts* about Modernity suffered by intellectuals, philosophers, and scientists in Europe and the U.S., the two crises are intertwined and their discourses complement each other. In a way, another aspect of their crisis lies in the very relaunching of the modernizing project in our countries. Therefore, an indispensable condition for thinking about a social project in Latin America in which economic and technologic modernization will not prevent nor replace a cultural modernity is that we take charge of this crisis. What relates this debate in a rather particular way to the *domain of communications* is the fact that not only is modernization being identified every day more explicitly with the development of information technologies, but also that communication appears as a strategic *place* in the reformulation of Modernity's currency and in the ways this reformulation announces Postmodernity.

In recent years, especially in the wealthier countries, communication has become crucial to imagining and naming new models for society. Such is the "information society," the one in which information has become the most valuable and costly raw material and in which communications has become the model of its own organization: a network of connections between all the circuits, the social spaces, and functions; a continuous *self-regulation* and *retroaction;* and transparency, which is the *convertibility* and translatability of all knowledge to the hegemonic information code (Baudrillard; Breton).

Paradoxically, communications has also become crucial in the opposite sense of its positioning in the information model. Jürgen Habermas has explicitly connected "communicative praxis" to the search for, and defense of, a noninstrumental rationality. Within this rationality Modernity's liberating dimensions—those which permit us to question the project's reduction to its purely technical and economic aspects—are still alive. In this way, at the center of social reflection, Communicative Reason appears to fill the void, the "epistemological orphanhood" produced by the crisis of the production and representation paradigms, and to provide society with a potential for resistance and moral orientation, which feeds new social movements, from ethnicity to ecology to feminism (Habermas). From the perspective opened up by Habermas, and beyond any critique of his idealization of Reason and communicative action in its radical exclusion of instrumental dimensions (Marramao; Alexander), what seems inescapable is the relevance that communication takes on in the renewal of the analytical models of social action, the renewal of research agendas, and in the epistemological and political reformulation of critical theory.

Communications also becomes relevant to another aspect of the crisis: that of the crisis of Modernity as both the announcement and commencement of Postmodernity. On the one hand, we have the changing of the guard in the communicative structure of postindustrial society: according to Jean-François Lyotard, far from being a mere instrument or mode of action, communications becomes, through the new relationships between science and technology, the constitutive element of the new conditions for knowledge. Knowledge no longer belongs to that ambitiously unifying modern Reason but rather to the Reason that moves between the opening of an unlimited horizon of exploration and the consciousness of the limited nature of all forms of knowledge, of the impossibility of master narratives, and of the irreducible local character of all discourse—this is where the structural change in the sense of *epochal change* is taking place. In the same vein, yet lacking Lyotard's austere optimism, Gianni Vattimo gauges this "communication society" by the emergence of the "weakening of the real," experienced by the urban dweller in the process of technologies' continuous mediation, the incessant crisscrossing of information, interpretations, and images produced by science and by the media. It is a society of the masses, understood as the declination of the force of values and the undermining of Modernity's central categories: tradition/innovation, progress/reaction, avant-garde/kitsch—due to the *question of the other*: the political and cultural thickening of ethnic, sexual, and regional differences.

The Social and Cultural Visibility of Modernity in Latin America

In its own way, Latin America is also living the ambiguous and strategic centrality of communications. During the so-called "lost decade" of the eighties, the only industry in which large investments were made and that had a noticeable development was the communications industry. The following examples may serve to prove the point: from the mid-seventies to the mid-eighties the number of television stations went from 400 to 1500; Brazil and Mexico acquired their own satellites; in most Latin American countries, radio and television established world links via satellite, as well as data networks, satellite dishes, cable television networks, and various regional television stations. Similarly, since the eighties, communications and computerization have turned into the prime target areas for the economic opening and a justification for the neoliberal model. This has become evident in the priority given to the privatization of telecommunications companies from Argentina to Peru (including Colombia's frustrated attempt to privatize its telecommunications companies), as well as in the privatization of national television in the few countries in which some public television stations have still been maintained, such as Mexico and Colombia.

Why this priority given to the privatization of communications businesses if not because this space has become strategic not only on the technological innovation level but also on the macroeconomic decision-making level? Or to put it another way: The technological and political enclave of communications has become decisive in the design and reorganization of the economy and society. At the same time this has implied, as a sort of given, the idea that the public authorities would be incapable of understanding and managing the range of bets and changes that technological innovations in the communications domain would entail. In this way, the initiative in this field is left to the market's movements while State intervention is seen as interference bordering on intentions of censorship. This ceremony of confusion has led to the point of pulling the rug from under what for years had been understood as a *public service*[1] and that has now become indispensable to rethink if we want democracy to have any meaning.

In Colombia, the eighties have also seen the deployment of the communications industry. We have one of the most modern radio systems in Latin America and a notably advanced level of technological and business development in television. We are witnessing the deployment of all the communications paraphernalia of the cellular phone, of optical fiber and the links between satellite systems, satellite dishes and cable networks. But at the same time, Colombia is going through one of the most profound ruptures in the communication of its communities with its social actors. In a flagrant paradox, the country is experiencing a not often seen assertive development of information means and technologies, while at the same it is time experiencing a profound crisis of coexistence, of *communication* between the collective groups that make up Colombia as a society and as a nation.

Some of the most perverse expressions and instrumentalizations of the crisis of coexistence are, precisely, in the communications domain. This is something that I have been trying to understand starting from a hypothesis I formulated at the end of the eighties (in "Comunicación y ciudad"): To a degree not seen in any other Latin American country, the Colombian media live off fear. People's fears are what has made it possible for the media, especially radio and television, to occupy such a decisive place in society, in politics, and in the culture (or the lack thereof) of the majority. The media have known how to take advantage of our fears—those fears that each day make us trust people less and shut ourselves in our homes more, those that allow television to absorb the communication which is impossible in public squares and in the street theater of politics. For this reason the modernization of television has become at the same time so strategic and so ambiguous (proven by the debate in Colombia on Law 182 regulating its privatization): In such a divided and torn country, television has become not only the sacrificial lamb responsible for the violence and demoralization that accosts us, but it is also the one strange and only place where Colombians vicariously and perversely arrange to meet.

On the basis of this panorama, an indication of the role that communication processes and technologies occupy in the scenario of modernization of Latin American societies, we are better able to understand the displacements the debate about *Modernity* has suffered in these countries. Until rather recently, Latin American Modernity was conceptualized as a mere prolongation of European Modernity, though, of course, misguided, deformed and even parodic. Yet, in the final analysis, it is always related to *the* Modernity of the Enlightenment and high culture (Ramos; Lander). However, today we see that in order to consider the crisis of Modernity from within, Latin America has as one condition dismantling this logic by asking ourselves if the Center's incapacity to recognize itself in diverse modernities does not demonstrate its incapacity to conceive of a difference that cannot be assimilated nor pushed away. This is the *decentering* that some sociologists have begun to take into account, for whom, Latin American Modernity as a *collective experience* has less to do with Enlightenment doctrines and high culture aesthetics than with mass education and the expansion of the culture industries, especially the media (Brunner; García Canclini; Ortiz). Latin American Modernity is thus structurally related to the process whereby the sources of cultural production—the community, the State, or the Church—have no longer fulfilled this function, which has been shifted onto specialized industries and apparatuses. The displacement of cultural production has first of all implied the secularization and internationalization of the symbolic worlds. Which means, on the one hand, an accelerated substitution of "exemplary lives" by the lifestyles proposed by advertising and fashion, nowadays the two models of globalization; and on the other hand, the progressive autonomy of the cultural sphere—from science to sexuality—in relation to that subjection to religious order that the Catholic Church had promoted in Latin America. The revitalization of Protestant, animistic, and Oriental beliefs in Latin America, without undercutting the noticeable growth of the autonomy of the cultural sphere and the weight that this domain has achieved in recent years in the very orientation of society, proves that this secularization has nothing to do with nineteenth century irreligiosity or with Hispanic anticlericalism (Morandé; González).

In a peculiar way, Latin American Modernity speaks to a profound fusion—the complicity and complexity of relations—between the orality that remains a primary cultural experience of the majorities and the "secondary orality" woven and organized by the grammar of electronic visuality.[2] How can we continue considering memory and Modernity as separated—especially the enlightened Modernity anchored in the book—when in Latin America the majorities access and appropriate Modernity without abandoning their oral culture? When the dynamics of the transformations that seep into the daily culture of the majorities come from the deterritorialization and cultural hybridizations that mass media provide and control in its disconcerting convergence with the "profound strata of collective memory brought to the surface by the brusque alterations of the social fabric that modernizing acceleration itself entails?" (Marramao 60).

Alonso Salazar found in investigating this *new orality* in the Medellín youth gangs that in this orality Modernity was hybridizing a thoroughly paisa culture—that of Colombian mule driver's (arriero) profit motive, his strong religiosity and retaliatory spirit—and that of the tango culture with its exaltations of macho values and the idealization of the mother. He also found that Modernity, in turn, is comprised of three ingredients. First, is a *fleeting sense of time*, which expresses itself by extending the short shelf life of the majority of objects to people—and thus, like the objects, making people disposable! Another expression is in the value that the present instant acquires when neither the past nor the future matters much, a value that changes the meaning of death and makes it the strongest experience in life. Second, is a modern sense of *consumption* that consists in becoming and exhibiting oneself as powerful and applying financial transactions to all areas of life? And finally, third is a *visually strong language* that permeates ways of dressing, of making music, and of speaking, all fragmented and full of images inspired by the visual mythologies of war, and cut through with the sound and gestural stridence of the punk culture (Salazar).

Nevertheless, it seems that institutions and the cultural politics, of searching for and preserving authenticity or denouncing the decadence of art and cultural confusion, have not noticed or given credit to this other Modernity. And this is not unusual, since the experience of Modernity that the Latin American majorities assimilate and incorporate is as far from the *conservative* worries of the traditionalists as it is from the experimentalisms of the avant-gardes. This Modernity, Postmodern in its own way, materializes by creating strong displacements in the compartments and exclusions instituted more than a century ago by the traditionalists. In other words, this Modernity takes place by generating hybridizations between the traditional and the modern, the autochthonous and the foreign, popular and high culture, and between both of the latter and mass culture. But these are all categories and demarcations that have become incapable of explaining the fabric that energizes the cultural world, the movement of integration, homogenization and differentiation that our societies are living now. Modernization, writes Néstor García Canclini

> relocates art and folklore, academic knowledge and industrialized culture, under relatively similar conditions. The work of the artist and that of the artisan approximate each other when one feels that the specific symbolic order in which it is nourished is redefined by the logic of the market. Less and less can they remove themselves from modern information and iconography, from the disenchantment of their self-centered worlds and from the reenchantment that is favored by the specularization of the media. (5)

Cultural experiences thus stop corresponding linearly and exclusively to the domains and repertoires of ethnicities or social classes. There is a traditionalism of the high culture elites that has little to do with the traditionalism of popular sectors, and a modernism in which part of the upper and middle classes, convoked by tastes molded by the culture industries, *communicate* with the popular sectors.

Some of these processes began a long time ago, with the modernization that started in the thirties, or even before, in some

Southern Cone countries. But even the modernization that began during those earlier years only became socially visible in the fifties with mass schooling and the development of culture industries. It is only since then that the professionalization of cultural producers and the organization and segmentation of the world of consumers has extended to the collective experience. This professionalization and specialization of producers and the fragmentation of audiences requires us to look at the culture industries not only from the perspective of the market but also from that of culture, thus assuming the culture industry and the mass media as spaces of the production and circulation of cultures, corresponding not only to technological innovations or to the movement of capital, but also to *new forms of sensibility*: new means of perception, appropriation and enjoyment. The new sensibility has its most decisive correlation in the new forms of sociability with which people today face the insurmountable symbolic heterogeneity of the city. This is so because it is through the new ways of "being together,"[3] but also of excluding, of recognizing and not recognizing each other, that what happens in and through the media and communication technologies acquires social density and cognitive relevance. It is from these new kinds of encounters and recognition that the mass media have begun to mediate in the production of a new imaginary which in a certain way integrates the citizen's tattered urban experience.

Thinking about the relationship between Modernity and communication in Latin America obliges us to let go of cumbersome theoretical legacies and ideological burdens that impede our analyzing the culture industries as matrices of the disorganization and reorganization of the social experience. Matrices which operate in the intersection of deterritorializations and relocalizations that social migrations and urban life's fragmentations bring with them. That well-maintained and legitimized separation that placed the mass production or industrialization of cultural goods in diametrical opposition to social development, thus permitting the elites to embrace technological Modernity in fascination while keeping their rejection and distaste for the dissemination of the centers of cultural power and the expansion and democratization of creativity gets buried by the urban experience. This same new urban experience that obliges us to rethink the relationships between culture and politics, to connect the question of cultural policies to the transformation of political culture, and to assume this political culture in its communicative density. A political culture is a way of interpellation among social actors, an interweaving fabric of interpellations and discourses by which these social actors become subjects (Landi). It is for this reason that the transformations of Modernity demand that we consider communications not only as a matter of markets and technologies but also as a decisive space in the construction of democracy.

Modern Images of the National and the New Latin American Imaginary

Constituted into nations to the rhythm of their transformation into "modern countries," it is not strange that one of the most contradictory dimensions of Latin American Modernity is to be found in the projects of nation and in the maladjustments vis-à-vis the notion of the national. In the twenties, the national was proposed as a synthesis of cultural particularity and political generality that "transforms the multiplicity of desires of different cultures into a single desire to participate in (be a part of) the national sentiment" (Noves 10). In the forties and fifties, nationalism was transmuted into populisms that consecrated the protagonism of the State to the detriment of the civil society—a protagonism that was rationalized as modernizing within both leftist ideology and rightist politics (Garretón). And in the eighties, when the affirmation of Modernity identified the substitution of the State by the market as the constructive agent of hegemony, will end up producing a profound devaluation of the national (Schwarz).

What role have the media and modes of communication played during this process? The modernization that we are going through now entails a radical change with respect to the position that the media held during that first Latin American modernization (the thirties through the fifties) which was guided by the populisms of Getulio Vargas in Brazil, Lázaro Cárdenas in Mexico, and Juan Perón in Argentina.[4] In that process the media was decisive in the formation and diffusion of national identity and sentiment. The idea of Modernity that sustains the project of constructing *modern nations* in the thirties, articulates an economic movement—the entrance of national economies into the international market—into a political project destined to forge nations by creating a *national* culture, identity, and sentiment. This project was only possible through communication between the urban masses and the State. The media, especially the radio, became the voice for the interpellation, which, through the State, aimed to turn the masses into a people and the people into a nation. Populist *caudillos* would find the radio as the means that would enable them to create a new mode of communication and a new political discourse which would break with the rhetoric of religious sermons and of parliament. Oscar Landi has studied the modernity of Perón's discourse, which, together with the discourses of the Mexican Revolution, contains the first interpellations of workers and farm laborers as *citizens*. This new discourse found through the radio a fundamental mediation with popular language's capacity to reelaborate orality and certain types of colloquial expressivity that connect the territorial with the discursive.

On the other hand, the media gave people from the provinces and the regions an everyday experience of integration, the translation of the idea of the nation into an everyday living experience. The radio in all Latin American countries (and in some, the cinema) mediated between rural cultures and the new urban culture of mass society, introducing into this society the elements of orality and expressivity of rural cultures, and likewise making it possible for the rural cultures to switch from the expressive-symbolic rationality to the informative-instrumental rationality that organizes Modernity (Muñizaga and Gutiérrez).

The process that we are experiencing today is not only different from that just described but largely reversed: The media are one of the most powerful agents for the devaluation of the national (Schwarz). What is configured from them today, in a more explicit way in the perception of young people, is the emergence of *cultures without territorial memory*, or cultures in which the territorial has become secondary. In contrast to those cultures whose axis is language and thus a territory, the new musical and visual cultures surpass that limitation and produce new communities, *tribes*, that are neither easily understood nor compared with territorial communities.[5] These new cultures, linked as they are to the stratagems of the transnational market of television, music or video, cannot be underestimated in what they imply for new ways of operating and perceiving identity. Such identities have shorter span, are more precarious, and have a plasticity that permits them to combine ingredients from very diverse cultural worlds; they are thus full of discontinuities and noncontemporaneous elements in which atavistic gestures, modernist residues, and radical ruptures coexist.

How difficult it is for us not to project the founding dichotomy of the national states onto these new deterritorialized sensibilities, making it even harder for us to communicate to the young the meaning and value that the national can still have! Nevertheless, today the media introduce another order of organization of the cultural that cannot be thought of in terms of the national/antinational, since what this organization generates is a contradictory movement between the globalization and fragmentation of worldwide culture and a revitalization of local culture. Today, the press and the radio, as well as and in ever more accelerated way television, are most interested in *differentiating* cultures, whether by regions or age groups, so as to at the same time connect each culture to global rhythms and images. As a consequence, the devaluation of the national does not solely come from the deterritorialization carried out by the circuits of the global interconnection between the economy and the culture-world, but also from the internal erosion produced by the *liberation of differences*, especially regional and generational differences.

As seen from the global culture point of view, national culture appears provincial and encumbered by State-level burdens. As seen from the point of view of the diversity of local cultures, national culture is identified with centralist homogenization and officialist stultification. The national in culture becomes a dimension overflowing in both directions, in this way reformulating the sense of *borders*. What meaning can geographic borders have in a world in which satellites can photograph the richness of the earth's subsoil and the information that influences economic decisions circulates through informal networks? There continue to be borders, of course, but aren't the old borders of class and race and the new technological and generational borders more insurmountable than national borders? This does not imply, however, that the national does not preserve its validity as an historic mediation of the long memory of nations, that which makes communication between generations possible—only if that validity is not confused with the intolerance that today returns in certain nationalisms and particularisms, empowered, perhaps, by the dissolving of borders especially experienced by the Western world.

What meaning can *Latin Americanness* have in this reinvention of images of the national? For many years the mass media has been an integral part of a Latin American imaginary. Film with its idols and radio with its music—*tango, ranchera, bolero*, and recently *salsa*—have been especially important for the Latin Americans to *feel united*. But the media and the culture industries of radio, film, and television operate today within an ever more paradoxical situation: the *integration of* Latin American countries today passes unavoidably through its *integration into* a world economy ruled by the purest and crudest market logic. Nowhere else is the unavoidable necessity of Latin American integration together with its difficulty surmountable contradictions as apparent as in the field of communications. If there is a powerful movement breaking down barriers and dissolving borders it is the one that flows through information and communication technologies (Drago). It is precisely these technologies that most strongly accelerate the integration of our countries into the world culture and economy through a *revolution* that turns the national into an increasingly insufficient framework to either take advantage of this revolution or defend us against it. At the same time this *revolution* reinforces and intensifies the inequality of the exchange: Developed countries experience an increase of conservation and substitution of raw materials, while these continue to be the key item for Latin American export, and the exchange is shifted toward goods and services with higher degrees of technological composition.

The contradictions that crisscross and sustain this Latin American integration come down to—in the communications field—the question of the importance of audiovisual industries to these processes. These industries operate in the strategic terrain of the production and reproduction of *the images that our nations create of themselves as well as with which they differentiate themselves from others*. From this perspective, what significance does the enormous and dispersed growth of television stations and scheduled programming hours or the fact that in several Latin American countries there are more VCRs than Belgium or Italy have, if all this is accompanied by a reduction in the percentage of internal production and by a rising homogenization of imports? Of course it is of consequence for the audiovisual milieu of the world that companies like Mexico's Televisa and Brazil's Redeglobo make their presence felt. What is disquieting is the fact that this presence is achieved at the expense of shaping the image of their own cultures in terms of ever more neutral and undifferentiated audiences. The end result is the dissolving of cultural differences in the most profitable yet tawdriest folklorism or exoticism.

Advertising and *telenovelas* (Latin American soap operas) serve as good indicators of the course the relation Modernity/media has taken in recent years. For advertising, *modern* means accelerated internationalization of content and displacement of the criteria of quality in favor of technical sophistication (Festa and Santoro). Beyond its economic force, advertising occupies a privileged place in the experimentation with images made possible by the computer, and thus in the renewal of the modes of *representation of Modernity*: images from advertising and videoclips—which in aesthetic terms come closer to each other every day—create the everyday mediation between technological innovation and narrative transformation. This mediation found its highest point in the images of the Persian Gulf War by inserting a strong system of primary identifications in an aesthetic of simulation and visual play dominated by seduction which makes painless the loss of cultural referents (Sarlo).

The *telenovela*, despite being weighed down with burdensome narrative schema and acting as an accomplice to strong ideological inertia, plays a crucial part in the mechanisms of modernization of the Latin American imaginary. It owes its success, at the very least among its audiences, largely to its capacity to turn an archaic narrative into a repository for the proposals modernizing some of life's facets (Martín Barbero, "De la telenovela"). New subjects and scope have been introduced throughout the genre's evolution and diversification. While the universe represented in *telenovelas* has its limits very strongly defined by the absence of those social conflicts that would break down its melodramatic scheme, which is what sustains the recognition and faithfulness of its audiences, this does not prevent the audience's complicity with the genre from also being encouraged by its porosity to life's transformations. For Colombians this became apparent with the appearance of *telenovelas* with "local color" such as *Gallito Ramírez, San Tropel*, and *El Divino*. The "local color" turned into Macondo in *Caballo viejo*, and became urban in *Café*. Of course, the modernity of the customs here depicted is clearly dressed up in so-called eternal values, and corseted in a variety of rituals; and, likewise, any changes are protected by their link to the myth of progress.

At any rate, what is interesting is that in a certain type of *telenovela* the shape of the hierarchies and social exclusions loses its rigidity as the social fabric of loyalties and submissions gets pluralized and more complicated. The distance between rich and poor, men and women, and adults and the young is at the same time laid out and disrupted by introducing mediations and movements that make visible the other side of the genre's fabric of humiliation and revenge. The genre thereby demonstrates that, even in the lowest social sectors, the struggle to "make it" is also a struggle to be someone and that neither dignity nor opportunism are confined to one social group. As the horizon of what can enter *telenovela* widens, new social actors and professions have appeared, new above all in the degree to which they are viewed as possible life-worlds, as figures revealing new forms of social relations, of cultural breakthroughs, and of moral conflicts. In the final analysis, these indicators of Modernity, which in many cases form part of the mechanics constructing the verisimilitude of the story—and thus of the renewal of the business—also indicate how the identity that flows through the world of *telenovela* is not a mere deceptive nostalgia but rather the dimension of living and dreaming with which Latin Americans construct the present.

Plural Communication in a Global Culture

When we think about the fabric and imagine the forms of democracy at the end of the twentieth century, the question of pluralism in communications has become crucial. But what do we really mean when we speak of pluralism? Do we mean an issue that concerns the *structure* of communication, whether at the level of recognition among peoples, ethnicities, races, ages, and sexes, and at the level of a flagrant inequality in the access to media suffered both by the majorities and the minorities? Or do we mean the postmodern *lightness* of a communication discharged, due to the technological miracle, of the heaviness of conflicts and the opacity of the social actors, in which "differences are disposed of," and everybody "communicates" without ever needing to meet one another?

From the Center, both in Europe and in the U.S., not a few and not unimportant thinkers affirm that the liberation of differences is the result of actions of the mass media. Making explicit what other intellectuals might be hesitant to express, Gianni Vattimo states: "The media have been the determining factor for the dissolution of centralized points of view . . . Despite any effort on the part of monopolies and large capitalist corporate headquarters, radio, television, and newspapers have become components of a generalized explosion and multiplication of worldviews" (*La sociedad transparente* 78-79). This leads Vattimo to a very unique reading of Walter Benjamin according to which the media would be the key to the postmodern *sensorium*, this is the pluralization that dissolves unitary points of view and unstoppably lets the voice of every kind of minority of the world emerge.

It would be shutting our eyes to reality if we tried to deny the shattering suffered today by the unitary visions of History and by totalitarian concepts. Likewise, it is impossible to ignore the fact that in Latin American societies the media, by making possible access to other world visions and customs, have contributed to cooling political and religious sectarianisms and to relaxing repressive wills and authoritarian tendencies. But tolerance, that defining characteristic of Modernity which is at the base of the current valorization of pluralism, has had a rocky road in these countries. "The history of Latin America," says Norbert Lechner in *Los patios interiores de la democracia*, "could be told as a continuous, reciprocal 'occupation of territory.' No physical border nor social limit grant any security. In this way, an ancestral fear of the invader, the other, and the different, whether coming from 'above' or from 'below,' is born and internalized from generation to generation" (99). This fear makes the collective order precarious and this order tends to be idealized rather than being built on a day to day basis, thereby generating a situation of mistrust and rejection of plurality, since plurality is perceived as disintegration, just as heterogeneity is felt to be the contamination and deformation of cultural purities.

According to Hilda Sábato, until quite recently the political and cultural debate in Latin America has been moving "between national essences and class identities" (2).[6] It was only after the crisis of the seventies that the model which held as a necessary condition for the construction of a political project ignoring or dissolving ethnic, gender, regional, or sectorial identities began to be questioned. The possibility of conceiving society as a plural entity is linked to the emergence of social movements that began to overcome a purely tactical notion of democracy, that is, democracy as a mere ruse for taking power. These are social movements in which the mediations of the civil society and the social sense of conflicts beyond their political formulation are revalorized, consequently making possible the emergence of ethnic groups, regions, sexes, and generations as social subjects. This in turn has implied a detotalizing of politics which does not imply only a desacralization of political principles but also that of the very idea of politics and of the stakes in the political game: the collective negotiation and construction of a social order. Politics can no longer pretend to fill every gap or flow through everything; rather, it has also found its limits, which differentiate it from ethics and culture.

It is at this time that pluralism, which had been confined to limited intellectual circles or restricted to periods of "liberal hegemony," is deployed in the Latin American countries, making possible the coexistence of Roman Catholicism and African American religions, the growing presence of Protestant sects, and the progressive secularization of customs and ideas. This in turn has made a new conception of identity composed less of essences and roots than of relations and interactions more visible and acceptable. Carlos Monsiváis sees the new Mexican identity in the following way:

> That which is Mexican is no longer an existential and cultural problem, and despite many discussions on the subject, national identity is not at risk. It is a changing identity, continuously enriched by the language of marginalized groups, contributions of mass media, academic innovations, ideological discussions, Americanization, and resistance to spreading poverty, an identity that is weakened by the reduction of the educational center's capacity, and by the institutionalization of a resignation to the absence of cultural stimuli. (192)

The media have much to do with these changes of sensibility, but in rather contradictory ways. The media, the uniquely expressive stage for this era's contradictions, expose us to a diversity of tastes and motivations daily. It exposes us, in other words, to difference, but also to *indifference*, to the growing integration of the heterogeneity of races, ethnicities, peoples, and sexes, in that *system of differences* with which, according to Jean Baudrillard, the West conjures, neutralizes, and makes functional *the others*: "Once we get beyond the mirror of alienation . . . structural differences multiply *ad infinitum*—in fashion, in mores, in culture. Crude otherness, hard otherness—the otherness of race, of madness, of poverty—are done with. Otherness, like everything else, has fallen under the law of the market, the law of supply and demand. It has become a rare item" (124). It is as if we could relate to other cultures only by submitting them to the *structural schema of differences* proposed by the West.

Are not the media one of the most efficient mechanisms of this schema? And this efficiency works through the most contrasting procedures. The mechanism of assimilation that brings cultures closer together, silences or thins out the most conflictive, heterogeneous, and challenging aspects of these cultures. In this way, there is no alternative but to stereotype and banalize the other, make him assimilable without any need to understand him. Is it not precisely with schematic and banal images of Indians, blacks, and the marginalized that most mass media discourses, especially television, "bring us closer" to others? The distancing mechanism functions in a similar way: The other is made exotic, folklorized, in a movement that affirms his heterogeneity which makes the other "interesting," while excluding the other from our universe by denying the capacity to interpellate the other and by denying the other to question us?[7]

But don't look for the reasons behind this scheme, tending to neutralize differences through media, in some perversion of the sensibility extolled by Vattimo. For, the rationality behind this schema is none other than the complementary movement of globalization and fragmentation that configures the *Modernity-world* of today's economy and culture, that is Modernity spatially and temporally decentered, delocalized from territorial contexts, and materialized in the mobility of information and technology (Ortiz, "Cultura e modernidade-mundo").

The space/time needed and produced by the market and new technologies is global. As was true of the nation-space since the end of the seventeenth century in Europe, the world-space[8] now constitutes itself as a horizon of economic and informational flow which has business as its axis, interdependent relations as its key, and the technological fabric of communications as its vehicle and support. In the globalization process the market holds the initiative: It is the market that now regulates relations between peoples, nations, and cultures, establishes models of communication, and energizes networks. What does the process of globalization mean for pluralism? Is it a way to combat both segregation and exclusion, or is it an expansion of the *non-place*, that world of transients and clients in which one is always and yet never "at home" (Augé 110ff.), and in which the abolition of distances and the erasure of memory produce not only a confusion of languages but also an increase of insignificance?

More than an opposite movement to globalization, but rather complementary to it, the world is experiencing an expansive process of *fragmentation* on all levels, from the breakup of nations to the proliferation of cults, from the revalorization of the local to the disintegration of the social. It is impossible to escape the question: Is the growth in the consciousness of diversity not leading to the relativization, even negation, of any community or sociability?[9] And does the uprootedness that this fragmentation supposes or produces—in the territorial or value domains—not constitute the basis for new essentialisms and fundamentalisms?

The praise of difference, so frequent among the postmoderns, speaks to a new perception of relativity and precariousness of ideologies and emancipation projects. But it also speaks of the vertigo of eclecticism which reduces everything, from aesthetics to politics, to the same value. Communications merchants take refuge in this confusion to carry out their business and make us believe, for example, that the diversity in television equals the number of channels, even if this very quantity does away with quality and offers but a hollow simulacrum of plurality.

Opposed to that deceptive pluralism that confuses diversity with fragmentation and also opposed to the fundamentalism of ethnic nationalists that convert identity into intolerance, pluralist communication means the challenge to take up heterogeneity as a value that can be articulated for the construction of a new collective fabric. Because in Latin America, as Lechner affirms, "heterogeneity will only produce a social dynamic linked to some notion of community." Certainly not a notion of community rescued from some idealized past, nor sustained with moralist principles and absolutist ideologies, but rather a notion of community in which it would be possible to recreate forms of civil deliberation and coexistence, renewing identities and ways of symbolizing conflicts and agreements from the opacity of today's hybridizations and reappropriations.

Notes

1. This is what studies collected in the following works suggest: E. Fox, ed., *Medios de comunicación y política en América Latina* (Barcelona, 1989) and H. Zemelman, ed., *Cultura y política en América Latina* (Mexico, 1991).

2. See G. Aneschi et al., *Videoculturas de fin de siglo* (Madrid, 1990) and Walter Ong, *Orality and Literacy: The Technologizing of the Word* (London, 1982).

3. On the new forms of sociability, see Michel Maffesoli, *Time of the Tribes: The Decline of Individualism in Mass Societies* (London, 1996).

4. See my book *De los medios a las mediaciones* (Mexico, 1987; trans. *Communication, Culture, and Hegemony: From Media to Mediations*, London: SAGE Publ., 1993), Part III, "Modernization and Mass Mediation in Latin America," 150ff.

5. See the development of this concept in Maffesoli. For a Latin American reflection on the concept, see M. Margulis et al., *La cultura de la noche: La vida nocturna de los jóvenes de Buenos Aires* (Buenos Aires, 1994) and R. Reguillo, *En la calle otra vez: Las Bandas: Identidad urbana y comunicación* (Guadalajara, 1991).

6. See also H. Schmucler, "Los rostros famosos del totalitarismo: nación, nacionalismo y pluralidad," *Punto de vista* 33 (1988).

7. On the "excluding difference," see Muñiz Sodre, *A verdade seduzida* (Rio de Janeiro, 1983).

8. See A. Mattelart, *La Comunication-monde*, especially Chap.10, "L'emprise de la géo-economie: la quête de la culture globale" (Paris, 1992), and Chap. 3, "Le scénario globale," in *L'Internationale publicitaire* (Paris, 1989).

9. On the dissolving of sociability by an "absolute differentialism," see A. Touraine, "Les postmodernismes," in *Critique de la modernité*. Vol. 2 (Paris, 1992).

Works Cited

Alexander, J. "Ensayo de revisión: la nueva teoría crítica de Habermas," in *Sociológica* 7-8 (1988).

Augé, Marc. *Non-places: Introduction to an Anthropology of Supermodernity.* London: Verso, 1995.

Baudrillard, Jean. *The Transparency of Evil: Essays on Extreme Phenomena.* Trans. James Benedict. London: Verso, 1993.

Breton, Philippe. *L'Utopie de la communication.* Paris: La Découverte, 1992.

Brunner, J. J. *Cartografías de la modernidad.* Santiago de Chile: Dolmen, 1994.

Festa, R. and L. F. Santoro. "A tercera edade da TV: o local e o internacional." *Rede imaginaria: televisão e democracia.* São Paulo: Companhia das Letras, 1991.

García Canclini, Néstor. *Hybrid Cultures: Strategies for Entering and Leaving Modernity.* Minneapolis: U of Minnesota P, 1995.

Garretón, M. A. *La cuestión nacional.* Santiago de Chile: ILET, 1984.

González, F. E. "Etica pública, sociedad moderna y secularización." *Una casa para todos.* Bogotá, 1991.

Habermas, Jürgen. *The Philosophical Discourse of Modernity: Twelve Lectures.* Cambridge, MA: MIT Press, 1987.

———. *The Theory of Communicative Action.* Boston: Beacon, 1984.

Lander, E., ed. *Modernidad & Universalismo.* Caracas: Nueva Sociedad, 1991.

Landi, Oscar. *Reconstrucciones: las nuevas formas de la cultura política.* Buenos Aires: Puntosur, 1988.

Lechner, N. "La democratización en el contexto de una cultura postmoderna." *Cultura política y democratización.* Santiago de Chile: FLACSO/CLACSO, 1987.

———. *Los patios interiores de la democracia.* Santiago de Chile: FLACSO, 1988.

Lyotard, Jean-François. *The Postmodern Condition: A Report on Knowledge.* Minneapolis: U of Minnesota P, 1984.

Marramao, G. "Más allá de los esquemas binarios acción/sistema y comunicación/estrategia," in *Razón, ética y política.* Barcelona: Anthropos, 1989.

Martín Barbero, Jesús. "Comunicación y ciudad: entre medios y miedos." In *Imágenes y reflexiones de la cultura en Colombia.* Bogotá, 1991.

———. "De la telenovela en Colombia a la telenovela colombiana." *Televisión y melodrama.* Bogotá: Tercer Mundo, 1992.

Monsiváis, Carlos. *De la cultura mexicana en vísperas del tratado de libre comercio.* Mexico: Nueva Imagen, 1992.

Morandé, Pedro. *Cultura y modernización en América Latina.* Santiago de Chile: Universidad Católica, 1984.

Muñizaga, G. and P. Gutiérrez. "Radio y cultura popular de masas." *Comunicación y culturas populares en Latinoamérica.* Mexico: G. Gili, 1987.

Noves, A. *O nacional e o popular na cultura brasileira.* São Paulo: Brasilense, 1983.

Ortiz, R. *A moderna tradição brasilera.* São Paulo: Brasilense, 1988.

———. "Cultura e modernidade-mundo," in *Mundialização e cultura.* São Paulo, 1994.

Ramos, J. *Desencuentros de la modernidad en América Latina.* Mexico: Fondo de Cultura Económica, 1989.

Sábato. Hilda. "Pluralismo y nación." *Punto de vista* 34 (1989): 2-5.

Salazar, Alonso. *No nacimos pa' semilla.* Bogotá: Cinep, 1990.

Sarlo, Beatriz. "La guerra del Golfo: representaciones postpolíticas y análisis cultural." *Punto de vista* 40 (1991): 28-31.

Schwarz, R. "Nacional por sustracción." *Punto de vista* 28 (1987): 15-22.

Vattimo, Gianni. *The End of Modernity: Nihilism and Hermeneutics in Postmodern Culture*. Baltimore: Johns Hopkins UP, 1988.

_____. *La sociedad transparente*. Barcelona: Paidós, 1990.

**Part II   Changing Identities, or "Where do we come from"
and "Where we are going?"**

◆ **4.**

The Challenges of Posmodernity and Globalization: Multiple or Fragmented Identities?

Fernando Ainsa

(*translated by Barbara Riess*)

Over the past two decades the accumulation of rhetoric and commonalities about identity, its importance, its defining typology's characteristics—ethnicity, "patrimonial" objectification, history, rituals, symbols and customs—and the idea of a "national being" in which a territory's inhabitants should recognize themselves, has left us with a seemingly salutary conceptual crisis within the postmodern and globalized framework in which we are immersed.

Certainly, the crisis we are living is due to the loss of identity's traditional telluric and biological referents and the disintegration of the metaconcept that unifies identity around the traditional notions of territory, of a people, of country, community and roots. We believe, however, that more than an annihilating obstacle, the effects of globalization would better be considered as a passionate challenge to the imagination, and as a new point of departure for the study of a notion that is an assignment rather than the gestation of a territorialized patrimony.

Possibilities, more than difficulties, are opened by participating in this debate, albeit critically and reactively, as we creatively place our bets. We must continue the inquiry by transgressing limits, not by repeating arguments that become simple slogans in our passive complacence with the given knowledge on the subject, but by producing distinct horizons and introducing new ideas with which to experiment. If not, intellectual reflection would be limited to a defensive withdrawal into a refuge of illusory derivatives of the nation, the confessional, or the tribe.

In addition, we believe that the ontological crisis of national belonging and the growing process of deterritorialization, incited by disappearing borders and multiplying circuits of movement and dissemination, although in the short term translate into the loss of identity referents due to globalization's presumed homogenization, in the long term can only "pave the way for one of the most exciting and potentially subversive cultural challenges of the moment" (Olalquiaga 93). In the following pages we intend to respond to this challenge.

Identity's New Frontiers

To this end, let's begin with the fact that the distinctive, what identifies us, is no longer synonymous with homogeneity and does not necessarily coincide with the limits of a determined territory. Moreover, it can no longer vindicate itself through collection of texts, objects to be conserved, well-defined roots, or immovable rituals and symbols fixed once and for all if not turned into stereotypes repeated without question.

The progressive disappearance of barriers throughout the world, the spread of communications, and the radical changes in the forms of production and circulation of cultural products formerly identified as "national," have lead to this process of "deterritorialization" in which one recognizes a certain kind of Postmodernity. All identifying systems—that is to say the set of cultural, social, or historical traditions to which a community belongs, and to whose destiny is bound for better or worse—can no longer be presumed organically contained. They are inevitably porous and can even end up having an osmotic relationship with other groups or systems that can impregnate, oppress, or favor them.

The restrictive notion of identity recedes as the resurgent individual dimension becomes characterized by the increasing mobility of a contemporary lifestyle more and more liberated from both biological and social organic dependencies, as well as territorial limitations and historical constraints. It must be remembered that having identity has been traditionally based on the presupposed belonging to a country, a city, or a people, even to a neighborhood, where an interchangeable sameness is shared with others. From this perspective, the distinguishable factor of a national identity has been the product of cultivating this territory so that it should coincide with the limits of a state, a language,[1] a religion, or an ethnicity. This "product" has generated behaviors and imprinted signs in which community members recognize themselves; a consciousness of similarity (the identical and the shared) that permits establishing differences with others, with all others that do not embody nor utilize the same codes.

The repertoires of common objects "that have a specific correspondence to the local forms adopted in the life of a community" and that are shared with others (those identical to oneself), and have ratified the idea of an organic identity and have founded the notion of *belonging* (García Canclini: 14). One belongs to a group and to a value system. This feeling[2] of having an identity is backed up with the security that belonging to a group's definition and cohesion rests on a common organic system of values and institutions. This belonging has brought about forms of *participation* at a national level (parties, unions, local associations) and the foundation of the political and legal referents of citizenship—the institutional characteristics of identity that are in crisis today.

The shared system, a common past more or less respected according to individuals or groups, has served as the norm of identity reference and has founded the *beliefs* upon which identity is supported and expressed. One believes in one's own culture, in a shared history, in the country or nation to which one belongs, in the limits and borders where this sameness begins and ends, and the mechanisms with which identity defends itself from contact or interchange. To this end, national documents and badges of identity are awarded, visas are required in passports, and border patrols are put into place. Many national identities have been formed in this way, thanks to the emphasis with which these differences have been marked out, most likely through conflicts or war with neighboring countries.

Presently, to the contrary, interaction and tension springing from difference, the onset of the subjects of alterity, marginality, exclusion, decentralization, and disorientation, have marked the crisis of the ontology of belonging in which we live, and have ended up in the reformulation of the notions of community and of heritage. The foreign penetrates political and economic borders, hybridizes the cultural reductions of identity, and mixes customs and behaviors. The "other" is no longer outside the limits of one's country, rather can be in the same city or even a neighbor in the building in which one lives. New borders (what metaphorically can be "asymmetrical frontiers") are installed in the interior of countries and cities and are blurred due to the multiplication of the transterritorial circulation of people, ideas and customs that relate them amongst themselves.

However, these changes are not produced without difficulties. They generate anxiety and dissatisfaction and produce a dislocation that some—the traditional owners of the identity territory—feel as a displacement towards the margin. From this, the good part of identity discourse, especially in the largest metropolises, opposes that of a threat to the heritage that some protect, to that of the demanding marginal discourse—that of immigrants, youth, minorities, or homeless—a discourse that has converted figures socially in the periphery as symbolically in the center.

On the other hand, this awareness of the vulnerability of inherited cultural identity brings certain sectors to a level of sensitivity, if not to violence, against any and all attempts at changing or altering what is considered their own. The talk and fear is of the loss of identity, although this identity in this case is nothing else but held prisoner by fundamentalist visions of ethnicities and cultures which claim identity as exclusive.

This concern manifests itself particularly in those societies that feel threatened by globalization, which they tend to confuse with homogenization or standardization. In Latin America's case, the primitive substrata of the mythic search for identity have lead some to a revindication of the native's (original, autochthonous) purity as opposed to foreign modernization, considered contaminating and alienating. Defense of the "popular/national" and of the axiological categories of the pre-modern and anti-industrial—whatever is represented as ones "own" or authentic—gives an archaic touch to identity's symbolization, defined by a past which, in some extreme cases, has become transformed into a real cult of origins. For indigenous societies this archaic symbolization dates back to the purity of the pre-Columbian. Everything that has happened after the "encounter of two worlds" in 1492 is nothing more than a long process of contamination, degradation and destruction of this original purity. All of this without affecting the problems of the autochthonous population, those who lived in American territories before the conquest and colonization, a population whose importance has been recognized by the United Nations in proclaiming the Decade of World Autochthonous Populations (1994-2004).

In the case of those countries constructed thanks to successive migratory fluxes, and ethnic and cultural miscegenation of every type, such as the River Plate countries, where beliefs mixed, there have been open and dynamic interchanges; they have no recourse to origins. In spite of this fact, the cult of the rooted proposes an identifying culture in charge of preserving a closed nationalism.

However, there is a preponderance of the inverse process. An alternative geography of belonging is being imposed on a large part of the world. Tracing this new cartography, based on the segmented and combined fluxes that redraw existing borders, is occurring through three parallel, independent and concurrent processes:

1. *A resurgence of truly diasporic cultures, resulting in the flow of cultural circulation proceeding the emigration from developing to developed countries.*

This implosion of the Third World in the First has lead to the development of multicultural societies (Rosaldo 9). The phenomenon of massive immigration and its consequent effects on the sociology of the family and on culture itself renders the identity debate increasingly more complex by incorporating more issues—integration, the "melting pot," insertion, acculturation, deculturation, among many others—into a discussion that is far from its conclusion. In any case, polarized views are brought to life: that of the fear of the acquired identity on the one hand and that of the "blessing" of the insertion of "life, energy and culture" celebrated by others.

Growing masses of refugees, with different characteristics yet similar effects of uprootedness, are obligated to cross the border of one country—often living in precarious conditions—to establish themselves in another, and are continuously modifying the planet's borders. If Asia and Africa seem to be the continents where the refugee problem assumes dramatic proportions, one cannot forget that Europe and Latin America have also suffered these difficulties. Problems have been added to those of the existing cultural and ethnic minorities because of emigration or the redrawing of borders; a new situation has become more evident with the loss of the traditional nation state's strength and the consciousness towards other emerging minorities' demands for rights.

Both immigrants and refugees have brought about, in the Latin American case, the resurgence of an identity mosaic in the continent's largest cities. In neighborhoods and even in streets that can be individualized without difficulty, fragments of the culture of origin are conserved after a massive diaspora reunites and reconstructs itself into the urban fabric. Dense zones of spontaneous eclosion preserve, many times thanks to a poverty that condemns them to the margins, components of the identity of origin, elements on the verge of extinction in other modernized areas of the same city. Neighborhoods that identify themselves with a certain ethnicity, veritable cultural ghettos proliferate, while marking unequivocal differences between themselves.

In this way cosmopolitan centers have become the quintessential scene for the multicultural society and it is there that new identity parameters are more evident. These metropolises, or the so called mega-capitals or global cities, sometimes associated with the "asphalt jungle," really a human jungle, are no longer a complex condensation of reality and memory, of histories selectively fixed in museums, monuments and street names, rather they are a permanent present that contains the world within its limits. Masses of human beings find themselves forced to commute long distances between the suburbs where they live and their workplace. In this incessant crossing over, usually in busses, metros, or in congested streets, it seems as if identity is dispersing into anonymity, while in reality what is happening is the birth of a new type of multiply fragmented individual, invited at every turn to wander erratically guided by chance, necessity or simple curiosity and to lose oneself among the cities' streets, terraces and shopping malls.

2. *The increasing importance of the figures of exodus and exile, the exhaltation of the nomadic condition, the notions of displacement and of the cultural fugitive as components of identity in the framework of the processes of globalization.*

The contemporary world has worsened the human being's stateless condition, to which Hegel referred describing those who live outside of the tribe or nation that protects them. This condition is inscribed by a relativist and cosmopolitan trend toward a humanistic secularism inaugurated with the Enlightenment. This can be made evident through a number of examples, among others, the "migratory artist," converted into one of the multiple transcultural links in a world under the sign of planetary nomadism. Numerous intellectuals and artists explore material and cultural diversity by incorporating themselves into other collectives in order to interchange ideas and aesthetic experiences.This permits overcoming—like Chilean painter Eugenio Dittborn proposes—"the sacrosanct emblems of identity, stereotyped distinctions of us as exotic victims" and forging a "multiple, polytheistic and *affordable*" (quoted from the English translation) perspective, which can open up a process of critical interaction with understood tradition as the memory of an historic past that should be continually revisited (Richard 200).

Encounters, mutual and interchanged (if not interchangeable) perspectives, intersections and separations provoke such disparate feelings as the flight from oneself and the need for contact and union with the other. These themes are extolled by writers who frequently have within themselves this ambivalent condition. Some call it being a fugitive in a foreign language; others, losing our own language in foreign lands. In any case, it is to always live as a foreigner, because one is lost in his or her own land. In the same vein, scholarships and postgraduate university courses promote contacts in a world that increasingly offers the possibility to live outside the place in which one was born and to integrate oneself into networks that have no exclusive national and cultural borders.

Other than an uprootedness, the figure of both the forced and voluntary exile also marks the increasing process of deterritorialization. One finds this figure to be a site of a concentration of memory, ambiguous and contradictory nostalgia, and above all the alchemy of interchanges and the fertility of meanings that originate in distance. According to the Albanian Ismail Kadare, who has lived the major part of his life in exile, although the exile's identity of origin may quiver, "there is not the slightest contradiction between the exile and the cultural identity of the writer . . . exile can strengthen this identity; at precisely the moment in which it appears to be weakening, the universal dimension that exile affords the identity of origin makes it more veritable" (21).

As an extension to these nomadic characteristics of identity, traveling proposes other typological variants (a trip to escape, of initiation, of peregrination, going back to ones roots, etc.) that underscore a symbolic and cultural traffic and the semantic register of the growing deterritorialization of acquired codes. In the case of Latin American identity, the function of the travel has not only been foundational (the conquest, colonization and subsequent immigrations) but in addition, an organic constituent. The necessary reflection in the European mirror has impelled the journey to take on various forms, both the journey of initiation as well as the search for difference, the recognition of alterity, or that which permits a discovery of one's own origins in "a far off place."[3]

One cannot leave out the concurrent forms of exalting nostalgia—just the opposite of the internationalized model of contemporary identity. The motifs *morriña, saudade, homesickness, Heimweh*, and *rodina*, that are accumulated in each language—Spanish, Portuguese, English, German and Russian—reveal a different nuance of torn intimacy. Writers who have made exile an almost natural condition for living have made literature an emotional reflection of this nostalgia. María Zambrano, for example, has said "Exile is my homeland."

3. *Multiplication of the modes of circulation and diffusion*

With the market's globalization and the progress in communications, individuals and peoples live in a permanent coexistence, without any sort of territorial base or barriers. Culture, instantly and simultaneously distributed reflects the event, the occurrence, the lived movement outside spatial and temporal referents. In this mode, contiguity is contingent, although the day to day doesn't cease to articulate an historical continuum and the unavoidable sensation of living, so put by television jargon, the "live and up to the moment news." This living up to date on a world level has lead the Swiss author Paul Nizon, a cultural nomad who has lived in Italy, France and Spain, to affirm: "If I am immersed in the present I am alive. I live in this world. I belong in my time. I am contemporary."

This condition of living in the present, the immediate as a way of life, is stimulated in a provocative form by circuits and intercultural networks of all types. The present installs itself as permanent. It doesn't want to be neither ephemeral nor fleeting. Because if, until recently, the past, memory and tradition were privileged, now the priority interest becomes focused on the present. José Luis Abellán, for this reason, has proposed that simultaneity be more deeply analyzed along with the current reflecting on globality.

This transversal interconnection is favored by the generalization of communications. The computer screen's intimacy, thanks to the Internet is developing the cyberspace culture, whose interactive territory of relations founds truly transnational virtual communities, where the real reality is lived in a type of world club of virtual reality as well as in the illusion of a new dimension of expressing identity. True conversation networks are constituted horizontally, displacing the vertical hierarchy of yesteryear. José Joaquín Brunner affirms that this horizontality has generated an interactive architecture of knowledge more complex than it was in the past. Even if the information available is increasing, a crisis in stability affects the certainties of knowledge. The limited knowledge of the past was clearer and more orderly than the present mass of information whose tracks are embroiled in the confusion of its multiple access.

If this supposes an opening In the foundational parameters of a new universality, with unknown limits until now, in the abolition of distances, in the generalization of access to the roots or the sources of knowledge and the loss of hierarchical power, the risks of an identity channel surfing become sharply evident, encouraged, partly, by a consumer society. Channel surfing that tends to go in the direction of postmodern discourse, of that of fragmented identity, the partial and the nonconclusive as an antitotalitarian virtuality of all texts that aspire to be totalizing. Identity fragmentation seems to be the process of deterritorialization and the multiplication of the circuits of circulation's most obvious risk, although at the same time they provide interpersonal cultural coexistence capable of feeding internal and external relations unimaginable until recently. In addition, the risk of forgetting that a million images will never constitute a concept becomes apparent, and that conceptual thought and the capability to rationalize and of critical thinking can not be substituted for ephemeral impressions. This "imperial of the ephemeral" with which Gilles Lipovetsky has defined our epoch, has also invited curiosity and openness.

Effectively, in the globalized world there is a growing functional interaction between such disperse economic and cultural activities, with many centers and a flexible articulation of parts and components of a diverse origin. This is reflected clearly in intercultural consumer habits, for example, the fact that many objects have lost their relationship with their point of origin. It suffices to think of many objects of internationally recognized brand names whose components are produced in various points on the globe and assembled in others.

In the case of "cultural industries," this montage further confuses the borders between popular culture, illustrated culture, and mass culture. The most rich manifestations of the evolution of this phenomenon are found in music and in the artistic representation where simultaneous polyphonic readings are possible and where a plurality of identity stories are represented within a thematic unity. A range of environments combine methods and trends in a fecund mix of rhythms and genres.

These multiple components present in the globalization of consumption can also be seen in the editorial sector (publishing houses with different poles of production, distribution and sales) and in the fashion sector with fashion design and marketing of trends (international brand names with different manufacturing centers). In speaking of the process of "clientization of the citizen"—as does Jürgen Habermas—it becomes evident that the legal and state's notion of the individual has been enriched by an opening up to multicultural diversity and differentiated pluralism. The traditional belief that it is impossible to be authentic and to evolve at the same time has given way to a society that sees itself as obligated to accepting not only difference, but also that which until recently seemed strange and even the opposite to the traditionally acceptable, to the point that the "new" can become more authentic and representative than the "old."

The New Identity Repertoires

The process through which the construction of identity is no longer necessarily founded in territorial, ethnic nor linguistic canons does not suppose that we devoutly accept the alienation subject to the worst effects of economic globalization and a Postmodernity that extols a fragmented culture.

In confronting this challenge, it becomes necessary to invent a way of looking at ourselves that is multiple, polyphonic and pluralist, capable of vacating from the signs of identity their accepted meanings. The important thing is to elaborate strategies for survival in the immersion of varied symbols and referents and to reconstruct the notion of identity on new bases, overcoming the rejection and monolithic fear of a multinational culture, what Buckminster Fuller calls onomatopoeically, *Grunch*, the monster.

The fall of walls and borders should invite globalization to be put to good use and reactivate an initiative of not solely defensive, but of creative thought. To that end, we must recuperate a foundational strategy for a line of thought that eliminates a nostalgia for the power of a paternalistic and omnipresent State, that seemed to cover identity until recently. At the same time this reactivated intellectual activity should help to correct the absolutism of the idea of a world market, an instrument of the drastic deregulation presently seen especially in the domain of the economy, labor and social security. There is an urgent need to elaborate strategies at the international level to confront these phenomena that some consider to be unavoidable, where an anticipatory vocation to which an utopic intention should not be a stranger.

In order to understand the breadth of this proposal, it is necessary to remember that each individual moves simultaneously in various identity circles, from the individual and familiar, to a wider sense of belonging to a community, religion, nation or country, through the political, labor or professional group in which he develops. Identity is displaced and is opened up in this circular space, superimposed, concentric or tangential, where each of the circles is always more reduced than the integral horizon of the person that embraces them.

The friction between the individual and the collective expressions of these different circles is inevitable, and their enlargement and reduction are variable and permanent. A broadening of the circles accentuates the pluralist character of identity and a reduction pushes for a fundamentalism and tribalization. While the circle of belonging maintains a nostalgia for the monocultural and for limited regional horizons, for pure languages and the unquestioned truths about origin, the circle that opens up, bets on dialogue and on an increased knowledge of the other.

It can be affirmed, then, that there are two forms of unity that coexist critically within the same identity: one that closes over itself and insists on a permanency, and other that affirms itself through a progressive integration of the new. This paradox's knot is found—as Albert Memmi suggests—in the fear that all change provokes, denied with desperation until it is integrated into the quotidian. What's more: what seems a fragility becomes transformed into the foundation for survival and evolution. Memmi states: "cultural identity is a dynamic equation where there is an inextricable combination of more or less stable elements with changing and relatively unpredictable elements" (100).

In this light, identity appears to be the result of variable positions and not founded in definitive form, a notion formed and deformed on various fronts, that is forged through confrontation and coincidence. Nor is it something homogeneous or fixed, rather it is a multiple and transitory condition that happens in conjunction with the always changing cross between cultures. It is far from being a clearly designed puzzle that can be put together with the cut fragments of a whole that can be reconstituted as a whole picture.

However, human beings need to grow and to persuade themselves as to the validity of their beliefs, especially in moments of great change. Human beings cannot live in a permanent state of fragility, relativity, and metamorphosis. So, the human being finds support in a common past that is invoked as identity's unalterable depth, although, in reality, it is the result of a idealistic reconstruction where readjusted beliefs are integrated with real elements, but also with symbols and imaginary elements. The feeling of the resulting identity requires a permanent adjustment of memory in order to be coherent and operational, and at the same time that it can endure the changes and the inevitable adaptations which this feeling will face. In this case, cultural identity would be a set of permanencies under constant change, although it is really about relative permanencies and continual adaptations. This complex process of opening, integration and closure is produced starting from a hybridization, characteristic of an increasingly interdependent world, where mixtures are synthesized and where the intercultural takes precedence.

These permanencies are even more relative among emigrants and exiles, where continual adaptations arise from an even larger problem of identity's adjusting to society: that which motivated and has driven one to emigrate into exile. Although the emigrant maintains ties and cultivates a nostalgia, the act that brings one to this separation and withdrawal from his/her origins, manifests that a desire for change, of being another in another place still exists. For this reason the emigrant's or exile's identity can reflect a process in which the desire to separate from a place, origin, or a territory, of withdrawing and constructing another identity, is stronger than that of conserving a closed and well defined identity that is impenetrable to surrounding influences.

This contemporary identity, then, is divided (and in some cases torn) into multiple loyalties. Although some find it difficult to accept this notion, where living "in between," in a "space between two worlds," as Daniel Sibony calls this distance a play *entre-deux identités*, it is part of a new repertoire of referents where a part of identity is permanently renegotiated and reconstructed from a multifocal perspective. Sibony warns of the risk that exists in wanting to enclose all emigrants and exiles in a trite identity of origin at all costs, in an authenticity that they should not stray from and to which they should recur when they encounter problems. In this way, one could better explain the increasing importance of dual nationalities, what we can ironically call Motherland bigamy, bi-patriotism, that characterizes the situation of a good part of exiles and immigrants. A double passport is not simply a comfortable way to cross borders, rather a document that translates a factual situation where one part of an identity has ceded its space to an adopted territory. Multiple loyalties are manifest as well in the complex relationship between citizens of autonomous regions and the nations that integrate them, or in bilingual communities divided in linguistic expression. Bilingualism does no more than reflect two cultural affiliations with their respective thought models, most evident in societies that accept the "cultural mosaic" principle as their own organic constituent.

The truth is that although this multicultural reality appears evident, the majority of governments of the countries affected by its impact refuse to reflect with any profundity on the changes produced in identity's behavior. The exceptions of legislation that channels and recognizes the phenomena of multiculturalism in Australia, Canada and the United States, the theoretical discussions in Germany that confirm the proposals in Daniel Cohn-Bendit and Thomas Schmid's *Heimat Babylon*, the provocative idea of the *World Bazaar* erupting into the *Gentlemen's Club* of the Indian theorist of *Post-Colonialism*, Homi Bhaba, are just the beginning of an inevitable end of the century debate.

This debate that should generate, above all, spaces for dialogue and educative systems open to knowing other cultural identities, and should establish outlets for communication between one another. Notions like "mutual respect" and "no discrimination," and the emphasis on the search for common meeting points that favor interdependency are fundamental. The traditional concept of cultural belonging can be complemented in this way with a multiple cultural belonging which would permit transcending the notion of simple pluralism and better explain identity's different levels and circles, as do the notions of multiple loyalties, bilingualism, and the varied cultural networks in which an individual can simultaneously participate.

However, not all multiculturalism comes about through passive means and even less through resignation, be it acceptance, patience, or tolerance. In principle, disagreement with different ideas and customs forms part of an authentically pluricultural society. Moreover, it is not always necessary to try to understand that which is different. Nor is it necessary to deliberately look for hybrids and racial mixtures. Acceptance and integration of the process of hybridization that synthesizes mixtures comes about according to the play between people and their common interests. Assimilation, when it occurs, should be voluntary and should vindicate the right to resist being integrated and the right to defend one's own parameters. In any case, to be capable of change does not necessarily imply one to stop being oneself to become the "other."

Coexisting within multiculturalism is more important than looking for a consensus or unions that can be transformed into coercive experiences, as these imply an artificial cohabiting. It is not necessary to autoidentify in a permanent form with the comfortable majority or with the vindication of minorities. For this reason, it is not so much about "living with the other" rather than knowing how to "live next to the other." It is not always necessary to identify oneself totally with the "foreign," or with what is foreign to ourselves. Nor is there a necessity to comprehend the other. Of primordial importance is to respect one another without the pretentious paternalistic intervention of "understanding." To respect does not always mean to understand, and even less to love. Nor does coexistence mean indifference. Without renouncing one's own convictions, but with respect to others and in the spirit of understanding, a community feeling of identity can be developed.

On the other hand, our identity is sometimes strange even to ourselves. The capacity to recognize this fact takes courage. An attraction to the foreign, a presumed love for the other many times feeds on a rejection of oneself. Those that excuse themselves for what they are and believe to save themselves before the rest through the feelings that they say they profess for difference, are only skirting a part of their own identity.

The multicultural collects the fragments and residuals of an identity that has exploded due to a confusing world without direction, in order to create another unity that invites a new culture made of diversity. In a society that has these characteristics, fragments emerge and disappear, an order is established or destroyed, projects are launched and collisions and collapses are produced like those between "the stars in the cosmos," a metaphor used by the Swiss writer Silvio Blater residing in the paradigmatic multicultural city, Los Angeles. Will Kymlicka, the specialist in plural citizenship takes the point even farther in maintaining that increasing globalization "has obligated that the majority, within each State, be more open to pluralism and to diversity" and that this has facilitated that "minorities maintain their own identity and collective life." The nation-state cannot vindicate the monocultural character with which it singled itself out in the past, including when it assumed a form of democratic nationalism.

This plural character is not a synonym for plurinational. The "national" aspect of identity can be that very same plural character, as is claimed by those peoples whose identity has been forged by ethnically and culturally diverse contributions. They are states that frame a multiplicity of fragments of nations articulated in cultural political unities functioning within their bosom. If some of these states are the mosaic of minorities that claim their own space, others are the result of an intense and heterogeneous migratory flow. In all of these, the important thing is how to harmonize the plurality within society's bosom, how to establish admissible borders of cultural diversity that a democracy is obligated to respect, how to articulate fundamental universally valid human rights with ethnic and cultural collectives' rights and with the expression of national minorities. In other words, conceiving pluralism as a form of coexistence between the particular and the greater good, that "civic friendship" that Kymlicka advocated for between multiculturally divergent identity expressions and the rights of the majority.

Actually, the multicultural is not a condition for the resurgence of new things, rather its precondition. It is permanent transition; no one ever asks themselves if they have been influenced by nor how they "naturally" live multiple aspects of multiculturalism. It is not about assuming different surroundings and, according to their proteic powers, of imitating oneself, of splitting oneself up and then reuniting oneself. It is not about falling into the chaos theory advocated by some, that explains how things and systems change. Chaos—according to theorists such as Ilya Prigogine, Norbert Wiener and Claude Shannon—is a particular and structured order of things, that changes as a whole and where the future conduct of its individual components is completely unpredictable. From this perspective, there is a narrow connection between chaos, chance and creativity. Chaos theory attempts to respond to the failure of scientific and historical explanations that presumed that thanks to order, certainty, and determinism, one could predict events.

Nor is it about falling into the other extreme, of a theory of complexity that others advocate in order to explain the margins of uncertainties that preside over the processes that were once thought predictable.[4] To explain this theory, Edgar Morin opposes the principle of simplicity that he supposes separates and reduces, abstracts and hides novelty and improvisation, with the principle of complexity that he claims reunites without failing to consider distinctiveness. Complex, according to Morin, means that "which is woven together." The complex line of thought is a belief that attempts to connect and to distinguish, but without separating. At the same time, it has to tackle uncertainty in a world where the dogma of determinism has been toppled. The universe is not subject to the absolute sovereignty of order, rather it is the field of a dialogical action (a relationship that is at once antagonistic, competitive and complementary) between order, disorder, and organization.

But without arriving at such extremes—chaos or complexity—it is evident that that which is not determined and that which is random guides a good part of the reflection about self-organizing possibilities of contemporary man's multiple identity. Identities constructed with Modernity's technological waste and thanks to the eclectic appropriation of various elements, many of those foreign or alien, permit renewed experiences. This identity collects—contrary to what had happened until recently—the possibilities of a re-found freedom among the wastes of oppressive and comprehensively totalizing systems in which we were immersed. If this forms part of a Postmodernist discourse, one cannot deny, as Kenneth J. Gergen affirms in *The Saturated Self* (1991), that now the doors to "the full expression of all discourses" are open, as in a free for all that "urges a heteroglossy of being, of living from the multiple voices in the whole sphere of human possibilities" (309).

It is beneficial to remember, as suggested by Ticio Escobar, that "this *bricolage*, this patient process that seeks to reorganize new identities out of residues and relics, is the task of all culture" (54). For this reason he recommends that Latin America "stress affinities, look for consensus, integrate common problems, come up with joint projects and even, for reasons of political or epistemological convenience, prepare the ground [in the artistic sense] only when it seems useful in order to strengthen positions or protect our recently born myths" (Richard 113). This task needs to take into account reflections on the cultural heterogeneity, that has characterized Latin American modernism, a heterodoxic modernity that juxtaposes unlike fragments of a social temporality in "a *collage* of memories and experiences" (Sánchez 160). An identity, that for Osvaldo Sánchez, is a *patchwork* or the *kitsch*, which he proposes for an alternative to the official discourse in Cuba: "[K]*itsch* is our way of appropriating for ourselves from all cultures, all movements, in a parodic reversal of our dependence . . . that being the last invited to dinner, we create our own menu . . . with fragments of works, with leftovers and scraps" (113). However, others remember that it is not necessary to equate this identity made up of fragments with postmodern problems in societies that haven't yet even consummated their own Modernity.

An individual with a greater capacity for movement and diverse (mobile) motives, usually plural, emerges slowly and breaks the classic identity model. Local and national loyalties give way to the projection of a new feeling of *belonging*, starting with participation in intercultural communities, in associative relationships that form part of a New World order of relations. New networks of interests, on the margin of national control or dependence, the scenes for the mixing of cultures, favor the creation of what can be called "authority networks" in interconnected fields like professional associations and nongovernmental organizations, editorial houses, magazines or universities that respond to different social sectors. In this dimension, the type of identity, chosen individually or collectively as a vital option assumed consciously and voluntarily, is essential. Identity is founded and recognized by a base of common sectarian interests, shared beliefs and coincidence, according to shared itineraries and common experiences. One identifies most with those that do and believe as one does and believes. In sum, identity components are now more related with one's "own time," individual, and shared with like beings with whom a "local space," community, neighborhood, or hometown is shared.

Redimensioning the Particular and the Universal

One of the most frequently heard criticisms of the current process of globalization stems from the belief that its explicit goal is to homogenize cultural diversity in one single mold for the whole planet. Culture's resulting uniformity would obey a strategic plan, in the name of which the enormous economic and technological potential of Western civilization, individualism, progress and well being will combine cultural diversity in the amorphous and impoverished "only culture."

However, when this position is taken to its extreme, the critical and reactive capacities of human beings are overlooked. The proof that the economic/financial and communications globalization is not automatically translated into a loss of identity, is found in the growing rebellion of varying "particularisms": minority rights and the claims for recognition by all types of identities that characterize the discourse of the late nineties. There are many opposite signs emerging presently in comparison to the prevailing discourse of the eighties, when globalism armed itself with the blatant onset of economic neo-liberalism. On the one hand, identity's conflation is converted into a cultural refuge where threatened values are protected, although generating exclusions, integrations and various fundamentalisms, especially those that are ethnic/nationalistic or religious, is not as anachronistic as it seems, nor is it just a return to the past, as its detractors schematically reduce it to being. What's more, these particualrist explosions are simply reactions and forms of resistance that look to retard or impede the convulsive globalist evolution of humanity and its characteristic abolition of distances and borders. The resulting tribalist tensions, the return to orthodox and ritualistic religions, are an effort in erecting new barriers where the globalization processes have attempted to demolish them, not only in the economic sense, but also in political and administrative interchanges. New borders—without falling into a vision of cultural difference that generates the "clash of civilizations" as Samuel Harrington has forecasted—where it is evident that antagonistic values that oppose one tribe against others are more cultural and religious than ideological, political, or economic, and they trace boundaries in the interior of existing national borders.

What's more, without ignoring the risk of homogenization, especially in economically weaker societies, there are those who see in globalization the possibility that a plural world diversification overstocks the big supermarket of images, leads to a plurality of choices in the cultural variety "on special" (cable or satellite television, for example), and to multiple sources of information. The problem that is proposed is exactly the opposite of what is feared. The problem is how to select, articulate, filter and organize this mass of "special offers" and information. Edgar Morin has proposed a true "reformation of thought" to teaching humans to navigate in the "incessant coming and going between certainty and uncertainly, between the elemental and the general, between the separable and the inseparable."

Actually, the diversification of the world is more fractionated than ever, a phenomenon that is felt most frequently in the cities and countries that most acutely live the processes of globalization and multiculturalism. It suffices to observe how objects and techniques of general use are incorporated into daily life and how they are naturally inserted into the particular, according to a selective individual process. Many of those objects and technologies become but mere instruments or facilitate behavior without necessarily altering the user's identity and even less making it uniform with other consumers.

However, it is important to emphasize that a multicultural equal presence in a society, whether or not a consequence of globalization, does not equal opportunity. In effect, "the multiplication of possibilities makes even more evident the inequality in opportunities"[5] for which the multicultural coexistence of different lifestyles should lead to an ethical reaction based on increased efforts for democratic pluralism—a pluralism that should decree the same rights and opportunities to all. "Maintain course without ignoring the discontented," advocate those who are convinced of the inevitable economic globalization, but that propose microeconomic and institutional reforms that correct globalism's most injurious edges.

Of primordial importance in responding to the question of how to reclaim cultural particularisms, is to concurrently take a straightforward look at planetary perspectives. Some have already done so, extolling the virtues of the "glocalization" (globallocalization) In using technologically powerful mass media communication—for example, regional television, longdistance learning, teleconferencing, and in the development of radio programs with listener's direct participation—the possibilities of inserting the local in the universal become apparent. Direct experiences of "glocalization" are being developed in Brazilian television, and the debate is extending into other Latin American countries like Mexico, Chile, Argentina and Colombia. In the case of television, a nationalization facilitated by the multiplication of channels, many of those directed to listeners of segmented interests and the mass offering of cable television and local and regional stations, make evident the increasing local programming over the canned imports. More than the "world village" predicted by McLuhan, it is possible to consider our progress towards a "village world federation."

The preceding proofs demonstrate that globalization is not antagonistic *per se* to the development of local and national cultural expression, rather, to the contrary, these are facilitated many times by the very technology and mass media communication that multiply contacts and interconnections. As Carlos Catalán concluded in a recent article about the globalization of television in Chile, the access to circuits and international communications products in no way means the decline in local expression's form or content, since "reality indicates that when the processes of globalization intensify, so do the citizens' demands that have to do with their most immediate surroundings, and with that what is the citizen's own, or most familiar—their country, city, or neighborhood—is integrated."

If, as we have seen throughout this essay, identity has lost many traditional territorial referents, it does not mean that the local dissolves in the global, nor do the different singular cultural expressions acquire a total, amorphous and standardized uniformity. Along the lines of a world without borders, but not impoverished or less varied, Edgar Morin, in *Terre-Patrie*, places his bet on *mestizaje* and on cosmopolitanism.

This is what will be the fundamental subject in the coming years: that of modernity's and identity's articulation within the framework of the current globalization processes. Under the psycho-social or solely cultural aspects of the debates already established, another more profound aspect can be brought forward: that of explaining the relationship between the particular and the universal.

In the individualized process of discovery and taking on an authentic identity—what Charles Taylor has called a "moral identity" upon which he builds his proposed "construction of modern identity"[6]— universalist options should increasingly outweigh the particularist and the territorial. In the name of the first, one shares different categories with other individuals beyond those of traditional geographical ones, the "hyper-good," notions of justice, the values inherent in human rights, feelings of responsibility, altruism, solidarity and tolerance, and, in addition, beliefs that surpass religious, ideological and political borders, and the values of modern life including those that are characterized as contemporary mankind's identity crisis.

Consequently it would become possible to speak of "globalization's second stage": that which should impose a universal ethic, a planetary macro-ethic that transcends traditional concerns of groups and national loyalties, to confront the emerging worldwide problems and challenges, due especially to the effects of the uncontrolled use of science and technology. An ethic of planetary responsibility that functions not only as a response to ecological problems, as Hans Jonas has proposed in *El principio de responsabilidad* [The Responsibility Principle], but in addition as regulatory mechanism of financial economic globalization and as a proposal for religious peace, according to Hans Küng's proposal.

The response to this necessary redimensioning of particularism and universality within the framework of new parameters of identity, especially from the traditionally open and plural Latin American perspective, is, as cited earlier, "one of the most exciting and potentially subversive cultural challenges of the moment." In addition, it would be counterproductive not to accept the challenge of rethinking these issues within the framework of the double processes of fragmentation and globalization in which we are all immersed. History, for now, does not leave us another alternative. We'd best face up to it.

Notes

1. Almost as if in a play on words, one could say that identity is the result of the sum of two elements: localization (locale) + locution (language, speech).

2. The Tunisian essayist, Alberto Memmi asks if it wouldn't be better to speak of a "feeling" of cultural identity rather than a cultural identity. In "Les fluctuations d'identité culturelle," he states: "To be French, German or Russian is a way of 'understanding' oneself, of defining oneself in relation to a cultural tradition or situation, however this relationship with oneself and these cultural elements are variable" (99).

3. I dedicate the second and third part of my book, *Identidad cultural de Iberamérica en su narrativa* [Cultural Identity in Ibero-American Narrative] (Madrid: Gredos, 1986) to developing this subject. On the "typology of the journey," see Fernando Ainsa, "Las dos orillas de la identitdad en la obra de Julio Cortázar. Significados del viaje iniciático," in the number dedicated to the conference on Cortázar in Mannheim of *INTI: Revista de literatura hispánica* 22-3(1985-1986).

4. Ilya Prigogine titles one of his most recent works *El fin de las certidumbres* [The End of Certainties], in which although it is conceived as a reformulation of scientific law where "possibilities" substitute certainties, his conclusions are also applied to "life's chance" as well as cultural fluctuations.

5. Javier Pérez de Cuéllar makes this observation at the end of his speech before the World Comission of Culture and Development, "Nuestra diversidad creativa," in *El correo de la UNESCO* (Paris: UNESCO). Now as "Prólogo del Presidente," in his *Nuestra diversidad creativa. Informe de la Comisión Mundial de Cultura y Desarrollo* (Madrid: Fundación Santa María/ Ediciones UNESCO, 1997) 9.

6. In Taylor's *Sources of the Self, the Making of the Modern Identity* he analyzes the causes for the so called contemporary man's identity crisis and the increasing importance of "proceduralism" (how one should proceed to act in life) as a declining of "substantialism" and of the "frames of reference" of traditional identity.

Works Cited

Balibar, Etienne and Immanuel Wallerstein. *Race, nation, classe. Les identités ambiguës*. Paris: Editions la Découverte, 1990.
Catalán, Carlos. "La globalocalización de la televisión," *El Mercurio* (Santiago de Chile) 1(1997). n.p.

Cubbit, Sean. Interview with Eugenio Dittborn. "An Airmail Interview." In Richard, 197-207.

Escobar, Ticio. "Identity, Myth: Today." In Richard, 43-56.

García Canclini, Néstor. "Scenes Without Territory. The Aesthetics of Migrations and Identities in Transition." In Richard 13-27.

Gergen, Kenneth J. *The Saturated Self. Dilemmas of Identity in Contemporary Life.* Basic Books, 1991.

Kadare, Ismail. "Ave de paso." *Los mundos del exilio. El correo de la UNESCO.* Paris: UNESCO, 1996.

Kymlicka, Will. *Ciudadanía multicultural.* Barcelona: Paidós, 1996.

Memmi, Alberto. "Les fluctuations d'identité culturelle." *Esprit* (Paris) January 1997.

Morin, Edgar. *Introduction à la pensé complexe.* Paris, 1990.

_____. "Por una reforma del pensamiento." *El correo de la UNESCO.* Paris: UNESCO, 1996.

Morin, Edgar and Anne-Gritte Kern. *Terre-Patrie.* Paris: Seuil, 1993.

Olalquiaga, Celeste. "Buitre-cultura. El reciclaje de imágenes en la posmodernidad." In Richard, 93.

Prigogine, Ilya. *El fin de las certidumbres.* Santiago: Andrés Bello, 1996.

Richard, Nelly, ed. *Art from Latin America: La cita transcultural.* Sydney: Museum of Contemporary Art, 1993.

Rosaldo, Renato. *Ideology, Place and People without Culture.* Stanford: Stanford UP, 1990.

Sánchez, Osvaldo. "Carnival, Politics and Kitsch." In Richard 160.

Sibony, Daniel. "Tous malades de l'éxil." *Libération* (1997); n.p.

Taylor, Charles. *Sources of the Self, the Making of the Modern Identity.* Cambridge: Harvard UP, 1989.

◆ 5.

Postmodernism and Latin American Identity

Jorge Larraín

Introduction

There is often a certain vagueness in the definitions of Postmodernism. This is understandable since it seems to refer to a complex phenomenon which has ramifications in disparate fields of knowledge and areas of human activity. Postmodernism claims to exist not only in art, architecture, literature, theology, philosophy and social sciences, but also as a new structure of feelings that pervades common people, as a particular way of experiencing, interpreting and being in the world which has undermined modernist sentiments (Darvey 53). It is then a good idea to introduce a distinction between the theoretical or academic discourse of Postmodernity which constitutes a social imaginary from which new meanings and significations are drawn, and the more concrete feelings, orientations and social practices of people which could be more or less postmodern if one compares them with the discursive claims.

Between the more rigorous discursive order and the more spontaneous and private order there exist, of course, many relationships. They cannot be conceived as two incommensurable worlds. In a way Postmodernist theories are elaborated starting with the new modes of feeling of common people, and also, they somehow influence the way in which people live and interpret the world. Yet, on the other hand, between the Postmodernist discourse and the emergent meanings and feelings which people have about the world there is no perfect correspondence. Even if Posmodernist discourses are born out of (and seek to explain) the new ways of experiencing the world, they do not, nevertheless, constitute the only plausible explanation, and do not entail, of themselves, a real power or decisive impact upon the complex social world that underlies them.

One has to avoid what Thompson has called the "fallacy of internalism" which is the tendency to "read off the consequences of cultural products from the products themselves" (105). The existence of Postmodernity as the definitive supersession of Modernity cannot be necessarily derived from the existence of Postmodernist discourse. For instance, one can distinctly detect in Postmodernist discourse a tendency to exaggerate the effects of the emergence of feelings of disunity, fragmentation, contingency, chaos, division, difference, discontinuity, meaninglessness and purposelessness as if they all were prevalent and widespread throughout society and had brought about the end of Modernity and the loss of the subject.

The distinction between articulated discourse and private feelings comes from a conception of culture which entails a double dimension (Williams 11-20). On the one hand, culture means arts and intellectual life, rigorous, articulate and elaborate discourse, that is to say, the cultivation of the human faculties and the most profound expressions of the human spirit. In this sense culture is universal. On the other hand, culture means the values and significations sedimented in the enormous variety of people's quotidian modes of life which produce different and specific practices and customs. The latter is the more sociological or anthropological level of culture, to which Herder contributes with the idea that more than culture there exist "cultures" which cannot be assimilated to one another. This means that the social processes of each people contribute to the creation of distinct modes of life or different cultures. This distinction is an important tool of analysis and I shall use it in order to better understand the problem of identity.

But let us define first what is the problem that confronts us. There seem to be two contradictory ways in which postmodern discourse relates itself to the issue of identity: On the one hand, it stresses the discovery of "otherness" and the right of the "other" to speak for itself. On the other hand, it underlines the decentering of the subject and the loss of its identity. On the one side, it highlights culture as a specific mode of life or being of a people and defends their right to express themselves, to manifest a truth that differs from others. But on the other side, it rejects the idea of a coherent and integrated personal identity because it rejects the idea of an autonomous subject, capable of constructing discourses. The subject does not produce ideas or discourses, s/he is rather produced or interpolated by discourses which constitute him/her as a subject. The plurality of discourses makes a centered subject impossible. The emphasis is put on discourse as the center of culture and social life. In this chapter I shall attempt to explore the way in which the Postmodernist discourse arrives at these two opposite results and shall examine critically their coherence and tenability. But first, it is necessary briefly to analyze how Modernity treats the problem of the "other."

Modernity and the Constitution of the Other

For a long time the modern philosophical conceptions of identity were based on the belief in the existence of a self or inner core which emerges at birth, like a soul or essence, which in spite of developing various potentialities in time, remains basically the same throughout life, thus providing a sense of continuity and self-recognition. The self was conceived as an essence inherent in the human being, and, as Taylor has maintained, it was constituted by a certain sense of the interior; the only source of moral strength and self-control (111). This given or *a priori* self could be conceived as a thinking metaphysical substance (Descartes, Leibniz) or as the sensuous continuity of consciousness over time which memory provides (Locke, Enlightened French philosophers), but in any case it presupposed a sense of the interior.

Thus Descartes sought to prove irrefutably the existence of an inner self as something given or *a priori* by arguing that if there is thought there is bound to be something that thinks: *cogito ergo sum.* Locke and the French philosophers of the Enlightenment, in their turn, wanted to leave metaphysics and the idea of substance behind and conceived of the self as that interior sense of conscious continuity given by memory, understood as something material. Although Leibniz thought that identity depended upon an immaterial substance, he also conceded an important role to memory. In general, it could be said that in spite of many differences between them, the seventeenth-century philosophers developed a conception of an individual and isolated subject which is also the point of departure for many eighteenth-century philosophers. Kant confirmed an abstract and supratemporal notion of the subject and although Hegel added to it a historical dimension and a dialectical reference to the other, it kept its abstract character insofar as real human beings and their relationships were replaced by the Idea.

It should not be believed, though, that Modernity totally neglected the role of social relations in the formation of identity. The idea of and concern for the "other" is not new and certainly does not arise for the first time with Postmodernist discourse. Well before the rise of Postmodernism Karl Marx, William James, George Mead and, in general sociology, understand identity not as a given interior essence, but as a socially constructed process in which the idea of the "other" is crucial. The self is not given but develops in an individual as a result of his/her social relations and experiences. Identity presupposes the prior existence of the social group.

Marx was one of the first authors within Modernity to attack the individualistic conception of the subject as an illusion derived from the "Robinsonades" of "eighteenth century prophets" (1973: 83). He argued against Feuerbach that if there is a human essence, this is in its very reality "the ensemble of the social relations" and not an "abstraction inherent in each single individual" (1976: 29). Human beings can individuate themselves only in the midst of society; they "become individuals only through the process of history" (1976: 494). William James, in his turn, asserted that the self was constituted by three elements. Apart from the spiritual element which consists of our psychic and mental capabilities and functions, he distinguished a material element which includes the possession of material objects and the acquisition of wealth, and a social element defined as the recognition that we obtain from other human beings.

Mead maintained that the conception of the self as a soul with which the individual was born had to be abandoned in order to study the "self in its dependence upon the social group to which it belongs" (1974: 1). The self is not given but develops in an individual as a result of his/her social experiences through language and communication. The subject internalizes the attitudes of others and makes them its own. However, the internalization of external attitudes does not make the self purely passive and receptive. The self is more than the mere organization of social attitudes. This is what Mead expresses through his distinction (which James had already made) between the "I" and the "me." The "I" is the response, the reaction of the individual to the attitudes of the others; the "me" is the organized set of attitudes of others which is constitutive of the self (175).

Mead accepts that because the self arises in the context of a variety of social experiences, it is very complex, full of aspects or dimensions which make reference to certain social relations and not to others. That is why it is even possible to speak of a variety of elemental selves. However, there is also a complete self which responds to the community as a whole or, at least, to the conjunction of significant others (142, 4). The unity and structure of the complete self reflect the unity and structure of the totality of the social processes in which the individual participates. In other words, the complete self responds to a "generalized other" which integrates the expectations and values of the significant others.

As it could be appreciated, these contributions understand identity as a process that develops in social interaction. The social character of identity possesses a double dimension. First, individuals define themselves or identify themselves with some qualities in terms of some shared social categories. Second, identity entails a reference to the "other." In forming their personal identities individuals share certain culturally defined affiliations, characteristics or group allegiances such as religion, gender, class, ethnicity, sexuality, nationality, etc., which contribute to specify the subject and its sense of identity. In this sense it can be affirmed that culture is one of the main determinants of personal identity. All personal identities are rooted in culturally determined collective contexts. This is how the idea of cultural identities emerges.

Cultural identities are historical categories which can change. Before Modernity most people defined themselves in terms of a relationship with God, and, therefore, religion was the fundamental cultural identity. In modern times the cultural identities which have had a most important influence in the formation of subjects are class and national identities. Today, these identities seem to be losing their relative importance before new emergent categories such as gender, ethnicity and sexuality.

Secondly, the construction of the self necessarily involves the existence of others in a double sense. The others are those whose opinions about us we internalize. But they are also those against which the self acquires its distinctiveness and specificity. The first sense entails that the subject internalizes the expectations or attitudes of others with respect to him/her, and these expectations of others are transformed into his or her own self-expectations. Hence, the subject defines himself or herself in terms of how others see him or her. However, only the evaluations of others who are in some way significant to the subject really count for the construction and maintenance of his/her self-image.

Yet, in second place, identity also presupposes the existence of others who have different modes of life, different values, customs, and ideas. In order to define oneself, the differences with others are accentuated. The definition of self always involves a distinction from the values, characteristics, and modes of life of others. In the construction of any version of identity, the comparison with the "other" and the utilization of mechanisms of differentiation with the "other" play a fundamental role: Some groups, values, and customs are presented as belonging outside the community. Sometimes, in order to define what is considered to be one's own, differences from what is someone else's are exaggerated. In these cases the normal process of differentiation is transformed in a process of opposition and hostility against the other. The process of differentiation from others is indispensable for the construction of one's own identity; the hostile opposition to others is not, and constitutes a danger of all identity construction process.

In the construction of European cultural identities from the sixteenth century onwards, the presence of the nonEuropean other was always crucial and, conversely, in the construction of nonEuropean identities, the presence of the European other was also crucial. The discovery and conquest of America in particular played a very important role because it coincided with the beginning of Modernity, the beginning of capitalism and the formation of the European nation-states.

The formation of European cultural identities during the beginning of Modernity took place in opposition to certain internal as much as external "others." In the first place, the other is the past, in opposition to which a new project is being built, it is the obsolete, the traditional, feudal society. In the second place, the other was also defined in the context of the very modern society in terms of those social sectors which did not totally comply with the requirements of reason. Wagner has suggested the examples of working classes, women and the mentally ill (1994: 39). The working classes were at the beginning considered dangerous classes with far too many boundless aspirations which introduced disorder in society. Women, in their turn, were systematically excluded from public and political life throughout the nineteenth century and a good part of the twentieth, because of their supposed emotiveness, lack of control and lack of rationality. Finally, mad and insane people also represented those irrational "others" which have no control over themselves. Disorder, emotiveness and lack of control constituted three categories contrary to reason. In the third place, the "other" is that who lives outside or comes from without, the barbarian or backward primitive who has still to be civilized. A more or less complete picture of the "others" of early Modernity and their specific lack of reason might be like this:

wildness	black people, savages, noncivilized peoples
tradition	nobility, priests
disorder	working classes, masses
emotiveness	women
insanity	mad people

It goes without saying that some of these social sectors later ceased to play the fundamental role of "other" and little by little were incorporated into the mainstream society. This is especially true of the working classes and women, the two sectors closer to society itself and numerically very important. Their incorporation was partly the result of their own successful struggles and partly the consequence of social pacts which gave them citizenship in exchange for moderation and order. The more advanced Modernity becomes, the more "otherness" becomes concentrated in the spatial dimension, including those who live outside or come from abroad. This is the reason why ethnic factors have acquired preponderance in the contemporary definition of otherness and, unfortunately, as could be seen in Europe today, hostile and aggressive forms of opposition have been gaining terrain.

Postmodernity, the Other and the Self

Postmodernist discourse no longer considers reason as the basis for the construction of identities and their others. In its view, reality has disintegrated into a multiplicity of simulacra and signifiers without meaning, direction or rational explanation. Chaos and fragmented images dominate: The entire system is fluctuating in indeterminacy, all of reality absorbed by the hyperreality of the code and of simulation. It is now a principle of simulation, and not of reality, that regulates social life. The finalities have disappeared; we are now engendered by models (Baudrillard 1988: 120). It is impossible to aspire to any unified representation of the world, or picture it as a totality full of meaning. Reality is no more than a conjunction of discontinued and perpetually shifting fragments and images which make illusory the existence of a superior and comprehensive vantage point which might find a global sense.

For Postmodernism this situation is related with the contemporary explosion of mass media. Culture has become increasingly affected to the point that some authors speak of the "mediazation" of modern culture: "the general process by which the transmission of symbolic forms becomes increasingly mediated by the technical and institutional apparatuses of the media industries (Thompson 4). Radio, television and newspapers have become the agents of a general explosion and proliferation of images and world views.

Somehow it is this violent expansion of signifiers which has made society more complex and chaotic. The enormous increase of information and images about reality from innumerable perspectives makes it increasingly difficult to conceive of a single reality. Vattimo reminds us that in the world of the mass media Nietzsche's prophecy is fulfilled: In the end the true world becomes a fable. We can no longer arrive at reality itself. Reality is no longer something simple concealed behind images, reality is rather the intersection of a multiplicity of images (Vattimo 7). Or, as Baudrillard says, one of the main characteristics of these signs is that they no longer refer to anything "real" beyond themselves. Hence the new world is characterized by hyperreality and simulation "in the sense that from now on signs will exchange among themselves exclusively, without interacting with the real" (Baudrillard 125).

In spite of the fact that the Postmodernist discourse is very critical of the modern discourses of emancipation,[1] Vattimo has argued that this very erosion of the principle of a meaningful reality is connected with a new sense of liberation and emancipation:

> Emancipation here consists of disorientation, which is at the same time also the liberation of differences, of local elements, of what could generally be called a dialect. With the demise of the idea of a central rationality in history, the world of generalized communication explodes like a multiplicity of "local" rationalities—ethnic, sexual, religious, cultural or aesthetic minorities—that finally speak up for themselves. They are no longer repressed into silence by the idea of a single true form of humanity. (8-9)

Thus the Postmodernist discourse allows "otherness" to emerge not just as the mere antagonist of well defined rational identities, but as the new protagonist of a plurality of discourses. Modernity, with its totalizing discourses of emancipation, "presumed to speak for others (colonized peoples, blacks, minorities, religious groups, women, the working class) with a unified voice" (Harvey 47-48). Postmodernism rejects these totalizing discourses, be them religious, Liberal, or Marxist. All groups have the right to speak for themselves, in their own voice or dialect, and this would show the pluralistic stance of Postmodernism. However, the paradox arises that together with this recognition of the other, Postmodernism seem to negate the subject's identity.

In effect, according to Postmodernist discourse, discontinuity, fragmentation, and incoherence affect not just the real world but also individuals themselves and their personalities. For Modernity the subject was thought to be well integrated, a coherent and centered self, the origin and cause of actions, ideas and texts. For Postmodernism, on the contrary, the subject is essentially fragmented and decentered in his/her inner being, internally divided, unable to unify his/her experiences. It is not the pre-given origin of meaning but rather is itself constituted by discourses. The idea of a well integrated and causal subject is an invention of Modernity, especially of the rationalism of the Enlightenment. Hence, the destruction of a single reality and the lack of meaning of history corresponds to a decentered subject which has lost its identity.

Foucault is one of the first authors to speak of the "decentering of the subject," a phenomenon which for him has been detected by the research of psychoanalysis, linguistics, and ethnology (1977: 13). The subject is constituted, it is not the starting point. Under the influence of both Nietzsche and Freud, Foucault argues that "the individual is not a pre-given entity which is seized on by the exercise of power. The individual, with his identity and characteristics, is the product of a relation of power exercised over bodies" (1980: 73-74).

In the work of Laclau and Mouffe, the very term "subject" is replaced by the notion of "subject positions" in order to indicate that a subject can only arise within a discursive structure, and that, consequently, it is eminently dependent, contingent, and temporal. Every discourse constitutes its own subject positions (115). Similarly, Lyotard argues that "a self does not amount to much, but no self is an island; each exists in a fabric of relations that is now more complex and mobile than ever before . . . a person is always located at 'nodal points' of specific communication circuits" (15). Baudrillard, in his turn, argues that the position of the subject has become untenable, since it can no longer control the world of objects as it used to. The objects are now in control, and this must be recognized by what he calls "fatal theory." The difference between a traditional, banal theory and the new, more adequate, fatal theory is that

> in the former the subject always believes itself to be more clever than the object, while in the latter the object is always taken to be more clever, more cynical, more ingenious than the subject, which it awaits at every turn. The metamorphoses, tactics and strategies of the object exceed the subject's understanding. (1988: 198)

In so far as the self is fragmented, it cannot unify the past, present and future of its own biographical experience or psychic life. The project of Modernity with its rationalism, determinism, and sense of historical progress, required that subjects have a sense of personal identity and coherence which allowed them to project themselves in time. The very critique of alienation (religious, political, and economic), so important for modern authors, presupposed a centered subject which somehow could be alienated by external factors which were essentially changeable. This was the sense of emancipation.

For Postmodernity, on the contrary, the subject is constructed in internal conflict, it exists in a radical incoherence of his/her personal identity and cannot therefore even picture or devise strategies to produce a radically different future. There is no sense in the question about a better future, about emancipation. The subject only lives in the present, surrounded by the spectacle of signifiers which have lost all connection with the signified. The loss of identity means that the subject cannot coherently act in the world.

This is then the paradox: The Postmodernist discourse seems to sanction the emergence of the other, of a different identity, but also seems to sanction the dislocation of the self. The "other" can now speak for him/herself but the self seems to be unable to speak for itself with a unified voice. The "other" appears to be integrated around a coherent, if local or different, identity, but the self seems to be fragmented in a variety of contradictory identities. Some crucial questions thus arise which Postmodernist discourse must answer: Is not the other, which speaks for her/himself with a unified voice, a coherent kind of identity? Why could there exist selves which are so dislocated if the selves of the others are not? Is there not a contradiction between this so-called discovery of the other and the announcement of the end of the coherent self? Before trying to see whether there are adequate answers to these questions within the Postmodernist perspective let us examine in greater detail each separate claim.

The Problems of Otherness and Latin America's Own Voice

What can be said about the discovery of otherness by Postmodernism? A first reaction tends naturally to be positive. If Postmodernism propounds concern for the other and opposition to total visions which reduce difference to uniformity, it must play a positive role. Modern totalizing theories are always in danger of believing that the particular, the local, and the historically specific acquire meaning only insofar as they are instances of the general. The belief in a general historical rationality may easily conceal the difference and autonomy of local rationalities. Postmodernism, on the contrary, seems to allow the cultural other a voice of its own, the right to be different and not to be subsumed by a general logic which eliminates its specificity.

I think here ultimately resides the cause of Postmodernism's enthusiastic reception in Latin America. For it would seem to be the only contemporary theory which allows Latin America its own voice and legitimates its right to be different. But the reason of its success cannot be reduced to this alone. I believe that, furthermore, Postmodernism has come to reinforce oppositional and essentialist positions on Latin American identity which since the military dictatorships of the 1970s, have been gaining terrain, especially in Chile. In effect, the failures of economic development in many Latin American countries and the military dictatorships that followed in their wake, led many intellectuals to a forceful and bitter critique of Western instrumental rationality and to a reappraisal of a different, supposedly original, kind of cultural identity, which would have been lost in the course of history. The main idea of the essentialist currents, be them neo-Indianist or religious fundamentalist, is that the processes of modernization, so desired and sought after in Latin America, could not but lead to failure insofar as they do not respect the Latin American identity, which even though forgotten, continues to be the true essence that has to be recovered.

Thus the idea begins to be developed that there is an opposition between two different cultural patterns: the European rational enlightened and the Latin American symbolic dramatic.[2] The former strongly believes in instrumental reason, that is to say, in reason as a means to master nature and bring about progress. The latter is suspicious of instrumental reason and has a religious-aesthetic approach to reality. The rational enlightened pattern emphasizes abstract and conceptual discourse and appeals to reason; the symbolic dramatic pattern emphasizes images, dramatic representations and rites, and appeals to sensations. Parker thinks that the nucleus of this model is popular religion which is characterized by its vitalism in the face of the enlightened intellectualism, by its expressionism in the face of the ruling cultures's formalism, and by its sense of the transcendental in the face of Cartesian-Positivist scientism.[3] In this way, emphasis is put upon the specificity of the Latin American cultural experience, upon that which separates it from other cultural models, especially the Enlightened one.

In this perspective, the Latin American future would depend upon its loyalty to some traditions or principles, be they of religious or Indian origin, which had been forgotten or marginalized by instrumental reason, by the alienated enlightened elite and by the neoliberal modernizing attempts. These traditions constitute a truly distinct type of rationality, which has some expressions in the Latin American people (for instance in popular religiosity) and which should be the basis for the construction of the future. It is this essentialist conception which opposes the Latin American cultural model to the European enlightened cultural model, encouraged by Postmodernism in the 1980s. Postmodernism seems to support the Latin American discourse which tries not to be reduced to European models and which asserts its unique character and its own specificity. An important aspect of this conjunction of interests is the Postmodernist attack on the Enlightenment and on the absolute character of Western reason. The critique of the Enlightenment as totalitarian and the rejection of Modernity as a reifying process, certainly represent those in Latin America who look for the causes of region's failures in its indefatigable search for an alien identity based on instrumental reason. Postmodernist discourse does not consider reason as the basic criterion for the construction of identities and their "others."

There are numerous contact points between European Postmodernism and the antirational conception of the Latin American identity. It is not just the common distrust of the subject-centered reason, it is also, as in Nietzsche, its replacement by its absolute other, the aesthetic experience which free from all constraints of cognition, purpose and utility, is the only means of communicating with the basic sources of social integration. It is also the common interest in ritual sacrifice, unproductive activities, and the free squandering of resources which Bataille studies with admiration in the Aztecs and which some Catholic intellectuals put at the center of the Latin American cultural identity: The human sacrifices of the Aztecs have only been replaced by hard labor, and ritual squandering has been continued in frequent religious festivities. It is also the sense that Latin America is the "other" that cannot be reduced, which possesses different parameters and proposes a different kind of discourse with its own truth.

The irony cannot help but be noticed in that the attempts at self-affirmation by the others of Latin America—for decades ignored by Europe and the developed world—should appear now to be defended by a European theory. The question arises, however, as to whether Postmodernist discourse truly defends the Latin American specificity and difference or whether a more careful and penetrating critical review of its premises might show that not all is as clear-cut as it seems.

Nelly Richard has developed a critical argument which precisely seeks to question the supposed openness of Postmodernism in the case of Latin America. According to her, Postmodernism appears to give Latin America a privileged position in so far as the heterogeneity and fragmentation typical of the Postmodern era would have been long standing Latin American characteristics. However, just as it appears that for once the Latin American periphery might have achieved the distinction of being Postmodernist *avant la lettre,* no sooner does it attain a synchronicity of forms with the international cultural discourses, than that very same Postmodernism abolishes any privilege which such a position might offer. Postmodernism dismantles the distinction between center and periphery, and in so doing nullifies its significance. Postmodernism defends itself against the destabilizing threat of the "other" by integrating it back into a framework which absorbs all differences and contradictions (Richard 1993: 467-68).

The critique seems to be that what Postmodernism concedes with one hand, it withdraws with the other, for it tends to abolish the traditional dichotomies with which Modernity used to work and which gave specificity to the Latin American situation: the original and the copy, center and periphery, colonial power and colony. My impression is that this is not a very fair critique and that it is based on a confusion of levels. Richard maintains that Postmodernism tries to convince us of the obsolescence of oppositions such as center-periphery, but when she tries to prove it, the texts she cites do not refer to the elimination of such distinctions but only propose a different assessment of its significance. Thus, for instance, one of the texts quoted as proof says: "Why should it be true that what comes first is more valuable that what comes after, that the original is worth more than the imitation, that what is central is more important than the peripheral?" (468).[4] The point seems to be, precisely, a revaluation of the copy, of the colony and the periphery, not an argument against these distinctions! In effect if one continues to read Schwarz's text, at least in its English version, one can see that he agrees with Foucault and Derrida and thinks that the revaluation of the copy "could increase the self-esteem and alleviate the anxiety of the underdeveloped world which sees itself as tributary to central countries" (6).

Hence, it is difficult to argue that Postmodernism eliminates the traditional dichotomies. What it does is to evaluate them in a different way which is more advantageous for Latin America. To maintain that Postmodernism defends itself from the "other" by integrating it in a frame which absorbs the differences and contradictions, is not an adequate interpretation. If anything, that was the technique of Modernity and its totalizing theories. Postmodernism is always in favor of exaggerating differences, not of absorbing them.

But my point is not to assert the total innocence of Postmodernism. I agree that Postmodernism tries to defend itself from the other, but not in the way Richard thinks; it uses a more subtle device which consists in exaggerating differences to the point that nothing in common is left, and the essence of what is supposed to be Latin American can no longer touch that other essence of what is supposed to be European. The defense is by exclusion, not by integration. Let us see how Postmodernism treats the "other" by contrasting its position to that of modern theories.

Modern universalistic theories have difficulties in understanding cultural differences because they conceive of history as a continuous series of universal stages through which everybody has to go. These theories emphasize the similarity of goals for all humankind, but have difficulties in respecting the other as different. Postmodernism has the opposite difficulty: it values differences and historical discontinuities but has difficulties in understanding the elements of shared humanity which underlie all cultures. Like all forms of historicism, Postmodernist discourses conceive of history as a segmented process or, as Foucault would put it, as "the space of a dispersion" (1977: 10). There is no unique center, principle or universal meaning that evolves, but a variety of different cultural essences which each nation develops with a logic of its own, discontinuous with the rest.

Universalistic theories tend to look at the "other" from the point of view of the European rational subject; they tend to apply a total pattern which postulates its own absolute truth and reduces all cultural differences to its own unity. Postmodernist discourses look at the "other" from the perspective of its unique and specific cultural setup, thus emphasizing cultural difference and historical discontinuity. There are dangers implicit in both positions. While the emphasis on absolute truth and historical continuity may lead to reductionism and neglect of the other's specificity, the emphasis on difference and discontinuity may lead to the construction of the other as less than human or inferior.

This is why the idea that modern theories tend to be intolerant and racist whereas postmodern theories tend to be pluralistic and tolerant is simplistic if not misleading. It is true that there is a form of racism which stems from universalistic theories which do not accept the other because they do not know how to recognize and respect its difference. But there is also another form of racism, perhaps more subtle, which stems from Postmodernist discourses, for although they allow the other to speak for itself, they do not want anything to do with it in so far as it is constructed as totally different, as belonging to an alien world that must remain distant. The other may be acknowledged in its right to exist and speak, but at the same time it can be suspected as culturally invasive and so different as to become unacceptable to one's own cultural standards.

The fact that Modern discourses tend to conceive of history as universal, unilinear and teleological progress, whereas Postmodernist theories conceive of history as a discontinuous, segmented, and purposeless process which has no universal direction, has effects on the conceptualization of identity. Paradoxically, the emphasis on historical discontinuity leads Postmodernist theories to conceive of cultural identity in a nonhistorical way, as an essence, as an immutable spirit which marks an unbridgeable difference between peoples and nations. Hence their affinity with the Latin American essentialist conceptions that wish to assert an identity opposite to the European one. The emphasis on history as universal and unilinear progress, on the contrary, tends to reduce cultural identities to being mere manifestations of a universal historical process and to neglect their differences.

A unilateral emphasis on difference may easily transform itself into a judgment of purity and a wish to exclude and keep the "others" separate: Different cultures are accepted as long as they remain in their places of origin and do not come to encroach on the cultures of the center. Postmodernist positions fail to appreciate the existence of the common ground between cultures, of hybridity. One can exactly question these positions as Said asked in *Orientalism*:

> Can one divide human reality, as indeed human reality seems to be genuinely divided, into clearly different cultures, histories, traditions, societies, even races, and survive the consequences humanly? By surviving the consequences humanly, I mean to ask whether there is any way of avoiding the hostility expressed by the division, say, of men into "u s" (Westerners) and "they" (Orientals). For such divisions are generalities whose use historically and actually has been to press the importance of the distinction between some men and some other men, usually towards not especially admirable ends. (45)

In the case of Latin America, Postmodernism seems to lend credibility to fundamentalist positions which reduce the question of a Latin American identity to an originating moment in the past and that wish to radicalize the differences from the "other": What is Latin America's own is understood as an immovable patrimony which values fiesta, rite, drama, intuition, religion and sapient knowledge. What is alien refers to an absolute "other": instrumental reason, logocentric discourse, Cartesian rationalism, Western Modernity or whatever other name one wishes to give it. Everything happens as if instrumental rationality were totally alien to the Latin American ethos or way of feeling, as if religious vitalism were totally alien to the European ethos. It is, in sum, the idea that there are totally different logics, in the same sense as Lyotard conceives of the incommensurability of language games (15).

Decentred Subject and Contradictory Identities

Stuart Hall has proposed a sort of historical progression of the concept of personal identity by distinguishing three stages within which three different conceptions of identity correspond to three different types of subject: the Enlightenment subject, the sociological subject and the postmodern subject. The Enlightenment subject was based on a conception of the human person as a fully centered, unified individual, endowed with the capacities of reason, consciousness and action. The self or human center was an inner core which came with the individual at birth and remained basically the same throughout life. The sociological subject goes beyond an individualistic conception of the subject to emphasize the fact that the inner core of the subject is not autonomous and self-sufficient but is formed in relation to significant others. The self could only be the result of the symbolic interaction between the subject and the others; the self is not given but develops in an individual as a result of his/her social experiences. Finally, the postmodern subject is conceptualized as not having a fixed and permanent identity, the subject has become fragmented and composed of a variety of identities which are contradictory or unresolved. Those identities are not unified around a coherent self. In fact, for Hall the coherent self is just a story, a fantasy we tell ourselves (275-77). Hall seems to privilege this version.

In accordance to this model there would have been a progression from the subject as an immutable essence to the subject as a social construction, and from this to the subject as divided, conceived of as a collection of disparate tendencies. From the point of view of identity, the progression would have been from identity as a fixed and given essence to identity as socio-communicative construction, and from this to the disappearance or break with identity altogether. If one surveys the history of modern philosophy, one can find many elements which seem to confirm this evolution.

We saw in the first section that the conception of identity evolves through various philosophers from the idea of a soul, or abstract essence inherent in the individual, to the idea of an identity constructed in social relations. But this main line of development coexisted with another more critical line. One of the first skeptical approaches came from David Hume, who maintained that personal identity was a fiction in so far as it was incompatible with the notion of change. A strikingly similar line of thought was taken by Nietzsche, who argued that "the 'subject' is the fiction that many similar states in us are the effect of one substratum" (269). In reality, "the 'subject' is not something given, it is something added and invented and projected behind what there is" (267).

From a different perspective, Freud's theory of the unconscious and of its importance in the formation of the self was clearly a new challenge to the whole tradition which had understood the self as a conscious subject, with absolute self-control. Freud revealed that the subject was shaped by forces of which it was not conscious, and this, of course, introduced the doubt about its postulated coherence and integration. Starting from Freud, but already influenced by structuralism, Lacan will later speak of the subject "in process," always incomplete, always being formed. Structuralism, especially in its connection with Saussurean linguistics, constituted another stage in the process of the dissolution of the subject, in as much as s/he loses its explanatory ability, his/her position as the creator of meanings, the ultimate cause of knowledge and culture. Instead of being the creator, the subject is deemed to be constructed by the external structure. As Lévi-Strauss argues, the "supposed totalizing continuity of the self seems to me to be an illusion sustained by the demands of social life . . . rather than the object of an apodictic experience" (254, 256).

As is well known, the dissolution of the subject even penetrates Marxist theory through Althusser's antihumanism, for which individuals are constituted as subjects in the process of being interpolated by ideology (160-70). This is the line of thought that reaches up to Foucault, Lyotard, and Baudrillard. This is a line which has systematically doubted the possibility of an underlying substance or unity in human beings which would be responsible for knowledge and practice. This skepticism about the subject has accompanied the development of Modernity almost from the beginning. However, for a long time this assault on the primacy of the subject was punctual and rather marginal with respect to the main modern intellectual currents. Little by little, though, it began to acquire importance and widen its sphere of influence, first with Structuralism, then with Poststructuralism, and getting finally to its culmination in present Postmodernist thought.

In a way, one could speak of a veritable crisis of the subject in contemporary social theory, which can only imply a crisis of identity. The Posmodernist proposal is that the fragmented subject corresponds to a decentered or dislocated identity. Stuart Hall's postmodern subject has no fixed or permanent identity, but assumes different identities at different times, identities which are contradictory and which cannot be unified (277). The new Postmodernist positions seem to be saying that in contemporary times the integration of the "generalized other" has failed, or, in Mead's terms, the "elementary selves" have become incompatible, and that for this reason the complete self is dislocated and decentered and incapable of achieving unity.

The cause of such a crisis of dissolution is not, of course, only a philosophical problem related to the emergence of Postmodernist thought. The Postmodernist discourse itself tries to respond to the accelerated changes in advanced societies, changes which may induce the belief that Modernity itself is being superseded. The loss of the subject is perceived as the result of the new feelings and practices brought about by unintended complex processes of rapid and chaotic change which seem to control individuals. New forms of globalization, space-time compression and the acceleration of changes in late Modernity seem to dislocate the sense of self and disintegrate the sense of identity. The true explosion of communications, images, and signifiers, and the vertiginous changes have made it more difficult to know what is true reality, and to prevent the subject from being oriented with respect to the world and to himself/herself. The proliferation of messages can lead to what Thompson has called "symbolic overload," which has disorienting effects (1995: 216).

The globalization of communications through electronic means has allowed the separation of social relations from the local contexts of interaction. This means not only that the number of "significant others" with whom each person can enter into relationships has substantially increased, but also that such others come to be known not by means of their physical presence but through the media, especially through televised images. Recent statistics tell us that almost throughout the world, children spend more hours annually in front of a TV set than at school. In this way, television is playing an increasing role in the structuring of contemporary identities. This means also that many people can now be aware of cultural differences, of how other peoples live and think. New "others" arise in relation to whom the self can be distinguished. This makes the construction of personal identity more complex and reflexive, more unstable and subject to changes.

The big social transformations brought about by globalization tend to uproot widely shared cultural identities and, therefore, alter the categories in terms of how subjects construct their identities. Processes of disarticulation and dislocation occur whereby many people cease to see themselves in terms of traditional collective contexts which provided a sense of identity. Thus, for instance, the cultural identities which had a most important influence upon the formation of subjects in early Modernity were class and national identities. Precisely these two have been affected by increased globalization. National identity has been losing its appeal due to the decline of nation-states and the erosion of their autonomy. The process of globalization spread nation-states throughout the world, but ended up by eroding their autonomy. Class identities have also declined due to the internationalization of the economy and the relative loss of importance of the national context. On the contrary, ethnic and sexual identities have acquired an extraordinary importance in Europe and increasingly so in Latin América.

Yet the question arising is whether this new changing reality can justify the disintegration of the sense of identity; whether the emergent new feelings are equivalent to a dislocated self; whether the Postmodernist discourse about the decentered subject is a reasonable explanation of what is going on. Are common people really living through an identity crisis? Although there is little doubt that the changes occurring in late Modernity are very momentous and deeply affect individuals, I do not believe that they really get to the point of producing decentered subjects with dislocated identities.

It is true that the construction of personal identities has become more complex and mediated by the media. As Kellner maintains "television and other cultural forms mediated by the media play a crucial role in the structuration of contemporary identities" (148). But from this point, there is a long way to accepting that the subject has become totally fragmented. In contemporary society, identity has not been totally dissolved, but has been rather reconstructed and redefined in new cultural contexts. However, for Kellner this redefinition of identity has a radical character. If modern identity was a "serious affair" (153) which defined an individual in fundamental aspects and could not be easily changed, postmodern identity seems a game of images and entertainment based upon appearances and consumption, which can be changed at will according to the leaps of fashion:

> Thus identity today has become a freely chosen game, a theatrical presentation of the self, in which one is able to present oneself in a variety of roles, images and activities, relatively unconcerned about shifts, transformations and dramatic changes. (158)

Kellner rescues identity from the total decentering proposed by Postmodernism, but does it by trivializing its role and by transforming it into a game whereby people freely choose, like in the theater, the roles they like to perform, only to change them for others when they wish. Kellner believes that in contemporary times people have increased their freedom to play with their own identity and to change their lives in a dramatic form, but he also understands that this can lead to a fragmented and disarticulated life subject to fashions and publicity campaigns.

On my part, I think that Kellner exaggerates and that really there is no such thing as total freedom to choose and change identity as one changes one's clothes. The problem is that Kellner seems to understand by identity a mere external appearance. It is true that one can play with one's own external appearance by trying to imitate cultural models—one can cultivate an image—but this does not always touch upon the most basic aspects of identity. With good reason Wagner has argued that one has to distinguish between wishful self-presentations and the actually ongoing social practices (168). As a professor in a British university, for many years I have seen many generations of students who tried to adopt a certain identity by means of earrings, hair-dos, dresses, tattoos and manners of speaking and moving. In the long run, neither them nor those who dress and act conventionally differ fundamentally with respect to studying responsibly, punctually complying with their commitments, reasoning in accordance to formal logic and aspiring to well paid jobs.

What has really happened in late Modernity is that the fundamental variables of self-definition have been disconnected from the traditional external appearances of style, dress and presentation. People can maintain their traditional identities, but wish to project a special and unconventional image. In overrating the dislocation of personal identity, Postmodernism confuses these planes and makes the integration of the "generalized other" impossible. Everything happens as if the individual was continually pulled apart by the internalization of different and mutually opposed others which can never be unified. What for Mead were isolated cases of schizophrenia, for Postmodernism seems to be normal.

This is the result of the Postmodernist overemphasis on discourse and its capacity to construct the subject. The plurality of discourses bombards the subject from different angles and constitutes him/her in a divided and contradictory form, thus making impossible a centered subject. The overrating of the causal role of discourses reduces the study of identity to a partial and simple problematic which ignores the complexity of the process of identification, and unduly presupposes that there is a total correspondence between discourses and the experiences of common people. Thus they fall in a unilateral and limited form of constructivism, a voluntarism of discourse which would allow the construction of antagonistic identities in a helpless subject.

Postmodernist constructivism does not conceive of the existence of conditions of any kind which could be outside discourse and which may help explain individual identities. Personal integration or dislocation is purely a discursive problem, a problem of interpolative capacity. Constructivism ignores the repeated practices and sedimented meanings in the life of people (from childhood) which condition his/her ability or possibility to be impacted by any discourse. Constructivist Postmodernism seems to presuppose that the necessary conditions for the early formation of an integrated identity in the child no longer exist and that, moreover, the already formed identities of adults easily collapse under the pressure of accelerated changes. I believe these two presuppositions are mistaken.

Young people continue to construct their identities in relation to significant others located in a variety of spheres of society (even if these others have considerably increased in numbers and are accessible only through the media) and can perfectly well integrate their various "elemental selves." Maybe this process is more complex than ever before and demands much more than what a child from a traditional agrarian society had to cope with, where the significant points of reference were the parents and a few more individuals. But in spite of the complexity, children continue forming more or less integrated identities. In adults, the image of self, although ultimately dependent upon the others' expectations, is normally strong enough to exist with some relative autonomy. The adult has already built his or her self-image on the basis of a long sequence of previous social expectations which leave a material imprint in the subject.

An adult totally dependent upon what others think of her/him (or upon the discourse of the moment), or whose identity crumbles before the impact of any new reality, would be totally inadequate, a puppet without substance. It is not that the others' opinions do not count any more when one is an adult. The self-image will always reflect the expectations of others, but only insofar as they are modified by our previously developed self (Gerth 85). This means that it has more stability and resilience than Postmodernism allows for. People who have suffered dramatic changes in their mode of life may experience feelings of bewilderment, disorientation, and discontinuity, but rarely adapt themselves to live in contradiction and always try to find some personal coherence.

Postmodernist Discourse and the Loss of the Subject

So far I have tried to show that Postmodernist positions about the "other" and about the "decentered subject" have serious problems when they are separately considered on their own merits. When one considers them together, though, new problems arise. Is it not contradictory to celebrate the discovery of the other that can speak for him/herself and, at the same time, to postulate the decentering of the subject? Is not the other in its turn, a subject in his/her own right? How can some subjects be dislocated and others be able to speak in their own name with a clear sense of identity? Postmodernism falls into this contradiction partly because it introduces too big a distance between the subject and the other. It tends to reduce otherness to sheer difference and opposition; it understands otherness as an alien world incommensurable with one's own, and is not able to recognize it as internalized or internalizable by the subject. This not only leads to an essentialist conception of cultural identity, but also makes it more difficult to conceive of a socially constructed identity.

In effect, in conceiving of the other as pure difference and opposition, it is impossible to understand how the subject can internalize and integrate the expectations of the significant others, and, therefore, the construction of identity is made impossible. On the other hand, in gazing at the other from the point of view of its unique and different cultural specificity, the cultural categories in relation to which personal identities are constructed tend to be essentialized: Nationality, religion, sexuality, gender and ethnicity—to mention only the more important—become absolute dividing principles between incommensurable essences. Catholic and Muslim, white and black, homosexual and heterosexual, man and woman, Israeli and Arab, cease to have shared worlds of humanity and only their cultural differences are accentuated. Thus a true fetishism of difference is instituted.

The latent danger of the fetishism of difference is the possible accentuation of its logic of exclusion. From marking a difference one can go to distrust, from distrust one can go to open hostility and from here to aggression. This process of increasing exclusion is not of itself necessary, but it has happened too many times in history to be ignored as a remote possibility. By following Hilberg, Bauman describes the logic sequence which ended up in the holocaust of the Jews: "It starts with the definition of the stranger. Once it has been defined, it can be separated. Once it has been separated, it can be deported. Once it has been deported, physical extermination could be the conclusion" (68). This is the same logic which has more recently operated between Hutus and Tutsis in Rwanda, or between Bosnian Muslims and Serbs in the old Yugoslavia.

The pretended decentering of the subject corresponds to the supposed triumph of objectivity, to the supposed inability of the subject to control objects. As we saw above, this is one of the central tenets of Baudrillard in his "Fatal Strategies." Objects (be they commodities, media, informations etc.), defeated the subject's ability to dominate them. Baudrillard proposes that individuals must surrender to the world of objects and abandon all projects of controlling them. Whereas Marx criticized the fetishism of commodity as an inversion between subject and object, Baudrillard seems to adopt it as the strategy to be followed: Objects acquire autonomous powers, develop more clever and shrewd strategies, and subjects must learn from them (Best 128-32).

This kind of objectivism dissociates personal identities from collective identities. Postmodernism dissolves personal identity but tends to hypostasize and reify collective identities as if they had an autonomous existence from subjects. It does not make sense that personal identities are shaped by culturally defined collective identities, but rather that the latter cannot exist separately from individuals. It is true that personal identities are not generated by social actors as individuals, because they need different "others" to contrast themselves with, and social categories such as nationality, ethnicity and class to define themselves, but such categories do not have an independent existence; they are continually recreated by individuals through the very means by which they express themselves as actors with an identity. There is no Chileanhood without individual actors who recreate it by means of their practices. Through their activities and their sense of personal identity, agents reproduce the socio-cultural conditions (collective identities) which make such activities possible. By paraphrasing Giddens it can be argued that collective identity is the means and the result of the conduct it recursively organizes (51).

Therefore, identity has neither a purely subjective character nor a mere objective character. Its mode of existence is multidimensional: It is internal to the subject but it is intrinsically determined from the outside, it is simultaneously individual and social or rather, it is internal in as much as it is social, and it is social in as much as it is internal. Thus, it is nonsensical to try to maintain the existence of essential collective identities together with the dissolution of personal identities. No one will deny the depth of contemporary changes and the existence of feelings of confusion and disorientation in individuals. But the Postmodernist explanation of such feelings in terms of the fragmentation and dislocation of the self is inadequate. It is possible to think of other, very different explanations. For a start, there are historical examples of other epochs of change and transition, like the one that brought about the triumph of capitalism and Modernity in the nineteenth century, which were explained otherwise. Let us see, for instance, how Marx and Engels were acutely aware of the magnitude and radicalism of those changes:

> Constant revolutionizing of production, uninterrupted disturbance of all social conditions, everlasting uncertainty and agitation distinguish the bourgeois epoch from all earlier

ones. All fixed, fast-frozen relations, with their train of ancient and venerable prejudices and opinions, are swept away, all new-formed ones become antiquated before they can ossify. All that is solid melts into air, all that is holy is profaned . . . (1970: 38)

This famous passage, so often quoted, refers to accelerated changes and to the rapid and profound dissolution of ideas and social relations as well as to the uncertainty and agitation that they provoke in people. It could have easily justified the idea that personal identities, socially determined as they are, were in danger of being dissolved with the disappearance of the last remnants of traditional society and the conjunction of social relations which underpinned them. However, Marx and Engels pursued their argument in a significantly different manner: "And man is at last compelled to face with sober senses, his real conditions of life, and his relations with his kind" (1970: 38). The idea of a dislocated identity is ruled out and the argument is rather that the process of change forces human beings to face their real conditions of existence with a clear mind. It seems to be a moment of discovery of the way in which social relations operate, a discovery of the way in which one's own identity is shaped.

In other words, it could be said that the dramatic changes that occurred with the triumph of capitalism and the globalization of Modernity brought about more reflexivity, a clearer consciousness about one's own identity, in the sense that individuals become aware of the social relations within which they live (including those which are not face-to-face but mediated through the media), and discover that their own identity is being constructed and that in this process they can choose symbolic resources within certain limits, thus acquiring a more clear notion about the changing conditions of their own identity. Although Postmodernists will surely argue that the world Marx and Engels knew has substantially changed and that the effects of the present forms of globalization and change are much more radical upon individuals, I still think that there are important analogies between the two cases.

The change from Medieval society to Modern society was also very radical and in certain moments traumatic. It was perceived by many as a fundamental disorder and decentering of all values and principles traditionally adhered to. It could be said that in that process, as much as in the present processes of change, great social transformations and revolutions uproot vastly shared cultural identities and bring about new ones. People cease to see themselves in terms of the traditional collective contexts which provided them with a sense of identity. But they do not remain empty-handed, new contexts appear which perform the same role and help reconstruct identity by means of new categories.

The old sources of cultural identity in feudal society, honor and religion, lost their importance with the arrival of Modernity, and nationhood and class emerged as more relevant sources of identification. I think the "radicalization of Modernity" (to use Gidden's expression which replaces the idea of Postmodernity) in recent years, brings about similar conditions (51). Nationhood and class are ceasing to be the most important cultural identities in the definition of individual selves, and new ethnic, gender and sexual identities emerge in association with new social movements (antiracist, feminist and homosexual movements). The explosion of communications and proliferation of electronic messages open up the self to new influences and alter the conditions in which it has to be formed.

Without a doubt, the above mentioned changes can and do produce disorientation and temporal confusion in people. The feeling that all is fleeting, contingent and discontinuous, that Postmodernism detects, has its correlation in the incredible time-space compression produced by the expansion of communications, rapid technological change and globalization. But all this does not justify a total and definitive dislocation or decentering of personal identities. Such assertions put in evidence a contradiction inherent in Postmodernism: While it attacks totalizing metanarratives as terroristic, it secretly reintroduces them through the back door with equally totalizing statements. Wagner is right when he maintains that absolute statements about the fragmentation of the subject "do not take the situation of actually living human beings really seriously, human beings who define their lives, act and are constrained from acting, in and by very real social contexts" (167).

Ultimately, to accept the Postmodernist premises in relation to identity is to accept the final loss of the subject as a conscious agent of construction and change, it is to accept the loss of value of all subjective purpose, to accept the inability of the subject to change circumstances and to propose an alternative rational future. It is the end of all genuine political practice of transformation. I do not believe that this has happened or that it could really happen, although I accept that it is more difficult than before for individuals to understand all that is going on and to have a clear sense of direction. The problem lies not so much in this difficulty, which is real, as in the ideological proclamation that the world of objects has triumphed over subjectivity and that subjects must no longer attempt to construct or change reality. All subjective intervention seems an arrogant assault against the wisdom of the objective world. I do not believe it is too farfetched to suspect that such "wisdom of the objective world" is nothing but the fetishized image of the invisible hand that harmonizes the market.[5]

Notes

1. Lyotard, for instance, argues that "the grand narrative has lost its credibility" or is breaking up; "most people have lost their nostalgia for the lost narrative." This is due to the fact that metanarratives have a totalitarian character: not only are they extreme simplifications, but also "terroristic" in so far as they legitimate the suppression of differences and try to impose their truth. All attempt to impose truth is terror. See J. F. Lyotard (1984: 37and 1974: 287), *Économie libidinale* (Paris: Les Editions de Minuit, 1974), 287.

2. I take this terminology from G. Sunkel, *Representations of the People in the Chilean Popular Press*, Ph.D. thesis, University of Birmingham, 1988, p. 42. It can also be found in C. Parker (1993: 370).

3. Parker enumerates six characteristics of popular religion (194-98).

4. The quoted text appears to come from R. Schwarz, "Nacional por substracción," *Punto de vista* (Buenos Aires) No. 28. No date nor page are given. (The article appeared in 1986. The quote comes from page 17 [Editor's Note]).

5. With this statement I mean to agree with Jameson's idea that Postmodernism is the cultural logic of late capitalism, especially in its neoliberal incarnation.

Works Cited

Althusser, L. *Lenin and Philosophy, and Other Essays.* London: New Left Books, 1971.

Bataille, G. "L'Amérique disparue." Oeuvres Complètes. Vol. 1. Paris: Gallimard, 1970. 152-58.

Baudrillard, J. *Selected Writings.* M. Poster, ed. Cambridge: Polity Press, 1988.

Bauman, Z. "Der Holocaust ist nich einmalig. Gespräch mit dem polnischen Soziologen Zygmunt Bauman" [The Holocaust is Not Unique. Interview with the Polish Sociologist Zygmunt Bauman]. *Die Zeit* 17(1983): n.p.

Best, S. and Kellner, D. *Post Modern Theory, Critical Interrogations.* London: Macmillan, 1991.

Foucault, M. *The Archeology of Knowledge.* London: Tavistock, 1977.

_____. "Questions on Geograpgy." C. Gordon, ed. *Michel Foucault, Power/Knowledge.* Brighton: Harvester Press, 1980.

Gerth, H. and Wright Mills, C. *Character and Social Structure.* New York: Harbinger Books, 1964.

Giddens, A. *The Consequences of Modernity.* Cambridge: Polity Press, 1990.

Hall, Stuart, Held, D., and T. McGrew. *Modernity and its Futures.* Cambridge: The Open University and Polity Press, 1992.

Harvey, D. *The Condition of Postmodernity.* Oxford: Blackwell, 1989.

James, W. *The Principles of Psychology.* London: Macmillan, 1890.

Jameson, F. "Postmodernism, or the Cultural Logic of Late Capitalism," *New Left Review* 146(1984) 53-92.

Kellner, D. "Popular Culture and the Construction of Postmodern Identities." *Modernity and Identity.* S. Lash and J Friedman, eds. Oxford: Blackwell, 1992.

Laclau, E. and Mouffe, Ch. *Hegemony and Socialist Strategy.* London: Verso, 1985.

Lévi-Strauss, C. *The Savage Mind.* London: Weidenfeld and Nicolson, 1974.

Lyotard, J. F. *The Postmodern Condition: A Report on Knowledge.* Manchester: Manchester UP, 1984.

_____. *Économie libidinale.* Paris: Les Éditions de Minuit, 1974.

Marx, Karl. *Grundrisse*. Harmondswoth: Penguin, 1977.

_____. "Theses on Feuerbach," The German Ideology, in K. Marx and F. Engels, *Collected Works.*, London: Lawrence and Wishart, 1976.

Marx, K. and Engels, F. *Selected Works in One Volume*. London: Lawrence and Wishart, 1970.

Mead, G. H. *Mind, Self, and Society*. Chicago: The U of Chicago P, 1974.

Nietzsche, F. *The Will to Power*. New York: Vintage Books, 1968.

Parker, C. *Otra lógica en América Latina: Religión popular y modernización capitalista*. Santiago: Fondo de Cultura Económica, 1993.

Richard, Nelly. "Postmodernism and the Periphery." *Postmodernism, A Reader*. T. Docherty, ed. Hemel Hempstead: Harvester Wheatsheaf, 1993.

Said, E. *Orientalism*. London: Penguin, 1985.

Schwarz, R. *Misplaced Ideas; Essays on Brazilian Culture*. London: Verso, 1992.

Taylor, Charles. *Sources of the Self, the Making of the Modern Identity*. Cambridge: Harvard UP, 1989.

Thompson, J. B. *Ideology and Modern Culture*. Cambridge: Polity Press, 1990.

_____. *The Media and Modernity, A Social Theory of the Media*. Cambridge: Polity Press, 1995.

Vattimo, G. *The Transparent Society*. Cambridge: Polity Press, 1992.

Wagner, Peter. *A Sociology of Modernity: Liberty and Discipline*. London: Routledge, 1994.

Williams, R. *Marxism and Literature*. Oxford: Oxford UP, 1977.

Latin American Identity—Dramatized

José Joaquín Brunner

(*translated by Shara Moseley*)

In this essay I propose to reflect upon that which we call Latin American identity, or rather when referring to lesser units, national identity, starting with the supposition that these are entities which only exist according to the forms we use to speak of them.

This presupposition implies that:

> the way in which people speak may create "objects," in the sense that there are many things that could not exist if people had never begun to speak in certain ways. Examples of such things are universities, contracts, government, the mechanisms of international monetary exchange, the traditions of historiography, revolutions in philosophy, etc. (Rorty 52)

Collective identities also pertain to this class of objects that are created by the way in which people speak of them. In truth, such identities—of peoples, ethnicities, nations or continents—lack substance; they are not out there, like something that we could apprehend beyond our ways of speaking of them. Rather, they are completely suspended above the fine web of words that name them; their substance is discourses, interpretations. To put it another way, identities and their signs are among us in the same way as are all of those meanings which we make exist—or which we maintain and transform through conversations, texts, discursive constructions and understanding. As seen from this angle, the identities of our present study, it can be said, are tributaries of the different manners in which we stage or dramatize them through discourses which, put into words, constitute, express and transform them. My essay will be limited to analyzing some of these dramatizations and their assumptions with relation to Modernity.

Before we begin to enter fully into this subject, however, we need to examine the concept of identity as has been employed in psychology (which is, after all, its locus of origin). According to Erik Erikson, we are dealing with a topic of common sense that is, at the same time, difficult to apprehend. It refers to a process located in the nucleus of a person and, at the same time, at the heart of communal culture. As such, we may agree that, in psychological terms:

> identity formation employs a process of simultaneous reflection and observation, a process taking place at all levels of mental functioning, by which the individual judges himself in the light of what he perceives to be the way in which others judge him in comparison to themselves and to a typology significant to them; meanwhile he judges their way of judging him in the light of how he perceives himself in comparison to them and to certain typologies that have become relevant to him. This process is, luckily, and necessarily, for the most part unconscious, except where inner conditions and outer circumstances combine to aggravate a painful, or elated "identity consciousness." (Erikson 22-23)

Likewise, it is not difficult to comprehend that this process is found in a state of permanent change and development. As Erikson shows us, "identity is never 'established' like an 'achievement' in the form of a personality armor, or of anything static and unchangeable" (24).

But, from whence comes the individual's need for identity? Erikson hesitates offering a reply that would be too simple or conclusive. It pertains, he says, to the necessity of a socio-genetic evolution of the species. Indeed, humans are only able to survive to the extent that they differentiate themselves in diverse groupings—into groups in which individuals develop their own identities independently.

Before we abandon Erikson completely, let us reflect a moment upon the way he speaks of identity—his lexicon. He shows that the use of this term [identity] opens itself up to a variety of connotations: a conscious sense of individual uniqueness, a continual unconscious search for personal experience, solidarity with the group's ideals, a way for the "I" to represent itself to itself, etc. Moreover, he adds, these ways of speaking about identity change according to the approaches that are employed, whether they use concepts from psychoanalysis or from sociology (208-9).

It becomes clear, through the possible interpretations of Eriksons' approaches to the configuration of this object which we call personal identity, that we cannot comfortably extend this notion to larger human collectives, even if it pertains to families, states, classes, nations or even supranational entities. In these cases, we lack a subject that predicates identity formation in this double process of self-recognition and of the self as recognized by others. Indeed, collectives lack a subconscious, a consciousness and a personality. They do not judge themselves, nor do they represent themselves as a single agent, nor do other collectives judge them.

Erikson's *communal culture*, mentioned as one of the poles of identity formation, is not necessarily an identity in the Eriksonian sense. Rather, it is an ensemble of evaluative practices—and their correspondent manifestations—in relation to which each one of us constructs our own perception of ourselves in interaction with the perception of others. In this sense one may speak, as does Erving Goffman, of the individual's social identity in opposition to his personal identity. While the latter causes each individual to be known as a single person by others, the former represents the category of person that we are "and the complement of attributes that are perceived as normal and natural by the members of each of these categories" (Goffman 12, 17). Erikson's *communal culture* is, therefore, a repertoire of virtual social identities that the group recognizes in its members, but not a separate group identity.

In spite of this, we persist in speaking of something that we call national identity or even Latin American regional identity. Our books and magazines are full of articles that invoke, exalt, analyze, question or acknowledge these identities. Today, as in the mid-twentieth century, and even a hundred years earlier in the nineteenth century—as we are reminded by Leopoldo Zea—Latin Americans are once again questioning the problem of their identity or its utopian possibility (Zea 481). Because of this, we speak of identity in numerous ways, and in this process, on a fragile web of words, we begin weaving our identity, or the problem of identity: its gashes and gaps, its promise and its conditions for birth.

We may now fully enter into the study of those identity dramatizations that have become pertinent to our analysis. The term "dramatization" functions as a way of approaching the ways of constituting the problem of our identity. We will concentrate in particular on four ways to speak of identity that we will call, successively, identity as origin, as evolution, as crisis, and as project. In each case we will use, with intentional arbitrariness, texts that illustrate our analysis as reminders that they merely constitute different "manners of speaking."

Identity as Origin

The response to the question, "Where do we come from?" has always been a source for speaking about identity. Historically, and even today, we speak of a Latin American (or national) identity in order to hallow discursive practices that outline a reality which wants to specify itself against the backdrop of the historical drama through which men and peoples appropriate nature and dote on it a particular meaning to create a way of life—a culture. This outline is not, of course, predominantly geographical, but geography does play an essential role as identity's "scenery." Nor does geography just deal with speaking about a localized identity; rather, above all, it is about highlighting a place of origin, an initial point of an identifying journey and about attributing time with a space populated with figures of identity.

It is amongst this tension between nature and culture, between heaven and earth, that the epic identity of the origin of the continent is constructed. This way of speaking about identity is susceptible to being condensed into one single focal point that, among a thousand other names, could be called *Macchu Picchu* or *Macondo*.

Identity as origin tells the tale, or in other words creates a reality, of an America that needs to be named in order to be shaped, cut out of the chaos, of the confusion of things and of time. For the same reason, it is a manner of speaking that finds its most eloquent expression in literature and, perhaps in Pablo Neruda's poetry, one of its major exponents: "I am here"—writes the poet in the beginning of *Canto general*—"to tell the story. My land without name, without America, / your aroma climbed my roots up to the glass / raised to my lips, up to the slenderest / world as yet unborn in my mouth" (14).

The operation by which the poet baptizes (names) reality, endeavoring to give it consistency, follows an itinerary from primordial Nature through History to Culture—a path in the course of which America acquires a name that we no longer invoke in vain. To this day, literature produces and recreates, changes and revises, celebrates and sings this identity of origin, to such an extent that many who are eager to analyze Latin America, search for it through its chroniclers, novelists and poets. Instead of accepting that these are stories rendering a fable, they tend to think that this literature has to do with expressions, deeper albeit than any others, that reflect something occult in reality, in the identity of America, our *Macondo* with a capital M. These kinds of manifestations of the collective soul seem to be found again and again in the writings of Arguedas, García Márquez, Vargas Llosa, Carpentier or Neruda, except few would employ such an anachronistic term as "collective soul" to explain their fascination.

On the other hand, how do we avoid this impression when many European and North Americans observers of Latin America read us, and we, too, read ourselves through this literature that proposes and specifies us in opposition to others? Above all, since the "Boom" we joined identity's image market—as is happening today with Eastern Europe and happened yesterday with African nations—through the "thin words" that construct an original way of being and a manner of existing in the world for us; therefore, a style, a language. In other words, this literature of identity offers us a way in which to speak of ourselves as we face our reading community. As Angel Rama said, "in the end, what is the Boom, if not the most extraordinary conscious awareness by the Latin American people of a part of its own identity?" (61). That the editorial marketplace made it possible for us to finally recognize our identity more profoundly is not the least of the contradictions in which we find ourselves in this revision of the ways of speaking about our identity.

We are confronted with another paradox when we speak of ourselves in the face of European or foreign mirrors. The writers of the Boom generation reached their momentum—entered orbit, one may say—only from the instant they were recognized by the outside world, from where the echo would arrive that established their "identity operations" before our very eyes.

Identity as Evolution

In a second sense, although connected with the first, we refer to identity in order to account for a solely Latin American socio-cultural genesis at the heart of the most ample constellation of the West. It is, above all, the identity of indigenous, Spanish, black and other ethnic groups whose particular contributions come together in the historical formation of Latin American culture.

The cultural personality of Latin America (or of its national societies) is what seeks to affirm itself in opposition to cultures whose components are similar but have different paths of development. For example, these personalities are seen in European or North American cultures where nature has a minor role and where everything, in contrast, is played out in the sphere of historical evolution. Here, identity is dramatized within the evolution of time; this way of speaking about identity answers the question of our mixed origin's destiny as seen through the drama of civilization.

Identity as evolution offers us a culturally displayed idea of ourselves. As such, it has been a preferred specialty of philosophers, essayists and historians who offered us their interpretations based on the shining world of preceding interpretations—each one of which deciphered, and continues to encode—the keys to our possible identity.

While writers create a reality by naming it, essayists recreate it through their continuous hermeneutic. Leopoldo Zea's voice stands out in this dialogue, above all in his work, *El pensamiento latinoamericano*, a text that opened up a new interpretative watershed to which others later have added their own interpretations of identity. At the basis of such an interpretive slant is the idea that Latin American society

> seems to be formed in superimposed levels with no possibility for assimilation. This superimposition was created and stimulated by the Western world in its expansion, conquest and domination of other peoples and men. This superimposition, and cultural as well as historical failure of assimilation, is reflected in a Latin America that seems to be in a state of permanent immaturity. (451)

Consequently, defects in identity result firstly because it is constructed on a negation—an unfinished accumulation that was never overcome—of its past (484). Secondly, and as a derivation of the first cause for its defects, is because identity is being plagued by contradictions and amputations; it is, therefore, a torn identity. And, it is defective, thirdly, due to its lack of productivity. The Spanish American could not really manage to change anything with his unconscious trapped in the past. His history would mask his impotence, his lack of profundity, his immaturity. "We, the Spanish Americans," writes Zea:

> still have the conqueror and the conquered, the colonial, the romantic liberal and all that was part of our past under our skin. Moreover, although we endeavor to be all of this we still continue without fully accomplishing it. We have only followed these attitudes in formal fields of study. In reality, such attitudes have not done anything but disguise, or cover up a fact, a reality not yet assimilated, the first one the Spanish American was conscious of—the colonial. This is its reality as dependent, its consciousness as an entity dependent on a reality that it still does not consider its own. The reality of its dependency is that it is to something which it considers foreign. (53)

It will be this last perspective, but in a different way of speaking than that suggested by Zea, that will be taken up once again by the school of thought that conceives of identity as a crisis of subordination or dependency. We will return to it later. For now, let us say that Zea's vision constitutes in itself a school of thought. Identity as disguise, as falsification, as product of a changing history constitutes, in effect, a topic in Latin American speech as relevant as that of the epic of the origin of our identity. Both serve to keep open "the problem of the possibility or the existence of a culture originally Latin American," in other words, our own organic expression of identity (Zea 482). Zea explores the long and zigzagging path covered by Latin American philosophers "in search of their identity"; an exploration that occurs, to paraphrase Erikson, at all levels of the collective mind: "through the history of ideas, and thought, through philosophy and culture, or even through the ontological search of man from this America" (Zea 476).

In conclusion, we search for that which has been disguised and distorted by History, above all by dominance and exclusion imposed on the structures of society. It is at this point that the interpretation of our identity, born out of the history of ideas and the philosophy of History, is connected to the following way of speaking about our identity; that which sprang from the field of social sciences.

Identity as Crisis

In this case, the term identity—or a lack thereof, its absence, confusion or crisis—is used to denote a developing region or, more frequently, to establish a critical discourse in opposition to the alienation and subordination imposed by colonialism, dependency and foreign invasion. In comparison to identity as dramatized through historical evolution, here the junctures, more than the evolution, become our point of interest. The distorted structures of society that determine the course of a negated identity are imbedded in origin and destiny. Where Nature has become absent, groups, classes and nations have burst on the scene; now social relations—hierarchies, asymmetries and hegemony, which they institute or impede—are everything. Identity, here, is spoken of within the unfolding drama of power in society.

The idea of identity as crisis, as a product of dependencies and deformations generated by it that explain "why we are not," is the modality through which the principal fields of Latin American sociology and economics dealt with this subject until very recently. As García Canclini indicates, "in the sixties and up to the mid-seventies, analyzing culture was equated to the description of domination strategies" (19). The cultural analysts of the period, most of all those that came out of social cciences, interpreted the Latin American identity with failure, weakness and impotence as its starting point. While identity as origin gave way to an epic, and identity thought of as an historical evolution reflected a search, the crisis of identity established by the social scientists pointed, instead, to a dead end or to some drastic alternative ranging from decadence to revolution. As Aníbal Quijano points out:

> The structural dependence of social formations submitted to imperialist domination . . . is not only present in the marginalizing process of growing social groups, but also in another phenomenon whose study has just begun, at least in the case of Latin America: that of the emergence of a "dependent culture" as a fragmentary adhesion to an ensemble of cultural models that the dominators diffuse, in a process by which the basis of one's own culture is abandoned without any possibility of effectively interiorizing the other. It is as if one forgets his own language and cannot sufficiently learn another. (38)

Out of this comes a manifest impossibility of identity, with pathological characteristics as stressed by Quijano: a true "schizophrenic acculturation." It is an identity crisis, therefore, that fragments, superimposes and causes its components to collide; in this case, as Edmundo O'Gorman would suggest much earlier, one wants to "be like others in order to be oneself."

Other authors that complement this reading speak of a culturally penetrated and subordinated identity that is, therefore, distorted. Out of this torn identity, in which the dominant internal groups imitate the cultural masters of the dominating groups, the dominated are subject to an implacable expropriation of their own traditional communal identity. Thus, "dominant culture, in itself incoherent and full of contradictions, penetrates, disintegrates, and dominates popular culture" (Lacayo 325).

Popular culture, on the other hand, constitutes a universe that could reflect, at its base, an erosion of popular identities giving way to

> particular subcultures, which provide a certain orientation in society, which are subordinated to the common orientation furnished by the "dominant culture" . . . In this way, what we may call a "popular subculture" is a universe of cultural elements that are derived from both subcultures of concrete social groups (class, for example), and from the dominant culture; yet it is characterized by its low level of formalized objectification, inasmuch as the social position of its own groups . . . excludes the possibility [that it] may develop its cognitive structures to the point of being capable of providing a highly elaborate objectification and formalization of its own cultural elements. (Quijano 28-29)

A muteness, therefore an absence of a true identity, peoples that do not exist independently. This absence of identity, as spoken of in the social sciences, is thus trapped in the structural determinants of dependency waiting for some resolution to the fundamental problems that render impossible its formation:

> In order for this to be possible, the radical modification of the cultural order of domination is necessary, for this 'popular subculture' to be placed in a dominant position . . . and this could only be possible through an equally radical alteration in the basic structure of social dominance. (29)

In sum: What was not and what is not, need to come into being, negating to this effect that which is, but that exists in a form distorted by dependence.

Identity as Project

In connection with the aforementioned discursive modalities, we also refer to identity as project as a way of calling to the fore what it is that needs to be done, only this time in proactive terms. It consists of a goal to be reached through constituting a (national or regional) reality in terms of its own potential. Here, identity is a frontier, a horizon, or even a utopia.

Many of the elements contained in the previously mentioned identity models are put into play in this dramatization of identity as project and reconciliation. For that is what identity as project entails: reconciling time and space, origin and destiny, nature and culture, man and humanity, heaven and earth. In fact, each of the former identity discourses has a specific way of presenting itself as an identity "project."

Identity as project responds to the question "Where we are going?" or, more accurately, "Where do we want and need to go?" It constitutes an environment where the preceding positions converge—each one in its own way of speaking—illuminating a possible, sought out, and longed for American identity. A utopian project, if you will, that would eventually reconcile the gaps and their shreads, origin, and destiny, and American words and their objects. Here, we are interested in the ways of speaking about an identity-of-the-future, above all, about how it comes into contact with Modernity or not. Or, in other words, how this project makes it possible to speak about Modernity in Latin America.

A utopian identity as origin resides in the reconciliation of nature and culture through the Word. This way of speaking of identity presupposes the recuperation of an American life that has been degraded by the exploits of History. "That is how your life was / denied, subdued, scratched, / stolen, young America," writes Neruda (167). Along with many other manifestations of continental literature, throughout Neruda's poetry numerous instances are found of a movement towards recuperating the "indestructible, the imperishable" life of man immersed in a nature that is, in the end, the strongest of all (35). *Macchu Picchu* is like an altar at the altitude where Neruda takes his first step in this utopian operation. It is from the "high site of the human dawn" where the failing and suffering history of America can be contemplated and it is to that high place where Neruda calls man [you] to climb "from the deep zone of your disseminated sorrow" (41). "I've come to speak through your dead mouths," exclaims the celebrated poet-priest: "Hasten to my veins and to my mouth. / Speak through my words and my blood" (41-42). Here, reconciliation takes on the form of a song or a story. It is by the Word that we may name a world and recognize in it a common belonging. The Word fuses Nature with man and makes culture, and this culture repeats tirelessly the gesture of the Word that names and recreates an identity.

> American sand, solemn
> plantation, red cordillera,
> children, brothers and sisters stripped
> by the old storms,
> let's join each living kernel
> before it returns to the earth,
> and may the new corn that comes forth
> have heard your words
> and repeat them and multiply.
> And may they sing to one another day and night,
> and bite and consume one another,
> and be scattered throughout the earth,
> and become, suddenly, silence,
> plunge beneath the stones,
> find the nocturnal doors,
> and again rise to be born,
> to be sown, to perform
> like bread, like hope,
> like the ships' air.
> The corn brings you my song,
> risen from my people's
> roots, to be born,
> to build, to sing,
> and to be seed again,
> more numerous in the storm. (286-87)

This utopian time, prior to being linear, successive or bearing notions of rupture and transition—all bases that involve thinking associated with Modernity—is, rather, mythic and cyclical in character, as often noted in connection with the novels of García Márquez, Arguedas and other Latin American writers. In reality, the drama of History—played out at this level—has little to do with Modernity and its artifices. This literature justly supposes a nondistancing from origin, space and other literatures. Identity is in the past, in the infancy of the continent, with the condition that it may be recuperated, even magically, in the present. Past peoples, and by extension all of those excluded, marginalized, trapped, exploited, and stigmatized are, in a way, those that best retain the marks of their origin, in other words, of their innocence. In making them speak, literature creates a reality that, according to some, is more real than the real: the Marvelous Real, insofar as it creates the marks of an identity that is waiting to be liberated and reconciled with America's vast and natural movement.

It is difficult to comprehend cities and machines, bureaucracies and industry, political parties and democracy, the marketplace and its transactions from this literature's point of view and way of speaking about our identity. The epic and original features of our identity remain trapped in that place of origin where Nature is larger than man and where the Word is married with Nature in a grandiose rite of fusion. Placed in origin and destiny, this paradise, without a doubt, excludes Modernity.

The utopian identity as historical evolution, the very field of essayists and philosophers, supposes, on the other hand, a reconciliation with a past that is found to be torn; however, it is more an historic operation than a mythic or poetic one.

It supposes a philosophy of history, however implicit it is found to be or, as in the case of Leopoldo Zea, entirely explicit. From this perspective, "once more the question is about the existence of the American man . . . [about] the profile of the concrete man of this part of the world, of humanity, of Latin America . . ." (Zea 474-75). In this context "the problem of the possibility or existence of an originally Latin American culture" emerges once again; therefore, the bearer of a specific identity emerges as well. In Zea's own words, in order for an "authentic philosophy of Latin American liberation" to be feasible, it is necessary that its axis be a critical assimilation and reconciliation of our present with the past as a basis for projecting the future: "It is necessary that we live the past in memory, in realized experience, in sum, in that which we are for having lived and not for that which we will be for continuing to live" (63).

This preoccupation for Latin America—"for its thinkers and philosophers"—is nothing new, as we have made clear through our glossing of Zea's text. However, during this entire trajectory, the central problem has not yet been resolved; it is that of the relationship of the American with his history. Only now could conciliation be possible between "the expressions of a culture (that an American) knows he is the son of, with the ineluctable reality of which he is also formed. And thus, while not ceasing to be American, (he is) also an active member of Western culture" (Zea 47).

This is rather a utopian conciliation, I admit, and as Zea proposed, it is merely possible because of "the path towards the universalization of [Latin American] thought." "Lifting oneself up, but counting on reality, seems to be the new philosophy's slogan," proclaims Zea. Octavio Paz wrote: "for the first time in our History we are the contemporaries of all men." For the first time then, Zea would add, it is possible to look at ourselves in the other's mirror without the distortions introduced by a nonassimilated past and a long situational succession of dependency. In this way the "reformation of consciousness," the product of philosophers, thinkers and social scientists, will be the platform from which a leap could be made to universality. Thus, the realization of the utopia of a Latin American identity that both "tends to the knowledge of that which is universal and, therefore, that which is common among all men" (49).

Perhaps this conclusion—Idealist Utopianism instead of Magic Realism—permits linking, although not without some tension, reflections on Latin American identity with those on Modernity. It is precisely the latter that, as least as a tendency, considers universality as identity difference (with all identities open to contact between each other in a state of constant exchange). This linkage notwithstanding, this identity project remains largely on the margins of Modernity. One illustrative example articulates this marginalization in the form of a question: What are the possibilities of developing a "Latin American thought," if we are, perhaps, incapable of developing—with the new millennium—science and technology to apply to production to solve our social problems, never mind to apply to the creation of a school of thought with universal importance? What role can we expect our universities and our companies that do not carry out research to play in this project, or for that matter, our scientists, who barely contribute one percent to the scientific publications on an international level?

So, this identity project, conceived as the utopian unfolding of our culture, seems to lack a modern base and leaves us, perhaps, with only some other form of speech and expression of hope, that is historically unable to become more concrete.

Lastly, identity as crisis, provoked by the framework of dominance and dependence such as that analyzed by Latin American social sciences, presupposes changing History, rather than just the understanding of history as philosophers do. A few years ago it was said more explicitly: Change presupposes revolution; today, however, language is nuanced and calls for—in the least—some form of liberation and the construction of a new alternate civilization in opposition to, or within the main current of, Western culture. Consequently, it may be said that it is in direct opposition to Modernity in which identity as crisis and its possible paths of utopian transcendence have been framed.

If there is a central characteristic introduced directly into our societies by the intricate interplay of dominance and dependence, it consists, according to Social Science discourse, of a heterogeneity of time, space, practices and discourses where everything seems to present itself simultaneously and synchronically. This had already been observed by Gino Germani who found it to be an inevitable consequence of the phenomena of modernization. But some authors point to less foreseen effects, showing, like Quijano, that

> Each time Latin America is in crisis, that which is behind this search for identity are those formative elements of our reality whose tense interrelationships cause the historical sedimentation that could make the ground of our social existence denser and firmer, to become a slower and more difficult process; each time consequentially the need to always be in search of identity becomes less compelling or recurring. (58)

Latin America's specificity, perhaps, resides here rather than in the intricate and degrading relationship between nature and culture, as suggested by the readings of poets and novelists of the continent:

> It pertains to a specificity, or if you prefer, to one of those meanings that are forming Latin American identity: the relationship between History and Time here is completely different from how it appears in Europe or the United States. What is sequence in other histories, is simultaneity in Latin America. Yet, it does not cease to be sequence . . . It pertains to a history separate from time. And a time separate from history. (Quijano 60-61)

It is at this point that social analysis connects to philosophical and literary analyses of the Latin American identity. As Quijano states, what this special relationship between History/Time/action signifies is that perhaps a peculiar rationality exists in Latin America, which, upon its unfolding, could create the possibility of a utopian reconciliation.

> Among us, the past is, or could be, a present, rather than nostalgic experience. The past is not a lost innocence, but an integrated wisdom, the union of life's tree of knowledge, that, as the seat of an alternative proposal to Rationality, defends us against Instrumental Rationalism. In this way, reality is seen,

and makes itself be seen as totality, in all its magic. Here, Rationality is not a disenchantment with the world, but the unintelligibility of its totality. (Quijano 62)

According to Quijano, such a utopia would require "the irruption of the dominated to the forefront of the scene." Such a condition would serve precisely to apprehend the totality of the new Latin American identity in the form of an alternative rationality which would integrate all the preexisting elements, reordering them and making them new and original. In conclusion,

The Latin American identity that cannot be defined in ontological terms is a complex history of the production of new historical meanings that depart from the legitimate and multiple heritage of Rationality. It is, thus, a utopia of a new association between Reason and liberation. (Quijano 69)

If the discourse of origin is impenetrable in the face Modernity's solicitations, and the discourse of History is connected with them only in exchange for the idealization of the reencounter with the past in order to repave the road from disguise to assimilation and the expression of the true Latin American identity; the discourse of identity in crisis establishes itself, in its own way, as a possible *habitat* of an "Other-Modernity," an alternative course of History where Reason finally would be joined with liberation.

In other words, the discourse of identity as crisis also does not rejoin us with the existing "real" Modernity, to paraphrase an outdated formula. What offers itself to us here is an "Other-Modernity" project, mounted upon an alternative rationality and, as such, far from bureaucracy, the market, formal democratic politics—let us conventionally call it "formal" to understand what we are referring to—and from mass culture established by the media.

In conclusion, our origin, history and crisis speak to us of a conflicting, unrealized, truncated or false identity, yet, in spite of this, one capable of founding reconciliation projects: utopias for writers, philosophers and social scientists, each one unraveling our identity and recreating it as a possibility through the very words that make it exist. No version, however, speaks readily about identity as Modernity in Latin America. Moreover, the ways of speaking about identity that have predominated until now, in the intellectual climate of Latin America, do not even allow us to glimpse, I believe, the continent into which we have been transforming. Our Modernity, ripped apart by its own constructive logic, power and dissemination, remains thus unnamed and without yet having begun to speak of itself as identity.

Perhaps this is why there was surprise and concern just a few years ago when the so-called "neo-liberals"—often economists, bankers and entrepreneurs—began to speak of a modern identity of Latin America. They frequently supplied this discursive gesture with an active destruction of the bases of these other forms of identity that we have intended to preserve in discourse. In the meantime, those other ways of speaking used by the Latin American intelligentsia—could we now call these intellectuals traditional?—have ended up permeating the very suppositions, prejudices and even the emotional tones that influence the theories and approaches they use in order to speak about identity. In this way, it is not surprising that these theories and approaches reproduce—with regard to intellectuals' emotion more than their reasoning—identity perceptions as fractures, as something from which we have been excluded, as masks and as lies. The source, therefore, of everything "pseudo" that we are: pseudo-modern, pseudo-civilized; and also the source of the promise of a continent inhabited obscurely and latently by something more real than this pseudo-reality that appears daily in our societies. Such discourses end up expressing a kind of impotent reality in the face of the potency of the dreams which speak to us of ourselves—which speak to us of something grander and hidden that is still waiting to be revealed.

The greatness within us, according to these discourses, is hidden or buried under simulation, dependence, and distortion: in a Nature that is waiting to be redeemed; in a forgotten peoples; in a History that we negate and that negates us; in the new populations that are already discerning an alternative rationality. Whatever the individual dream, these buried identities speak to us of a "new West" that we would carry within us as a utopia that we have just barely dared to name. Some think it could be an epicenter for a renewed Christianization of the world; and others, humanity's ecological reserve; still others dream of a new balance between Modernity, magic and re-enchantment in a world finally liberated and united.

That such dreams are able to be maintained in spite of the pressure of Modernity—things like the bustling cities, the internationalization of culture, the unequal advance of education, the new forms adopted by economies inserted in global markets, the destruction of the environment, the erosion of the past, the growing secularism, the exclusion of indigenous peoples, massive poverty, etc.—speaks for the force of these dreams and the discourses that feed them.

This does not guarantee, however, that these ways of speaking about our identity shall be saved from the pressure of Modernity. Nor does it exclude the possibility that we are witnessing the end of these same discourses, and that they may be substituted soon by other ways of speaking—and creating—our identities: those furnished by mass communication, particularly television, and by the multiple languages that are generated with urban life, by the changes in the cultural market, and by the new ways in which countries enter the world economy.

Works Cited

Erikson, Erik H. *Identity, Youth & Crisis.* New York: W.W. Norton, 1968.

García Canclini, Néstor. "Cultura transnacional y culturas populares." *Cultura transnacional y culturas populares.* Eds. N. García Canclini and R. Rancagliolo. Lima: IPAL, 1988.

Goffman, Erving. *Estigma.* Buenos Aires: Amorrortu, 1970.

Lacayo, Francisco. "Políticas culturales en la revolución popular sandinista." *Cultura transnacional y culturas populares.* Eds. N. García Canclini and R. Rancagliolo. Lima: IPAL, 1988.

Neruda, Pablo. *Canto General.* Trans. Jack Schmitt. Berkeley: U of California P, 1991.

Quijano, Aníbal. *Modernidad, identidad y utopía en América Latina.* Lima: Sociedad Política, 1988.

_____. *Dominación y cultura. Lo cholo y el conflicto cultural en el Perú.* Lima: Mosca Azul, 1980.

Rama, Angel. "El boom en perspectiva." *Más allá del Boom: Literatura y mercado.* Ed. Angel Rama. Buenos Aires: Folios, 1984.

Rorty, Richard. *Contingency, Irony and Solidarity.* New York: Cambridge UP, 1989.

Zea, Leopoldo. *El pensamiento latinoamericano.* Barcelona: Ariel, 1976.

Part III   **Changing Realities, Politics, Arts: Strategies of/for Resistance**

◆ **7.**

Autochthonous Cultures and the Global Market

Mario Roberto Morales

(*translated by Eva L. Ramírez*)

> *Reporter: –Are you a Mod or a Rocker?*
> *Ringo Starr: –I'm a mocker . . .*

Rural Metropolis, Globalized Community and Tourist Religiosity: Negotiation of Identities in the (Pre/Post)Modern Multi-Ethnic Spaces in Guatemala

An examination of the intercultural dynamics of a country such as Guatemala in its relationship with economic and cultural globalization, and, consequently, with central as well as local Modernity and Postmodernity, implies proposing the study of popular cultures as processes located differentially outside of the circulation of the messages of popular (mass) culture, in order to place them in the spaces of hybridization in which icons and contents are fused and con-fused with the iconographies and imaginaries produced by the culture industry for the masses. Yet this industry is also *popular*, because it is consumed by the people, and is also *culture*, because it constructs *meanings* which perform social functions of identification, cohesion, and legitimization.[1] Likewise, it implies situating the analysis of the production and consumption (reception) of traditional cultures in the space and dynamics of the market, since the market constitutes the main mediator that permits the circulation of symbolic goods and the creation of conglomerates of consumers of culture. The market creates the necessary conditions for the *creative and contestatory consumption* of the culture industry's symbolic goods, carried out on certain occasions by the popular conglomerates of Latin America, thanks to the positionalities sui generis they assume in the globalizing market (García Canclini, *Consumidores*).

Consumption is the market's mechanism for perpetuating its productive dynamics, and consumerism, through the conversion of the activity of consumption into a value, constitutes its ideology. It is in this ideological space where the hybrid and negotiable identities of large popular conglomerates are articulated. The market is also the space where the negotiation of cultural codes of senders and receivers of messages takes place. Both the production of objects of popular culture and the religious traditions of indigenous communities turned into tourist attractions, along with the consumption of globalized audiovisual contents and forms in these same communities imply, on the one hand, a translation of the popular-ethnic to the codes and needs of the metropolitan consumer, and, on the other hand, "translation" of the Western "cultured" and *pop* strata to the codes and needs of the subaltern consumer. What happens here is that this latter translation is not performed by the producers of those contents but by the receivers, constrained by their socioeconomic position which does not correspond to that of the consumer for whom these contents were originally created. In spite of that, those contents circulate with lavishness and intensity in the indigenous villages as well as in Third-World cities, and in this respect, we have to say that the metropolitan mass media are every day more in charge of adapting—"translating"—its contents for the expanding markets (Martín Barbero and Muñoz). The result of these movements is a rich intercultural and inter-identitarian hybridity and *mestizaje* (crossbreeding) challenging all binary theorizations of culture, identity, and subalternity, as we will be able to prove in the case of Guatemala.

The analysis of intercultural relationships in Guatemala implies, from the transdisciplinary perspective of Latin American Cultural Studies, first, identifying the spaces in which the traditional cultures meet the transnational culture industry and, second, describing the transculturalization and hybridization processes that take place in that encounter. In this way one can account for the articulation of the hybrid identities in continuous negotiation, that operate in those spaces of ideological and cultural resignification and re-articulation which, in turn, relativize notions such as "the people," "cultural resistance," and "otherness" as synonyms of "difference." All this supposes that there are no mono-identities or pure identities, solid and compact, opposed to each other in a binary and irreconcilable form. This is the situation at the factual level. However, at that of the traditional mentalities and fundamentalist ideologies, essentialist and racist, both from the side of *ladinidad* as well as from the *indianidad*, binary notions are still in use.[2]

All this takes us to the definition of the popular subject and hegemony, both with respect to ideological and cultural production and consumption, and to class position.[3] This definition would take into account the fact that ethnic, class, and cultural positionalities are movable and negotiable, since they are articulated, operate, are found and interact in the hybridization areas mediated by the market and by the production and consumption of symbolic goods and merchandise. That is to say that the popular subject is inter- and transcultural on the one hand and can be inter- and transclassist on the other, if we so define him in terms of his positionality with respect to the mediations which make possible his interaction with other subjects and with other cultural and ideological productions and consumptions. This can make him also an inter- and transnational subject.[4]

The position of a poor ladino in Guatemala can be conceptualized as hegemonic with respect to poor Indians; however, the position of the same ladino in Los Angeles, New York, or Miami can be in fact viewed as subaltern and as shared with the Guatemalan Indians there. The ladino we are talking about may well live ten months of each year in the United States and two months in Guatemala, and can be related to other subjects in the Guatemalan hybridization areas as a hegemonic subject and, in the North American areas, as a subaltern subject. Hegemony as part of the globalizing movements is, in that case, also an ever-changing exercise, negotiable and possibly hybrid and ambivalent in its own way, according to the changes in the positionality of the hegemonic or counterhegemonic subject. Furthermore, the hegemonic position can become counterhegemonic and vice versa; and the same subject can negotiate within himself by a sort of schizophrenia of power, or by a necessary transvestism of power, that allows him to live as the trans-bordered subject in which he has been transformed by globalization. And this is so not only because he is a consumer, but also because he is a subject producer of culture, of ideology.

We know that Los Angeles and New York are now spaces as crucial for the Guatemalan economy as is the Southern coastal plain in that country, with its large agricultural plantations and farming. This fact defines the ladino subject we mentioned before as a transterritorialized, and, at the same time, as a Guatemalan subject. The question would be: Is this a popular subject or not, and how and with respect to what does he articulate his hybrid identity in those two environments? And which is his "true" environment in the case that both would not be considered as true, complementary and natural for him? If they were, then we would be facing a ladino case of negotiated identity, since this subject adapts his ladino (ethnic) identity vis-à-vis the Indians and ladinos in Guatemala differently from how he adapts his (political) Guatemalan identity in Los Angeles vis-à-vis other Latin Americans, vis-à-vis the *gringos*, and together—and this happens often—with the Guatemalan Indians there. He is hegemonic in his own country and subaltern abroad. This dual identity is assumed by our hybrid subject as something natural and experienced in his own life, although it may be conflictive for him.[5]

In Guatemala, *ladinidad* is hegemonic and *indianidad* is subaltern in the ideological realm, although both may be dominant or dominated at a given moment in the economic sphere. For example, there is a minority indigenous middle class allied, in social class terms, with the ladino middle class, whose business, among others, is the manufacture and export of textiles. If we place ourselves in the perspective of Cultural Studies, the following fact must never be forgotten: The negotiation of identities and their hybridizations are performed always in a frame of disadvantage for the indigenous part. It has always occurred that way, from the Colonial period, through the Liberal revolution, the Democratic revolution, and the revolutionary war, to today's Globalization. However, one cannot forget either that, always, throughout History, there have been power niches in which the polarities hegemony/counterhegemony were often negotiated inversely, as it occurred during colonial and republican times with some ennobled and/or enriched Indians, or with some rebel Indians. This was the case recently with the large number of indigenous guerrillas and with the large number of indigenous high officers in the genocidal Guatemalan army. The possibilities for the hegemonic and counterhegemonic articulation realized by the same subject in those scenarios are very diverse.

It is known that popular culture and its products are mediated by the market and by its mechanisms in their production, circulation, and consumption. Just as there is an indigenous bourgeoisie which produces and exports "typical" textiles, there are also cases such as that of a North American man in Panajachel, owner of a crafts store, who has created designs and has introduced new colors in the manufacture of indigenous fabrics: the natives of Salcajá make the fabrics with his new designs and colors in wooden looms which produce them by the yard. This North American entrepreneur has customers in the United States and in other countries. This is a case in which the adaptations of popular culture to the transnationalized demand of cultural goods do not originate from its producers but from an outsider. In this case, popular culture is neither the space of preservation nor of resistance, and not even of autochthonous transformation, but a receptacle of exogenous modifications. On the other hand, some indigenous entrepreneurs owning stores in San Jose, Costa Rica, produce the fabrics and articles in Guatemala and sell them in San Jose with the label *Made in Costa Rica*. The fabrics no longer follow traditional designs and are even very different from those worn originally by the Indians. All this helps the national transvestism which makes it possible that "typical" Guatemalan articles can come from Costa Rica, Mexico, Ecuador, Pakistan, India, or Greece, as happens at international crafts stores.

Hybridizations have been occurring since way before today's globalization, and constitute a sign of traditional popular cultures' diversity. The best example is precisely indigenous dress.[6]

> The expressions of traditional popular culture move between the poles of Indian and *mestizo* expression, depending on localities and occasions of performance [of the position of the popular subject]. There is no clear and simple division, just as the search for a purely Indian expression is romantic and antihistorical, and actually leaves the Indians deprived not only of those dimensions of their culture which the Conquest destroyed, but also of the European materials and technologies which they appropriated for their own use. (Rowe and Schelling 73)

In spite of the fact that this conceptualization still establishes a difference between the indigenous and the *mestizo* expressions (because the popular is conceived as a compact space resistant to Modernity, and is reduced to the defense of memory) and, as a result, the indigenous is considered as pure in opposition to the *mestizo* (which is impure because it is mixed), the idea that to deny hybridization implies shortchanging the achievements of indigenous cultures, seems to me illuminating, and helps us to accept assertions such as the following: "Popular cultures: that artifact does not exist in a pure state" (Sarlo 109).

I am not going to reflect on the difference in focus among Cultural Studies and anthropology, but it is useful to say that the notions used locally to think Guatemalan interculturality are owed to leftist as well as rightist North American anthropologists. Notions such as "reverse racism," "right to difference," etc., and the term "Maya" itself, which populate the academic lexicon of the present debate on multiculturality, are owed to them. I don't want to say with this that the "Mayan" academics do not think for themselves. What I mean to say is that their works have that referent in common. Moreover, this referent operates within the theoretical frameworks of Postcolonial Studies, dubiously applicable to Latin America and to Guatemala, since their independence from colonialism was obtained more than a century and a half ago, and their cultural problematic is not the same as that of the recently emancipated African countries.

The concept of the people and of the popular is often limited in anthropology to what is considered aboriginal, and, in that sense, we must rethink it from its very foundations because the "aboriginal" today operates in the spaces of television, radio, and cinema, and in other modern and postmodern spaces of cultural consumption in which it articulates its hybrid and negotiable identities. The aboriginal moves, then, within the market, and it is in that space that it negotiates its identity with transnationalized (Post)Modernity. This is not new. In the 1970s I met the father of the Guatemalan indigenous novelist Luis de Lión, who would define him amusingly as a "sculptor of antiquities" because he used to make small animal stone figures, bury them in their house patio in San Juan del Obispo, and in a few months he would sell them to the tourists.

Also in the 1970s, and as a result of the interest shown by foreign tourists in the textile crafts, the shawls called *perrajes* became fashionable among Guatemalan ladino women who began to wear them at parties and at elegant gatherings. The ladino artist Marco Augusto Quiroa set up an exhibition of paintings entitled precisely "*El perraje*" in which he showed the possibilities for the use of that garment, which he amusingly defined as an "indigenous garment used by ladino women to look like gringas," thus synthesizing the possible identitarian usages of the *perraje*, and with it the subject's mobile positions and identities negotiated by cultural consumption, in this case, that of an object of traditional culture refunctionalized by fashion (the market).

I have chosen some spaces of cultural hybridization in order to examine negotiable identities—or those in the process of negotiation—in Guatemala in the context of the relationship established between globalization, production, and consumption of popular culture, and the active consumption of globalized messages of the mass media and of the culture industry in general among the indigenous people.

In the itinerant mappings which describe realities I could observe during the summers of 1995, 1996, and 1997, I will try, as much as possible, to apply the analytical criterion of creative or "anthropophagous" consumption. In other words, I will follow the criterion of the indigenization of the homogenizing cultural projects of globalization.[7] That is, of a defensive, and therefore resignifying, consumption. I will use personal testimonial interviews in order to establish the presence or absence of resistances in a given type of consumption. In any case, I intend to question the validity of the officious defense of *cultural difference per se*, in order to introduce the political possibility of passage into (Post)Modernity of all cultural differences, considered, however, as negotiable, movable, hybrid, and autotransformable.

To posit oneself on the vertex of differences implies looking analytically not only *towards* but also *from* the articulation of ethnic and cultural differences. Or, it implies analyzing a national geographic space *from* and *at* the points of intercultural *mestizaje* in which the differences are articulated in order to generate hybridizations and *mestizajes*. But to do that implies an even bigger task, already foreseen by Fredric Jameson: "to achieve, in other words, a type of thinking that would be capable of grasping the demonstrably baleful features of capitalism along with its extraordinary and liberating dynamism simultaneously, within a single thought, and without attenuating any of the force of either judgment" (*Postmodernism* 86). This, as Jameson notices, leaves out the much more comfortable possibility of moralism, so common in an academe given to solidarity with marginal, subaltern, and exploited cultures, since "the urgency of the subject demands that we make at least some effort to think the cultural evolution of late capitalism dialectically, as catastrophe and progress all together" (86). In other words, we cannot fall into culturalist and paternalist preservationisms against the brutal regulatory reality of the market in the production and consumption of popular cultures. Nor can we continually find cultural resistances in the minimal gestures of the subaltern, who often simulates them, because resistances (or an illusion of resistances created intentionally for consumption by the solidary groups) are marketable. This is a question that often turns solidarity communities into those of consumers of the simulacra of resistances. In such sense, the solidarities with counterhegemonic expressions must take into account the displacements of what is hegemonic and what is not, as well as its constant negotiation of positionalities.

All this, as Jameson also observes, raises the question about any "'moment of truth' within the more evident 'moments of falsehood' of postmodern culture" (86), in order to go further and be able to articulate a critique consistent with what he calls late capitalism. It is in this sense that we are going to carry out our itinerant mapping as a first step towards thinking interethnicity and interculturality not only as a chaos, but also as the beginning of a new paradigmatic, more democratic, order. According to Jameson, "The political form of postmodernism, if there ever is any, will have as its vocation the invention and projection of a global cognitive mapping, on a social as well as spatial scale" (92), and, for our purposes, also on the international and global scale, which is therefore national and *glocal.*

Indigenous People Working in the City: Occupations and Identities

We should start by deconstructing some presuppositions about the essence of the popular-cultural. Bastos and Camus (*Indígenas*) review the urban occupations of subsistence practiced by Indians as Indians, and which therefore constitute spaces of reproduction and transformation of ethnic identity:

> Another field where indigenous presence is significant is the tortilla factory where manufacture and sales are combined . . .

It also represents a clear case in which the dwelling and production unit are united, blurring domestic and labor boundaries: the food is prepared in the same fire as the tortillas, the female workers share the house with the family business owners, the house chores (done by women) are mixed with work in which the owner participates as one more worker . . . For all that, the tortilla factory becomes a special environment as far as the preservation of ethnic traits is concerned . . . Not only because the workers hardly speak Spanish and rather use their native languages, more functional in this case, but because being a women's space, even when there are not any, the tendency to preserve traditions and customs is greater. (64-65)

The gender problem is self-evident here since the custody of traditional culture held by women constitutes a clear case of *machista* oppression. However, the main idea of the authors is that "Human capital and domestic space are the pillars of their subsistence" (65). Perhaps that is why they state, "Discrete traits—language and dress—may be lost in this different environment, but the cultural substrate to confront survival remains. Their behavior will continue to be indigenous in spite of the fact that they may not be identified as such from their appearance" (65). In this regard, the space that must be studied is that of the mechanisms of globalized symbolic goods, which articulate hybrid identities, because that activity modifies what the authors call "the cultural substrate" which, according to them, remains probably unchanged. They also state, in another book, that ethnic identity "may take up new contents without losing its *essence*" (emphasis added; Bastos and Camus *Los mayas*, 13).

Another interesting idea expressed by these authors is their "position not to consider 'ladinos' as the nonindigenous people," a position, they argue, that began to take shape when they observed that "the relationships of this group with indigenous people did not correspond to the behavior of the ladino stereotype" (*Indígenas* 67-68). This idea is central to us since it expresses the universe of hybrid identities in which stereotypical polarities Indian-ladino do not function anymore, and where, on the contrary, the new range of identities, moreover negotiable ones, is very wide. It also matters because it is precisely the ladino stereotype what serves as axis to the *Mayista* discourse (that is, to the current ethnicist essentialism of some indigenous intellectuals educated in the United States and in Europe) in order to articulate its concept of Mayan identity in terms of a cultural and ethnic purism, as opposed to the ladinidad, considered by them as racist, essentially bad, opportunistic, hypocritical, cruel, exploiting, oppressive, etc. That is, as another essence.

With regard to the relationships between indigenous and nonindigenous people in the popular spaces, the authors state that "The worsening of the crisis can provoke a competition for economic spaces, pushing the nonindigenous people to see the indigenous ones as strangers who hold the positions belonging to them." What could be the consequences of an Indian-ladino confrontation for economic space and what does it have to do with identity? The authors say that "it could come to an isolation and a new awareness of identity by the urban indigenous people" (69), as is already happening in the case of the small streetcorner stores.[8] Although the authors condition this to the possibility of swelling nationalism among the indigenous people of the capital, it would be more interesting to consider the possibility that an affirmation of ethnic identities would spring up, unrelated to Mayismo, as a spontaneous phenomenon, not prefabricated by an intellectual avant-garde. Another possibility worth considering is the strengthening of the popular movement due to the economic crisis, over and beyond ethnic differences.

In another book (*Los mayas*), Bastos and Camus devise a sort of taxonomy of ethnic identities in the city, and although they do not state them as hybrid or negotiable, and they assign a more or less fixed position to each classification, there are various passages in which one can see that they glimpse the negotiable mobility of hybrid identities. All this, of course, without considering the role of consumption in the articulation of the new identities. The first division established is that of the "de-ethnicized Indians," i.e. those who have distanced themselves from their ethnic traditions but keep (or not) the self-identification as indigenous. Interestingly, the authors state that "the ethnic ceases to be relevant for them, whether by their own active decision or by a passive attitude, but it does not necessarily presume an automatic assumption of the identity of the 'other'" (144). The phrasing expresses the authors' essentialist perception of identity. On the one hand, it is clear that the loss of relevance of the ethnic elements of an identity does not imply automatic assumption of the identity of the other because that assumption does not depend on will. It is negotiation, not the masks, that is imposed upon them. On the other hand, the identity of the other is equally negotiable in many aspects and is not fixed, and thus the problem is posed of what type of other identity is assumed by the Indian, since he is immersed in a universe of intensely interacting hybridizations in which he can adopt diverse elements of the ladino or Western otherness. However, the authors sense the negotiation of identity when they affirm that the culture in those spaces "is a product of crossbreeding," and the subjects involved in them "continue to collaborate in the recreation of that mixed culture in which the indigenous is present" (14). Later they talk about "the hidden urban Indians," that is, those indigenous people who do not forsake being indigenous by assuming urban identities: "The success of their chameleon strategy should be based on knowing how to separate or to complement their environments" (14). That is, on negotiating their already hybrid identities.

The "evident urban Indians" are, according to the authors, those who not only assume their indigenous identity but also exteriorize it consciously and deliberately. The "semi-urbanized" are those who maintain rural mentalities in the city, and for whom "The identification of the indigenous with the peasant leads to a perception of ethnicity as something opposed to the urban and, therefore, endows a negative connotation to an identity which is so evident they cannot reject it" (149). They call "rural/urban Indians" those who "are integrated to the city only temporarily" and "maintain their home and their traditional rural occupation," although they can also be craftsmen who commute to and from the capital.

The most recent studies about the Indians who work in the urban space have been done with this fixed system of categories. Next, we will analyze those indigenous people who consume in the urban space in order to relativize those criteria, and to place ourselves in the intersection of the cultural boundaries.

The Indians Already Came Down from the Hill: Popular-Consumerist Resignification of the Urban Space

The commonly called Parque Central emblematizes the city of Guatemala as the *locus* of the hybridization and negotiation of subaltern identities. On Sundays—when Indian housemaids as well as other indigenous people who work or do their military service have the day off—the Parque Central, the center point of what is still considered—in spite of the architectural deprecation it has been subjected to—the historical downtown area of the city, is crowded with hundreds of young women wearing their regional attires and young men with military haircuts dressed in Western clothes. Before the counterinsurgency war, the gathering place for the indigenous men and women in the capital was the "Obelisco," the plaza commemorating the Independence, located in what until the eighties was the elegant residential area of the city. Today, that area—called "*Zona viva*"—is intensely commercial and (post)modern, and it has replaced the historical downtown area in its old urban business functions. The downtown has been left behind as a residue space of exchange for the low income middle class and for the populace, i.e. the conglomerates excluded from the advantages of full citizenship. Consequently, the cinemas, coffee shops, and transnationalized recreational spaces such as McDonald's, Burger King, and their epigones local fast food restaurants, such as Frankfurt and Jimmy's, have been literally overtaken by the populace (by the "mob"), although only on Sundays. The rest of the week, the historical downtown area functions as the site of public and private buildings where many people must conduct all sorts of transactions, although today's use of an important part of the historical downtown area is already limited to its neighborhood.

On Sundays, then, the downtown area becomes the space for the populace, to the extreme that certain middle class people would not even think about (though it is only an expression) going to the cinema or a coffee shop there. The downtown streets are full of merchandise with labels from Levi's, Wrangler, Lee, Reebock, L.A. Gear, Adidas, Fila, Calvin Klein, etc., and, of course, one can see plenty of citizens of all ages—indigenous and ladinos—dressed in those clothes, buying them from the street vendors, and listening to heavy rock pouring out of big boom-boxes carried by young men on their shoulders, flaunting a condition of transnationalized consumers of an international culture.[9] Their hairdos may or may not be punk; nevertheless, they are North American style. In the downtown cinemas people can watch films featuring Bruce Willis, Arnold Schwarzenegger, Steven Segal, or Sylvester Stallone, and, afterwards, listen to the movie enthusiasts express how good the films are according to the type and degree of violence displayed. Young workers and soldiers usually take their girlfriends (domestic employees) to watch those films, and later they eat something at Pizza Hut, for example, although, as I said, there are local, less expensive, alternatives for fast food such as the greatly popular *Pollo Campero*, whose advertisements maintain that that fried chicken is "as Guatemalan as you are," offering people, including the Indians, the hegemonic political identity as an *instant made* gourmet dish, through local consumption emulating "international" consumptions, in an atmosphere that also emulates "international" ambiances.

García Canclini states that "social urban life does not take place only in the historical or traditional centers of the cities but also in the modern shopping malls of the periphery," and that "strolls shift from the specific parks in each city to the shopping malls that imitate themselves across the planet" (*Consumidores* 86). The case we are describing poses the need for an analysis more suitable at least to Central America. The assertion made by García Canclini is valid for the middle classes but not for the indigenous and ladino Guatemalan masses who have overtaken the city's historical downtown area for their massified consumption. Of course, that is the space that somehow has been assigned to them, and has been remodeled, duplicating the shopping malls in the United States, in order to promote among them the urbanized consumption of the transnational culture industry. However, the shopping malls, replicating those in the United States, are reserved for the affluent or semiaffluent middle classes.

In any case, it would be interesting to establish how the populace, through their transnationalized consumptions, resignifies the homogenized objects and messages, and how it adopts them to their hybrid needs of cohesion, identification, and legitimation. By establishing this, it would be possible to show how much popular consumptions can constitute spaces of cultural resistance, transculturation, or acculturation. At a glance, it would appear as ambivalent consumption; but perhaps what follows may help to illustrate the contrary.

One of the functions of this space—the Parque Central and the adjacent streets—is to serve as an inter-and intraethnic communication bridge, since it is the congregation place for indigenous peoples of all ethnic groups who communicate among themselves in the *lingua franca* of Spanish or Quiché. This also takes place in the markets, but without the same hybridizing implications. In the Parque Central area there is an abundance of street vendors who are also indigenous, and who no longer negotiate their identities in a traumatic way in military quarters but rather in the marginal areas of the city. Some of these areas were formed before and some after the counterinsurgency war which reached its peak in 1980-1984, and they represent the excessive and disorderly urban growth caused by the "scorched land" policy of the military. From 1982 to 1984, the city's population grew from one million to three million people, and presently it has reached three and a half million. A large number of these inhabitants were uprooted from their communities by the war, and they settled down in the marginal zones of the city with their children—now adolescents or adults—who constitute the most dramatic example of hybridized identities.

The human landscape is intense and colorful: Young women (and this is not new) wear their autochthonous dresses combined with Western clothes such as industrially manufactured sweaters, high heels, plastic earrings, and diadems. Young men dress in the North American fashion, with caps worn backwards and with T-shirts sporting North American brands and emblems, articles which were probably brought illegally from the Panama Canal zone, or were manufactured in the *maquiladoras* of San Juan Sacatepéquez where several indigenous families have become rich thanks to using local indigenous workforce in their factories (Mayén). Much of that indigenous youth no longer speak their vernacular languages; they work in temporary and unstable jobs, such as washing cars and selling inexpensive merchandise, or they enlist themselves in organized (and unorganized) crime gangs in order to steal goods from automobiles and homes, or they hold up people on the streets, or find other forms of subsistence. Those gangs are known as *maras*, and they are closely linked to the problem of the street children, their chronic drug addiction (mainly by inhaling industrial cement), their systematic extermination by the police, and particularly by those who consider them as a source of shame for the city and for the country (Levenson).

Consumption constitutes subjects with new identities since some of these individuals did not exist as human beings with contestatory identities before their particular cinematographic and musical consumptions, and because their identity is defined by the sort of product consumed in the determining frame—of course—of poverty and unemployment in which they live. Poverty conditions the active consumption of music, movies, clothes, type of food, etc., and these items visibly articulate new hybrid identities in those conglomerates, identities negotiated in complex and complicated ways.[10]

An example of how consumption has altered traditional customs of communities when their members are transplanted to the urban environment is the city courtship among indigenous people which contain all the elaborate forms of rural courtesy and in which Spanish and the dialects are used interchangeably. For instance, after holding hands or kissing—while watching the movie screen literally bleeding in a North American thriller projected in one of the many downtown cinemas—the girlfriend will be invited to have pizza or hamburgers, while listening to heavy metal rhythms.

That has been the experience of Candelaria, for example, a young Quiché woman whose indigenous boyfriend is a *Kaibil* (member of the special troops that massacred Indians during the counterinsurgency war); she always carries a key ring with her boyfriend's picture in military uniform, and she attends an Evangelical church, the Gospel Outreach. Efraín Ríos Montt, under whose leadership the troops perpetrated the worst massacres of Indians and for whose political party she and her boyfriend would have to vote in the November 1995 elections, belongs to a church of the same denomination. Candelaria would usually go to the Parque Central to meet with her boyfriend on Sundays. But she left her maid job at the beginning of that year. When her boss went to look for her at a semimarginal neighborhood in the city to ask her to go back, she found Candelaria's brother living in a two-story block and cement house, dressed as ladino. She also found that in the same house another sister who wore autochthonous attire, and that both their spouses and their children lived there. Apparently, Candelaria had run away with her boyfriend and nobody had heard from her for several weeks. Normally, when this happens, the young woman returns home when she is already carrying her first born in her arms. The seduction, then, functions in the middle of the globalizing hybridizations, and, because of them, the negotiation of identities achieves its objectives, although in a nontraditional way. A relationship such as this, as can be seen in the testimony by Rigoberta Menchú (Burgos-Debray), is carried out in a totally different fashion in the rural community area.

The case of Parque Central and the historical downtown area of Guatemala City, their use and consumption by the urbanized indigenous population, as well as the hybridization and negotiation of identities they propitiate, lead us to revisit diverse reflections, frequently rejected because they are not totally understood. How is an identity negotiated? First one has to establish who is the subject whose identity is being considered. Let us say that it is an indigenous woman who comes from the *altiplano* looking for a job as domestic worker in the city as Candelaria did. At the LASA convention of September 1995, held in Washington, Demetrio Cojtí (an indigenous intellectual and UNICEF official) gave as an example of racism in Guatemala the fact that an indigenous woman often must forsake her autochthonous attire to secure a job at a ladino home. I could offer a variant of said example illustrating, from my angle, ladino ethnocentrism: Many ladino housewives like to have domestic workers who are *inditas* (little Indians) and *envueltas* (term used to designate women who wear the indigenous skirt or cut) because they are considered "less spoiled" than those who roam the streets wearing the make-up and high heels, and who, precisely because of that, are not seen as indigenous people, either because they have never been that and come from the East (for example), or because they are not "indigenous" anymore due to the hybridization with which they assume their identity; or better said, their negotiable identity.

In other words, either because a woman changes her attire in order to obtain a job or because she changes it just because she wants to change it, and that is precisely what would make getting a job difficult, that woman is negotiating her identity to survive economically, culturally, and ideologically, in an interethnic country in which the intercultural problem has not been democratically solved. Candelaria did not change her attire, but many of her friends did, and they did it in a generalized practice that people carry out as fast as needed, and with a mimetic ability more and more precise each time, evidencing countless possibilities for hybridization.

We all, in one way or another, negotiate our identity. This, in turn, means that we have not one but various identities according to the needs for identity negotiation we may face. The ladino guerrillas used to negotiate their identity whenever they would try to win over militants; they would make an effort to speak like the peasants, to use their expressions of courtesy, and to adopt their manners. They would imitate them and try to be like them, in order to achieve indigenous people's support and activism.

What is posited by the negotiation of identities, or better said, what is posited by the fact that identities are negotiable, and therefore flexible and hybrid, is that they are self-transformable: they come closer to or separate from their original forms in various degrees and modalities according to the needs set forth by the subject's economic, cultural, and ideological subsistence. In this way, the spaces of hybridization appear as shadowy, amorphous, and gelatinous zones, where nothing or almost nothing is secure and unmovable and much less eternal and suprahistoric. Consequently, where are the firm identities from which, as if from a trench, we would judge the other and define ourselves according to set differences?

There is no doubt that there are Indians and ladinos in Guatemala, or, if you prefer, "Mayas" and *mestizos*. But where are they and who are they exactly? If we rely only on the principle of and right to self-denomination, all I can do is say that I am ladino to be considered ladino, and all Alfredo Tay, Estuardo Zapeta, Demetrio Cojtí or Humberto Ak'abal can say is that they are Maya to be considered Maya. In Costa Rica and in the United States I am referred to as Indian or at least Indian-like (*aindiado*). I believe that those *Mayista* intellectuals I have just mentioned could be easily taken for ladinos in Guatemala, if they did not mention that they are not ladinos, because their physical traits are like those of ninety percent of Guatemalans. But, what is the Indian-like identity? Is it only a physical trait? And, what is the ladino-like identity? Is it a set of visible traits such as clothing, Western culture, and Western manners? It is clear that the notion of single identities does not help in answering these questions.

The Parque Central of the city of Guatemala—where on Sunday afternoons some rich indigenous families can also be seen descending from their vehicles to drink *atole* and enjoy other delicacies of the popular cuisine, and where the youth of both sexes can be seen dressed in their indigenous attires, listening to Selena, Los Tigres del Norte, or Whitney Houston from the headphones in their walkman or discman—is the country's easiest and most accessible display window for observing live the intense identity negotiations possible in urban consumption spaces. Those negotiations show that intercultural crossbreeding is no longer a subject reduced to the very limited scope of the binary duality Indian-ladino, but that it is projected towards the internationalization and transnationalization of globalized cultural consumption in which the popular and ethnic subject is diversified in its identity to the limit of the impossibility of being apprehended in one single word, whether it be indigenous, Indian or Maya, or ladino. That is to say, in one single identity.

But this dynamic of hybridization cannot be observed only in the city. In the rural communities also, the effects of economic and communicational globalization have changed the codes of identity negotiation due to globalized consumption.

Lake Atitlán Turns (Post)modern: Globalization Comes to San Lucas Tolimán

In 1994, the Mayor of San Lucas Tolimán bought a parabolic antenna. A while later the municipality began to sell cable television service to the local community. Soon the cable service enterprise became a prosperous business in that beautiful town.[11] The interesting thing, however, was that together with the screams and bizarre gestures of Gloria Trevi, Thalía, Shakira, Chayanne, Ricky Martin, or Michael Jackson, who began to invade the townspeople's imaginary, the Mayor would suddenly appear on television sending political messages to the community. Subsequently, the Mayor created an organization to preserve local traditions which he began to promote by broadcasting videos recorded by a technician he hired to manage and expand the enterprise.

Globalization and promotion of traditional cultures constitutes, as a coalition of simultaneous activities, a (post)modern contradiction explained by means of a marketing technique: the translation of the codes of the "otherness" to the codes of the consumer of "other" symbolic goods. On the one hand, the uniform message of the mass media tends to homogenize the taste for certain audio-visual goods, and thus it is homogenizing the demand for an equally homogenized supply; on the other hand, in the presence of the uniform supply of culture for the masses, which offers new identity possibilities, traditions tend to transform themselves or disappear as elements of social cohesion, political legitimation, or grantors of identity profiles. Traditional cultures become refunctionalized by the transnational demand of consumption of symbolic goods, turning them, in many cases, if they are lucky, into tourist attractions for consumption, or into receptacles of knowledge of otherness, encapsulated in the codes of the consumer's culture and logic. Accordingly, documentaries about indigenous peoples in Latin America are explained with relationship to the Euro-North American culture, and the traditions, turned into tourist attractions, conform their contents to those of the consumer in order to facilitate their consumption. Apparently, this is the only way traditions can survive: as cultural heritage for tourism (Ashworth).

What is happening in San Lucas Tolimán is a very clear example of how cultural hybridization in multiethnic countries of the so-called Third World is taking place at the time of globalization and globalized consumptions. In the same manner, the Confraternity of Maximón in Santiago Atitlán functions today as a tourist attraction more than as a traditional cohesive factor of identity for the townspeople. The municipal project to create an organization to preserve the traditions of San Lucas, using cable television with its transnationalized contents as a means, illustrates the violent changes and refunctionalizations that globalization is producing in traditional cultures, through the intensification of already existing processes of hybridization and intercultural *mestizaje* in this country.

The majority of television channels now viewed in San Lucas are Mexican, and the townspeople have already adopted many of the patterns of culture for the masses offered by Televisa and other companies affiliated—or not—with Televisa, for example, dances, hair styles, clothing and lyrics of popular songs. The mexicanization of San Lucas is the gate of its strange access to cultural globalization. This by itself suggests a radical restatement of approaching the study of Guatemalan traditional cultures by placing them in an intense and dynamic relationship with the culture industry launched by the globalizing mass media, which homogenizes the taste of consumers, and, with it, demands a supply that is already packaged like fast food or pop music.

The so-called municipal channel (channel nine) works by interrupting some of the regular cable channels on Mondays and Thursdays, from six to seven at night, broadcasting prerecorded Evangelical services, soccer games, telethons, ecological messages, weddings, anniversaries, funerals, and also traditional festivities and autochthonous ceremonies, in order to stimulate the preservation of confraternities and other cultural institutions, which are now in danger of extinction due to their rejection by a growing fundamentalist Protestantism. The main demand of consumers (about three hundred out of fifteen thousand inhabitants, in addition to those who steal the signal) is for the Univisión channel, which broadcasts the preferred soap operas. Whenever the broadcasting signal has been interrupted there have been attempts at serious disturbances against the municipal authorities. The television signal reaches only the city boundary, but there are plans to take it to the most distant villages.

Television and video games (one arcade is located in the park), in fact, affect local culture because suddenly men wear ponytails and earrings, listen to music in English, and inhale cement, smoke marijuana, and even come to use cocaine. In addition to this, many do not want to speak Cackchiquel because everything in school is taught in Spanish, and many parents do not want their children to speak the autochthonous language, so they can better fit in the ladino world. Used clothes, or *ropa de paca* (clothes from bales coming from the United States), have made men definitely lose their indigenous attire, since those North American clothes are cheaper, are in fashion, and appear on television. Some of the townspeople work in the United States, and, therefore, in many homes they have videocassette recorders sent by their relatives, so that they can see them on videocassettes. These forms of audio-visual consumption in indigenous communities conflict with the aspirations of their pretended organic academics, who would seem to think that simply by being masses, people would transform the contents of mass media:

> Television does not have to be used like that. It would be wonderful if our humble people had access to these means of communication: television, radio, the written media and all kinds of oral media. I am sure they would use them differently. They would create new generations that are sensitive to life. Instead of a grandfather passing on wisdom solely to his grandson, he could teach society as well. Television might be able to spread knowledge of our traditions without having them manipulated, ridiculed and belittled by folklore. (Menchú 220, adapted following the original)[12]

In addition to the video game arcade located in the park in San Lucas, there is a movie theater, which at the time of my interviews was showing a Kung-Fu movie with David Carradine. The music most heard on the radio was that of Los Bukis, Bronco, Los Temerarios, Selena, Olga Tañón and Los Tigres del Norte. The radio station's name was "Galaxia Súper Estéreo," and most of the indigenous and ladino population listened to it.

In search of less hybridized traditions, I went to the local Confraternity of Maximón. When I arrived, the brothers showed me his coffin, and, for ten *quetzals* (about a dollar fifty), they placed the image in a sitting position, so I could take his picture. Maximón is a deity whose confraternities can be found in various corners of the altiplano, and he is an excellent expression of intercultural *mestizaje* and negotiated identities: "While he is known, in part, as San Andrés, San Miguel, or San Pedro, not to mention Pedro de Alvarado, the Guatemalan conqueror, he is also known by the name of *Mam*, the Old God, whom, according to bishop Landa and other sources, the ancient Mayans revered during the last five days of the pre-Columbian calendar" (Mendelson 137).

Faced by this type of phenomena, one has to realize that there is a deep gap between what is going on in reality (the factual level) and the ethnicist slogans set forth by the *Mayista* intellectuals, transfixed with the idea of the popular as a space of frontal resistance, which is supposed to enter (Post)Modernity as an unequivocally differentiated culture. Vis-à-vis such phenomena as I have adduced, where are the pan-Mayanist purisms, the fundamentalisms that demand a manifest destiny and a unilateral right over the Guatemalan territory and its resources for the *Mayanidad*? What is left of the argument that ladinos are *mestizos* (crossbred/hybrid) and that Indians are simply "Mayas," without any intercultural *mestizaje*?

What the case of San Lucas Tolimán shows is the spontaneous entry of the indigenous and ladino populations into the unavoidable (but not necessarily pleasant) coordinates of (Post)Modernity, prescribed for us without any alternative options by the North (with a capital N). My point here is to avoid appealing to archaeological criteria, or to the unmovability of the past in order to package, ideologically, the right of the indigenous people to enter (Post)Modernity together with their distinctive culture and ethnicity, and rather to begin speaking about those claims in terms of fair and egalitarian hybridization and *mestizaje*, so that all the cultures forming this cultural and ethnic ensemble called Guatemala can evolve and be able to express themselves in equal conditions. It is true, then, that globalization does not end the traditional or the local, but it does transform and refunctionalize them to the point that they may become unrecognizable.

Postmodern Transfiguration of Kukulkán and the *Maximón's Syndrome*

Perhaps the most popular deity as a genuine case of cultural resistance has been, till recently, Maximón, a god-saint with multiple identities which he negotiates at his convenience. Supposedly, he is also a transfiguration of Kukulkán (the Plumed Serpent) in his enemy, James the Apostle, in order to deceive him. Maximón is, physically, a clay mask with a small body (his height is barely over one meter) made out of rags, *perrajes*, and scarves. He always wears two or three hats one on top of the other, and his priests give him something to smoke uninterruptedly while his believers, kneeling before him, kiss the scarves of his body and have long talks to him or pray, helped by strong sips of liquor.

Until the counterinsurgency and the arrival of the fundamentalist Protestant Churches, Maximón was the primary element of cultural cohesion, legitimation and identity for the townspeople of Santiago Atitlán. Everything changed with the arrival of the Protestant Churches after the counterinsurgency massacres in the area of Santiago. The Confraternity of Maximón and its parishioners were reduced to a few people. The Confraternity (which used to sell liquor) went bankrupt when the Evangelical Church prohibited drinking. Today, the saint's festival, a beautiful ceremony called *La traída de la fruta* ("The Delivery of the Fruit") continues only thanks to the groups of Japanese, German, and North American tourists who visit the city mainly during Holy Week. That is how Maximón's ritual is now financed.

This deity is very complex, as Mendelson makes clear: "This Maximón, who is the father of the worshippers, master of insanity and some other things . . . is not an easy figure to analyze. I have called him 'the traitor', keeping in mind his betrayal of the indigenous people as Alvarado, and his betrayal of Christ as Judas, and, incidentally, as Peter" (159-60). The traitor syndrome suggested by Mendelson can be expanded. Thus, the Conquest would become an act of divine betrayal and the *ladinization* a simple development of the same. The negotiation of identity, identity transvestism, a transvestism perceived conflictively as treason, is what I would like to call *Maximón's syndrome*, and thus propose the saint himself as an expression of the conflicting self-perception of the indigenous people oppressed (and seduced) by colonization and ladinization; this expression extends to the self-perception of the ladino as someone whose identity constitution is articulated based on an indigenous cultural nucleus assumed with difficulty. Thus, Maximón, in all his variants, expresses the intercultural *mestizaje* of Guatemala as well as its conflictive condition. Therefore, I believe that the local neurosis about identity and culture denotes a symptomatology of ambivalence: denial-assumption, shame-pride of the own *mestizo* being, that is what I would like to call *Maximón's syndrome*.

It could be argued, in this sense, that what the "Mayan" constructionist conscience and identity do is to deny—asserting it indirectly—Maximón's syndrome by fabricating supra- and transhistorical cultural contents to fill not only the void created by colonial oppression, but, above all, the historical void (or lack of information) before the tenth century, in order to throw itself into cultural, economic, social, and ideological negotiation in more favorable terms. The "touristified" Maximón is the paramount negotiation because it is the negotiated "essence": religion, gods, faith, and the arrival to the power of the West, all negotiated with Maximón's mask. In this sense, Maximón is, essentially, a mask, a perennial translation; it does not have a body, and its volume and appearance are volatile and ethereal, made out of scarves, at least in Santiago Atitlán's version, where he is dressed sometimes as ladino, always with his hats on top of each other, and, other times, wearing an indigenous attire.

The Confraternity ended in bankruptcy when the saint was no longer the factor of social cohesion in his town, and the fundamentalist Evangelical god occupied that center. Nevertheless, the enormous ability of mimetic refunctionalization for survival faced by traditions allowed the deity to survive, this time as a tourist attraction subject to the rules of the spectacle, but not as an element of identity and cultural resistance.

The mentalities of those who maintain traditions are also rooted in (Post)Modernity and the market, understanding the latter both as a marketplace and in its more complex version. Only for us—the ladino intellectuals—this hybrid, borderline situation presents itself as some kind of a "problem."

Viewed as elements of ideological Modernity, the Evangelical fundamentalist Churches of all kinds constitute the leading element of the religious convulsion on the Guatemalan altiplano since the inrush of the Catholic Church in the days of the so-called Discovery and Conquest. In order to establish analogies between that epoch and the current religious situation of the Guatemalan Indians, one has to observe that fundamentalist Protestantism is mainly centered in the altiplano villages which were part of the battleground in the armed struggle between the insurgents and counterinsurgents, and that the spiritual proposition it made to the terrified conglomerate of inhabitants implied a violent refunctionalization of their traditions and convictions; that is, a refunctionalization of their syncretic culture which had emerged in colonial times. Today, the fundamentalist Churches encourage their parishioners to enter the world of employment and enterprise, particularly in the religious marketplace, since it is very easy to succeed in the Evangelical ministries. This is a determining factor in the vertiginous multiplication of the Churches and of their financial resources, and, in turn, explains the fall of Catholicism, which is ultra hierarchical, verticalist, and classist. It is a well-known fact that the poor people attend the Catholic church while the middle class and the rich of the town, Indians and ladinos, attend the Evangelical churches.

Further, since the groups of *Acción Católica* were the vehicle for the mass incorporation of the civil population into the guerrilla movement on the altiplano, the peace and spiritual consolation offered by the Evangelical fundamentalism contrasted naturally with Catholicism as a whole (not only Liberation Theology), which was then perceived as the cause of the many sufferings of the community.

Christianity in its catholic-colonial version forced the Indians to refunctionalize and transfigure their gods, obliging Kukulkán to disguise himself as his enemy, the conquistador, and later to become Maximón. In a similar way Christianity, in its Protestant version, forced Maximón to give up power and ideological influence over his people for the benefit of Jehovah, and to survive by charging a fee to the tourists for seeing him and taking his pictures. Maximón, then, has turned into an impresario.

What does this mimetic capacity show? Force or weakness? It is difficult to answer that because traditions survive thanks to the weakness and backwardness of local capitalism. But one thing is for sure: The bankruptcy of Maximón belongs in the past, because his Confraternity is now a prosperous communal business. And even if he has lost the all-embracing power over his people, his Confraternity is pretty busy now that it has become an international tourist attraction.

The transit of Maximón from heaven to the market emblematizes the journey on which all the religious ceremonies of the Guatemalan indigenous altiplano have embarked, as evidenced by the rituals of "Mayan spirituality" staged lavishly and repeatedly here, as well as, surely, in all the indigenous communities of Latin America.

When one stops at one of the numerous elevated sites of Santiago Atitlán and manages to catch a general view of the town, what springs to the eye is the boom in the construction of Evangelical churches and the absence of bars and drunkards, which previously constituted the typical scene. When, on Sunday mornings, the atmosphere fills with echos of religious hymns, the suspicion creeps in that the townspeople live their lives striving to appease all the quarrelsome gods that inhabit their richly disorganized and exuberant Olympus. And, of course, one can only reflect on the considerable international finances fomenting development programs for "Mayan" culture and spirituality among the marginalized ethnic groups, apparently (and only apparently) against the tendencies of the globalizing processes, which are clearly pointing to refunctionalizing traditions through tourism and religious homogenization.

It would seem that international determination to revive the disappeared Mayas, at the same time that the residues of the colonial hybridization vertiginously become (post)modernized, by turning into spectacles and/or simulacra of otherness subsidized from the outside, can only respond to ideological objectives aimed at deproblematizing and standardizing the syncretic worldviews of the indigenous peoples, in order to homogenize the demand for a spiritual product which could satisfy the need for transcendence without granting excessive concessions to the cultural particularities vindicated today as part of Multiculturalism. With the objective of incorporating those types of cultural otherness into the global market, turning them and their human groups into producers and consumers of a very salable product called *cultural heritage,* the tourist industry offers a marketable package, "otherness" translated to the proper codes of the (tourist) consumer.

In Santiago Atitlán, the conflictive cohabitation of different religions expresses the irruption of Postmodernity also via religious pluralism. A tense pluralism of spaces in which traditions and breaking the tradition contend, drawing borderlines in which individuals posit themselves to negotiate their religious identities in the most astute ways possible, but never as passive receivers.

Urban Behaviors in the Rural Areas

The young Tzutuhil student from the San Carlos University, Gerardo López Cotuc, who introduced me to his community, San Juan La

Laguna, told me that he no longer looks forward to going to his hometown, situated on the shores of Lake Atitlán, because the indigenous youngsters who have come to work in the city return to their communities to organize *maras* and antagonize people through robbery, holdups, and unwarranted intimidations. This is a case which clearly illustrates how, particularly in urban areas, the articulation of young people's identities is achieved through messages and forms offered to a consumer standardized by the mass media as well as by the marginal behaviors of young people previously settled in those areas. The behaviors observed on the margins of the central power reveal a tendency to affirm individual and collective identities whose main traits are its hybrid nature and authoritarianism. Naturally, in this case, hybridization is of the type that tends to annul the distinctively indigenous components (as such already *mestizados* or mixed) from the structure of those identities. It is not difficult to note that the organization of *maras* in San Juan La Laguna, for example, constitutes a foreign incrustation on the idiosyncrasy of the communities along the shores of Lake Atitlán. However, the alien nature of the phenomenon is not enough to restrain it, and illustrates how social and economic conditions of a country are elements of the growing formation of new identities. The young Indians are not exempt—they couldn't be—from the influence of the elements of the urban marginality which is in itself already *mestizo* culturally.

San Juan de La Laguna is an example of urban marginal behaviors which have arrived to the rural areas, erasing the old divisions and transterritorializing the (pre/post)modern conflicts only now experienced amid the cornfields and at the foothills of volcanoes. On the other hand, who could deny with any certainty that the gang's know-how does not come directly, say, from Los Angeles, where some young men from San Juan could have spent time washing dishes at a restaurant, and not necessarily from the Guatemalan epigones of the Hispanic gangs? The transnational circulation of capital, people, and cultures views cultural locations as overflowing national spaces (Bhabha). That is why *Mayismo* and other manifestations of the articulation of popular culture and the market must be studied in its globalized and globalizing dimension.

Macondista Fundamentalism

One indigenous intellectual, mathematician and editor of school textbooks in Guatemala City, told me that once he was not admitted to a meeting of "Mayas" because he did not fulfill two out of three conditions which were put before him as a proof for anybody to be considered a Maya: one was to speak any of the Maya languages, which he fulfilled plentifully; the second was to be married to a Maya woman, and the third was not to have any ladino friends. He did not fulfill these two last conditions and, therefore, he was not regarded as a "Maya" and was not admitted to the meeting. This case illustrates the chasm between the *Mayista* leadership, with their concept of identity as something immovable, essential, and monolithic, on the one hand, and, on the other, as something that takes place on the factual level, where identity is crisscrossed by negotiations realized in most tangles ways.[13]

This takes us to the problem of learned ideologies implanted as enclaves, through the international academic tradition, into Latin American subaltern thinking. García Canclini writes:

> I ask myself if, given the shift of national monoidentities toward global multiculturality, fundamentalism does not try to survive as Latinamericanism. As we have seen in politics there continue to exist ethnic and nationalistic movements that attempt to justify themselves by supposedly distinctive national and symbolic patrimonies. However, it seems to me that the operation that achieved closest verisimilitude is the *Macondista* fundamentalism: it freezes the "Latin American" as a sanctuary of the premodern nature and sublimates this continent as a place in which social violence is under the spell of emotions. It puts together texts from most diverse countries . . . and streamlines them into one single paradigm of reception, which is also a single way of situating Latin American heterogeneity into cultural globalization. (94-95)

The question is how do the ideologies of fundamentalism and globalization coexist? And not only how but also what for? What are the objectives of the simultaneous promotion of Indian fundamentalisms among the leadership and intellectual elites, bent on representing the subalterns, and of transnational tastes among the masses of those very subalterns? And also, how do the communities such as Santiago Atitlán, San Lucas Tolimán or San Juan La Laguna (where there is also cable TV) respond to this duality of messages? Because "the referents of identity are formed nowadays . . . in relation with textual and iconographic repertories provided by electronic media of communication and by the globalization of urban life," or by the globalizing urbanization of rural life, as in the case of San Lucas. "In this process, what do the imaginary constructions that contradict it mean?" (García Canclini 95). Do they strengthen it, since they affirm Latin American *Macondism* before the very eyes of central (Post)Modernity?[14] Or do they constitute spaces of resistance? And if so, what type of resistance is it?

Neither Memory nor Resistance

One ladina friend of mine writes me the following note (from November 20, 1995):

> Three years ago I went to the Museum of Anthropology [in Guatemala]. For the first time I saw three indigenous women visiting that place. They asked me what I knew about the Mayas, and so we began talking. Two things struck me: 1. that they were there, something that was not seen before in Guatemala; and 2. that when I told them what the Mayas had done, they said: "This means that our forefathers did all this, and that we come from them. I did not know that! It means that we were powerful then."

I answered to my friend: "There is no memory and no resistance. There is oppression, domination, and subjugation. That's what this situation makes clear." She responded, offended: "There is no memory because: a. official history does not say anything; b. since the moment that their history 'does not exist,' how can there be any memory? If we add illiteracy and lack of access to culture or to places where culture is exhibited, how can they know about the past and their roots?" And I thought: "No memory. No resistance."

As long as brutal facts such as these are not admitted and the guilt is adjudicated unilaterally to ladino domination, we will not be able to think adequately much less to solve the problem of our interculturality.[15]

Spirituality and Cultural Heritage for the Tourist Market: Chichicastenango

The "Mayan" priests who now proliferate thanks to the enormous amount of dubious NGOs (*Organizaciones No Gubernamentales*, the so-called Non-Governmental Organizations) that have sprung up in the country, particularly after the signing of the peace agreements (there is now a consortium of the NGOs of "Mayan" priests), go on inventing all sorts of new rituals and attires (feathers, necklaces, etc.) for their ceremonies, presumably kept intact since pre-Columbian times. These ceremonies can be seen in plazas, or at archaeological sites, baptisms, weddings, inaugurations, etc. Consequently, in Chichicastenango, the ceremony of *Pascual Abah*, which was previously considered sacred and was circumscribed to a specific date, is now staged at least every Sunday at a "secret location in the mountains" where the tourists, walking on the plaza, are invited to go and see it "in secret," for a sum of money paid to the guide who can be either an adult or a child.

On the stairs of the church, one or more "Mayan" priests may usually be seen dressed in ritual attires which—pitifully—are the same ones worn by the bellboys at a near hotel. At the marketplace, and in adjacent streets, the tourist is faced with an oversaturation of hybridized handicrafts he has to push out of his way while going through the frequently dark corridors created by the street booths conforming the market, which already overflows the plaza and branches out into the streets of the central area. Some "Mayan" priests, showing off their beautiful ritual attires, pose for the tourists' cameras, while the tourist guides recommend the already mentioned "secret ceremony" in the mountains.

Chichicastenango has become a setting where the local indigenous bourgeoisie have established their businesses which compete among themselves as well as with some more popular ways to market culture such as those of individual street vendors, improvised tour guides, and small scale artisans. Old properties owned by local Indians have been transformed into parking lots attended by the owner families; consequently, spontaneous ways of making the most of the tourist industry have become the axis of the local life and culture production. As part of this shift to the market, the cosmogonies and worldviews as well as the ceremonies claimed as inherent to the "Mayan" culture by the "Mayan" priests organized in NGOs, who use them to reassert a trans- and suprahistorical subject insisting on absolute "otherness" and on natural rights over the Guatemalan territory, are spontaneously staged for tourists by the Chichicastenango townspeople. These simulacra of ceremonies would seem more profitable than the ways in which those same traditions were financed in the past: with contributions from people who were still attached to its contents. However, this is not entirely contradictory if we analyze the phenomenon of "Maya" cultural activism also from the viewpoint of its shift to the market. In that sense, the *Mayista* culturalist and identitarian constructionism may be seen as an adaptation of one's own culture to the demands of the ideological market and to the demands of the political market of international organizations and Churches that understand the world in the jargon of ecologism, feminism, multiculturalism, democracy, human rights, and "political correctness."

From this perspective, discourses can also be considered as merchandise offered to the ideological market. That is why it is so interesting to analyze the ambivalent discourse of Rigoberta Menchú in *Rigoberta: la nieta de los mayas* (*Crossing Borders: Rigoberta Menchú*), where she sends messages to the different ideological markets in which she negotiates her content: international cooperation, international and human rights organizations, feminism, ecologism, the North American Academy and Churches, and European governments. The ambivalence of her discourse oscillates from one pole where she defends intercultural *mestizaje*, to another where she reasserts, in an essentialist way, the Mayan culture. The need to please one consumer or another determines the transvestism of her discourse and the concessions she makes to her readers. This ambivalence is articulated throughout the text.

As far as Demetrio Cojtí's discourse is concerned, it could be seen as a product offered to the market of international organizations, such as UNICEF, where he is an advisor, and not so much to the academic market, as it would appear. The discourse of Vitalino Similox is a product offered to the market of the fundamentalist Protestant religiosity (which he wants to reconcile with "Mayan spirituality"). Rosalina Tuyuc's discourse is directed to the human rights international market. And the discourse of the solidary North American intellectuals on the interethnic issues in Guatemala is a product—without any doubt—meant for the North American academic market.

There is, then, a way of being "Maya": that of marketing the product called *cultural heritage*, independently of the fact whether it is real or fictitious, or includes both components in varying degrees, according to the situation and the product. This phenomenon expresses, undoubtedly, the way the Indians—born traders by external, economic and cultural, determination—spontaneously participate in globalization, offering the best product they have: their culture, real or invented, or real and invented. In the market, indigenous people found the main incentive to assume their own culture (inventing it to a large degree) within the frame of (Post)Modernity, without having to go through the tortuous road of ladinization and overcoming the feeling of being torn apart which so tormented Luis de Lión (who exposed it intensely in his novel *El tiempo principia en Xibalbá*). It remains to be seen what happens when the interests of tourism entrepreneurs, ladinos or foreigners, enter in conflict with those of the Indians in the negotiation over the management of the tourist product called *cultural heritage*. Most probably we will have a negotiation in which interethnic business partnerships will be put in charge of selling the country as a tourist attraction.

Potpourri

The marketing of popular cultures and traditions has other variants. In Antigua, for example, former president De León's wife reactivated the *loas* or dramatizations of biblical passages, lives of saints, and other things of that sort. Their staging would be announced in the cultural sections of the newspapers. The entire city of Antigua is a *setting* where the tourists may consume artificial colonial and indigenous environment as well as autochthonous and international dishes in an atmosphere filled with the circulation of drugs, and the proliferation of discotheques, art galleries, and other forms glamorizing the old and decrepit and the ancient and venerated. In Tikal, likewise, "Mayan" ceremonies for tourists are celebrated. In these stagings, "Mayan" poets, painters, and artists can be seen dressed in "typical" shirts, "typical" vests, "typical" thread bracelets, "typical" caps, long hair and sandals, in order to offer a Mayan *look* harmonizing with the tourist's expectations of the country and of its cultural heritage.

When one attends traditional festivities, it is not strange to see indigenous people dressed as Christians and Moors, arriving at the plaza on bicycles or motorcycles, wearing Reebock tennis shoes and Cassio watches. It is not strange either to hear massages and cures being offered under the moonlight, according to "Mayan" therapeutic techniques. The Dance of the Conquest, a tradition dating from colonial times (Milla; Fuentes y Guzmán), is sometimes represented in a way that the Moors carry the Spanish flag, and the Guatemalan flag is flaunted by Tecún Umán. Likewise, in Panajachel, when the dance of the *Negritos* is staged on the 20th of February, the day of Tecún Umán, one can see indigenous children disguised as Disney characters and even those who usually dress as ladinos, disguised as Mayas or as Indians wearing "typical" outfits. These hybridized translations which precede the globalization wave, contradict categorically the binary and essentialist discourses of the *Mayista* intellectuals. As is well known, on December 12, the day of the Virgin of Guadalupe, parents dress their children as Juan Diego, the Mexican Indian to whom the Virgin appeared at the Tepeyac hill. Today, indigenous children in some communities also dress up as Juan Diego, since the rest of the year their clothing is "western."

Touristization has also reached the Central American Left. The former *comandante* Edén Pastora owns a business offering fishing tours to the tourists who visit the San Juan River. The price is higher when the ex-*comandante* personally accompanies the group and chats with its members. Another, and more successful, form of commercialization of the Left, is the image of *subcomandante* Marcos on cigarette lighters, pens, and on clay crafts made by Indians. In its turn, the URNG (Guatemalan National Revolutionary Union) has entered the world of the market by signing the peace accords, and one of the products it will offer to the political market will be its indigenous political base.

Unquestionably, some stereotypes collapse once we see the Indians as conglomerates immersed in the (post)modern dynamics of cultural production and consumption and not as some groups of robots endowed with an ancient and immobile culture. When one listens to an Indian Quiché telling his son: "Don't be a moron, you look like a Cackchiquel," or how one friend tells another "You left me waiting at the park *like an idiot*" (*con cara de quiché*, literally "with a Quiché face"), one understands not only that ethnocentrism is a very important factor for the cohesion of a community, but that mutual discrimination functions in a more pluralistic way than the one restricted to the binary opposition of Indian-ladino. The criteria become relativized regarding humanization of the Indians (to see them as human beings and not as some superhuman entities) when one thinks that used clothes (*ropa de paca*) may turn into a factor of the women's resistance against *machismo* since many women in the Indian communities assert their right to comfort, low cost, and lesser effort involved in wearing used North American clothes. However, this is detrimental to the tradition of which men have made them guardians, thus putting another heavy burden on the women's shoulders. No matter how idealized it might be by culturalist preservationism, this burden is undoubtedly an element of patriarchal oppression. It is also interesting to observe how the indigenous and ladino women employed at the capital's *maquiladoras* unite in the political identity of "Guatemalans" in order to confront the abuses by the South Korean male owners, notorious for their cruelty towards women workers. Indigenous women broaden their field of action in the *maquiladoras*, although (and precisely because) they wear used clothes and negotiate their identities with their ladino coworkers. This, undoubtedly, offends the indigenous patriarchal system, particularly if it is essentialist.

The way in which indigenous people adapt themselves and their culture to the wave of globalization gives rise to certain mimetic identities that express attitudes and behaviors which would seem to comprise, as a whole, an appropriate form for creatively confronting globalization from the positionalities of their particular cultures. For these intercultural popular subjects, the only natural defense against the invasion of their imaginary is their ability to absorb, decode, and subvert globalized messages through active and creative consumption of symbolic goods. To a certain degree, this is a variant of the traditional notion of transculturation of the subaltern populations, now turned into communities that consume globalized symbolic goods. This mimetism of identity is, then, an active answer—sometimes contestatory, sometimes acculturated—from an active consumer. It implies a negotiation, among themselves, of class, ethnic, national, and gender identities. Or, better, a continually shifting negotiation of the class, ethnic, national, and gender aspects of those identities which, in Guatemala, offer us an intense and often incredibe display of their intrinsicly movable, negotiable, and transpositional character.

Neither Freedom Nor Death, But Negotiation

All the cases we have been analyzing illustrate the fact that "we are moving away from the epic assertion of popular identities as part of national societies, to the acknowledgment of transnational conflicts and negotiations in the constitution of the popular and all other identities" (García Canclini, *Consumidores* 168). Although, who knows if what is happening is not perhaps that we are witnessing a coexistence of the epic affirmation of telluric identities with the pre-post-modern transcultural negotiations. If it is the case of coexistence and not of a shift from the old to the new models of practicing identity, the space of hybridization would appear as suitable for testing—as García Canclini wants—cultural policies that would account for the hybrid subjects and the negotiable identities, and would, naturally, propitiate the free democratized flow of hybridizations. Besides, this way the role of the State in multi-ethnic problems would be reasserted, and the role of the intellectuals as designers of the hybrid, intercultural, negotiable, and mobile policy, would be redefined. However, the problem cannot be reduced to the control of the intensity of hybridizations through the State and intellectuals, but must be extended to the field of participative and democratic interethnic negotiation.

In theory, intercultural dynamics seem to be taking a coherent form. In reality it has got it already, only we are not yet capable of thinking of it in terms of its own and original coherence, simply because it implies adopting a new *episteme*, situated beyond the comfortable polarities to which we became accustomed during the years of political struggle in which we have invested more than half of our lives and the outcomes of which could not have been foreseen by us. The plain truth is that what was for us in stock in this political struggle was neither freedom, nor death, as the slogan went, but negotiation. And in place of the all-solving macrosystems, what is left is the market (absurdly idealized by neoliberalism) in which, whether we like it or not, we will now have to enjoy the pleasures of bargaining as we sell ourselves, like *petates de muerto* (the straw mats for the dead) we used to frighten each other with, back in those days when we, both rightist and leftists, were exhilarated, driven by the dream of eliminating one another. We need, then, to turn the market in our favor although our ideological and financial capital may be meager. In order to increase that capital, we must begin to play following the market's rules of the game, the same way the indigenous people are spontaneously doing it, although their discourse is ambivalent.[16] In that sense, this discourse needs to be corrected, and that is the aim of this work.

It is time, then, to begin accepting the fact that there are no pure identities, only negotiable ones (live or extinct). On this basis we will be able to explore just how free some identities are when they negotiate the terms for their survival in the codes of domination and/or hegemony, and to what degree the negotiation is, nowadays, the only possible form of resistance.[17] In other words, how and how much the subaltern, in fact, not only speaks but writes, expresses, and constructs himself as subject in the midst of a world that negates him by affirming him, and that affirms him by negating him, because he is needed there, as situated, in the position of the subaltern. Perhaps to explore this situation is one of the tasks before the intellectuals in this phase of the search for the components with which to articulate a more intelligent utopia, less demagogic, less dreamy, and more realistic than the one just unravelled.

Notes

1. A first version of this essay was published in *Istmica* (Universidad Nacional, Heredia, Costa Rica) 3-4 (1997-1998): 13-37.

2. The differentiation between Indians and ladinos emerged during the Colonial period. Ladinos were, at the beginning, the Indians who had learned Spanish and were versed in Spanish customs. Later, the term continued being used to refer to any person who would not identify himself or herself as Indian or indigenous, independently of their physiognomy (Batres Jáuregui 81-94, 357).

3. "We shall use the term *popular subject position* to refer to the position that is constituted on the basis of dividing the political space into two antagonistic camps; and *democratic subject position* to refer to the locus of a clearly delimited antagonism which does not divide society in that way" (Laclau and Mouffe 131). The use that might be given to the first category may refer either to class origin or to class ideology (or ideology for a class).

4. "As more people arrive in Indiantown from different Guatemala Mayan communities, a sense of Pan-Mayanism is emerging. In an important sense, Indiantown is a place where Guatemalan Maya have become American Maya who take their place alongside other ethnic groups that are economically tied to the low paying jobs in migrant agriculture and construction" (Burns 131). Indiantown is in Florida.

5. ". . . any hegemony is not only an articulation of positionalities: it is an articulation of positions in a field furrowed by antagonisms" (Laclau, *Tesis* 23). And it is also furrowed by negotiations of those antagonisms.

6. "Those clothes were not, and could not be, pre-Hispanic. Not only because this is proven by colonial documents, but because many of their garments are of European origin, as are many of their ornamental motifs and resources, and because some of their materials were elaborated or imported after the Conquest—wool, silk, etc. Nor can it be affirmed that such clothing is Hispanic. First, because many of their clothes were made then as they are partially manufactured today, with autochthonous instruments and techniques. Second, because in the Indian attire there appear garments which belong to the pre-Hispanic attire. Third, because colonial documentation reveals that the transformation of Indian apparel was very slow" (Martínez Peláez 605-6).

7. "The central problem of today's global interactions is the tension between cultural homogenization and cultural heterogenization. Most often, the

homogenization argument subspeciates into either an argument about Americanization, or an argument about 'commoditization,' and very often the two arguments are closely linked. What these arguments fail to consider is that at least as rapidly as forces from various metropolises are brought into new societies, they tend to become indigenized in one or other way. The dynamics of such indigenization have just begun to be explored in a sophisticated manner. But it is worth noting that for the people of Irian Jaya, Indionesianisation may be more worrisome than Americanization . . . " (Appadurai 295).

8. In a newspaper article I alluded to the topic of "the small streetcorner stores," selling groceries and various products, which today constitute an expanding business almost exclusively controlled by Indians.

9. "The difference between the slum kids of Medellin who consume punk rock and the unemployed British working-class youth on the dole who invented it is not all that significant in class (or linguistic or musical) terms. They are both part of a postfordist transnational subproletariat in formation" (Beverley 7-8).

10. In fact, the clothing as well as the visible behaviors and consumptions, for example at the video games arcade in the historical center, show that those conglomerates already fully participate in some elements of the "obscenity" which Baudrillard assigns to the "ecstasy" in which electronic communication plunges us, since, if their dress and other habits denote that they watch television commercials, they must also be watching *El show de Cristina* and other talk shows more or less revealing of the middle-class domestic intimacy: "the spectacle, even if alienated, is never obscene. Obscenity begins when there is no more spectacle . . . when everything becomes immediately transparent, visible, exposed in the raw and inexorable light of information and communication . . . We are in the ecstasy of communication. And this ecstasy is obscene. Obscene is that which eliminates the gaze, the image and every representation . . . It is no longer the obscenity of the hidden, the repressed, the obscure, but that of the visible, the all-too-visible, the more-visible-than-visible" (Baudrillard 21-22). It would be interesting to find out how much those conglomerates find themselves in the alienation and/or the ecstasy of communication and how much the mass media-based simulacra and its "obscene" exposure constitute central elements of their hybrid identities, which, in general, are negotiated in the environment of delinquency.

11. It was the social worker Lizeth Jiménez who introduced me to the community of San Lucas and the local authorities. The work she did there before my visit and her knowledge of the place facilitated my interpretation of consumptions and indigenous cultural hybridizations.

12. ". . . television only *functions* as it assumes—and by assuming it legitimizes—the demands from the groups of receivers; but in turn, it cannot legitimize those demands without resignifying them as functions of the hegemonic social discourse" (Martín Barbero 20).

13. "Many social and political movements put absolute value on the original territory of ethnic groups and nations, affirming dogmatically biological and telluric traits associated with that origin, as if they were alien to historical vicissitudes and contemporary changes. In the interethnic and international conflicts we find obstinate tendencies to conceive each identity as a hard nucleus, compact and resistant; consequently, they demand absolute loyalty from the members of each group and demonize those who exercise criticism or dissidence. Defense of purity, in many countries, is imposed upon those modern currents seeking to relativize the specificity of each ethnic and nation group in order to construct democratic forms of

multicultural cohabitation, complementation and governability" (García Canclini 92).

14. "Macondo has become a catchword, alluding to all that we do not understand or do not know or that surprises us by its novelty. Moreover, a catchword that helps us remember what we want to continue dreaming with when 'we are no longer what we wanted to be' . . . From there, *Macondism* has extended, together with the Boom, among a sector of Latin American intelligentsia that does not want to renounce making America a land of promised wonders. The land of dreams and utopias; the new world out of which an 'alternative rationality' will emerge for the West, divested of its instrumental, Protestant and Faustian character of the rationality-axis of Modernity" (Brunner 52-53).

I personally believe that Latin America can be thought of as the utopian space for the emergence of an alternative rationality, without falling into the colonized coordinates of *Macondism*, if we start by giving our interculturality a different way out than that of *Multiculturalism*, by promoting the democratization of the processes of hybridization and negotiation of identities toward the constitution of an intercultural *mestizaje*, created in the process of free and equalitarian practice of cultural inter- and intraethnic differences.

15. "From the most political and voluntarist aspects of Gramscian thought, a hardly verifiable autonomy and resistance of the popular classes was proclaimed. Much of the research became a biased register of acts in which the popular sectors would give continuity to their traditions in opposition to hegemonic ideology and politics . . . The defeat of popular movements during the last years poses, at the center of the debate, a question ignored by those who base their research and their political practices in this hypothesis of popular autonomy associated with a revolutionary or insurrectional voluntarism. The question is, why do subaltern classes collaborate so often with their oppressors? Why do they vote for them in elections, and form alliances with them in everyday life and in political confrontations?" (García Canclini 173). In the case of Guatemala, it would be very interesting to investigate the phenomenon of Ríos Montt, particularly related to the presidential elections of November 1995, when his party—the FRG (Frente Republicano Guatemalteco)—was left in second place and competed in the second round, on January 7, 1996, against the right-wing neoliberal party—the PAN (Partido de Avanzada Nacional)—which won the first round and ultimately also the second round, thus establishing an opposition between an extremist right and the right-wing favoring private enterprise and privatization. The popularity of Ríos Montt continues unabated after the signing of the peace agreements in December 1996, particularly among the indigenous communities where the armed struggle was most intense and where most people died in the counterinsurgency war unleashed by this Evangelical general. [In January 2000, Montt's party won the second round and is now in power, wreaking havoc on the country, writes Morales in February 2001. Editor's Note].

16. "We are a community great in culture, with plenty of beauty. If we all become ladinos, whom are the intellectuals going to watch?" (Tezahuic 7).

17. "As in Fanon's version of the master/slave dialectic, as in postmodern theory, resistance, if it is ever to be conceptualized effectively in the current period, must be generated at the interior of the very discourses which make its articulation most problematic . . . we look to the collage of Latin America as a constructivist combinational system that points toward original oppositions, political articulations, and sources of creative possibility" (Marc Zimmerman 87-88).

Works Cited

Appadurai, Arjun. "Disjuncture and Difference in the Global Cultural Economy." *Theory, Culture & Society*. Vol. 7. London: SAGE, 1990.

Ashworth, G. J. "From History to Heritage - From Heritage to Identity. In Search of Concepts and Models." G. J. Ashworth and P. J. Jarkman, eds. *Tourism, Culture and Identity in the New Europe*. London-New York: Routlege, 1994. 13-29.

Bastos, Santiago and Manuela Camus. "Indígenas en la ciudad de Guatemala: Subsistencia y cambio étnico." *Debate*, 6. Guatemala: FLACSO, 1990.

_____. *Los mayas de la capital: Un estudio sobre identidad étnica y mundo urbano*. Guatemala: FLACSO, 1995.

Batres Jáuregui, Antonio. *Vicios del lenguaje y provincialismos de Guatemala*. Guatemala: Encuadernación y Tipografía Nacional, 1982.

Baudrillard, Jean. *The Ecstasy of Communication*. New York: Columbia UP, 1988.

Beverley, John. *Against Literature*. Minneapolis: U of Minnesota P, 1993.

Bhabha, Homi. *The Location of Culture*. London-New York: Routlege, 1994.

Brunner, José Joaquín. *América Latina: Cultura y modernidad*. México: Grijalbo, 1992.

Burgos Debray, Elizabeth. *Me llamo Rigoberta Menchú*. La Habana: Casa de las Américas, 1984.

Bums, Allan F. *Maya in Exile: Guatemalans in Florida*. Philadelphia: Temple UP, 1993.

De Lión, Luis. *El tiempo principia en Xibalbá*. Guatemala: Editorial Cultura, 1996.

Fuentes y Guzmán, Francisco Antonio de. *Recordación Florida*. Madrid: Luis Navarro Editor, 1882.

Garcia Canclini, Néstor. *Consumidores y ciudadanos. Conflictos multiculturales de la globalización*. México: Grijalbo, 1995.

Jameson, Fredric. "Postmodemism or The Cultural Logic of Late Capitalism." *New Left Review* 146 (1989): 53-92.

Laclau, Ernesto and Chantal Mouffe. *Hegemony & Socialist Strategy. Towards a Radical Democratic Politics*. London: Verso, 1985.

Laclau, Ernesto. "Tesis acerca de la forma hegemónica en la política." In Julio Labastida Martín del Campo, coord. *Hegemonía y alternativas políticas én América Latina*. México: Siglo XXI, 1985.

Levenson, Deborah. "Por sí mismos: un estudio preliminar de las 'maras' en la ciudad de Guatemala." *Cuadernos de investigación*, 4. Guatemala: AVANSCO, 1988.

Martín Barbero, Jesús. "El proyecto: producción, composición y usos del melodrama televisivo." In Jesús Martín Barbero, and Sonia Muñoz, coord. *Televisión y melodrama*. Bogotá: Tercer Mundo Editores, 1992.

Martínez Peláez, Severo. *La patria del criollo*. Guatemala: Editorial Universitaria, 1970.

Menchú, Rigoberta, Dante Liano and Gianni Minà. *Rigoberta: la nieta de los mayas*. Madrid:

Aguilar, 1998 (*Crossing Borders: Rigoberta Menchú*. Trans. and ed. Ann Wright. London-New York: Verso, 1998).

Mendelson, E. Michael. *Los escándalos de Maximón. Un estudio sobre la religión y la visión del mundo en Santiago Atitlán*. Guatemala: Tipografía Nacional, 1965.

Milla, José. *El visitador*. Guatemala: Piedra Santa, 1977.

Morales, Mario Roberto. "Las explosivas tiendecitas de la esquina." *Siglo Veintiuno* (Guatemala June 7, 1996).

Rowe, William and Vivian Schelling. *Memory and Modernity. Popular Culture in Latin America*. London: Verso, 1991.

Sarlo, Beatriz. *Escenas de pudor y liviandad*. Buenos Aires: Ariel, 1994.

Tezahuic, Francisco. "Los indígenas queremos ser hermanos de todos los guatemaltecos." Entrevista con Ursula Reyes. *Magazine 21. Siglo Veintiuno*. August 4, 1996.

Zimmerman, Marc. "Tropicalizing Hegemony in Latin America: Transculturations, Fatal Attractions, Neo Colonial Capitulations, and Postmodern Transactions." *Postmodernism and New Cultural Tendencies in Latin America*. San Francisco: San Francisco State University, 1993.

◆ **8.**

Post-Cities and Politics: New Urban Movements in the Two Americas

Armando Silva

(*translated by Mary Louise Babineau*)

Introduction: Post-Ideological Origins

In the past twenty years, important and at times imperceptible events have occurred in urban behavior and in the construction of cities in the two Americas. This set of events presages the consolidation of two urban forms, and at the same time gives way to logistical foundations; at least it would seem that each one grows in fear of being assimilated by the other and for this reason they are essentially indebted to one another. I believe the cities being built presently in the U.S., in particular in southern California, to be authentic "post-cities" in the sense that they represent what comes after centrally and historically organized modern urban life; that is, they have become a new regime of exacerbating corporate planning. Meanwhile, I prefer to interpret what is being experienced in various South American cities as a "trans-city" phenomenon in the sense that they correspond to cross sections of the various simultaneous influences under which the metropolises grow, without having resolved their previous historical stages, and in which their refounding characteristic is to develop amidst urban chaos. This has led them to assimilate all that they embrace in their unconstrained growth, whether in terms of their physical size or their precipitate and fierce assimilation of new technology.

However, in both the U.S. post-cities and the South American trans-cities, new practices have appeared within different sectors—sectors which had lived before in anonymity, such as mothers, women or the middle-class youth—and these practices have assumed the city with its social and political connections in a new way. Such experiences are accompanied by resources that in a more general sense could be described as postmodern, as they transform street spectacles or the use of media into their new space of confrontation and vindication; and irony, jokes or cynicism into their instruments of struggle which are then interwoven with old ways of confronting authority. This paper proposes a reading of some of these new movements which converge as the result of esthetic concerns other than those related to the harmony of parts. They participate, rather, in the strange rituals that have summoned other citizens to witness a certain rebirth of popular opinion with which to debut the next millennium. Urban postmodernism advances by way of incorporating new strategies of resistence and representation alongside the growth and development of global society's media and technology. We can glimpse some disturbing efficacies proclaimed by postmodernists within the very dry and rigid organizations of present technocratic societies for the economic globalization, cultural postmodernism, and social technocracy to be understood as mutually supporting and interactive terms.

I begin by presenting a few Latin American practices that have brought about an extraordinary political effectiveness, and then concentrate on certain experiences within United States' metropolises that in turn have revealed what is meant by the authentic post-city project: a Republican utopia conceived in the United States to combat the growing urban disorder within central metropolises.

New Political Practices

Visual Rituals of the Madres de Mayo in Argentina

To begin, I think that the extent of symbolic resistance which occurred in Argentina after the 24th of March, 1976—when the process of "National Reorganization" was initiated by the Military Junta after the coup d'état—is exemplary, and as such has become a model for other ludic experiences within the continent. While the Junta was in power, the citizens were suspected of being subversives. The Junta attempted to reorient the Argentine society beneath the slogan: a change of mentality. Nothing more, nothing less. In doing so, the same Junta introduced various imaginary components which, in light of the reaction that they caused, are worth taking into account.

Perhaps visual forms of denouncement would not have reached, as in the Argentina of that time, the colossal dimension that Miriam Casco conceives it to have had (according to a list that I take upon myself to update), since they encompassed nearly an entire civil society in rituals that projected the construction of a collective image of the citizenry. Faced with the impossibility of having their demands heard by traditional means—courts, precincts, etc.—the relatives of the disappeared began creating alternative ways to demand an explanation from the dictatorship within the only space which allowed them to be heard: the street. The situation is original. When faced with an imposed silence by the dictatorship, the mothers respond in kind: they do not speak. They seek to demonstrate their real presence, undisappeared.

The mothers' rounds of the *Pirámide*—a national monument which recalls the struggle for independence from Spain—were situated in the center of the *Plaza de Mayo*, famous for being the center of important labor union and popular protests. The rounds are rituals intended to show their presence, to appear as though dancing alone in silence. There they appear every Thursday at four in the afternoon, like ghosts that have grown old. Now they are not mothers but grandmothers. Let us recall that a general baptized them "the crazy women of the *Plaza de Mayo*," an incredible urban metaphor to discredit the rationality of a protest. "The rounds are doubly effective: they mock censorship since their demonstrations speak, but they also insert themselves within the urban landscape, establishing their presence. The passer-by sees them." He has to see them. They make themselves seen and cause a disturbance in the street.

The mothers wear a triangular white handkerchief with the names of the disappeared and the date of their disappearance. When one of those handkerchiefs is found in the street, it is like graffiti or a statement of conscience. It is a performance device. The mothers used to walk with people who covered their faces with white masks, without holes, and as such their eyes remained hidden. The existing photographic documents capture the impact that is caused by masks without eyes alongside mothers with handkerchiefs on their heads, demanding their children. This theatric device is interesting; a person appears who represents, theatrically, the disappeared. The mask is a symbolic device of protest that also has archaeologic traces: they send us back to an unpleasant and unknown origin.

On the walls of Buenos Aires and in some other cities in the country, silhouettes are drawn of an approximate natural size. Within these silhouettes the names of the disappeared also appear. That is to say that by metonymy, the silhouette also takes the place of the absent. We find ourselves before an elliptic action: appearing through absence. It so happens that "if the silhouette is drawn on the ground, passers-by avoid stepping on it," out of respect for the disappeared.

In other street manifestations the *Madres* have worn posters with blown-up pictures of their loved ones that they have never seen again. This construction of collective memory exists so that the disappeared are not forgotten.

The mothers in these protest groups and in other manifestations wear photos of their children on their chests and backs. The photos are hung with pins and string, once again devices with which to revive memory. In different publications that adhered to the cause of the disappeared, pictures of the victims were published in graphic testimony of a person who does not rest in peace with their relatives. The effect is harsh and expressive. And above all, massive.

In December of 1993, in Bogotá, a poetic exercise was carried out that called to mind the silhouette strategy in the way of urban ritual: Faced with the shocking abandon in which the city has been submerged by its administrators, various groups of young people began making silhouettes of the mayor Jaime Castro. The evocative exercise continued, but in another way: The potholes in the city, which had provoked the most protest and nonconformism, were painted with distinct figures: frogs, reptiles, clowns, men in space or walking through craters on the moon. The results were outstanding. Within a few days the mayor announced a plan to pave the roads and fill the potholes. These new means of expression, which recover a certain dialogue, are based more on expressive effects than on wise speeches.

Urban Appearances in Peru, Brazil, and Venezuela

In Peru, since Fujimori's suspension of legislative power in 1993, we have witnessed some fairly spectacular acts (to put it theatrically as the facts well merit). Abimael Guzmán, *President Gonzalo*, was captured and appeared in a press conference as a caged tiger. His black and white horizontally striped outfit represented a prisoner's traditional zebra outfit, however due to its exaggerated colors and dimensions it became ridiculous and mocking. The discussions concerning his terrorist acts which forced him to speak and defend himself were promoted by government personnel and presented as spontaneous citizen criticism.

It was actually a ritual, duly rehearsed and presented to the media like a play, through which President Fujimori sought revenge not only against the violent and ruthless actions of guerrilla fighters, but also against the esthetic exercises of the *senderistas*. These included turning off all lights in Lima so that the inhabitants feel the darkness, and hiding their faces and vanishing after having carried out military action.

The Peruvian writer Abelardo Sánchez proposes some new arrivals on Peru's urban iconography which I will reelaborate presently with observations that I have been making about Colombia: television animators, informal sector workers, drug dealers, subversives, and kidnappers.

All of the previous characters possess certain common traits in that they lack mediators, but have a strong presence in the cultural life in Lima and other Peruvian cities. These are characters that refute the ideal model of the educated, well-mannered, and frenchified middle-class that is moved by, shall we say, an educated imaginary. "The image of a robust mestizo adorned with a loose-fitting shirt (*guayabera*), a moustache, and sideburns inside a brand new vehicle is widely propagated. Furthermore: there could not be a mestizo with money unless he were a drug dealer."

One must recognize that these characters appear in Latin America in the midst of social chaos. It is also true that the media, driven by the facts, must record them. The so-called informal sector workers appear permanently in labor strikes or different acts within the city. Soap operas and other television programs infinitely portray and recreate them. At this point I think that the popular sectors are favored by the quantitative measures spurred into action by the North American company Nielsen: To the extent that there is a greater popular sector, most of the programming is directed toward it as it represents the greatest number of televisions in use.

What is certain is that in Lima—perhaps more than in any other city in those countries characterized by the greatest violent conflict in Latin America—"the forgotten" (*los olvidados*), as Buñuel would say, make themselves heard and felt. Even guerrilla strategies, like those of the *senderistas*, touch upon symbolic elements such as turning out the lights so that the path may appear. The group of poor who became rich and make themselves noticed in the streets is very clear in cities such as Cochabamba, Cuenca in Ecuador, Medellín, Lima, and Cali. In time these suggestive phenomena must be analyzed, because although they have always been seen as a problem of public order, it is tempting to understand other such exercises as cultural, social, and esthetic facts. A number of these new characters do not allow themselves to be seen in order to stand out by their absence (elipsis), or on the contrary they mark their presence emphatically, as occurs in Bogotá on Sundays when popular sectors occupy Seventh Avenue.

But to make one's presence seen and felt in the media is not strictly a subversive act. Peru's television is one of the most dominated by popular culture on the continent, and one may be surprised by its take on the most marginal sectors in contest, and in programs of opinion and of humor. Through this media one can see their appearance, their clothing, and their colors, all within an environment that is part rural and part urban. This creates the sensation of a popular avalanche, especially if one compares it to the appearance of the well-educated and well represented by television in neighboring countries: Colombia and Venezuela, the beauty queen countries.

One must also consider, along with the esthetic, a political analysis of the new authoritarianism behind the marginal presence in Andean countries. Abilio Vergara points out this authoritarianism in present-day Peru. Both Abimael Guzmán's April 9, 1980 speech, one month before beginning his armed struggle, and President Fujimori's speech when he addressed the nation after the auto-coup on February 6th, 1993, were titled "We Are the Initiators." In both cases the violent epithets, hierarchical and excluding, are forms of authoritarianism. These discourses "function as plans for action and they are characteristic of political discourse, especially that of the authoritarian: a daily attempt to instill order in not only the words, but also the actions, of civilians. It is desired that this discourse be not only a model for other discourses, but rather that it replace them." Thus, we find ourselves once again before the excluded Other, in the midst of an environment of publicized international plurality.

In Brazil, the fall of Collor de Melo was preceded by youth manifestations that succeeded in transforming various carnival events into a party opposing a president accused of corruption. Without violence, by means of marches, hullabaloos, and street games, the accused had to endure the avalanche of criticism imparted through humor and sarcasm. Traditional graffiti gave way to notices with the motto *fuora Color* attached to peoples' bodies, clothing, or on tape that sealed peoples' mouths. In this case the party was organized by the people, mainly from the middle-class sectors.

A similar case occurred in Venezuela, where not only did young students from secondary schools and universities reunite and attack government representatives and the military with stones, but they were also joined by another force. Housewives banged pots together to produce irritating sounds, reminding president Pérez that economic development is worthless without social well-being, and finally overthrowing him.

The cases of Brazil and Venezuela are significant within the context of the expression of urban protest in Latin America. They represent two relatively stable and wealthy countries without any recent history of popular struggle. But their kinds of struggle are also novel, touching on symbolic rather than violent aspects. They also represent a connection between the majority of popular sectors, the media, and on occasion even some elite sectors, which all together demanded the resignation of their governors. The great marches, the festive ambiance, and the participation of young people teach a lesson on the ways in which our civil society is mobilized, especially for those official politicians and leftists who consider popular participation to be an obligation that does not include ethical commitments nor aesthetic provocations. For this reason union and revolutionary manifestations which were carried out by means of flamboyant speeches and street parades have been replaced. New actors appear with other innovative languages.

Trans-Cities and the Emblem of the Circus

Latin America, where a number of the biggest cities of the world are located, is by very definition characterized by multitudes and by excesses of people. Human bodies live daily with the sense of being squeezed and stretched. The human body in the southern continent is amalgamated, tumultuous, assaulted, tired, surrounded by all sorts of sounds and shouts, street-sellers, the noise of cars, and every imaginable kind of obstacle and inconvenience. It is not the kind of cared-for and solitary body that I will consider next; perhaps its speed is more like that of an obstacle course, proceeding by fits and starts. Their city streets are overused and instead of immaculate order, one lives in a permanent state of chaos that has now become a daily threat. There is something different about the Californian post-city built by corporations among deserts and isolated areas only connected by automotive routes, electronic registers and nets, when compared to those concentrated conglomerates of Latin American cities. The latter I propose be understood as trans-cities, where urban areas sprawl out unplanned, growing and spreading at will, taking over a number of rural zones, and where the city becomes a particularly imaginary adventure.

One of the most cited experiences in Latin America, which has as a distant model the *Madres de Mayo* in Argentina, occurred in Bogotá, when in 1994 a university professor became mayor and promised to change the city by means of the use and exhibition of symbols of his own invention framed within an educative-city proposal. At the end of his term however, it seemed that the symbolic sources that inspired him did not produce the proposed results. Nonetheless, his new way of doing politics has had repercussions in other Colombian cities as well as in other countries within the continent.

When Antanas Mockus was nominated as mayor I cautioned that he had succeeded in arriving at this position because he knew how to create the illusion of not being real: a mayor born of actual fiction. His tactical problem, as I understood it, was to convince us that he could be real, but not so much so as his spited predecessors. Mockus entered the mayor's office with tremendous popularity, and in particular with two characteristics which civilians attributed to him. Firstly, he did not belong to the political class and, therefore, was not a thief. And secondly, he was irreverent, different, came from a university ghetto, and had the conceit of an artist. His platform was based on education. But the city that he directed (and continues to manage today as ex-mayor) is mental, theoretical, and its ambition is epistemological, if you will. It involves changing reality, the harsh Bogotá reality, by means of mental exercises that lead us to an ideal and magnificent city. Mockus is an idealist. But also a mental provoker. His path as a provoker (and no longer an agitator) worked to a certain degree until, it seems to me, he became tangled up in his own circus. Before, when he pulled his pants down in front of his hecklers and showed them his bottom naked, all this on television, his actions unleashed the most powerful graffiti in the Colombia of that time as a result of the scandal that it caused within the ruling class, which rejected him with bitter moral comments, even asking for his resignation as rector. The result was the following university graffiti: "While this country crumbles down the President doesn't give a stitch."[1] But his boldness bit its own tail, and a most irritating antisymbol was recorded when he was married in a circus.

The circus is a symbol: the protagonist, the mayor himself; the audience, the citizens. It does not cease to be strange that a mayor should be married there and that he summon the people like submissive subjects to come and adore him. But, what violation is this? Why does an educated mayor who bases his government on a civic education program summon his citizens to a circus? At the very least one could recognize a type of exhibitionism: the pleasure of being looked at by others (transposing), and a private act made public (the wedding) constitutes perverse behavior. We find ourselves before a narcissistic exhibition; a return to what Freud called primary narcissism, when the child discovers the figure of the Other, his mother at first, to be admired. In addition to psychological motives we also find ourselves before another social conduct, the eruption of the private into the public, the making of a private act into an occurrence for collective memory. In other words, it is to situate someone, a public official himself, as a public object. To go to the circus—a territory quintessentially representative of the people's tradition, a place where modes of expression include laughter and jokes packaged in magic and happiness, where lions, tigers, and elephants impress by their savage imposition, clowns pretend to fall in order to make us laugh, and magicians alter our perception of the world and of the laws of credibility—is different from the mayor's circus because instead of this ambiguous perception between the playful and the fantastic, he placed himself in the center of the spectacle as a reality to be imagined. As an example of one of his daring episodes, his entrance mounted on an elephant with the sign "just married" (emulating the gringo's just married) was neither a violation nor an alternative, because the truth is that he was getting married: it is reality itself that does not even succeed in being presented as ironic because its reference, the act of getting married, was taking place and therefore the act (perlocutive of language) had its effect on the action. It seems to me that pretending to fall, as clowns do, is the opposite of simulating that one is not pretending. Better said, Mockus's circus did not appear to erupt in order to represent an aesthetic or enchanting city; it was rather more like an anti-circus, because it denied the very base of the circus: it created the illusion that the outside world (that of the city) can suspend itself with a magic wand. Therefore, it made of the outside city a faithful representation of what is inside the tent: a circus. What I could imagine, i.e. the world of the circus as a metaphor for another city, is now hopelessly lost: the mayor, who is the official voice and image of the city, is converted into an agent and protagonist of the circus, displacing its actors. And what is left as a lesson for the outside city is to live chaotically, like a sad circus with no real magic. Would the circus be, rather, a mask to distract or hide what is really out there?

Antanas's circus became his great synthetic image; the different acts in which he appeared, his superman costume, his priestly attire, and even his street mimes well demonstrated it. But it was also his great lapsus where private gesture makes itself evident and is not assumed to be a social response. His bursts and installations have not had the shock that was produced in Irvine by a defecating ghost who, as I will examine further along, succeeded overwhelmingly in converting his physical action into the social testimony of an ideology, racist and plastic like Disney, that scorns whomever should enter into contact with its unique organization. In the case of Bogotá, what kind of profound imaginary has brought the city's people to seek a mayor-installer to take them out of the chaos and corruption that reign in their cities? In principle, one would believe that what is sought is the exact opposite of chaos and disorder. What disorder demands, at least it was believed, is the law. We have already been living in a circus for a long time. Instead of a father, the mayor presented himself to us as a good brother. This sense of brotherhood, daringly playful and above all horizontal, characterized our mayor. And here the paradox arises between knowing whether or not the people of Bogotá, in an authentic postmodern gesture, incited their mayor to be a friend and thus to participate in their love of disorder in order to experience such an explosive encounter with their leader, or whether we have another means to reach order by the accentuation rather than the negation of circus life. In this way the circus would be a paradigm of chaotic urban life, but in this way desired or at least accommodated.

The Post-Cities of the Other America and the Emblem of Disney

The founding of various cities in the south of California barely forty years ago was preceded by certain propaganda in keeping with new desires to create an authentic metropolis as close to perfection as possible. Such is demonstrated in a governmentally generated text:

"Orange County is the closest thing to the movies, to a dream . . . its cars are new, its stores, schools and mountains are also new. Even the land and the ocean look new. There is no other place more like your new home than Orange County." Within the various small cities that compose Orange County, there is one in particular that stands out for its sense of hygiene and efficiency. It is Irvine, one of the first corporate cities in the history of humankind, "thought of as a model for the future development of Western Civilization" by companies such as the Irvine Company, Mobil Oil Corporation, Henry Ford II and others, according to what was stated in Fortune magazine (December 1989) by Senator Zalamic. The Irvine family still maintains close to fifty percent of the property of the city, and also owns a lifestyle and manages a new Republican utopia that combines, politically, a certain socialist, fascist, and capitalist democratic regime. The authoritarian regime can be noticed by whomever lives there. The colors of the houses are limited to only three variations of pastel renaissance invocations; in some areas houses are sold without the land, which continues to be the company's property; grass must be cut to the same height in the entire city; traffic zones are strictly marked, and commercial zones and their destinies were determined from the very beginning. The official propaganda by the Chamber of Commerce invites one to live in Irvine, the "city where fear is not a part of your daily life."

Thus, the original plan is converted into a regulated document in which at any moment one's neighbor stands out if they do not adhere to strict citizen behavior. The golden rule everyone must know is this: Work defines the urban. One could be tempted to transform the Marxist maxim, stating that religion is the opiate of the masses, into a new and very Californian one: Work is everything, including God (something like the passion of daily life). Alongside work, industry develops its support mechanisms. The most valuable object of all is the actual human body. But in Orange County the body is only an extension of work. It is maintained to improve production. Going to the gym is converted into something of a religious practice. One gets up early in the morning and discovers various athletic bodies in search of earthly purity; women and men running, often desperate because of some extra kilo that may quickly be censured. The body deserves attention, and the most successful industry—after the electronics industry—is perhaps the one that sells exercise for every anatomical part, age and moment, because the body is presented in perfect fragmentation just like the city. It is not by chance that elderly people do not live in Irvine, as their bodies do not present the vitality and challenge that this city demands of young athletes.

After the human body, another element that satisfies—the spirit this time—is religion. Everyone adheres to a religion, sect, or belief: Any means is optimal to speak with God. It is not odd that the only promoters who can roam easily within closed areas, like the university campus, are the brothers of all religions who come to invite everyone to readings from their sacred books. Religion, like the body, is another ally of the painstaking truth. A healthy and well-intentioned person presides. The absence of God in Irvine could be suspicious. Atheists have no place, because part of social control is exerted by churches. The political theme *par excellence* is that of migrations, and in the end Irvine is made up of foreigners. As can be seen, only a dominant race which is "no other than the white race" can possess so much purity, because what is being valued as legitimate are the first migrations. Those that came afterwards—the Asian, the Latin—are out of place, although to varying degrees. The Asians are better assimilated than the Latins—or, more precisely, the Mexicans—for various reasons that can be synthesized as follows: Asians work, are quiet, do not protest, are more willing to forget their country of origin and when they are rich, and like some of the Koreans who arrived after the poor Vietnamese, they bring new money. The Mexicans are the opposite. They do not forget their homeland, are poor, insist on speaking Spanish and, in addition, it is a historical fact that they are the true owners of California. Thus, what arises in California as a consequence of this purist and excluding ideology is an enormous wall to defend oneself against the Mexicans, a wall which began being built in February of 1996 on the eve of presidential elections, which served to demonstrate the political magnitude of this hot topic.

The idea of a dominant white culture is not accidental, but rather it sets "color as ethnicity against white as transparency," as stated by Dean MacCannell. The result is a form of racism that is perhaps not obvious, but constitutes part of what I call the original plan which only legitimizes whites or those who are not white but who adapt to their way of being, because being white is not so much a question of race as it is a cultural invocation. Any undesirable conduct is immediately associated with the Other, as has occurred in the pathetic story of the "anonymous defecator" and urban installer who has driven the authorities of the Irvine university campus crazy in their efforts to identify him as a criminal. In tracing their proceedings, we can expose clear ideological differences among the perceptions of the inhabitants, classify them, and use science and technology for puritanical detective purposes. Let us examine the juicy story.

Since the end of 1995 loose samples of feces began to appear in different locations on campus. This continued in spite of being brought to public attention several times by the community newspaper, *Verano Gazette*, edited by the administration. Little by little the complaints increased as the defecating ghost could not be found. On the contrary, the aforementioned discovered new locations that some mornings appeared more disgusting than others. In the January 26th, 1996 edition, in an extra issue in Spanish, Chinese, and

Vietnamese (the three poor groups that reside there, in spite of the fact that many other languages are spoken on campus), a message entitled URGENT appeared. The Spanish part states: "Someone has been defecating . . . we request your immediate cooperation to put a stop to this unacceptable behavior." In the February 2nd edition, some results are shown from laboratories and from continuous and systematic observation carried out by social scientists. They wrote the following: "Reports on the excrements indicate that the time of defecation varies, but the majority of the deposits occur in the morning. The feces are now covered with napkins or bathroom tissue, decorating their shape: the majority have been located in the following places . . . We still do not know if they are specimens from children or adults, some are very long and others are very small." But what followed was even more telling. The administration office arrived at a conclusion which could not be published due to the results: The defecator was identified as Asian. The laboratory had found the remains of vegetables which Asians consume. In addition, the very elongated shape of the feces signaled an Asian diet that cleanses the stomach with vegetables. The next step consisted in inventing a chemical that would explode so as to attack the anonymous defecator's private parts when he did his deed, leaving him with an itch that would make his illicit act unpleasant. They also considered installing hidden television cameras to prevent future defecation by people who might have been be inspired by the success of the elusive original offender.

The World of Disney: the Clean and Orderly City. Smile for the Camera

There would be a model to better understand these new urban formations where the body is commercialized, religion is translated into concrete fantasy, and happiness—although without lasting pleasure—is the offer for admission. It is Disney. To say "I'm going to Disney World," is like saying one is going to the world of pleasure. Disney is the utopia of pleasure and of well-being. The garden city would be the physical paradigm that presages the Disney space: the theme city as studied by Michel Sorkis. The idea of a garden city appears first in Europe, presented initially by Ebenezer Howard in 1902 in a revolt against the Le Corbusier city, which is considered to be an icon of alienation and uncleanliness due to its industry and pollution. Disney is organized around a center which it produces itself, "occupied by the totemic castle of fantasy." Its spaces are organized by specific themes: Tomorrowland, Adventureland, Fantasyland, etc. In turn, everything is made not for comfort, but to be bought and consumed. The citadel belongs to a global marketplace, but especially for the sale of Disney's own products. There are perhaps three characteristics of Disney that can be traced back to the new post-cities: its relationship to space, its sense of cinematography, and the absence of conflict in its daily life.

The Disney in Orlando, as well as the one in Anaheim, exist in a gravitational mode with the airports. For this reason, one arrives by means of the freeways—the "new ceremonial arrival from reality to fantasy"—a ritual of the runner and of velocity. And secondly, the most explicit recognition that can be given to Disney is its sense of cinematography. Cinematographic reality of pleasure, diversion, simulation, and above all a reality that is not what it used to be: it is not historic but rather that of the future. In this way, where Disney works best is in creating the utopia of a new space, a "city without geography," without a place. Perhaps this is what most likens it to the movies, and for this reason its space is imagined, with very different characteristics than the more literary spaces of Europe or Latin America. Thus, a "theme city" (I prefer to say post-city) refers to a package where various things take place as expressions of an exhibition park and of daily diversion. In a city in southern California, one generally encounters (themes such as) freeways, entrances, gas stations, fast food chains such as MacDonald's, motels such as the Holiday Inn, etc. Everyone, upon arriving at these places, believes they are repeating themselves. Businesses require that their branches have the same design. If one enters any Albertson's Superstore or Carl Junior hamburger joint, they are all are the same: the same distribution of space, restrooms in the same place, tables facing the same direction, even the employees' service and words are exactly the same. Therefore one experiences a strange sensation, as though dreaming of an image being reiterated frenetically, neurotically, and that one is but a part of this infinite repetition: the very client reproduced. This idea of perfection and repetition is reinforced by a new industry that appears in these lands: that of the friendly smile, greetings with a smile as the expression of a culture without conflict. A salesperson who does not smile for his clients can be fired in any number of these friendly businesses. Even rituals in public matters such as the driver's license photo require that one appear smiling, as anyone who reads these observations can confirm. The photographer is obligated to make sure the citizen looks happy in his license photo which, as is well known, is the United States' identification document.

Disney, in the end, like Orange County, is an urbanism that does not produce a city as described by M. Sorkis. In terms of nomadic cities it is one of citizens in passing, citizens but not residents. Citizens who buy and who travel on their freeways many times daily, but without a guaranteed space. Citizens who were previously cut off from public space, because what was public is now corporate. And that which is usually called public space, for the use and enjoyment of all—sidewalks, streets, urban furniture, public transportation—does not have a social function in the new city. It also must be recognized that functional and productive efficiency is evident in these post-cities. In Irvine, things undoubtedly work: Bureaucracy functions, cars move and people are decent. Is that what humanity wants? If this is so, the future has already begun. The rest is learning how it is done. Irvine is the perfect model, there is no doubt about it. If you, the citizen, seek perfection, it is waiting for you there. That city, desired by many, already has a name and is starting to be imitated in many metropolises, including parts of Mexico City, Santiago, São Paolo, Guayaquil, Caracas, Bogotá, or even Buenos Aires and others within the continent. Post-cities no longer suggest urbanization, but rather an "Irvinization" of the world. Welcome semicitizens: the disorder has ended. The defecator that I described previously can be understood in this context as an anonymous and vengeful person who succeeded by means of his actions in stripping white purism: He put color in the *caca*, revealing a fascist ideology.

The post-city lives within and outside of itself, since if something is impoverished in actual urban societies, that place is no longer associated with geographic space. As such, the "post" and "trans" envelop and run through us simultaneously in the different functions of daily life. I conclude by saying that the two types of cities that I have described are becoming surrounding utopias fed by different objectives: in one, the post-city, the northern city, there is an excess of reality while the other, the trans-city, the southern city, is dominated by an imaginary projection which tends to embrace itself. But both are being redefined and have been intermixed in the past few years as a final hope. And the hope is to establish a new urban utopia to bring in the next millennium.

Note

1. Original "mientras el país se derrumba al presidente le importa un culo" plays on ambiguity: *importar un culo* would normally mean "not to give a damn" about something; but in the context of Mockus's provocation and the ensuing scandal in which the president of the Republic had to intervene, the literal meaning also comes out ('to be concerned about an ass'). [Editor's Note].

◆ **9.**

Modern and Postmodern Aesthetics in Contemporary Argentine Theater (1985-1997)

Osvaldo Pelletieri

(*translated by Mary Louise Babineau*)

Introduction

Fredric Jameson (1991: 18) has pointed out that Postmodernism in central countries is the dominant cultural feature of late capitalism. Therefore, one must question: In Latin America, in Argentina, what is it? Could there exist such a thing as a Postmodernism of the excluded or, in any case, of those on the fringe of Postmodernism? Would it be part of our chronic dependency? Could it be like the obsolete technology or the discarded drugs that we invariably receive? Will the same thing happen with Postmodernity that already has occurred with the modernization we have generally accepted without criticism, ceasing to be what we were in order to become like others? Will we be able to ignore it, refusing to recognize growing globalization?

In Buenos Aires—as had occurred previously with the modernization of theater in the thirties and in the sixties—Postmodernism has been met during the past ten years enthusiastically and without criticism by the so-called emerging sectors, and with strong resistance by those sectors associated with the "theater of art" or "modern social theater," heir to the Independent Theater (1930-1969).

The objective of this paper is to analyze the evolution of this esthetic and ideological trend—the renowned postmodern condition—and to observe its indigent condition at a social and theatrical level. In Argentina, this indigence has a strong historical emphasis because our theater has always been "displaced," "peripheral" and "marginal." This paper, which attempts to read this phenomenon from within our own theatrical system, includes a final diagnosis of this trend which is already advanced in its initial stages.

The study of our theatrical system includes its attempts at rupture and continuity. We will focus on its productivity, not ignoring the phenomenon of productive reception, but placing an emphasis on our theater's ability to produce its own dynamic. We believe this clarification to be pertinent because the majority of the analyses that approach this topic do so from the Euro-North American intertext only, underestimating, regrettably, the peculiarity of our theater.

Antecedents

In the thirties and then in the sixties, two modernizations occurred within Argentine theater (Pellettieri 1997). Both gave way to what we call "marginal Modernity" because it remained on the fringes of European Modernity, and its peculiarity was that it did not generate an avant-garde which sought to include theater within its social practices (Bürger). Its failure—contrary to what occurred with the theatric avant-garde of central countries, which consisted of not having been able to break the esthetic institution—was partial. It triumphed in having created in Buenos Aires and in other cities the "theater of art," but it was defeated because it was not able to fulfill the social utopia that sustained it. This utopia involved changing society, the country, through the practice of social theater. On the contrary, as the years went by critics, the institution, the tastes of the bourgeois public and the official artists, tamed social modernism. They crystallized it, taking away its aggressive attitude and leaving only gestures of its previous belligerency. This taming experienced its canonical moment when Kive Staiff was hired as director of the General San Martín Municipal Theater during the *Proceso* (1976-1983), that created a cultural island amidst the political and social horror.

On the other hand, in both the first and second modernizations of our theater, traditional devices and tendencies appeared blended with modern texts. Two cases can clarify our affirmation: First, in the thirties, the dramatic works of a modernizing playwright such as Roberto Arlt always had an outcome destined to prove a realist thesis; and second, during the sixties, reflexive and neoavant-garde realists could not keep their discourses from being infiltrated by costumbrist devices and even the social realism of Florencio Sánchez's drama (Pellettieri 1997: 176-77).

In the thirties and then later in the sixties, the marginal modernity of Buenos Aires' theater was primarily characterized by its presentation of a fundamental utopia: The destruction of end-of-the century models, cosmopolitanism and the emphasis on originality. According to this concept, theater was considered to be basically a testimonial and didactic phenomenon. (Pellettieri 1990)

Our Theater in the Past Thirty Years

With regard to its semantics, we can establish three moments in the evolution of our theater during the past thirty years:

1. The modern existentialist period is characterized by the practice of the semantics of alienation (1960-1967). It implied the "revolt of subjectivity against the staging of bourgeois forms, against the restrictions and rituals entrenched in the way of life" (Heller 1987/8: 22). This semantics questioned the political and social limitations of the middle class, its self-sufficiency and its members distancing themselves from reality by throwing themselves into work, politics, religion, social gatherings, etc. The period also coincided with the consolidation of reflexive realism and the absurdist neo-avant-guarde movement: "It underlines textual as well as ideological decadence, alienation, and disintegration" (Pellettieri 1997: 200).

2. The political period, of a decidedly optimistic nature in its initial stages, is characterized by the practice of the semantics of fervor for revolutionary changes (1967-1976). The majority of its creators were also involved in militancy, either with the Peronist left or simply the left. Its textuality revealed

the belief in the fact that art signified "an aid" for society in the sense of "healing" itself from its alienation. During this period, drama discovered a "redeeming" class: the popular sector. It went from negating the possibility of change—*Soledad para cuatro* (1961), by Ricardo Halac; *Nuestro fin de semana* (1964), by Roberto Cossa—to a limited hope in individual transformation and rebelion against the "sensible life" of the characters in *Hablemos a calzón quitado* (1970), by Guillermo Gentile; *Cien veces no debo* (1974), by Ricardo Talesnik or *Simón Blumenstein* (1979) by Germán Rozenmacher . . . and to the confidence in social transformations that people would achieve with their dynamics and ability to ironically unmask the bourgeois in texts such as

El avión negro (1970), by the Grupo de Autores, or *Historia tendenciosa de la clase media argentina* (1971), by Ricardo Monti (from parodic theater to the political intertext). (Pellettieri 1997: 247)

This period coincides with that of an exchange of devices between the two aforementioned modern movements: the absurdist neo-avant-guarde movement and reflexive realism.

Its second stage (1976-1985) coincided almost perfectly with the "Process of National Reorganization." It corresponds with that which we have classified as the Open Theater Cycle, which constituted the canonic moment of Argentine theatric modernity and its later transition toward epigonization. It includes the texts from the *Teatro Abierto* movement (1981-1985) and those that appeared between 1976-1985 inscribed within an esthetic ideology close to that of *Teatro Abierto*. These represented a militant theater that obliquely questioned power, using theatrical devices in an attempt to demonstrate a realist thesis, and generally parodying dictatorial power and its multiple projections within society (Pellettieri 1992a: 3-12). Both the modern existentialist and the political movements considered freedom to be something worth achieving.

3. The Postmodern Intertext Period, of a generally pessimistic nature, with variations which we will enumerate, is characterized as favoring irony and eluding denunciation. Reigadas has observed this movement which spans from 1985 to 1997 with great critical insight as national post-*Proceso* period:

based on repentance and disillusionment—but also on fear and horror due to what had been experienced—the advocacy for the "new man," the revolution and the Third World, has been substituted by democratic neoilluminism or by the growing depoliticizing in postmodern tones. (1988: 116)

We suggest that the move toward change was already present in our theatric system, in its own dynamics and authority (Pellettieri 1995: 66). Based on this concept, we note that in the seventies, marginal modernity was already being questioned. In Buenos Aires, a movement deconstructing modern theater was detained, interrupted in 1976 by the painful diaspora that the military process caused in our intellectual circles. This process of deconstruction presaged our theater of the eighties and nineties. Toward the end of the sixties, plays such as *Fuego asoma* (1969), by José María Paolantonio and Luis Verdi appear in the theater of the Torcuato Di Tella Center for Audiovisual Experimentation which was already a mixed theater where singing, dance, music, cinema, and theater came together with satirical, social and esthetic purposes.

A very clear case is that of collective creations such as *Porca miseria,* which opened in Buenos Aires in August of 1975 with the Grupo Teatro-Circo formed by Hernán González, Lorenzo Quinteros, Tina Serrano, and Rubén Szuchmacher in the theater of the CAYC. *Porca miseria* was a dramatic text—an antecedent to theater of parody and inquiry—that challenged "serious theater," and that worked with the stylization and parody of the *criollo sainete* and grotesque dramatic texts. In the search for a histrionic and caricatured theatrical effect, it did not disdain comic stock characters or verbal jokes, and it parodied the tics of modern theater. It was, at the same time, a ferocious satire of social context. The mix of genres already constituted its constructive beginning (Pellettieri 1989: 89).

With the fall of the dictatorship, another wave of questioning marginal modernity was witnessed that had to do with changes in the social context (acceptance of liberal democracy and the disappearance of the enemy which the military *Proceso* represented).

This change that took place in Buenos Aires theater responded to internal needs, and became mixed with elements from the semantics of Postmodernism (the questioning of History as "a true story," adherence to theater of resistance, predominance of nostalgia, irony, and ambiguity). To a lesser extent, it also became mixed with devices of the same trend: the favoring of parody, the assumption of a mixed culture and the inclusion of image as a base of representation.

In another sense, still concerning the contemporary situation of our theater, it is important to clarify that "postmodern theater" is an expression rarely used in intellectual circles of Buenos Aires, especially by the creators. We believe, least among ourselves, that there are not enough elements to qualify an actor, director, or author as postmodern, even though almost ten years have passed since the appearance of this intertext in our theater (Pellettieri 1996: 65-67).

We can even affirm that from the mid-eighties to the nineties dramatic texts of a postmodern intertext were not produced in our city. With the appearance of the dramatic works by Daniel Veronese and Rafael Spregelburd among others, this absence was limited. Until this moment there were only positions that responded to this model, due to the way in which directors used dramatic texts. For a complete understanding of the theater to which we are referring, it is essential to describe the social context, mediated by intellectual circles, in which said theater was produced.

Indigent Postmodernism

In a previous work (Pellettieri 1995: 57-70) we refer, with regard to this topic, to a seminal essay by Dotti (1993). We believe that many of his ideas continue even today—more than four years later—explaining the phenomenon of our social life in an exemplary way. Dotti underlines various points:

In Argentina, daily life is included in postmodernity, which he qualifies as "indigent" because "it denotes a delay and marginal character in comparison with the First World."

Also, in Argentina mercantilism is the hegemonic element because it endows the basic semantic nuclei that make up social coexistence or collective imagination and shape ways of life. This is even true today, after the results of the October 26, 1997 elections to partially replace the Chamber of Deputies, in which the opposition united creating the Alliance that succeeded in overthrowing Peronism in the government for the first time. This occurred in the midst of growing socioeconomic deterioration in the country, which was evidenced by massive layoffs and subsequent unemployment, the decrease in salaries, recession and popular protests, and adjustment and convertibility (one peso=one dollar) that for public opinion continued to be the guarantee against disaster. So much so that the most conspicuous members of the Alliance had to clarify, before the elections, that they too believed in the adjustment and the convertibility. That is to say, mercantilism has a stabilizing function because it can lower the criteria of behavior considered to be desirable, rational and transmissible.

In Argentine social coexistence the modern concept of crisis has been banished:

> this does not mean that conflicts do not occur, violent situations that are profound in their severity and novelty. But the postmodern aspect of our reality is that this data is categorized by the opinion of the majority as mere dysfunctional elements of not entirely successful market dynamics, but that will be eliminated once they become stronger . . . Today, the indifferent acceptance (not without a certain discredit) of "the politicians" and "parlimentarianism" prevail as such. Confidence lies, however, in the free "market" as though it were the North Star towards which all efforts to overcome Argentine backwardness must be directed, with disregard for the social costs of such programs. (Dotti 1993: 7-8)

It is to be noted that during the month of December of 1993, severe acts of social violence were carried out which included the burning of the government building in the province of Santiago del Estero, one of the poorest in the country, and where the provincial government owed various months' salaries to their administrative employees. Due to the structural characteristics of Santiago del Estero and the "adjustment" work of the national government, public administration has become the most important employer of personnel in the northeastern provinces of Argentina. Far from acknowledging the crisis, Domingo Carvallo, the Minister of Economy at the time, gave as an explanation, in the December 1, 1994 edition of *Clarín*—which received next to no reply from the opposition—the fact that only "in provinces where adjustments are not carried out is there the threat of outbursts." In conclusion, Dotti underlines a fact with which we fully coincide:

> The relative success of the neo-liberal economic plan is not the cause but rather the effect of a profound change in the criteria of sociability with which generalized common sense and public opinion comprehend their own reality. This change sustains itself by what has been called the hegemonic function of mercantilism in the social imaginary of the Argentines. (8)

And so, the same as a second Modernity appears in Buenos Aires at the end of the 1950s, with the Frondizist developmentalism, the development of technology, the rise to government of the individualistic middle class, the growth of social sciences and the affirmation of cinema art, in short, with the appearance of a new metaphor of the country and its relationship with the world and its inhabitants, it can be said that the theater of postmodern intertext makes itself known hand in hand with the hegemonic function of mercantilism, Menemism, the free market, the disintegration of society, the proletarianizing of the middle class, the lumpenization of the proletariat, the limitation of the welfare state, the crisis of the working society, and the advent of an intense cultural manipulation by the economic powers which control the information directed to the public at their discretion.

Faced with these new rules of social coexistence, two fundamental types of attitudes arise—that imply intermediate and premodern positions, which as we said we will not discuss here—at the heart of Buenos Aires theater after the experiences of the military dictatorship and the advent of democracy in 1983. Both tendencies, contrary to what occurred before 1976, coincide in accepting political liberalism as a base for Argentine coexistence, but they are opposed to actual crude economic liberalism. In this situation, a "hidden polemic" is produced between a group of authors, directors and actors which dominate the theatrical system—group representing Modernity and whose ideology we could name as "anti-postmodern"—and a series of emerging experiences that we classify as of the postmodern intertext. We will proceed to attempt to characterize these positions.

Modern Realist Position

This includes the greater part of the predominant theater in Buenos Aires, that which was solidified in the sixties, which produced an interchange of realist and absurdist devices in the seventies, and whose most notable protagonist was *Teatro Abierto* in the 1980s.

This trend still occupies—in spite of the esthetic exhaustion that we underlined in the introduction of this work—a central place in the intellectual field concerned with theater due to the hegemony that it maintains in the eye of the public, newspaper critics, and scholars. The most active group is found in the Somi Foundation (apocope of the disappeared author Carlos Somigliana), which includes some of the principal modern playwrights: Roberto Cossa, Eduardo Rovner, Bernardo Carey, Osvaldo Dragún, Carlos Pais, Roberto Perinelli, Marta Degracia. Its objective is to stimulate theatrical authors and it periodically gives its opinion on its own movement. Its attitude within the media is canonizing and legitimating. During recent times a series of plays have become integrated militantly within this trend. Its fundamental exponent in 1997 was *Teatro Nuestro*, which included authors—Carlos Gorostiza and Roberto Cossa—actors—María Rossa Gallo, Pepe Soriano, Lito Cruz, Cipe Lincovsky, Juan Carlos Gené, Ulises Dumont, Alicia Zanca—and directors—Rubens Correa, José María Paolantonio, Roberto Castro—of this trend.

The plays' stagings (with singularities and variations within the model) also present a series of distinct formal and semantic characteristics, which respond to Postmodernism—to its esthetic and its semantics—intensifying its meaning. With regard to its superficial structure or its intrigue, they sustain an adherence to the realist thesis based always on a social and individual utopia, on the belief in the necessity and rationality of historical facts, and on the concept of crises as "moments of truth" in the social process, a thesis demonstrated through a clear dramatic development, which takes shape through various central facts:

a. The dramatic text continues to be fundamental for staging.

b. This text is "respected" and completely controlled by the director. The dramatic work is closed and self-sufficient.

c. The realist thesis is reiterated in the end vision of the performance, closing its meaning. It always implies a questioning and didactic vision of Argentine social life, a sought-out ideological appraisal of the world that questions indigent Postmodernity.

d. The staging functions as a very precise hegemonic entity in which the notion of totality, a visible theatricality and also a "coherent development" that allows the audience to draw their conclusions predominate. The staging is absolutely referential.

e. It is founded on an idea that is completely communicational and objectifies the relationship between audience and performance.

f. It presents a total predominance of ideological and political interpretation in every nucleus of the performance: its production, circulation and reception.

g. The texts and stagings are constructed from the certainty that "there is no need for the past." They establish an ironic intertextual relationship of opposition with the past, as in the case of *Cocinando con Elisa* (1997) by Lucía Laragione and the Argentine "white comedy" of the thirties.

h. It is an ideologically and politically committed theater.

Postmodern Intertext: Theater of Resistance

The other trend to which we refer as "postmodern intertextuality," rejects the modern sense of the word "realist," showing in its dramatic texts that it has ceased to be "credible" and "theatrical." It uses some of the European and North American postmodern devices, but fundamentally, it concurs with the semantics of postmodern texts.

This trend is divided into two branches: theater of resistance and theater of disintegration. First, we will describe the differences between the two and later, a series of traits common to both.

Theater of resistance: This esthetic and ideological branch has as paradigms the shows that Ricardo Bartís directed, starting with *Postales argentinas* (1988) and which were: *Hamlet* (1991), an adaptation of Shakespeare's text; *Muñeca* (1994), an adaptation of Armando Discépolo's piece; and *El corte* (1966). In these dramatic texts, an ambiguous version of social reality can be noted. They propose the deconstruction of modern staging but they recuperate some of its devices. In this way, they create a theatrical model in which modern discourse becomes refunctionalized by suppressing form/content, realist/formalist, and high-culture/popular culture oppositions (Pellettieri 1992b: 63-64).

These texts begin with the notion that Argentine theatrical modernity is an incomplete project and attempts to rescue theater from its domestication. Its resistance is exposed particularly in *Postales argentinas* and *El corte* as well as Bartís' metatexts and is found within the concrete social context of present-day Argentina and directed against official culture.

In *Postales argentinas* it was sensed that its director had not yet abandoned the idea of critical theater, but rather redefined it from the postmodern optic. It questioned, in the handling of the actors and of the intrigue (as these were incomplete and lacked synthesis between the modern and the traditional), the modernization of the thirties and the sixties. The work rejected this modernization's resounding negation of the past, and its appeal to constant and elitist modernization. The proposal of *Postales argentinas* objected to the rationalization and the standardization of "the new" as being the trivialization of culture. At the same time, the appearance of *Postales argentinas*, with its deconstructive conception and its manipulation of textual corruption, indicated the advent of the postmodern intertext in our theater.

Charles Jencks postulates notions for postmodern architecture that may be useful in examining Bartís' theater. It is bifocal, which is to say that it looks in two directions simultaneously: "toward the traditional codes of slow evolution and the particular ethnic meanings of its surroundings, and toward the changing codes of style and professionalism" (1977: 97). This is a typical attitude of the great renovators of completed Modernity, which our marginal Modernity never achieved.

The rest of Bartís' work maintained a gesture of opposition towards marginal Modernity, but also towards the defeatist climate of indigent Postmodernism. Its pessimism is constantly limited and this limitation is founded in its revalidation and re-semantization of Argentine popular theater.

There is an intention to approach full Modernity at the crossroad of what is "ours" and what is "the other's"—which evidently Bartís believes is something to achieve—that appears in *Hamlet* and in *Muñeca*. In the latter, an attempt is made to deconstruct Discepolian theater which consists in pointing out aspects that had not been observed in the staging and criticism of the work: its machismo, for example. Its staging retrieves meanings from the text that were "suppressed" by the totalitarian arrogance of reason. *Muñeca* (Bartís' version) implies an assumption of uncertainty of criticism, research and the very performers, as opposed to a text with a guaranteed certainty.

An interesting turn of events occurred in the last production by Bartís and his group, the *Sportivo Teatral* of Buenos Aires, *El corte*. In it, referential contextualization, mixed with postmodern devices, turned out to be exemplary in describing the director's esthetic. In this case we agree with the critique that our disciples of the GETEA (*Grupo de Estudio de Teatro Argentino e Iberoamericano*) made of this performance, in *Nuevos Espacios* (1997: 52-54): It is not difficult to notice the reflection in *El corte*'s butcher shop, the sad indigent Postmodernism of our country: a family which morbidly repeats the traumatic scenes of our past. Undoubtedly, the naturalist intrigue with postmodern functionality wants to settle an old score with Argentina's past: "Parents take out their own inoperability and symbolic shortcomings on their son in the form of bodily punishment" (52). For *El corte,* retrieving the past is fundamental, "designing artistic forms that allow us to critically retrieve our past and construct other possible identities" (53). In the text, there is another, more intense, underlining of the questioning of the writing of Argentine realism and of its desperate clinging attachment to words. The shortcomings in its esthetics are duly noted in such reflections as "no one is convinced by pamphleteer fables" (53). It becomes evident that theater of resistance wants to show us that, in any case, our Postmodernity is peculiar, but it participates in the advent of new times, in the crisis of Modernity.

The proposal of these plays is to take Postmodernism "starting with ourselves," beginning with Argentine theater and including our limitations and perplexities and attempting to include it within our own identity. For example, starting with what we could call "our poverty," and adding the uncontainable type of pathos found in *Postales argentinas* allows it to dialogue with other greats in our theater: Arlt or Discépolo. What is common to these phases of Argentine theater is that in them all things are deprived, as in the case of our urban life. For this reason, this drama questions without a doubt our indigent Postmodernism. This is evident in that in texts such as *Postales argentinas* and *El corte* "rather than constituting a specific trend of thought and research [their postmodern attempts] have contributed to challenging, reformulating and enriching the analyses of modernity" (García Canclini 1992: 19).

Postmodern Intertext: Theater of Disintegration

The paradigm for this esthetic is established by the author and director Rafael Spregelburd (*Destino de dos cosas o de tres,* 1993, *Cucha de almas,* 1992, *Remanente de invierno,* 1995, *La tiniebla,* 1994, *Raspando la cruz,*1997, director Rubén Szuchmacher (*Música rota,* 1994, based on three texts by Daniel Veronese, *Palomitas blancas,* 1998, by Manuel Cruz, and *Polvo eres,* 1997, by Harold Pinter, among many others and, very especially, the playwright and codirector of El Periférico de Objetos, Daniel Veronese (*Crónica de la caída de uno de los hombres de ella,* 1990, *Cámara Gesel,* 1993, *Circonegro,* 1996 and *El líquido táctil,* 1997, among others).

These dramaturgs and directors essentially take the lead, since the early nineties, in Argentine theater's "new entry into the world." In an environment that was limited for years to "living on our own" theatrically, they have achieved a productive reception and have allowed the intertext of a series of fundamental authors on today's scene to circulate in our theater, such as Heiner Müller, Philippe

Minyana, Valere Novarina, and Raymond Carver. Their theater is the result of a very productive mix of these intertexts with the neo-avant-garde theater of the absurd, whose last late modern exponent appeared in the sixties and among whose radicals were Griselda Gámbaro, Eduardo Pavlovsky, Jorge Petraglia and Roberto Villanueva.

This theater of disintegration is, in our opinion, the esthetic and ideological continuation of the absurd, which was, in turn, the continuation of the irrational-pessimistic tradition of the grotesque. The difference lies in that the absurd tried to demonstrate the absurdity of human existence in society. It still believed in the notion of meaning, demanded an interpretation, and strengthened meaning even more.

The theater of disintegration took from the absurd the abstract nature of theatrical language and the dissolution of the character as a psychological entity. But it does not pretend to demonstrate anything, it believes that the meaning of the text, which is absolutely referential, must be determined almost exclusively by the spectator. The character not only "pronounces" the discourse, but also is deconstructed and psychologically disintegrated. The universe of this theater is not only a dreamless universe, but it also appears to us as though possessed by a vertical dwindling of the senses, of passions. The characters are transients in a nightmare. All of this appears within the fragments of the intrigue, which contrasts with the neo-avant-garde illusion of totality, and which has repercussions on the staging's conception.

The pessimism in this type of theater is absolute. One could say that the dramaturgs, especially Veronese, work with a nihilist esthetic. It is a theater that is not ashamed of its elitism, and that rejects the *chatura*, the low class of our society. Its cultivators are competent polemicists (especially Spregelburd), contradictory, contemptuous, and who find sufficient reasons to question the absurdity of the end of our century. Its metatexts maintain a high coherency with its texts (Cruz-Pacheco 1997: 14-15; Weinschelbaum 1997: 10-12; Chaer 1995: 40-42).

This theater, that not only demonstrates disintegration, familial incommunication, ferocious consumerism, gratuitous violence, and the absence of love in postmodern coexistence, but is also intertextual with its social context, with the Menemist neo-conservatism that has broken away from the norms of social life. It is the emerging facet of our indigent Postmodernism. The answer to all of this is the perfect simulacrum esthetic: eclecticism combined with anti-esthetics and modern illusions that are observed in all texts and metatexts in the sense that they consider themselves to be radically innovative.

This merits an explanation: We have already said that they are contradictory, consciously contradictory. They are anti avant-garde because they reject the basic concern of the avant-garde—which is still present in theater of resistance—that of creating a new art in an alternative society, and rather negates the avant-garde's pretending to be the center of experimentation. At the same time, they avoid reflecting upon the problems that the exhaustion of modernism, the "theater of art," and community theater are causing Argentine theater and society. They also distinguish themselves from theater of resistance in this respect.

In this sense it is important to clarify that another difference is that theater of disintegration is an author's theater, whose director considers the dramatic text to be a guide, while that of resistance works without a previous text, like a theater created collectively, oriented by the director.

In synthesis, the theater of disintegration is not concerned with recuperating aspects of modern theater. It is evident that for its followers we are in a moment of total change within the theatrical system. Argentine theatrical modernity "already was" and, therefore, we cannot expect any "unfinished project." It is for this reason that they are not worried about criticizing reality, because for them popular theater, in the same way as "cultured theater," can only be a useful addition to the mix. They do not reject popular theater, rather, it is dissolved in the deconstruction of styles and it is useful in creating other things.

These authors' plays are close to monologues, as the characters have little or no connection between each other. The text closely resembles an empty eggshell, it is seamless with very limited spatial references. It is self-referential, meaning it uses the devices (as defined by Krysinski) "of the verbal plenitude of an autonomous language in as much as it systematically permits the impossible." In this way, "the incongruent principle subverts correct communication," and it involves the use of shock, surprise, the improbable, the fantastic, and the absurd." It results in the destruction of mimetic referentiality and the autonomy of the dramatic text. It must therefore be affirmed that just as the neo-avant-garde absurdism of the sixties was the most homogeneous modern expression of our theater, today the theater of disintegration is the most postmodern exponent of the Buenos Aires scene.

It is important to make some references to Szuchmacher in closing this part of the paper, as the majority of what has been presented here applies basically to the poetics of the authors. Without a doubt, Szuchmacher incarnates a new type of scenic director, a return to the ingenious arbitrarities of the "masters of the scene"—Pavis' words—of Augusto Fernandes and Jaime Kogan, for example, and more closely to the notion of a mediator between the distinct components of the rehearsal. It is evident that according to this conception, the director has exchanged global for technical responsibility. The direction has become decentralized and has produced a greater participation by the actors and other participants in the theatrical circuit.

Even directing a text from the so-called theater of resistance like *La china* (1995), by Sergio Bizzio and Daniel Guebel, or the already mentioned *Palomitas blancas*—curiously a reflexive realistic text, modern marginal to the core—Szuchmacher succeeds in having the staging question the cult of the receptor's interpretation. In opposition to the interested gaze of anti-Postmodernism, or the critical vision of Modernity that is postulated by the theater of resistance, his stagings attempt to retrieve an impartial view of the text. We do not find in them "evidence of meaning"; they are neutral. The receptor may or may not give them meaning. The theatrical aspects remain hidden by the commentary on the facts, by the undetermined. The direction remains on the surface, it does not get "in-depth." Some time ago, Szuchmacher told us that some of his works implied "a staging without a concept." We are in agreement: He lets the characters do and talk; there is not an all-encompassing view in his works. Without arriving at the nihilist or deconstuctionist notion of theatrical communication, he proposes an integral or radical relativism that "relegates to a second level theatrical meanings and the intellectual comprehension of the show, giving priority in a unilateral way to the perceptive and emotional processes of the spectators" (De Marinis).

His works entail an ambiguous version of the text and its self-referential nature, and generally by means of an ironic reproduction of forms of common living that are not as such, intensify the places of indetermination of the texts that he brings to the stage.

The modern director clarified the text, his work implied a truth about the social life of the spectator; but this new type of director "problematizes" the ambiguity of daily life. Without a doubt, Szuchmacher is a director that has found his path in the theater of disintegration.

Common Traits in Both Trends

At any rate, both theater of resistence, as well as theater of disintegration, participate in a fundamental change within our theatrical system. It is for this reason that it is important, after underlining their differences, to point out their common traits:

1. The idea of staging as a "simulacrum." In this way, the text does not adhere to the true/false opposition found in theatrical modernity.

2. The staging seeks to deconstruct language and reason, and as such, certainty. It digs into the intrigues of differences of a text until it succeeds in deconstructing it.

3. Both types of theater are opposed to the dogmatism of reason. They infer that there are various meanings in texts, and that the question of meaning must remain open. In this case, there is a notorious limitation in the evidence supporting its meaning.

4. This situation forces the play to present itself as fragmentary, inconclusive, complex.

5. The text and the staging are intertextual. The intertextual relationship is not established with an individual text, as occurred with modern intertextuality, but rather with a genre or trend.

6. Originality is not sought, the old is rewritten (a joke, a vaudeville, etc.), but in a new way. The old textuality acquires new meaning thanks to the new text.

Conclusions

Already advanced in its initial stage, one must weigh postmodern intertextual theater's progress and diagnose its evolution. In spite of its aforementioned limitations, this trend has brought a series of positive elements:

It has permitted, as in any period of change, that there be a moment of self-reflection on the Argentine scene. The theater of postmodern intertext has allowed us to critically look, from another perspective, at modern textualities that we found satisfying until very recently. We observe their limitations and thus acquire a broader perspective. On the other hand, in a theatrical system as prejudiced and malignant toward popular theater as ours, the new system has empowered us to note that the distance between it and "theater of art" is no longer as relevant as it was in the past. Furthermore there is another perception of the history of Argentine theater, among those who are or are not scholars in the field: We perceive that we have overcome linear and "progressive" notions, unique and chronological, "based on truth." Posmodernity has brought us to realize that each of us can create his or her story without unique assumptions or utopian goals that lead us to believe that theater will save the country. We are overcoming determinism and accepting our limitations as critics and historians.

With regard to the questions which were put forth in the introduction, we must add that only time will tell if a completed modernity (theater of resistance) will become explicit in the second phase of the theater of postmodern intertext, or if we will become completely integrated in Postmodernity (theater of disintegration) or if, as has occurred until now, the historical constant of realism will triumph. In addition, we find that new questions arise. What characteristics will the second phase of this trend have? Will esthetic forms develop which are totally different from modern ones? As early 1989 we postulated the following response to these questions:

> We cannot guarantee it, because the future of Argentine theater will "create itself." At any rate, we trust that the emphases placed on present-day Argentine theater will be found correct, because from them we have established hypotheses concerning the future. We hope to not have been completely wrong.

Works Cited

Bartís, R. "Problemáticas y perspectivas de la experimentación estética en el teatro actual." *Teatro XXI* 2:3(1996): 18-20.
Bürger, P. *Teoría de la vanguardia.* Barcelona: Península, 1987.
Chaer S. and C. Pacheco. "El teatro argentino no se hace cargo de la contemporaneidad." *La Maga* (February 15, 1995): 40-42.
Cruz, A. and C. Pacheco. "Ricardo Bartís. Maestro de actores." *La Maga* (February 26 1997): 10-12.
_____. "Rafael Spregelburd. Actor/dramaturgo/director." *La Maga* (March 5, 1997): 14-15.
De Marinis, M. "Problemas de la semiótica teatral. La relación espectáculo-espectador." *Gestos* 1 (1986): 11-24.
Dotti, J. "Nuestra posmodernidad indigente." *Espacios de crítica y producción* 12 (1993): 3-8.
García Canclini, N. "Después del posmodernismo: la reapertura del debate sobre la modernidad." *Imaginarios urbanos.* Buenos Aires: Eudeba, 1992.
Heller, A. "Los momentos culturales como vehículo del cambio." *Letra internacional,* Madrid 8(1987/8): 22.
Jameson, F. "El posmodernismo como lógica cultural del capitalismo tardío." *Ensayo sobre posmodernismo.* Buenos Aires: Imago Mundi, 1991.
Jencks, Ch. A. *The Language of Postmodern Architecture.* New York: Rizzoli, 1997.
Krysinski, W. "La manipulación referencial en el drama moderno." *Gestos* 7 (1989): 9-31.
Nuevos Espacios. "*El corte,* un cuestionamiento a la estética realista." *Teatro XXI* 3: 4 (1997): 52-54.
Pelletieri, O. "Notas 1975-1985: las puestas más representativas." *La escena latinoamericana,* 2(1989): 89-90.
_____. "El teatro latinoamericano del futuro." O. Pelletieri (ed.) *Teatro argentino actual.* Cuaderno de GETEA no.1. Ottawa: Girol Books-Espacio, 3-16.
_____. "El sonido y la furia: panorama del teatro de los 80 en la Argentina." *Latin American Theater Review* 25: 2 (1992): 3-12.

_____. "Postales argentinas: deconstrucción y continuidad en el sistema teatral argentino." J. Dubatti (comp.) *Comparatística: Estudios de literatura y teatro.* Buenos Aires: Biblos, 1992. Reedited in *Teatro argentino contemporáneo.* Buenos Aires: Galerna, 1994. 151-64.

_____. "*Los Macocos* y el teatro nacional." J. Dubatti (comp). *Teatro 90: El nuevo teatro en Buenos Aires.* Buenos Aires: Libros de Quirquincho, 1992. 71-72.

_____. "Posmodernidad y tradición en el teatro actual de Buenos Aires." *Gestos* 10:19 (1995): 57-70.

_____. "La puesta en escena actual en Buenos Aires." O. Pellettieri and E. Rovner (eds.). *La puesta en escena en Latinoamérica: Teoría y práctica teatral.* Buenos Aires: Galerna/CITI, 1996. 65-78.

_____. *Una historia interrumpida: Teatro argentino moderno (1949-1976).* Buenos Aires: Galerna, 1997.

_____. "Dramaturgia argentina (1985-1995)." *La dramaturgia en Iberoamérica: Teoría y práctica teatral.* O.Pellettieri and E.Rovner (eds.). Buenos Aires: Galerna/GETEA/CITI. 1998.

Reigadas, M. C. "Neomodernidad y posmodernidad: preguntando desde América Latina. *In Posmodernidad?*" Buenos Aires: Biblos, 1988. 113-45.

Sikora, Marina F. "La aparente homogeneidad de la dramaturgia emergente en Bar Ada y Martha Stutz." *Teatro XXI* 3: 5 (1997): 61-63.

Weinschelbaum, V. "Daniel Veronese: una mirada transversal." *Magazin literario* 3 (September): 10-11.

◆ **10.**

Polarized Modernity: Latin America at the Postmodern Juncture

Raúl Bueno

(translated by Cynthia M. Tompkins)

How does Latin America enter into Postmodernism? Extreme positions remain after a decade of discussion on the controversial issue. Some argue that the region has not only entered into Postmodernism but, as proven by the work of Borges and García Márquez, also foreshadowed it culturally and aesthetically.[1] Conversely, others argue that since Latin America has not effectively entered into Modernity, it is senseless to talk about its entrance into Postmodernism.[2] Perhaps intermediate positions, which posit an unequal, selective, asymmetrical and restricted (to certain sectors and lines of action) entrance into Modernity and a critical exit, which resembles an ideological project rather than a realized program, are the most accurate.[3]

Despite good social intentions and collective desire, upon discovery, Latin America entered into the dark side of Modernity, for it was immediately subjected to the logocentric and universalizing rationality of the raging capitalism of the time.[4] Furthermore, contemporary resistance to the imposed Modernity, combined with attempts at representing its historical absurdities and mimetic expressions of decentralization, resulted in *a sui generis* critical Postmodernism which is therefore rooted in the domination it opposed. However, the notion of Modernity itself needs to be re-examined, bracketing the connotations that link it to recent periods, and even to the twentieth century.[5] This re-examination also requires reconnecting Modernity to the Modern Age, to the very inception of processes of rationalization such as Copernican heliocentrism, Renaissance perspectivism, the financial capitalism of the Era of Discovery and Colonization, social utopias, and the impact of Machiaveli—for it constitutes the foundations of social, economic, scientific, and artistic Modernity. It also requires reviewing the hermeneutical implications of Dependency Theory, a discussion which is still pending because it failed to offer a viable exit from domination, as proven by the fact that Cardoso, one of its proponents, wound up supporting the demands of neoliberalism.[6] The fatalistic response to backwardness of certain plaintive versions of Dependency Theory may have also aborted the discussion. Though perhaps other issues simply took over the spotlight of Latin American cultural and social studies. The re-examination of Modernity also requires reactivating the opposition between Center and Periphery, for it appears to have been relegated to an epistemological limbo from which it tends to emerge either as an obvious or a shared assumption. Incidentally, this article is also part of that discussion.

Partial Modernity

Indeed, according to most of the literature on Latin America vis-à-vis the spheres of rationality (science, art, government, society, law, the economy, labor) mentioned in Habermas' discussion of Weber,[7] ours is a partial Modernity.[8] The thesis of a partial Modernity is further reinforced by considering the three "logics" of Modernity (capitalism, or the universalization of the market; industrialization, or the universalization of the modes of production; democracy and the ordering of civil life, or the universalization of the rights of man and the citizen) José Ignacio López Soria refers to in his assessment of Agnes Heller's work.[9] For a modern subject, or a subject undergoing the process of modernization, the region is found lacking in all of these respects. This is especially true regarding the highly unsatisfactory state both of the industrial apparatus and the organization of public life, generally reduced to scripts which fail to be enacted. Conversely, capitalism fully penetrated most of the region following a colonial blueprint according to which Latin Americans were reserved the role of exporters of raw materials (exploited or not) and docile consumers of manufactured products. The resulting injustices were unequivocally foreshadowed by the social and economic unbalance generated by mercantilism as unequivocally sketched in Columbus's diaries.[10] Clearly, however, nineteenth-century liberalism, as scripted in the concluding pages of *Facundo,* offered no release.[11] Both the process of globalization and the neo-liberal tornado that currently rage over our lands reinforce so-called modernizing capitalism. Yet, to date, no one has been able to prove that these winds offer a desirable modernization that actually favors the dispossessed masses of Latin America. To the contrary, in most cases, these winds have made us regress to the most undesirable conditions of Latin America's pre-Modernity.[12]

Moreover, an examination of the cultural contexts of the canonical fields of Latin America's Modernity reveals not only glaringly insufficient and tendentious colonizing versions, but also ostensible irregularities in geographical distribution and noticeable budgetary contradictions. If culture is the symbolic locus for both the economic (production and distribution of goods) and the social base (regulation of collective life), modern society should appear as a coherent and relatively uniform culture. In reality, this does not occur, far less in Latin America. Indeed, in these lands, the field of cultural production, which represents very different social traditions and expectations as well as opposing projects of economic development, is pretty asymmetrical and broken. I am referring not only to elitist cultural discourse, but also and especially, to traditional and popular discourses and social practices that, fictive or not, aim at maintaining the stability and continuity of communal and private life, which in our case, configure a rather fragmented, heterogeneous and contradictory schema. More specifically, I refer to the distance and disharmony between elite and survival culture.

Elite culture is undoubtedly modern given the functionality and rationality of the expressive system. It is also capable of developing cosmopolitan systems of great formal and thematic complexity, free from the demands of survival as well as from the urgencies of the dispossessed (e.g. *Ariel*).[13] Conversely, the culture of the better part of the population is not cosmopolitan. Nor can it detach itself from the basic needs of life, such as food, clothing, housing, and work. This is illustrated by transition cultural practices such as the lyrics of Peruvian "chicha," Mexican "cumbia ranchera" or "azteca," and Argentine "cuartetazo" or "bailantas," which embody hybridity by positing the desire for modernization as they articulate the subject of enunciation's needs. In other words, these practices showcase the difference between subjects who are modern and those who are not.[14] To a certain point this is also proven by ethnic and testimonial literatures, which not only introduce us to other racial and cultural inequalities in addition to those of class but also manage to express the fractures resulting from the enslaving intrusion of neocolonial Modernity (e.g. Rigoberta Menchú's moving denunciation).[15]

Thus, from the perspective of Latin American social life and its discursive representations, we may conclude that Latin American Modernity is not only questioned or even denied by unequal development and flaws within the paradigm itself (the region's western or westernized society), but also by the sharp contrasts generated by the ongoing presence of "different historical times" in the region. These times refer back to specific locations of Latin America such as Chiapas, the Quiché region, Ayacucho, or the shanty towns that encircle capital cities, which not only appear to be anchored in pre-Modernity but also to recede into subhuman living conditions given the effect of servitude, exploitation, abuse, and other scars of domination. However, these conditions do not necessarily lead to a loss of highly desirable social values—as J. M. Arguedas and A. Rama would say[16]—but to the contrary, are advantageous as regards resistance movements as well as the affirmation of collective values, and the defense of tradition, which have been at the center both of testimonial literature and the critique of heterogeneous and transcultural literatures.[17]

In short, the Weberian version of Modernity barely reaches certain but not all Latin American regions. And the parts it does reach, are affected (or benefited, depending on the beholder) only partially and asymmetrically.

Plural Modernities

Despite the humanistic slant of the discourse of Modernity, the gaps, flaws, asymmetries, inequalities, lacks and distortions of Latin American Modernity articulate the essence—Chomsky would say the "deep structure"—of a highly hierarchic and discriminatory Modernity. A Modernity that had international and global projections from its very inception. A Modernity that solidified dependent premodernities and imposed partial modernities in the periphery to suit its interests.

Freely drawing from the title of a book by Sarlo,[18] we could say that Latin America, not only Buenos Aires or Argentina, presents an ample and complex case of "peripheric Modernity." Any explanation requires examining the imperialist condition of central Modernity, for the material (monetary) resources of Euro-American Modernity resulted from the different colonizations. In other words, Euro-American modernism would not have become what it is without capitalism, political empires, mercantilism, neo-colonization, transnationals, economic imperialism, and dependency. In sum, without the flaws and shortcomings brought about by the exercise of power of nations that possess a powerful war machine, which thereby become rich, over defenseless nations, which thereby become impoverished. Thus, domination is a *sine qua non* prerequisite for diverse aspects (industrial, economic, infrastructure, and conspicuous consumption) of Modernity in developed nations. This also applies to the development of civil society, as illustrated by Carpentier's *El siglo de las luces* (1962), C. L. R. James' "The Black Jacobins"

(1963) and A. Césaire's "Discours sur le colonialisme" (1955),[19] which examine the double standard—metropolitan and colonial—applied to the rights of man and the citizen, as well as to the value of modernization. As producers and processors of raw materials, and maximizing production through minimum wages, precarious living conditions, and environmental deterioration, in sum, as providers of the quality with which the First World pampers itself, underdeveloped nations have entered the dark, dirty and unfair, underside of Modernity.

Thus, countries of the so-called Third World, and among them those of Latin America, embody the unsolicited and shameful part of a superstructure that has allow for the First World's enjoyment of Modernity. More precisely, this superstructure has determined that the First World be the "presentable" side of Modernity. In other words, the Center's Modernity has cast its social and economic pre-Modernity toward the periphery; its development depends on the pre-modern conditions of dependent countries. Therefore, against their wishes, many regions of the world remain condemned to material pre-Modernity because such a fate is necessary for the Center's Modernity. The process, which has gone on for centuries, continuously adjusts itself to the prevailing economic and political conditions always counting on the support of local oligarchies (landowning, government, banking, trade, mass media, and now, the assembly subindustry), who act as the great capital's agent who benefit from, while at the same time control the drainage of the resources of the Third World. This is why we Latin Americans find ourselves at the juncture of a polarized Modernity, and why we show the other—the dirty, undeveloped, underdeveloped, unequally and contradictorily developed—face of Modernity. Ours is then a submerged Modernity, a kind of deficit sub-Modernity, required by the Center's "conspicuous" Modernity.

In its climaxing century, two relevant phenomena prove the polarizing and hierarchic nature of material Modernity: the presence of pre-modernities and sub-modernities in the bosom of the Center's Modernity, and the presence of pseudo-modernities, or elite modernities, in the landscape of sub-Modernity. In both cases nodules function as a synecdoche of the global phenomena, by locally maintaining the same polarity that encompasses them nationally.

Indeed, the Center's Modernity does not always succeed in removing its undesirable pre-(or sub-) Modernity. Undeveloped or underdeveloped regions remain in Europe (Greece, Bosnia, the South of Spain and of Italy) and the U.S. (the Appalachia, Native American reservations, the "inner cities"). Ghettoes and hovels also remain, and in dark times, concentration camps and crematories. Even though the goddess Modernity is aesthetically panoramic in that she strives to free the landscape from certain intolerable blemishes, she cannot completely conceal—not even on her own grounds—Modernity's basic disadjustments, nor the hierarchic, discriminatory, antidemocratic, and even genocidal principles, which appear whenever her corset is pulled too tightly.

On the other hand, a bird's eye view of the metropolitan centers of Latin America and the Third World reveals an order of center and periphery, or privileged areas encircled by shantytowns. This is only further proof of the cellular and contradictory nature of polarized Modernity.

The arbitrary manipulation of our fate, historically effected by the Center with the support of the local sector in power, further proves the polarizing streak of Modernity. The imposed social and political order has gone against our needs and desires. Governments and dictatorships have been installed (Estrada Cabrera, the Trujillos, Batista, Pérez Jiménez, Odría, the first Pinochet, Videla, etc.). Democracies have been undermined (the ostensible cases of Madero and Allende), and pseudo-democracies have been imposed (the flagrant case of the second Pinochet), in accordance with the wishes of transnationals such as United Fruit Co., ITT and of agencies controlling the health of the Center's Modernity (such as the International Monetary Bank).

Our own oligarchies and elites in power also offer ample proof of this polarization. As they actively take on their privileged roles within the colonial schema (maintaining colonialism's feelings and hierarchic system to continue the exploitation with old and new arguments) they become watchdogs of global polarization and agents of subsidiary polarizations, or (as per Burgos-Debray)[20] internal colonization (in a sense that differs from Habermas' term). The ideological apparatus of conquest and control designed at the beginning of the Modern Age is now being enforced as a colonial effect in areas of infra-Modernity. It filters and propels resources, benefits, quality and values in one direction, and scarcity, need, inferiority feelings, backwardness, and other negative values in the opposite direction. This process, obviously, takes place among the mediations and convenient modernizations it is forced to install between the Modernity of the Center and sub-Modernity. The colonial effect also generates and shelters the agents it requires. Not only the elite in power who keep Latin America's veins open[21] (the Artemio Cruz-like characters of the continent)[22] but also the useful fools who persist, honestly or not, in a modernization that repeats the central model and, needless to say, its inconveniences. In any case, they are necessary byproducts of global Modernity and agents assigned to the process of polarization as understood in this essay. Their removal implies positing a different, alternate Modernity, adjusted to local realities, which overcomes the vices of canonical

Modernity and avoids the dangers of globalization. This Modernity, often labeled utopic, regressive, archaic, and anti-historic, is yet to be.

We may thus infer that the mimetic modernization of Latin America has become a distopia, not only because it implanted a desire which ultimately results in a growing subjection and dependency, but also because at the level of an inspiration, it implies an unattainable desire: namely, the quest for a presentable, generalized, socially gratifying Modernity, in a certain way equal to that of the Center. Impossible because the agenda of central Modernity does not include dismantling the hierarchic system that supports it to allow for the real development of the regions on which its privileged position hinges. I insist: The pleasant and polished Modernity of dominant countries depends on the (pre-modern, anti-modern, and sub-modern) conditions of Latin America and the so-called Third World. From this perspective, the desire of Futurist avant-garde Spanish American writers (Maples Arce, Oquendo de Amat, González Lanuza among others),[23] who domesticated mechanical language to approach, at least discursively, the benefits of industrial Modernity, resulted in a sterile, inconsequential, lost cause, based as it was on an illusion that revealed its ignorance about the forces which, even to this day control the processes of history. Luckily, other less effervescent and more autonomous Latin American avant-garde writers such as Vallejo, Neruda, or Asturias, proved to be more interested in mankind than in the instruments at their service.[24] They realized that the kinetic avant-garde did not promote modernization beyond the horizon of the symbolic, and thus, posited an instrumental use of avant-garde language to represent the human condition facing the historical juncture, rather than opting for a self-centered and reverent cult of the European (Modernist) avant-garde.

Postmodernities

> [. . .] paradoxically, "the postmodern condition," expression of the most advanced capitalism, appears not to have a better historical model than the Third World's crippled and deformed subcapitalism.
> Antonio Cornejo Polar[25]

Literature on Postmodernism appears to agree on an important point: Rather than surpassing Modernity, which has certainly not been declared defunct, Postmodernism revises the meaning and the values of Modernity, or at least the manner in which these have been implemented. It is more like an indictment, which tends to recycle and rearticulate Modernity, to free it from its vices and errors, and to posit it as a viable possibility for the future. The pulsion of Postmodernism at the center marks the rhythm and increases the resonance of Third

World intellectual movements which have long discussed imbalances and other excesses (centralism, hierarchic modes, drainage of resources, foreign control) Modernity imposes on the periphery. I am referring not only to national liberation movements, cultural resistance, the affirmation of ethnic plurality, democratization of the international order, recovery of identities, and the democratization of resources, but, above all, to those confronting the abuses resulting from the great capital and the laws of the market, especially in the current era of globalization and the rule of neoliberal policies. As we shall see, however, there are basic differences between Postmodernism's central and peripheric pulsions.

Indeed, when the subject of the Center questions his/her Modernity, s/he does it from a more aesthetic and philosophical than material standpoint. Furthermore, s/he knows that at bottom, his/her critique is not aimed at dissolving the system that supports him/her (even though s/he may resort to an apocalyptic tone to refer to the end of history and of the grand récits) but rather to fine tune the cultural paradigm and the programs it generates. That is why his/her actions (which may be disguised by verbal scandal) tend to confront questions that, though important, were until recently deemed invisible or superfluous (i.e. cultural relativism, defense of the environment, integration of minorities, usage of socially and politically correct rhetoric, etc.). In the meantime, this subject becomes aware of the mercilessly overbearing advance of the globalization of the economy and the cultural industry, as well as of the resulting increase in political interventionism. In short, s/he is reduced to a mere witness of an overwhelming process that deprives him/her of any real possibility of agency.

Instead, when the colonized, the neo-colonized, the Latin American, the Third-World subject, questions Modernity (ethnocentric rationality which invades the cultural landscape, the universality of double standard values and the validity of the metanarratives that flow with the expansive wave of capitalism and colonialism (cf. Shakespeare's *The Tempest*!), s/he does so out of historical necessity. S/he does so not only to change the cultural paradigms and the world order but also to free him/herself from the shackles of dependency. Admitedly, given the conditions of globalization, at times the Third World experiences the echoes of central Postmodernism, especially culturally and artistically. But this does not always happen as a mere reflection of an emerging rhetorics (such as the "postmodern" architecture à la Pompidou Center, which sprouts in the Latin American capitals) but rather, attuned to a decentralizing and antihierarchical impulse which is increasingly becoming the norm. Furthermore, it may occur as a reaction against the unequal and contradictory efforts of local modernization, as proven by internal migration, riots, the shantytowns that encircle metropolitan centers, informal economies or the deliberate return to pre-modern forms of social organization and co-ops.

Thus, Latin America meets its infamous Modernity (slit open by modernizing measures that actually lead to regression—as García Canclini would say),[26] maintaining several of its pre-modern conditions (orality, reciprocity, barter, native communalism, etc.), while it experiences a unique Postmodernism, adapted to its colonial and dependent status, which developed historically as a counter discourse to colonialism, domination, and the absurdities resulting from global Modernity. According to the surfacing signs and the desires of the elite in power, fate favors a homogeneous Modernity. However, below the water line, reality reveals itself as a complex iceberg, which is not as docile as the bureaucrats of the World Bank and their local straw men would wish. In the meantime the anti-Menem coalition won in most of Argentina and the masses show their dissatisfaction with the neoliberal model.[27] A sign that unequivocaly points at the agency of the Latin American masses—they are subjects, not merely objects—of an "Other" Modernity. A different, humanizing, profoundly democratic Modernity, attuned to our conditions and respectful of tradition, heterogeneity, plurality, and even—though it may sound as a truism—of the common good. The discovery of this complex and fair design, which offers a way out of unsatisfactory pre and sub-modernities, while it prevents us from falling into the excesses of central Modernity, is the main duty—the meaning and justification—of our *sui generis* Postmodernism [Hanover, New Hampshire, November 1997. Footnotes were included in July 1999].

Notes

1. The following are some of the necessary sources from the extensive bibliography: Douwe Fokkema, *Literary History, Modernism and Postmodernism* (Amsterdam-Philadelphia: J. Benjamins Pub. Co., 1984); David Buehrer, "'A Second Chance on Earth': the Postmodern and Post-Apocalyptic in García Márquez's *Love in the Time of Cholera*," *Critique: Studies in Contemporary Fiction* 32.1 (1990); George Yúdice, "Postmodernity and Transnational Capitalism in Latin America," in G. Yúdice, J. Franco and J. Flores, eds., *On Edge: The Crisis of Contemporary Latin American Culture* (Minneapolis and London: U. of Minnesota P, 1992); Carlos Rincón, "The Peripheral Center of Postmodernism: On Borges, García Márquez and Alterity," *Boundary 2: An International Journal of Literature and Culture* 20. 3 (1993); Carlos J. Alonso, "The Mourning After: García Márquez, Fuentes and the Meaning of Postmodernity in Latin America," *Modern Language Notes* 109.2 (1994); Graciela Keiser, "Modernism/Postmodernism in 'The Library of Babel': Jorge Luis Borges's Fiction as Borderland," *Hispanófila* 115 (1995).

2. For Nelson Osorio's position in the debate on "Corrientes en la crítica y la literatura latinoamericana" held at the Conference on "Latin America: New Directions

in Literary Theory and Criticism," Dartmouth College, April 1988, see Proceedings in *Revista de Crítica Literaria Latinoamericana* 15.29 (1999): 146-48.

3. Consider George Yúdice's response to Nelson Osorio in the above issue pages 105-28. More elaborated and recent versions may be found in G. Yúdice, "Postmodernity and Transnational Capitalism in Latin America," John Beverley et al, eds., *The Postmodernism Debate in Latin America* (Durham and London: Duke University Press, 1995). See also, Richard A. Young, ed. *Latin American Postmodernisms* (Amsterdam, Netherlands: Editions Rodopi B. V., 1997).

4. I posited this view among a group of colleagues at the conference Jornadas Andinas de Cultura Latinoamericana (JALLA), in Tucumán, 1995. Professor Silvia Spitta encouraged me to develop it. Later, I discovered that it had been advanced by Enrique Dussel's convincing "Eurocentrism and Modernity (Introduction to the Frankfurt Lectures)," published in J. Beverley et al (pp. 65-76) and in the book titled *The Invention of the Americas. Eclipse of "the Other" and the Myth of Modernity* (New York: Continuum, 1995). However, I soon found out that our views had different—though complementary—trajectories. While Dussel's work presents a philosophical conceptualization of Modernity and of the modern subject, mine explores the conditions of Modernity *outside* of the so-called modern and developed world. Whereas his offers a universal and dialectic definition inclusive of the undeveloped world which appears to withdraw from and deny it, mine questions the benefits central Modernity accrues from its impositions on the undeveloped world. Whereas Dussels' work focuses on the construction of the modern subject (at the Center), based on an alterity that insures the legitimization of cultural practices, mine focuses on the construction of a subjectivity that resists Modernity's dominating and centralizing logos. My work also emphasizes the highly hierarchic and dehumanizing function of Modernity (regardless of its proclaimed humanizing rationality), which not only establishes areas of center and periphery in the global panorama of nations, but also different levels of Modernity, even in the developed world.

5. According to Juan Poblete's reading of Marshall Berman, Modernity would only reach its climax in the twentieth century, at the culmination of the process of modernization initiated during the first industrial revolution. See Poblete's discussion of Berman's ideas in "Homogeneización y heterogeneización en el debate sobre la modernidad y la postmodernidad," *Revista de Crítica Literaria Latinoamericana* 42 (1995): 115-30.

6. This theory focuses on the impact of economic, political, historical, external overdetermination on nation-states. The most important source is Fernando Henrique Cardoso and Enzo Faletto, *Dependency and Development in Latin America*, Marjory M. Urquidi, trans. (Berkeley: U of California P, 1979). Dependency Theory has been critiqued for falling into mechanistic schemas that "overemphasize the role of external components over internal ones" (Marcos Kaplan, "Las relaciones internacionales y el enfoque de la dependencia," in Octavio Ianni and M.K. *América Latina y Estados Unidos: Relaciones políticas internacionales y dependencia* (Lima: Instituto de Estudios Peruanos, 1973) 137.

7. Among the articles closest to our work we should mention José Ignacio López Soria, "La modernidad en el Perú," the conclusion of "Las lógicas de la modernidad," *Revista de la Facultad de Arquitectura, Urbanismo y Artes de la Universidad Nacional de Ingeniería* 2 (April 1988): 2-9, and David Sobrevilla, "¿Tradición, modernidad, o post-modernidad?" *Kachkaniraqmi* 8 (March 1993): 20-22.

8. Jürgen Habermas, *The Theory of Communicative Action. Volume One. Reason and the Rationalization of Society* (Beacon Press, 1984) 157.

9. José Ignacio López Soria, "Las lógicas de la modernidad" specifically refers to Heller's "History Retrieved?" in Agnes Heller, *A Theory of History* (London: Boston and Henley, Routledge & Kegan Paul, 1982) 281-98.

10. According to Beatriz Pastor's analysis in "Christopher Columbus and the Definition of America as Booty" (9-49) in *The Armature of Conquest. Spanish Accounts of the Discovery of America 1492-1589*, Lydia Hunt, trans. (Stanford: Stanford University Press, 1992).

11. In *Facundo, o civilización y barbarie* [1845] (Caracas: Biblioteca Ayacucho, No. 12, 1985), Chapter Fifteen "Presente y porvenir" [Present and Future], Domingo F. Sarmiento states that Argentina's "ignorant tyrant" Juan Manuel de Rosas prevents "Europe from penetrating the heart of America to obtain the resources we are unable to exploit." Later, more explicitly on the same page: "On the other hand, we Spaniards are neither industrious nor seafarers, and Europe will provide us, for centuries to come, with its artifacts in exchange for our raw materials" (232).

12. The widening gap between the rich and the poor in Latin America, especially in countries such as Perú and Argentina, which have most obediently applied the requirements both of the International Monetary Fund and of the external debt creditor countries, is hardly a secret. Once subsidies for basic needs disappear, the population's purchasing capacity is dramatically reduced. Elimination of incentives to internal production and reduction of tariffs on imports lead to massive bankruptcy of local industries and to massive layoffs. Enter transnationals, the middle class becomes impoverished, etc. True, fiscal management is orderly, but after ten years of neo-liberal prescriptions, it's clear that as the saying goes, "peor es el remedio que la enfermedad" [the medicine is worse than the sickness]. As G. Yúdice, J. Franco and J. Flores state: "Democracy and capitalism have proved time and again to sing a poor duet because they elide questions of social justice. Dramatic changes in the past two decades have put developmentalism and social justice in inverse relationship" ("Introduction" to *On Edge: The Crisis of Contemporary Latin American Culture,* viii).

13. José Enrique Rodó, *Ariel* [1900] translated, with an introductory essay, by F. J. Stimson (Boston and New York: Houghton, Mifflin company, 1922). Indeed, Rodó directs his eloquent nationalistic and modernizing discourse at the Latin American intellectual elite (obviously white and "criolla" [of Spanish descent]). The working classes are not included in his project (he rejects them because of their ugliness). Nor does he mention the racial and cultural plurality of the Latin American subcontinent.

14. Concocting a hybrid Andean and Afro-Caribbean music, the singer of the Peruvian "lírica chicha" almost invariably expresses the desire to conquer the Center. According to the lyrics, the Andean migrant resorts to all means to triumph in the great city; however, all he encounters is instability, margination, and poverty, "Fui minero, albañil y carpintero, / chofercito, ayudante y cobrador, / fui zapatero, sastre y mozo de bar, / ambulante, comerciante y panadero. // Fui y soy sólo un obrero / marginado y maltratado /. Fui y soy sólo un obrero / olvidado por la sociedad." Band "El Pumita y sus Geniales [I worked as a miner, construction worker, and carpenter, / driver, assistant, and collector, shoemender, tailor, and waiter, / street vendor, merchant and baker. // I was and I still am a marginalized and mistreated worker. / I was and I still am a worker / forgotten by society]. For this type of cultural hybrids, which I would term "self-reflexive" because they rationalize the social context and conditions of production, see among others, William Rowe and Vivian Schelling,

Memory and Modernity. Popular Culture in Latin America (London-New York: Verso, 1991), especially Chapter Two: "Urban Contexts."

15. Rigoberta Menchú (and Elisabeth Burgos-Debray, ed.), *I, Rigoberta Menchú: An Indian Woman in Guatemala,* Ann Wright, trans. (London: Verso, 1984).

16. Rama writes the following about José María Arguedas views on the relationship between Peruvian indigenous and *mestizo* culture: "Arguedas views the problem from the perspective of cultural anthropology rather than that of sociology. He is concerned about preserving national identity, as well as ethical and philosophical values of the indigenous culture, which he considers superior, such as the notions of property, labor, group solidarity, nature, and humanism). Rather than viewing *mestizo* culture as superior to the shielded culture of indigenous peoples . . . he views it as an efficient locus for the partial preservation of these values" Angel Rama, *Transculturación narrativa en América Latina* (México: Siglo XXI, 1982) 188.

17. See, among other sources, Angel Rama (ibid.); Antonio Cornejo Polar, *Escribir en el aire. Ensayo sobre la heterogeneidad socio-cultural en las literaturas andinas* (Lima: Editorial Horizonte, 1994); John Beverley and Hugo Achugar, eds., *La voz del otro: Testimonio, subalternidad y verdad narrativa,* special issue of *Revista de crítica literaria latinoamericana* 18.36 (1992).

18. Beatriz Sarlo, *Una modernidad periférica: Buenos Aires 1920-1930* (Buenos Aires: Ediciones Nueva Visión SAIC, 1988).

19. Alejo Carpentier's novel has been translated by John Sturrock as *Explosion in a Cathedral* (New York: The Noonday Press, 1963). C.L.R. James' work is titled *The Black Jacobins. Toussant L'Ouverture and the San Domingo Revolution* (New York: Vintage Books, 1989). Aimée Cesaire's essay has been translated by John Pinkham as *Discourse on Colonialism* (New York: Monthly Review Press, 1972).

20. In the "Introduction" to *I Rigoberta Menchú,* Elizabeth Burgos-Debray uses the term "internal colonization" to refer to profoundly heterogenous realities such as those of Guatemala, where a racial and cultural sector establishes relations of "domination and exclusion" of the others (xiii). In *The Theory of Communicative Action. Volume Two. Lifeworld and System: A Critique of Functionalist Reason* (Boston: Beacon Press, 1987), Jürgen Habermas resorts to the term "internal colonization" to refer to the control exerted by the economy, the state, and bureaucracies, over the sphere of civil life (lifeworld) in "developed capitalist societies" (356).

21. Eduardo Galeano, *Open Veins of Latin America: Five Centuries of the Pillage of a Continent,* C. Belfrage, trans. (New York and London: Monthly Review Press, 1973). According to Galeano: "Latin America is the region of open veins. Everything, from the discovery until our times, has always transmuted into European—or later United States—capital, and as such has accumulated in distant centers of power. Everything: the soil, its fruits, and its mineral-rich depths, the people and their capacity to work and to consume, natural resources and human resources" (12).

22. The protagonist of Carlos Fuentes's novel *The Death of Artemio Cruz,* A. MacAdam, trans. (New York: Farrar, Straus and Giroux, 1991), represents a sector of Latin American economic power which cloaks the transnational exploitation of local resources with apparent legality.

23. Rather than articulating aesthetic impressions derived from machinery, industrial production and speed, the work of these poets aimed at appropriating the most visible aspects of Modernity. See my article "La máquina como metáfora de modernización en la vanguardia latinoamericana" *Revista de crítica literaria latinoamericana* 48 (1998): 25-37.

24. See above article, section "El desencanto" (31-34).

25. Antonio Cornejo Polar, "Introduction," *Esribir en el aire* (Lima: Horizonte, 1994).

26. In "Una modernización que atrasa. La cultura bajo la regresión conservadora," (*Casa de las Américas* 34.193: 3-12), García Canclini refers to the neoliberal modernization which rages over Latin America toward the end of the millennium.

27. This is a reference to the 1997 election of the Argentine House of Representatives. According to a friend, "the defeat of President Menem's party allowed for the consolidation of the Alianza as a coalition of progressive parties which critique the neoliberal model imposed by the IMF (International Monetary Fund) and the World Bank. [. . .] While the Alianza celebrated partial victories in certain provinces such as San Juan and Neuquén, Menem's party won in other provinces such as Salta and Tucumán, where misguided local governments support metropolitan and centralizing economic policies rather than the local economy. The Alianza's is moderate program. It could not be otherwise since fragility and dependency currently drag Argentina down given its 140,000 billion dollar debt. A radical reform would unleash a financial coup d'état, similar to the one experienced during the last semester of Alfonsín's administration."

◆ 11.

The Latin American Writer in These Postmodern Times

Abelardo Castillo

(*translated by Cynthia M. Tompkins*)

In the nineteenth century, Nietzsche asked himself, "What is modern man?" He replied, "All that is disoriented, everything that is completely confused, that is modern man." Dostoyevsky begins *Notes from Underground*, that notable book which, I believe, laid the foundation for a new trend in contemporary literature, with the following words: "I am a sick man. I am evil." Dostoyevsky is not speaking about himself. As a writer, he is referring to himself, but he is referring to the condition of modern man, and he articulates it clearly toward the end of the Prologue, the true beginning of *Notes from Underground*. He considers the nineteenth century man an incomplete man, an unfulfilled man. According to Lev Shestov, this book was the *Critique of Pure Reason* of our time, a rebellion against reason; that is, against all those theories inherited from the Enlightenment, which have currently been critiqued by the so-called Postmodernity. I have quoted Dostoyevsky, and I could add Edgar Allan Poe. I am not the first to notice that the tone of Poe's *Eureka* is very similar to *Notes from Underground*, that *Eureka* constitutes an extremely violent critique of all modern man thought he could achieve through reason and science. I mention these writers because my topic is that of the writer in these postmodern times, and because the concept of Postmodernity—I'm referring to the *concept*, not to the term—is certainly not an idea that arose some weeks ago, or even in the last few years. It was foreseen by nineteenth century writers and poets, and it was even profoundly examined by thinkers of the twentieth century, such as Nikolai Berdiaev, Martin Buber, or Max Scheler, all of whom certainly preceded the so-called philosophers of Postmodernity.

Let me set the record straight. Postmodernity and Postmodernism appear to be synonymous. Accordingly, much has been said—chatted as Heidegger would say—about "Postmodernism" without taking into account that if Postmodernism is something at all, it is at most a theory of aesthetics, of recent date, linked to architecture, to dance, and to the theatre successively. It appears in the United States and travels to Europe. It can hardly explain the literary and philosophical phenomena of our time. Yet, Postmodernist art, Postmodernist literature, and even Postmodernist philosophy are current terms.

I shall not dwell on Postmodernism, but on *Postmodernity*.

What is Postmodernity, then? Strictly, Postmodernity is simply the era that supersedes Modernity. In other words, it's something that happens in history. Not as an "ism," not as a mere aesthetic theory, but as phenomenon in a certain global sense (though, not in another sense, as we shall see), a phenomenon that cannot be understood if we elude "history," even if certain postmodern philosophers may attempt to do so.

How would that Postmodernity be defined? The postmodern world would be marked by the acceleration of technological advances and by the appearance of the mass media. Consumption would be understood as the basic economic criterion, and it would displace knowledge, or in the words of one of its theorists, postmodern knowledge would hinge on the feasibility of transferring knowledge into information technology. According to this argument, science has reached its farthest limit. It no longer searches for truth—something communal, for all humans—rather, it becomes an organization of the knowledge that can be applied to technology, and it is therefore linked to the interest of the great corporations. Postmodern knowledge would appeal to certain philosophical trends—basically certain theories from Nietzsche, Heidegger, and Wittgenstein—which would link up with certain scientific disciplines to articulate a new pragmatic type of knowledge. Culturally, it would also imply two other things: a controversy with the theorists of the postindustrial state: Aron, Touraine, Bell, etc.—and at a deeper level, the negation of the paradigms of Enlightenment, i.e., reason, unlimited progress, and science—the founding principles of modern man. The denial of the Renaissance conception of freedom, as I would call it, which was deployed against superstition and the medieval order, appears to have catastrophically arrived at its limit. This conception of freedom which even nineteenth-century man deployed to realize the great doctrines, the great causes of peace and social justice, has at present become one of the *grands récits* [metanarratives], almost in the sense according to which we define narrative as fiction, in other words, as a fable.

Is this condition of Postmodern man, which is presented as universal, really universal? Are these historical transitions from one era to another really universal?

Let's think about the Renaissance, the environment that gave rise to modern man. The Renaissance was a historical phenomenon, mainly a *Central European* historical phenomenon. The Renaissance can no longer be understood merely as an aesthetic movement, as the recuperation of the values of antiquity. It was a vast and complex historical event, which *also* encompassed aesthetic disciplines, and installed a new conception of man in rupture with the conception of medieval man. But, did this Renaissance affect everyone? No, it did not even happen in all European nations. When we refer to the Renaissance, we basically mean the German and the Italian Renaissance. Can we speak of a Russian Renaissance? of a Spanish Renaissance? European peripheric peoples did not experience any renaissance whatsoever because they did not go through the historical process of the Renaissance. As for us Latin Americans, what do we have to do with the Renaissance? Undoubtedly, the voyages of Conquest, the so-called discovery of America—discovery from a European standpoint, since for thousands of years America had been discovered by Mayas, Aztecs, Incas, and Araucans—are a phenomenon of the Renaissance in the European sense. But, what did they have to do with our cultures, except in a few cases, with their destruction?

The question would be: What does this Postmodernity, which Central Europe and the United States refer to, have to do with Latin Americans? Or with Argentines? I do believe, however, though it may seem paradoxical, that it has a lot to do with us.

In contrast to the Enlightenment and Modernity, which were, as it were, broad but focalized phenomena, today we all experience the postmodern era. We are "post-modern" precisely by the "postmodern" facts and features which I consider negative.

If a Renaissance man, if Leonardo or Piero Della Francesca were resurrected today, they could believe that the great dreams of the Renaissance had been achieved in the twentieth century. Interplanetary voyages, information technology, the media that allows us to know about events almost at the same time they are taking place in another continent, the advances of physical and mathematical sciences and the spectacular discoveries of biology and medicine, give us the impression of being the culmination, and in some way they are, of the dreams of the unfettered Renaissance man, who fought against obscurantism and false religiosity (and I say false religiosity because I believe that to fight against religious feeling is one of the dangers of our time), of that modern man who wanted to achieve peace and social justice in this world. If Leonardo were resurrected and lived for a while on our planet, he could think that the Renaissance had in fact materialized in the twentieth century. But, is our century only that? Our century is also the century of the two World Wars, the century of the Holocaust, and I am not only referring to the Jewish holocaust—which has yielded significant dividends in cinema and TV lately—but to the holocaust of humanity in general, the Armenian holocaust, the Gypsy holocaust, the sixty or seventy million dead of World War II, to our thirty thousand disappeared, the one and a half million dead of the Spanish Civil War, to what is currently taking place in Bosnia and Chechnya, and in Rwanda and in the most undeveloped nations, to our "children of the street," and to all the people who die before they achieve their "natural" destiny, which is, if we believe in the Biblical words of King David, the age of seventy. No other century was as savage as ours. In our century we have killed more human beings than in all previous wars and plagues in history. That is also our era, this is our contemporary world, and it is also Postmodernity.

These are the negative features that affect us all. But there are also others. At present, a war would be a war of total annihilation. Up to now, only metaphorically can we talk about World Wars. These world wars were only nominal, they were not planetary. World War II did not affect us Latin Americans, World War I was a European conflict. If a world war were to take place nowadays, and if contemporary man deployed his weapons of destruction, it would be the end of the species. No one would be spared from that genocide, not even those who had not participated. Certain diseases—the so called Black Plague, for instance—which in their own time were considered divine punishments or universal calamities, were no more than very local phenomena. A disease like AIDS *is* universal. Whether we carry it or not, whether we are homosexual or not, whether we are drug addicts or not, no one is free from AIDS. The possible shortage of food in our planet in the next fifty years, the irrational felling of forests, the contamination of rivers and seas, the Ozone hole in Antarctica, any one of these events, even isolated, would be enough to end the world as we know it. What happens to us, then, who live with all of these threats, when we feel that they can be triggered, either individually or collectively, at any point?

But I don't want to continue without setting the record straight. I am neither a millennial nor an apocalyptic writer. I have a great sense of humor, which allows me not to be pessimistic. I am not a professional of catastrophe. I am simply stating facts.

I say that in *this* sense, Postmodernity encompasses all of us. In the other, undoubtedly not. What does information technology mean to Rwanda? What does interdisciplinarity mean to Chechnya? What does access to the First World mean to Latin America? A dream, a utopia, or perhaps the hope of arriving at Modernity at some point, especially given that most countries of the world are still to arrive at Modernity. It is the negative events that describe the contemporary world that really affect us all.

At a later point I shall discuss why mankind is at the brink of disaster, almost without a return ticket. Now I want to discuss the philosophical and metaphysical environment, the spiritual reality that surrounds this material reality we live in.

Renaissance mystics invented a beautiful metaphor to define the universe. They called it *Amplissima Domus*, the big house. The great house of man. Living in this house, man also had what they called *imago mundi*, an image of the world. For the Renaissance man, as complex as it might have become, the universe could still be sketched, as it were. The stars and their displacements in heaven were conceivable. It was not a Copernican heaven, it was even clearer, it was simpler. Kepler only needed three laws to cipher the universe. It was possible to know the house we lived in, and, in a certain way, we could map it. We lived in a comprehensible house.

No matter how wise, scientific, or even how "universal" contemporary man may be, he has no idea about the universe. He cannot know what it looks like, or how long it will last, nor the reason for its existence, nor anything about the house he is living in. This leads to an overwhelming feeling of being orphaned, which Martin Buber described in referring to the spiritual crisis that results when the pact between man and the universe is broken. It is not necessary to be a theist—I think I am an atheist—to feel the religious truth of Buber's phrase. The covenant with God or with the universe has been rescinded, it has broken down. We no longer know in which house we live, we don't know which world we inhabit, and we don't even know what life is for.

When I was fifteen, if anyone would have asked the members of my generation: What will the world look like in the twenty-first century? We would have had an answer. There might have been arbitrary, childish, or science fiction answers, but there would have been answers. For some the world would be as Ray Bradbury described it; for others, the stability of the beautiful socialist theories would have finally materialized. That these ideas were absurd or childish doesn't matter, what does matter is that it was possible to think about the year 2000 when I was fifteen. But I was fifteen in 1950, i.e., there still was half a century to go until the year 2000. If today one were to ask a kid, or a man, what the world would be like in fifty years, they would be clueless; moreover, they would not be able to think about the world fifty years hence. And I would say that the younger generations are not even interested in thinking about it. This leads me to the ahistoric feeling of the lack of a project, which also defines the Postmodern man. The Postmodern man does not know what will happen next. He is not interested in what may happen, nor can he even conceive of it. This feeling of insecurity results in privileging individualist and personalist theories, not in Mounier's sense of personalism (I'm referring to the French Christian philosopher who may have preceded Sartre in establishing the notion of engagement, and who understood the term "person" not as an isolated individual but as social singularity within a community), but in the broad sense of selfishness. This state of things has led to the *carpe diem* morale: to the feeling that all that man has is the present.

This famous appellation of *carpe diem* is, as everyone knows, a verse from Horace that has been traversing history for the last two thousand years. At one point or another, we have all felt that *carpe diem* described the essential truth of our predicament. Catullus' *Vivamus, mia Lesbia*, Hamlet's monolog before Yorick's grave, Ronsard's sonnet to Helen, are other manifestations of this *carpe diem*. In fact, being objective, what do we have but the present? We are here, that is all. Rather than being a great discovery, this is the most trivial description of what we call living.

When this is transposed to a general theory of a "non-project," of a "non-future," it begins to become the philosophy of the "What do I care." Today, we don't know what the world is, nor the reason for our being in the world. The *imago mundi*, the map of the world in the scientific and metaphysical sense, has disappeared.

But, and to go back to the pending question: What is it, in this chaos, that allows us not to become pessimistic?

I believe it is precisely this catastrophic—and for writers such as Ernesto Sábato—even apocalyptic moment we are living. It is precisely due to those negative universal facts that we can reconstruct what the ancients called the *amplissima domus*. There is a spiritual force that appears only at critical junctions, a very mysterious force which has made philosophers think, perhaps candidly, but at least not without reason, that man is essentially good. I don't know if essentially good or essentially evil, but I do know that in certain moments, not historical but familiar or quotidian moments, events such as the following occur. We may detest our neighbor, disdain him, or refuse to acknowledge him. We may even live in a huge apartment complex where we know no one. If this complex were to be on fire, we would find ourselves saving the life of the son of that man we weren't interested in, or even his TV, or his clothing. Likewise, when a ship sinks, women and children, no matter *who* they may happen to be, are the first to be saved. Because there is a notion, very much above the moral sense, which is the ethical sense, which thinks of, and privileges, the species over the individual. In a society undergoing a catastrophe, such as a city hit by an earthquake, if a building is on fire, or about to collapse, one tends to cooperate and help others, and one accepts naturally that others will collaborate with us. This would never happen if we were not essentially communal beings. The attention of several nations may be focused on the fate of a child trapped under the ruins of a collapsed building. It happens all the time. It happened when the AMIA was blown up.[1] We were all glued to the TV, wondering: "Is there anyone left? Will s/he be saved? Did they hear anyone breathing?" In those crucial and dramatic moments, the communal sense of the species is re-established. If we understand the contemporary world as a collapsing house or a sinking ship—as we should come to understand it before long—we are doubtless going to re-establish from its ruins, the Renaissance man's *amplissima domus.* We are going to realize: This is our home, the only home we have, and it is collapsing. We have to prop it up somehow.

All of the contemporary ecological theories, all the feelings of solidarity regarding nature and the respect for the animal species result from the discovery of that principle. I would add, that all of the emancipatory theories of our time are also related to this.

In the contemporary world the inclusion of women as providers of solutions, also speaks to the same issue. Women are closer to nature. My generation was raised disdaining women and disdaining nature. To the great thinkers that formed us, illustrious men who appeared to have total knowledge of the world, generous men, nature was always something negative, the "other," or the antihuman. Marx came to say that nature was reactionary. Thomas Mann and Sartre felt it was stupid. For men like Freud, it didn't even exist: What did exist was the secret man, the unconscious. Women are closer to nature and they have taught us that nature exists. It is the women who speak to plants, and water them. Women teach us to take care of animals and have an almost corporeal relationship with the world. If we pay attention to these larval theories we may be paying attention to the continued life of our planet. This is not a childish expression of desire, it is something that is undoubtedly happening and it is happening in the world at large.

Regarding the other, the significance of accelerated communication, computers, Internet connections, microcomputers and chips—the so called positive features of the postindustrial era of developed nations—I am under the impression that in Latin America these topics are part of a discussion that is still lagging. Latin America has not arrived at Modernity and it may have to skip the Modern Age to arrive at the future. Latin America is still a barbaric territory. But it is, at the same time, the land of dreams and of utopia.

Another topic of the theorists of Postmodernity is that of the end of utopia and the death of ideologies. They don't seem to have thought that the theoretical discourse of Postmodernity is nothing but an ideology. It's no more than what Lyotard would term a *récit* [a narrative], though I doubt Lyotard would consider what he tells us about Postmodernity a narrative. It is a narrative with the difference that it is not a metanarrative as the heroic narrative of social emancipation, it is a small narrative, analogous to the narrative that power has always articulated when it has become established with universal laws as absolute, the thought of a class or of the caste in power. Hegel, in his own way, did it when he placed the Prussian State practically on the cusp of his philosophy; North American and European theoreticians do it when they say, "utopias are over." What are they trying to tell us? That communal utopias are over. "The death of ideologies." Of which ideologies? Of the ideologies of emancipation and freedom. "The end of history." Of which history? Of socialist history. In short, what are they telling us? Let's leave things as they are. They are OK. We are in power, we have a car, a TV, access to the Internet. We have fought long enough to obtain a place in the party of the Millennium. And the poor of the world . . . ? Well, what can one do? The poor are a calamity that will have to be borne until they become extinct. Power refuses to say what it thinks. And it thinks the world would be much better off if, once and for all, the poor, the unnecessary poor would, all of a sudden, disappear. If someone were to decide to articulate this idea, the great repression would undoubtedly return, the new holocausts and the massive crimes, would recur, as they have so many times in history.

Which is, then, the function of the writer in this world? First, to point out the problem. It doesn't seem much, but as De Quincey would say, discovering a problem is no less than finding a solution. Second, not to abdicate of his condition as an intellectual. In other words: to become naturally, once again, what at some point used to be called an engaged intellectual.

I will return to what I understand by intellectual engagement despite my denial of an "engaged" literature.[2] The term intellectual was marked by disdain from its very inception. It was born in France, during the famous Manifesto of 1898, and it was a term that Clemenceau, the director of the *Aurora* newspaper, used to describe that protest: the *Manifesto of the Intellectuals*. Maurice Barrés, a kind of *avant la lettre* fascist, replied by stating there was nothing worse than these gangs of semi-intellectuals, aristocrats of thought, poor devils who would be ashamed of thinking simply as the French would. In other words, intellectuals were idiots who didn't know reality but offered their opinions about it. As that manifesto had been massively signed by writers—Emile Zola, Anatole France, Marcel Proust—who are now paradigmatic figures of French literature, since then it has been assumed that the intellectual is essentially a writer. This is more or less true, which also means it is more or less false. Not only is the writer an intellectual. A professor is also an intellectual, a reporter, a teacher, a lawyer, or a psychoanalyst, are also intellectuals. And if by intellectual we consider the man who resorts to his intelligence to do his work, one could almost say that the number of intellectuals in the world is much greater than what we may have thought. To use his diestock, a plumber has to resort to his strength, but he also has to execute some precise mental operations, he has to use his head. Conversely, a chess player—I am not looking down on chess, a game I worship and to which I devote my free time, when I am not obliged to think about Postmodernity—practically does nothing other than think. Yet, can he be called an intellectual? A chess player almost doesn't have to use his body, he could play the same game without looking at the pieces, and at times, the pieces become an obstacle in analyzing certain positions. To think then, is a necessary but not sufficient condition to designate an intellectual. There are men who think all day, yet they are not intellectuals. But a professor, a teacher, a psychoanalyst think and they are also intellectuals. What is then, an intellectual? Is he simply defined by his actions? He's more or less defined by his actions. It's not a social class, nor a craft. It's something like a caste. An intermediate caste between common man and what we call the "State," in other words, between average man and Power. But the State or Power cannot be confused with the government. I use "state" in Gramsci's sense. Today our State is the president and his ministers, as well as all of those who have money and retain real power. Beneath them, a strata of professors, physicians, psychoanalysts, writers, reporters, are the intellectuals, and they are, almost by definition, those destined to transfer the ideas of the powers that be to the average man, or to state it with the ancient term, the ideas of the dominant caste to the dispossessed, and to make believe, at times, that these ideas are the Absolute Idea of a definitive society, finalized forever without the possibility of change. This is the traditional intellectual, the intellectual used by the powers that be, and who, in a way or another, also belongs to that power.

But there is another type of intellectual, the intellectual defined by Gramsci, by Sartre, and by a postmodern thinker such as Jürgen Habermas. An intellectual who is not defined by acceptance of the moral and political norms of power, but by his opposition to these norms. This is the concept of the intellectual we can still recover, and I would say, we must recover. To do so, we have to be aware of the different ethical problems that appear in reality as if they were absolute truths.

When a psychoanalyst cures—or we assume he cures—an ill person, what is he really doing? He is returning that man to the society that made him sick; if that society made him ill, he will become ill again. The psychoanalyst is under the obligation of—this is not an idea of mine, Cooper and Laing and so many others said this in the 1960s—of thinking through the problem to see if all he can do as an intellectual is therapy, or if there is something more. When a lawyer establishes certain parameters of justice, he should consider whether he is merely a professional prosecutor or a defendant at any price for whomsoever has paid for his services, or rather, if he is someone who articulates the ethical principles of justice. And a writer—I am not talking about teachers and professors who face the problem daily—a writer is a man who, at least, has to start thinking about the purpose of words, that which Edgar Allan Poe called "the force of words," not only the poetic but also the transformative and mobilizing power of words. This power has manifested itself throughout the ages, because, to give only one example, the French Revolution was not only carried out with weapons or with the masses who took over the streets. It was the intellectuals, the Encyclopedists who formulated it first, the same way than our American revolutions always counted on their poets and writers to transform society. If we do not take into account what words are for, instead of trying "the power of words" we shall simply continue to be the *words of those in power.*

Today, we are led to believe that writers should limit themselves to imagining fictions, and poets to writing poems, but above all, to thinking about the problems of the market. Today, what is wanted is a generation of artists for whom the market may be something like a moral law. As the old writers of the generation of 1960, as writers and poets who are like museum pieces, I think we still have the right to establish *what* words are still *for.*

To conclude, I'll restrict myself to repeating an answer I gave to this problem some time ago. The question is: What is the place of the writer, in the contemporary world, or in the postmodern world? I said it would be easier to answer the question—and the answer would be more disenchanting—if we asked ourselves about the place of art in general. If by place we mean influence or practical importance, art occupies no place at all. In the 1960s or even in the 1970s, one could speak about the mission of the writer, of his fate, his engagement with history. One would talk about literature as a weapon, as a tool, or as a mode of knowledge. As a kind of aesthetic artifact, in sum, destined—even in the long run—to influence people or to change the world. It doesn't matter that these ideas were false. It doesn't matter that a novel cannot change the world. What does matter is that these ideas *could be thought* and above all, that they allowed the writer to write. Writing poetry, writing fiction, was always a secretly shameful craft. The problem of the contemporary writer is that he no longer asks himself what literature is for, and he doesn't ask himself the question for fear of the answer. As a writer, one cannot ponder the general meaning of literature without considering the specific meaning of *my* literature. The traditional writer solved that problem imagining that, at least, he was necessary. A kind of marginal worker, or a marginal philosopher, but none the less, necessary. Today, he suspects that this is a false alibi, and with feigned humility, he becomes pragmatic: He sees himself as a pure object of the market economy. A book, he thinks, is something for sale; therefore, its author is a producer of consumer goods. The goal of a novel is not to live on, nor to provide a testimony on the world, not even to be read. The goal of a novel is to be sold. Editors and literary supplements have accustomed us to that. There are no lists of the best books. No one lists the best books. There are best seller lists. There are no indicators of value. If sometime someone were to hold a slightly heterogeneous competition and placed TVs, marihuana, computers, and novels on the same rank, doubtless, books would disappear from the best seller lists. In a country where fiction, and let's not even talk about poetry, sells no more than two or three thousand volumes, and this when it becomes a kind of national success, it is hard, being a writer, to imagine that one still occupies a place. Who is to blame? I admit I don't know. And I confess I am not very interested in the publishing angle of the problem.

We are experiencing what I would call a universal crisis of meaning. Neither religion, nor science, nor art, provide answers any longer. The end of history, the end of ideologies and the death of utopias, simply mean that we fail to understand the meaning of the world. The question would then be: What is the meaning of literature in a world that has lost its meaning? There can only be two answers. The first: no meaning. The second is precisely the one that seems to be out of fashion nowadays: The meaning of literature, as the meaning of art, is to imagine a meaning for the world, and therefore, for the writer or the artist that produces that literature or that art. In this, the contemporary Argentine writer, the writer of the nineteenth century, or of the 1960s and the writer in Dante's times, are exactly alike. The writer of fictions writes to establish a new meaning for the world. As Unamuno would say: "To return it to God in order." To make, with the fragments of this broken world, some "other" thing, which, in the aesthetic field is called the poetic object, and in the categories of thought will continue to be considered ideology, politics, and ethics.

I said before that art occupies no place at all. This also seems to be a good answer, a metaphoric and therefore literary answer. We all know that utopia means precisely that: no place. A writer is not only someone who publishes books and signs contracts and appears on TV. A writer is a man who establishes his place in utopia.

Notes

1. In the July 18, 1994, bombing of the AMIA (Asociación Mutua Israelita Argentina [Israeli Mutual Association in Argentina], 86 people lost their lives, dozens were injured and the building was demolished. [Translator's Note].

2. The question of engagement was discussed in subsequent conversations. This essay was read at the Feria del libro [Book Fair], held in Córdoba, Argentina, 1996. Summing it up briefly, I understand it as follows: Poetry and fiction, as aesthetic objects, do not have to be engaged; it is the writer or the poet, as an intellectual, who shows his engagements by means of his opinions and actions.

Part IV   Changing Cultural Dossier:
Some Classic Texts from the 1990s

◆ **12.**

Variations on Postmodernity, or, What Does the Latin American Postboom Mean?

Mempo Giardinelli

(*translated by Daniel Joseph Smith*)

I will begin by confessing my prejudices, my fears, and my confusion. As such, I hope that my words are taken only on the basis of these assertions.[1] I would also hope that what I may say is taken provisionally, as the simple reflection of a Latin American intellectual, a writer who endeavors to explain—through self-analysis—the time and place in which he produces his work. I must say that every time I find myself before the need to articulate definitions, I feel a panic come over me, and a vehement desire to resist them wins over. To me, everything that is defined begins to die. To me, every explanation, every conclusion, is a death. Therefore, I believe that possibilities are life, and for this reason every time someone sets out to define something I feel a mix of envy and misgiving. Regarding literary movements, I feel that every time someone defines one, in reality he is speaking of something that has already existed for a long time even though the definer considers himself a pioneer of his time.

Did this not happen, already, with the so-called *boom* of the 1960s, with surrealism before that? Those who were defining them believed that they were discovering what already had been discovered by Rabelais, Hieronymus Bosch or Cervantes. Or one could point to Christopher Columbus himself who, in his obstinance and monumental error was the true founder of the so-called Latin American Magic Realism. Five hundred years ago, not thirty. And we have as proof his memorable Journal of the First Voyage.

Does this remind you of something similar happening now? What defines Postmodernism? Minimalism, intensity, existentialism, discouragement, a hatred of so-called moral values? Compressed form and the opposition to the Baroque? The presence of audiovisual devices? The decline in reading ability and its substitute—a very simplified and simple thought process, as seen in contemporary societies? Or, perhaps it is the 1968 fiasco, Vietnam, the lost Latin American social revolution, and the so-called death of utopias? All of this and a whole lot more, as seen in the general decadence of our societies: the deterioration of the quality of life, irrational urban violence (it would be fitting to wonder, above all here in Colombia, if some violence exists that is "rational"), the disregard for one's own life and therefore for the life of another, and sharpened social resentment, are all elements of Postmodernity, according to what we read from many authors. As is also not believing in God, nor in one's mother, nor in politics, nor in progress, nor in ethics, and then to think "who cares?" or "we have already passed that stage." A context, by the way, in which it is natural that drugs appear to be the way to false, illusory nirvanas.

Have I by any chance failed to mention something else that defines Postmodernity? Well, if that ensemble somehow results in an idea of a contemporary aesthetic, it does not seem that bad to me, it seems unavoidable. Even though I would love to see if we could judge that aesthetic in thirty or forty years—which would be the prudent thing to—I think perhaps considering these aspects here and now is unavoidable, simply because they make up the world in which we operate and in which we produce our works.

Of course as an author myself, I want to clarify the fact that I do not presume this aesthetic to revolutionize anything, nor that it is that original. It is that it never ceases to be a *melange*, and it is that because it is an indicator of the mix in which we live. That which we Argentines, using tango slang, call *cambalache*, that is to say an absurd but possible mix of the Bible and boiler, Carnera champion, and San Martín.[2]

Postmodernism, then, would be a *summa*, an accumulation of existential and everyday circumstances that is outlining its own aesthetic and philosophy. In this sense, one understands the coexistence of epigons such as Beckett or Carver or Bukowski all mixed-up with Almodóvar and Eliseo Subiela, with Madonna, and with Sting.

In my opinion, all these characteristics—interchangeable, intertwining, dynamic—have every right (I would say the necessity) to be expressed. And they are expressed, in effect, as part of this aesthetic that we are checking out, assimilating and some, many, are resisting. Which is not my case. To the contrary, I believe that we have to avoid resisting, and require, as I usually do of myself, understanding before any judgment. And in order to be able to understand I have to go back to a revision of my own culture. And I ask myself: Is it not true that we come from a culture that at least since the Second World War seems compelled to celebrate hypocrisy and ignorance? Is not this a culture which justifies stupidity, lack of effort, and falsification? Were not my parents—many parents—hopelessly mediocre in leaving us an irrational and unmerciful world, in schizophrenic contrast with attractive discourses, and a generalized political attitude of corruption and oversimplifications? Haven't we seen a mediocre actor, whom Aeschylus would have disdained, governing the most powerful nation on Earth? Are we not products of an education that sanctified the poor distribution of wealth, that preached peace while making war and that showed us gods to fear rather than to adore?

I do not feel frightened nor overwhelmed by all this. I admit to being an idealist, and I aspire to be a passionate witness-protagonist of this time. It seems to me, then, that certain projects, certain iconoclastic attitudes of some postmodern youth in my country, who scorn and reject all which is established and more or less recognized, famous or consecrated, are in a certain way attitudes of rebellion. Why not think then, I propose, that maybe Postmodernity is a scream of possible rebellion at the end of the millennium? And why not think, also, that like all screams it is at the same time one of impotence and of pain, and a request for help, a desire for redemption?

This issue of Postmodernity also seems to me, at times, a little tricky. And let me say why: Because it would seem to presume to establish an unnecessary and futile limit: One has to be on one side or on the other. It pretends that the *postmodern* is in and what is modern becomes old and therefore *out*. I do not like this, because it does not seem to me to be a legitimate intellectual attitude. To cut, to segment, to schematize, can be a good method of investigation, analysis, and criticism, but to me it does not seem a valid method in understanding an aesthetic. A lot less valid, I would say, since all aesthetic should be considered and looked at globally, universally and in its totality.

Moreover, I am convinced that to be modern—or to presume to be—is a way to rebel, to question, and to protest against the establishment. To be modern is to question and to protest and to transgress, and this has occurred at every time and every place because it makes up the constitution of the intellectual and of the artist. Therefore, I suspect that since one can't avoid the sensation of amazement produced by the world in which we live, a world that is overwhelmingly, distressingly and exasperatingly modern to the point of suffocation, then it would seem that we must be postmodern. From which one infers that Postmodernity would be something like the modernity of Modernity. Marilyne Robinson has said it best in her excellent work on Raymond Carver's short stories: "The idea of the modern is so, so old, that it has had to be re-labeled as *postmodern*, and with the guarantee that the new product is even more arid, more cynical, more abysmal than the product to which we are accustomed."[3]

As you can see, what I am doing is a simple variation on a theme that worries me, and for which I am hard pressed to give a full judgment. It worries me because, like it or not, it is the aesthetic of my time, the time in which I live and write. And because my own work—although it is not up to me to speak about it—is immersed in, accompanies, and traverses this aesthetic, despite my best intentions. It is because I myself, when I search and question, when I make literature in order to know why I make it, when I rack my poor brain in order to reach a little understanding, am entering into this modernity of Modernity. And entering with guts, with force, with everything, because for me to write is to transgress, to question, to protest, and to denounce; in the same way it is to suggest and to shake-up, because one writes from one's own desperation.

Of course I distance myself from the overbearing attitude of immature postmoderns (in my country we call such attitude *canchera, sobradora*). I mean to say that I work to keep far away from the iconoclastic attitude of some of the petty rebels that abound in my country. It is just that I do not share the skepticism of a pseudo-Nietzschean pose. I do not share the iconoclasm nor the "don't give a damn" attitude, which is essentially nihilistic. Rather, I believe in Postmodernity as the modernity of Modernity but with a renovating spirit overflowing with projects that do not shoot down the utopias by decree, but rather rethink them in order to update them and adapt them—meaning modernize them—to the times of our lives.

If I were told that Postmodernity equals reductionism, as if to be postmodern meant to be minimalist, I am opposed. If I were told Postmodernity only consists of a return to the existentialism of Samuel Beckett—full of atrocities, skepticism, disenchantment, fatalism, and that "don't give a damn," "being past that" or "who cares" attitude—I confess that I do not like it, and that I continue to prefer Sartrean existentialism. If I were told that Postmodernity in literature is the grotesque, disillusioned, and incoherent lyricism, fictionalization based on the lack of adjectives and on cryptic minimalism, it does not seem to me to be sufficient.

But I do confess to be postmodern and to accept its postulates, if Postmodernity is understood as an *attitude* of rebellion and purposeful inconformity. *If Postmodernity is—as I believe it to be—an enduring Modernity.*

It is in this sense that I have understood for some time the so-called *postboom*, a designation that is perhaps not very felicitous, and which of course is not of my choosing. This is what I wrote between 1984 and 1985 in some articles in my country, and said in various lectures I gave at North American universities since then. And when I speak in this sense I am referring to the fact that this is a type of writing that contains a high charge of frustration, of pain and of sadness for all that happened to us in the 1970s and 1980s; the charge of unease, anger and rebellion (that is to say, Modernity) because of the world which came out of all that, which we inhabit and do not like. However, it is also a literature (and this is to me a central aspect) that does not contain self-deprecation nor humiliation. There is no self-pity, nor winks of complicity, nor exaggeration, nor anything even close to exoticism, so that North America and Europe may read in us what they want to see and with some prejudice what they already know about us: that we are disorganized, idle, corrupt, *machista*, racist, mulatta-chasing, authoritarian, and incapable of living in a democracy.

To me, in literature, Postmodernity, postboom, or whatever you want to call it, is a writing of pain and of rebellion but without demagogic poses, without becoming accomplished at the art of disdain, at complacency, exile, at anything. In other words, to be postmodern is to be forever modern, forever young, forever a rebel, forever a transgressor, and a nonconformist with a fighter's spirit, steadfast aesthetic and ethical attitude.

Even though—I insist—I avoid defining postmodern writing, given the character of this forum, I would like to share with you some considerations which, in my opinion, could help to round out the concept. These observations, which are provisional, are the following:

1) Postmodern writing abandons certain now classic attributes of a Borges, Cortázar, and García Márquez type of writing. Presently, there is not as much delicate wordsmithing, nor rhetorical narcissism (as Juan Manuel Marcos has called it) that seduces the reader who is dazzled more by the artistry of the author than by the actual narrated material. In distancing itself from this type of virtuosity, postmodern writing strives to immerse itself in the recovery of oral voices, in certain simplicity of exposition, and in avoiding a forced, exaggerated depiction of the characters' traits. Postmodern style is less sophisticated.

2) Exile—interior or exterior—is a product of our nations being torn apart, and is almost unavoidably present in our prose works. Our pain, anger, and our impotence because of the dead that we have suffered, stand out in a more timid and cautious type of writing. At the same time this writing suggests itself, I believe, as an exhortation to reflect, to reevaluate life far from dogmatic considerations. It is evident that Postmodernity is aloof from politically committed discourses and does not pretend to create a literature in the service of any ideology or revolution. Perhaps that is why we have become so solemn without appearing so, less capable of verbal play. And perhaps, therefore, our sense of humor is sometimes rather parodic

and essentially so sad. Just as other generations have defined themselves by great world wars, by the dictators of the *belle époque*, or by the Cuban revolution, I believe that the writing of the *postboom* stands politically for democracy, for peaceful coexistence, and for social justice as a slow and steady construction. Cautious and less flamboyant, the contemporary Latin American writers have sympathized in an almost unanimous way—yet not dogmatically—with Sandinista Nicaragua, in the same way that they condemn abuses and disappearances (that damned euphemism of our time) and fight for the return of the exiled to their home countries.

3) Postmodern writing reveals a marked influence of audiovisual mass media. In contemporary literature, there is an almost unavoidable cinematographic vision, and one sees it in the return to the short sentence, precise framing, the uncomplicated metaphor, direct poetic tone, and to atmospheric portrayal. It is necessary to mention that there were several precursors from the late sixties and in the seventies. At least three come to mind: Manuel Puig in Argentina; Antonio Skármeta in Chile, and José Agustín in Mexico. Perhaps we could add here the late Colombian Andrés Caicedo.

4) Postmodern writing does not seem to wander into Magic Realism, or into the Marvelous Real. At least one does not see it as a determinant aspect. Today, forms and structures seem more simple and compressed (minimalist), in the same way that the contents tend to be more rooted in recent memory, in a shared life experience with the reader. There is a return to realism, and to the oral quality revealed by the strong presence of detective literature as a vehicle for describing our societies. The *noir* detective genre in some way drives home its expressive code, based on the vertiginous aspect of the action, its continuous sequence, on the constant use of dialogue and the characters' harshness and/or lack of feelings. This writing is less grounded in myths and legends (even though it can contain them), and it is far away from limitlessness and exaggeration. *Postboom* writing has no use for the old, literary, mythical nineteenth-century dictator, a character bordering on a caricature—paternalistic, involuntarily sympathetic, the head of some banana republic, playful and comically arbitrary and corrupt. No, our today's dictators are cold-blooded and intelligent assassins, well educated, who know how to speak in public, and who resist being judged. They are no longer those likable villains, the simple scoundrels who marveled the European readers, but rather all too human oppressors, recognizable authoritarians. Dictatorships are a somber presence that looms over the texts without explication, without description.

5) During the *postboom* one witnesses the end to *machista* literature. Models and preoccupations have changed. Women in literature, in the service of the *macho* and the kitchen, are no longer invented, nor admitted. Traditional *machismo* is a true symbol

of previous generations. In Postmodernity, the female characters no longer appear stratified as prostitutes, unfaithful, subdued, authoritarian, castrating, ambitious, snobby, objects of pleasure or witches. And even better, now women writers have a place in literature unlike in any previous generation. María Luisa Puga and Ethel Krauze in Mexico; Angélica Gorodischer, Reina Roffé, and Ana María Shúa in Argentina; Cristina Peri-Rossi in Uruguay, Isabel Allende in Chile, Rosario Ferré and Ana Lydia Vega in Puerto Rico, and many others that surely I am forgetting, occupy a place that decades ago was denied such writers as Rosario Castellanos, Eunice Odio, Herminia Brumana or Silvina Ocampo.

6) Postmodern writing works with quite unpleasant topics that are in no way treated in a pleasant manner: death, violence, rape, genocide, as well as desperation, alienation, brutalization, and the indifferent contemplation of the world's collapse. Everything is more real and tangible (Carver's style); death is something suffered, seen and palpable. It is a type of writing that gives a mirror reflection to contemplating a horrible face in which pessimism stands out. Corruption, crimes of the state, lowered ethical standards, perversion, profit, and transgression, are constants. But there is not always an unavoidable condemnation in these texts. Many of us do not want to admit that things cannot change, or that the government of calamities and exuberance cannot be rooted out.

7) We are marked by new, end-of-the-century motifs: cybernetics, the so-called "low intensity" clandestine wars, the political lie turned style, the alienation caused by television turned virtue and the simplification of the present day world that divides everything into either good or bad, black or white, communists or freedom fighters. We are overwhelmed by external debt, the loss of readers, and racism vs. sexism. It is for this reason that there is resignation and pessimism in postmodern writing. However, the teachings of some of the masters' narratives, whose works seemed to encourage the possibility of change, when in reality they confirmed one's resignation, have been abandoned. The literary allusion, as it seems to me that all narrative texts are, in the *postboom* has become more subtle, that is to say, less evident, less moralizing, less sententious. That unbearable urge that seemed to keep the masters of the *boom* up at night, the urge to write "The Great Latin American Novel," has been forgotten, thank God.

8) I believe that the role of the author in and of itself has changed. There is not as much stardom seeking among contemporary authors. There are no great figures, and although there are interesting works, no one dares to come forth as nurturer of the myth of the writer (of which I am glad). I believe that today the great majority of the 200, 300, 500 or more writers that make up this so-called *postboom*, do not hold that vocation to *be exotic and to show it off,*

which seemed so common among famous writers that were young 30 years ago, and who enjoyed the fruits of the *boom*.

9) Finally, as Ricardo Piglia has pointed out, in Latin America today we write *against* politics. It seems to me, without doubt, that this also sets us apart. Today we attempt to take politics out of our fiction, we try to stop it from irrupting into our pages. We have respect for politics: we practice it, we have suffered it and *because of it* we have exiled ourselves. And that is precisely why we do not want it to infiltrate our works. We want our fictions to be only that: an expression of the imagination, pure invention. And nevertheless, this is impossible for us, and I would say that this constitutes our daily conflict: I myself, as a writer, admit that even though I usually demand that politics not enter into my works, it almost inevitably filters in. And I will add that in Latin America—and particularly in Argentina—we continue to write today in order to rid ourselves of fear, to defeat it. For this reason I would complete Piglia's formulation and say that we write *not only against politics, but also against fear and forgetfulness*. In other words: I believe that, to the contrary of the *boom*, we now do not write to satisfy, to please, or to be loved. Today we write to question, to experiment, to know and to discover. But also, and above all, *to remember* and perhaps, in this way, *to survive*.

Notes

1. This paper was read at the 3rd Annual International Literature Congress of Bogotá, the 5th of May, 1990, under the title of "Postmodernity and Postboom in Latin American Literature."

2. Carnera, the Argentine heavyweight champion; general San Martín, the liberator of Chile and Peru. [Translator's Note].

3. See *Quimera* number 4, Latin American edition.

13.

Latin America and Postmodernity

Nelly Richards

(*translated by Cynthia M. Tompkins*)[1]

Which "Postmodernity" and from Which "Us"?

An analysis of the convergence and divergence of the interrelation between Latin America and Postmodernity is complex:

> 1. Because of the elusive nature of the traits that name the disperse configuration labeled Postmodernity which lacks the guarantee of a faithful definition. A medley of *moods* (suspicion in philosophy, parody and simulacrum in aesthetics, deconstruction in theory and criticism, skepticism in politics, relativity in ethics and syncretism in culture) and *fashions* (a collage of styles and references to the past in architecture, post-Marxist disenchantment, narcissistic playfulness and *cool* relaxation, a neutral eclecticism in cultural judgment, a bland pluralism in social consensus, etc.), leads to the confusion between Postmodernity and Postmodernism(s), which becomes the enveloping sign of a diffuse feeling accompanying epoch-making changes marked by the *dissemination* and *contamination* of meaning, namely, the crisis of the totality and the pluralization of the fragment, the crisis of univocity and the multiplication of differences, the crisis of centrality and the overflowing proliferation of the margins.

2. Because of the unevenness of the Latin American integration of the nonequivalent historic and cultural processes that shape each country. Neither Perú, nor Chile or Argentina share the same antecedents regarding "modernity," "modernizations" and "modernism." Not only did these tendencies not develop uniformly, but the sedimentation of the fusion between myth and history, rites and progress, tradition and the market, was dissimilar as well. Furthermore, the disposition of each context regarding the Postmodern exigency of a critical balance of the accomplishments and frustrations of Modernity precludes comparison and the effect of the dynamic of forces and resistances is too variable and specific.

Perhaps we could agree on a representative marking of the category "Postmodernity" by synthesizing its predominant traits: the fracturing of ideals (the subject, history, and progress as absolutes of rationality) that monolithically regulated the civilizing process of the dominant Western Modernity; the resulting heterogeneity of signs and the multiplicity of meanings; the transformation from the macro-social phase of integrative forces of power to the micro-social phase of disintegrating forces; the abandonment of certainties and the resignation to partiality and relativity as shattered horizons of a new theoretical and cultural landscape located under the vacillating sign of doubt; the decorporeality of social reality converted into a mass media artifice through images whose specificity and temporality have lost historical texture and density, etc. But our physiognomy (as the Latin American site of the question on whether and *how* Postmodernity affects us) is so different that it fragments the subject of enunciation into parts that are not always compatible. Still, even as a polemical notation of a difference to be activated against the international postmodern dominant—"Latin America" designates an area of experience (named marginality, dependency, subalternity, decentering), common to the countries located at the margin of the dominant Western model of centralized Modernity. Therefore, one of the questions raised in this essay is: How does the postmodern discourse that theorizes the failure of centralized Modernity (disorganize, reformulate) intervene on the ways Latin Americans imagined themselves under modernist dependency?

How Can We Talk About What's "Ours" If the Repertoire of Our Terms Is Borrowed?

In Latin America, the extent of the trauma of colonization, and the subsequent struggle to break from peripheric subordination influences the transfer of cultural systems from abroad, which are received with distrust, with the suspicion that taints the transfer mechanism between the foreign and the national, the imported and the local, the international and the domestic.

In Latin America, discussion on Postmodernity is still viewed as an imitative tic, an alienated copy, as falling prey to an international fad, copying the last fact promoted by the information market, surrendering to the foreign impulse by mimicry. This disqualification tends to be supported by a complementary argument to prevent the transplant. Upon comparing realities, the contrast between *overabundance* (the postindustrial context of hyper-consumerism and information overflow that leads to the examination of the shattering or the exhaustion of international Modernity) and *lack* (the Latin America landscape is still marked by the stigma of poverty, oppression and violence), is extreme. The social and economic inequality between hyperabundance and lack (morally) precludes a comparison between these two poles of experience and impairs the transfer of the critical and theoretical content of the discussion.

There would also be a certain insolence in addressing Postmodernism from our standpoint, due to the way postmodern discourse attacks the Latin American generation that heroically subscribed to the Third-World faith in the revolution and the "New Man."[2] As a *theory of excess* and an *aesthetics of indifference* (resulting from hyped mass-media overexposure and the shattering of the self-fulfilled images of the market) Postmodernism violates two basic tenets of solidarity in underdeveloped countries: poverty and social and political commitment, which served as vindicating banners of the Latin American social conscience of the 1960s. That same revolutionary and utopian intelligentsia resents the mockery of postmodern irony because it discredits the ethical backbone of their militant discourse. Indeed, there would be a "certain legitimacy in arguing that in countries where poverty, hunger, unemployment and illiteracy are endemic, the issue of Postmodernism may appear to be an exotic luxury,"[3] and perhaps a perverse one too. But only if we remain within a mechanistic paradigm that explains economic and social development and cultural processes through linear interdependencies between phenomena and events. We know that the serial nature of culture and society leads to an interaction marked by imbalance, contradiction, and asymmetry. Given that the history of the avant-garde movements in Latin America reveals multiple and productive "imbalances between cultural modernism and social modernization,"[4] it is unnecessary to reproduce the structure of First World Postmodernism to allow for Latin American cultural thought to include in its aesthetic and theoretical folds, motifs *obliquely* linked to Postmodernism, for its shadows and nooks will be examined due to the incitement to think them through the lens of ambiguity, surprise, and incongruity. The evidence that the language that describes

Postmodernity in its international phase does not belong to the same register (of reasons and explanations) as the seemingly corresponding signs, appearing as analogies or simulations in Latin America, is not sufficient to disallow local reflection on Postmodernism.

Let us get beyond the obvious incompatibility between the socioeconomic determinants that affect the crisis at each geographic point of the axis of power (center-periphery), to surrender to the subtle play between continuities and gaps that attracts us to the bifurcating ramification of the multilinear nature of Postmodernism. The turning around and the to and fro movement between what the international discourse shapes and patents as postmodern concepts and the fractions of our reality that these terms allow to describe even as they resist them, also allows us to try out names that may be useful as we attempt to "re-cognize" ourselves as part of the crisis of meaning, but as interested parties in reverting that crisis purporting, as we are, to name ourselves.

Modernity, Tradition, Postmodernity: The Latin American Collage

Postmodern discourse gathers the periodizing signs that define our present, either from the symptoms of its crisis (as discomfort) or from the theatricality of its artifice (as spectacle). But this epoch-marking discourse follows the zigzagging rhythm of a transhistoric sensitivity. Belying the order assigned by the *post* prefix, Postmodernity does not follow Modernity (as its most recent and perfect "ending," its polished "perfection"). Rather, it offers a pretext to reread it from the vantage point of the suspicion that historically weighs over the cognitive and instrumental articulations of its universal design.

Several of our authors have accepted the postmodern challenge by engaging in a critical revision of Latin American Modernity: its particular constitution and varieties of development, its programmatic flaws or unfulfilled goals, its accidental unfolding, its resolving and dissolving movements. This is a strategic revision since Latin American Modernity is still in the process of rethinking itself, and thus continues to be open to new configurations of meaning resulting from the alternatives to the present that recreate the past according to present wagers.

Various divergences appear in the arguments posited by these authors on the issue of peripheric Modernity: a Modernity unhinged from its European matrix by the asynchrony of the process of cultural formation and social instrumentation that displaced the metropolitan design of the uniform series of advancement/progress. The unresolved tensions between Modernity and tradition may be the most striking counterpoint. On the one hand, the functionalist rationality of European Modernity and its secularizing paradigm are considered to have censored the rituals of a *mestizo* culture that expresses its Latin American identity through the ethical and religious contents of its faith. And both the ideology of the structure and technical aspects of the market are considered to have deculturalized the popular traditions that guard the Latin American ethos.[5] On the other, it prizes the heterogeneity of social and cultural effects of Latin America's Modernity, resulting from the interactions between the transnational market and the mixture of codes recombined by the clash between networks of consumerism (North American hegemony) and popular symbols and daily rituals, that succeed in contradicting (through opacity, delay, and resistance) the tendency towards uniformity of the international Modernity's progress vector.[6]

But if something should be learned from the postmodern flexion, (about the way it realigns the temporal order of precedence and succession), that is precisely its capacity to fragment and recombine historical memories in discontinuous and haphazard ways. Tradition and Modernity—in postmodern language—are no longer opposed under the sign of rupture between the antagonism of the old (repetition) and the new (transformation). Postmodernity disorganizes and reorganizes the process of its phases due to the transversal vectors that alternate pasts and presents in sequences disrupted by the operation of historical citation. Accordingly, Modernity did not arrive to substitute tradition but to *intermingle* with it in a mass of signs that link backwardness and development, oral culture and telecommunication, folklore and industry, myth and ideology, ritual and simulacrum. All of these half-obscurantist and half-enlightened signs share the asynchronicity of a *collage* resulting from the sedimentation, juxtaposition, and cross-breeding of indigenous traditions, "Catholic Hispanism, and modern political, educational and communicational activities [through] an inter-class *mestizaje* that generated hybrid forms at all societal levels."[7] Latin American cultural heterogeneity (*mestizaje* of identities, hybridity of traditions, fusion of languages), may have arrived (by fragmentation and dissemination) at a kind of *avant la lettre* Postmodernism, according to which Latin America, traditionally subordinate and imitative, would be a precursor of what postmodern culture consecrates as a novelty. By the admixture of signs, the transplants and grafts of disjointed historical and cultural codes, the Latin American mosaic would have foreshadowed the postmodern *collage*. In this sense, Latin American Postmodernity would never be the conclusive "afterward" of an all too unfinished Modernity. It is the translinear exacerbation of what this Modernity already contained as heteroclite and mixed—the figural paroxysm of its variegated multitemporality of disconnected references and fragmented memories.

The Postmodern Wink: Politics and Aesthetics

It is possible to argue in favor of a Latin American interest in the postmodern debate by stating that we are an interdependent part of a global network of influences linked by the communicational here-and-now of the receptor subjects disseminated in the center and the periphery of cultural information. This globalization of culture would, in and of itself, force us to take a position so as not to lose our situational awareness.

But other authors prefer to point out certain similarities that, allusively, link Latin American factions to postmodern angles, to defend the relevance of a critical link between international figuration and local casts, either following the complications of an identical script, or unraveling the hints of its misunderstandings through mistaken similarities or pseudo-likenesses. The first area of similarity brings *politics* to the limelight. It is not very hard to relate, even if the frame of the comparison may seem twisted or warped, the "dissolution of the social link" which results in the incoherence of any sketch of univocity under postmodern conditions there, and the fragmentation of the communal fabric, dislocated by the violence of the institutional fracture typical of regions subjected to oppressive powers, here. Most of what crumbles up the postmodern façade (from the rupture of the social nexus to the emptying of the referents—leadership for mobilization and struggle) is reflected among us, though darkened by the drama of a historical convulsion (dictatorship), which shakes up the thesis of a relaxed "end of history" currently espoused by "integrated apocalyptics."[8]

The failure of history as an ascending continuum, the decline of the totalizing ideals of social revolution projected as end in themselves, the crisis of absolutes and the consequent fracture of the political/revolutionary image of an awareness that embodied truth as dogma (class struggle or party), the revalorization of democracy as an antitotalitarian response, and the pluralist framework of the social contract, the reformulation of combatant roles based on the demystification of the proletariat as the only key to liberating victory and the rise of new diversified social subjects who claim their minority right to difference, are factors of the postdictatorial experience of Latin American states that narrow the gap between their new political horizon and the detotalizing changes of state-power-society-institutions ciphered on the micro-social postmodern theory.

There is another set of markers—no longer political but cultural—which recur in all of the Latin American aesthetic and critical production, which are considered to be similar to the styles of the postmodern repertoire. All these markers are related to the culture of reproduction in which—due to an addiction to imitation or mania for simulation—each image is an image of a copy, recycled until its originality (the cult of the exclusivity of the model as origin and perfection) degenerates into substitution and bastardization, restylized by the kitsch passion for ornamenting the fake. The sum total of rhetorical maneuvers (parody, irony, and reappropriation) that a subordinate culture must fine-tune to mock the colonial sanction of *dejá vu* by exaggerating its ironic mimicry of dubbing, coincides with the postmodern notions of the culture of pastiche and simulacrum. Culture is embodied here in a sign-mask, which makes up for the deficit of one's own by resorting to the trick of borrowing, stealing or plundering. Citation is the intertextual mechanism that undercuts and dismantles the discourse of authority by subverting the scaffolding of its finished sentences. Hence, the fragmentation of the quote does not serve the sole purpose of denouncing *totality* as a theoretical/philosophical artifact of a tradition only guilty of phallogocentrism. It also denounces the *Eurocentric* subterfuge that posits the closure of the total system (of the totality of the system) as an undeniable guarantee of the universality of meaning. Beyond the stylistic wink which admits certain similarities between Latin American collage and postmodernist montage, fragmentation and recombination allow us to deconstruct the imperialistic self-referential closure of the model that protects the dogma of its own perfection.

Center/Periphery: Stage Inversions?

The center/periphery axis was designed by Modernity to subject the signs and functions of the international exchange to the metropolitan regulation of a Center empowered *to decide* whereas the periphery was limited *to execute*. If postmodern theory appears to question the normativity of the center-legitimized functions of Modernity, we should expect it to alter the system of hierarchies and dependencies sustained by the modernist axis of center and periphery. What is redefined regarding cultural roles (power structures and peripheric conditionings) with the postmodern critique of the Centers and the resulting re-examination of the margins as borders of a system in the alleged process of decentering authority?

A first theoretical opening of postmodern discourse would seem to favor an unexpected protagonistic role for Latin America. The postmodern vindication of alterity and difference would allow for an anti-hegemonic celebration of the cultural periphery censured, up to now, by Western Europe's dominance and its universalizing assumption of a self-centered representation. One of the postmodern hypothesis which decrees the end of Eurocentrism indicates that the critique of Modernity and the condemnation of its legacies (the ultimate meanings of historical conclusiveness, homogeneous rationality of transcendental categories, and progressive linear uniform logic, etc.), led to the weakening of its certainties and the relativity of its universalizing pretensions, thus vulnerating the superiority of the European model. The disbelief in absolutes that currently appears in the guise of cool relaxation after having freed itself from the tyrannical dogmas would announce, according to some, the crumbling of the Western-dominant model. This would favor the subcultures of the margin or the periphery which have now been invited by the Center to form part of the new anti-totalitarian non-hierarchical model. Especially since the Center has multiplied and fragmented itself into dissident micro-territories that transverse it as proliferating and ubiquitous margins. That semantic and operational explosion of the image of the Center as a unifying pole now overflowing with nomadic divergencies would render the center/periphery opposition obsolete and, consequently, to continue posing as victims of colonialism would sound more regressive than ever.

All of these reasons derived from the crisis of the Center-totality, would seem to argue for a re-evaluation of peripheral culture, which would play the protagonist's role in the new postmodern decentralized narrative. However, those who developed the de-centering hypothesis react as if they owned it, and supervise its functions from the stage of the competence of an 'I' legitimized by the cultural tradition of a domain of meaning, and ruling on its validity from an experience of the crisis which continues to become paradigmatic beyond the boundaries that limit the meaning of its how and its why, rendering the *crisis* into another *universal metanarrative*.

The perverse flexion that, thanks to the fractured syntaxis of Postmodernity, resulted in the Center's being the first to ponder its own crisis and in vindicating the transversal proliferation of the margins, forces the periphery (one of those margins now reintegrated into the rhetorical complex of disintegration) to redesign the axis of its polemical confrontation.

Some old and new questions: Is it possible to conceive of ourselves as modern without having completed the historical and cultural passage into full Modernity nor having participated in its European self-referential categories of understanding? Can we define ourselves as postmodern without having been in sync with the postindustrial phase, the requirement fixed by the European and North American trends to experience the vertigo resulting from the overexposure of images, the interchangeability of effects, the superflousness of the sign and the indifference to values? And regarding heterogeneity, fragmentation, and plurality, how can we deconstruct the emblematic difference to open it to the multiple differential of cultures not encompassed within its area of theoretical/cultural prestige?

Notes

1. In collaboration with Heidi Ann García and Barbara D. Riess, who worked on an earlier version. [Translator's Note].

2. On the "New Man" ("Hombre nuevo") see Ernesto "Che" Guevara's *El socialismo y el hombre nuevo*. Francesc de Carreras, ed. (Barcelona: Editorial Anagrama, 1975). [Translator's Note].

3. Follari, Roberto A. *Modernidad y postmodernidad: una óptica desde América Latina* (Colección Cuadernos, Buenos Aires: Aique Grupo Editor, 1990) 140.

4. García Canclini, Néstor. "La modernidad después de la posmodernidad." *Modernidade: Vanguardas artísticas na América Latina*. Ed. Ana María de Moraes Belluzzo (São Paolo: Memorial UNESP, 1990).

5. Morandé, Pedro. *Cultura y modernización en América Latina* (Santiago: Universidad Católica de Chile, 1984).

6. Brunner, José Joaquín. *Un espejo trizado: Ensayos sobre cultura y políticas culturales* (Santiago de Chile: Flacso, 1988).

7. García Canclini, ibid.

8. Reference to Humberto Eco's influential book *Apocalittici e integrati* (1964), opposing celebratory optimism of intellectuals "integrated" in the unstoppable rise of mass culture and apocalyptic attitude of intellectuals nostalgic of the irretrievably lost ground of high culture. [Editor's Note].

◆ **14.**

Critique of Global Philosophy, Five Hundred Years Later

Rafael Ángel Herra

(*translated by Sukhada Kilambi*)

The Spanish perception of celebrating the Fifth Centennial is curiously expressed in the commemoration's emblem: a five and two zeros. The zeros represent two entwined spheres, on one of them, the one in the center, a crown is raised. Is it because of the graphic configuration's formal exigencies that the crown bestows a visual privilege to the central sphere, while the other zero as well as the five are subordinated to it graphically? I do not think so. The official emblem of the meeting of two cultures embodies a hierarchical reading of History and not a critical point of view.

Is it not urgent, that finally, after five hundred years since the discovery of America, we discover the value of and (if there exists) that which is a truly Latin American philosophy? What are the results of the "meeting of two worlds" in the field of philosophy today? These questions, formulated by Zdeněk Kouřím, restate the question about philosophy in and from a Latin American country, that is to say, in the context of intercultural relations predominated by the gravitational force of Western philosophy. The considerations that I formulate summarize, in part, my opinion of Z. Kouřím's questions.[1]

The act of questioning oneself about the possibility of a philosophy of philosophy from the perspective of intercultural relations and in the context of Hispanic heritage in America, poses a foundational difficulty: The question itself is conditioned and the answer—it intends to be philosophical—tends to look for Western ears. This conditioning comes from Western philosophy/ies' globalizing and centripetal role and establishes in History what can be called a global philosophy. Its power to dominate is associated with multiple factors: 1) Philosophical reflection in the West has been forged concomitantly with the West itself, generally in conflict with other civilizations and forms of thought. 2) The successful maturing of the West as the producer of instruments of domination (techniques, strategies, ideologies of legitimization, philosophy) has favored the triumph of its material and imaginary products, from metaphysics and religions, to the techniques and artifacts of modern science, to rock music. Add to this the West's own writing of its History, the history of the dominated people and the history of this domination. 3) There is a drama that repeats itself incessantly: The West has suppressed other civilizations, it has degraded or baptized them and, whenever at all profitable, it has appropriated parts of them, but Westernizing them.

The success of the West, based on a certain kind of violence, reveals a constant or an impulse towards globalization, examples of which are very varied. Let us examine a few:

a. Rudolf Euchen's book titled *Geschichte der philosophischen Terminologie im Umriss* (*1964*), just to mention here the casuistry of philosophical vocabulary, shows that there is no such thing among Western philosophers as a particular interest to look for terms outside the strictly Greco-Latin, the Medieval, and the modern Anglo-Saxon traditions. The words used in modern languages are derived from Latin. German philosophical vocabulary is generally constructed according to the Greco-Latin model. A classification of contemporary philosophical terminology would yield results similar to those that are extracted from Euchen's *Umriss*. The West has not been inclined to promote philosophical exchange;

b. The obsessive practice of considering as barbarous all those who belong to other cultures acts as an ideological inhibitor of equal relations. The Aristotelian syndrome of underhumanization of the foreigner, the barbarous, the slave, the Indian, still continues to be an obsession not completely overcome in the Western psychic phantasmagoria. Surely the logic imposed here is that of belonging to the "in group" which resolves any identity crisis by opposing its own image to that of an enemy.

The long list of conflicts in European History is rich in examples. In the Middle Ages, a syndrome of religious stereotypes is developed. Salvation is possible thanks to the pagan, the heretic, and the infidel (imaginary, as that of Buenaventura or real, as that of the Crusades), and the practice consists in combating, judging, and burning at the stake, creating imaginary Antichrist societies such as the gog, the magog and the Tartars (C. Kappler). The latter, in medieval bestiaries, fed on putrefied things, like the devil Eurinomo. The conquest of the

American civilizations was inspired by the very stereotypes dominated by the sign of the Cross.

The Rousseauist nostalgia of the noble savage is not precisely an exception, but rather, being an exception of the good monster, it is equivalent of modern European society's self-criticism represented in a myth set in tropical scenery. Equally critical is the Voltairean derision, in *Candide*, of the "best of all possible worlds," that is, of the West. America was tirelessly fascinating, not because of its cultures, but because of its natural womb: First it was the Paradise in Columbus' dreams, and later, El Dorado, the object of the conquistadors' obsessive search. The common linguistic origin of "cannibal" and "Caribbean" clearly shows the European perception of the American Man.

Nowadays, there is the Third World. This term, from the Western perspective, dons heavy and strange connotations. "Third World" is a concept clearly definable in a single sense: as a title of that which is not the West or that which is only partly West. But that diversity of nations, peoples and states is so vast that to group them together under the designation of Third World is to fabricate a beast. In reality the Third World is another Frankenstein, the strange creature that is born of the forced union of many parts. The ideologization of the Third World tends to hide the fact that North-South relations have provoked perhaps the most important conflict in History since 1492.

c. A particular example of the relationship of the Western way of being with other cultures is the crime of the Guatemalan Indian, Julián Tzul, who is punished by the *ladino* (Europeanized) justice system for an act of violence that this justice cannot understand in its own socio-cultural context. The legal corpus of Guatemala that laid the base for his condemnation opposes the *Weltanschauung* of the majority of the indigenous population. The Indian Julián Tzul is a victim of these laws, which punish him for defending himself against the malignant nightly threats of a sorcerer, who uses special rites and tools. This very sorcerer, in front of Tzul, assumes the responsibility for the death of his wife, also by means of witchcraft. The (white) court does not consider as legitimate defense (a European legal concept made universal by criminal law) the magical terror that possessed the Indian on having surprised the powerful enemy who was calling the demons and wishing him evil. The desperation of that instant facilitated his homicidal act. This judgment documents "the impossibility for a (monocultural) State Law like the Hispanic to do justice for the people who live in a Quiché cultural climate and use a set of values that belongs to the precolonial period" (Albertina Saravia Enríquez, "El delito de Julián Tzul").[2]

Let's go back to the beginning. I was saying, with a radical approach, that the question about the philosophy of philosophy from an intercultural perspective is conditioned and the answer is necessarily heard with occidental ears. The question is conditioned from the beginning: Why? By whom?

Its condition originates from the questioning itself: "To question," here, is thinking like a Westener, that is to say, with pragmatić, teleological (in German: *zweckrational*) interest. The logical concatenation that links subjects and predicates, contains a *telos*, namely, the domination of nature, of societies, and of the conscience (in the West, adding the adjective "rational" to the noun "domination" is usually a tautology). To think is to do and to foresee; and to foresee in order to do. In the Western tradition, questioning no longer conserves those nonutilitarian and powerful remains of the Greek admiring of self, of the *thaumadsein*. Actually, the *thaumadsein* marks the transition from myth to the Western logos: Gradually the spontaneous ingenuity of admiration is lost and gives way to the controlled question.

The question is born with a direction, a specific weight, and a social demand. It can be seen that, because of this, he who interrogates is marked by the question. And the response owes itself to those conditionings. Even when the West questions itself through magic, it does so armed with analytical and teleological resources to respond. And with this, it interferes in that which it tries to identify; it modifies it, that is, it gets to know it under the conditions of its means of observation. An analogous example is that of psychoanalysis and its scholastic variants. The deciphering process is definitely an interference.

The answer is necessarily heard with Western ears: What does this signify? It means, firstly, that the question predetermines the manner of responding and, secondly, that this manner involves talking and hearing with Western signs. Or, to express it in less rhetorical terms: A question asked from a global philosophical perspective, in order to be understood and to be formulated, should be posed—and of course responded to—through supporting evidence taken from the conceptual resources of that philosophy. The very act that interrogates the philosophy of philosophy from an intercultural perspective is a Western, globalizing, and an exclusive act. To perform this act is to get caught up in that philosophy.

Let us assume that act: Edmund Husserl sees the development of modern Europe as a process linked to the reign of the Galilean model for the mathematization of the world. The physical world is a world constituted by the mathematic-technologic *a priori*. The Western world is a constituted and thereby, a constituent world, a global and cosmopolitan world which gets implanted outside Europe. This world no longer recognizes the right of other cultures and values except under special conditions: the other cultures are only conditionally free, they are put, so to speak, on parole.

Since the Renaissance, the European West is the Hegelian spirit that doubles itself, it is the idealist conscience that produces everything, if is the subjective/objective principle that creates the sense of reality. The West monopolizes the discourse by making it cosmopolitan. And philosophizing is, in fact, the initiation into this cosmopolitanism.

What is left then?

The act of questioning the philosophy of philosophy from an intercultural perspective must be a critical act. Explanation: As the question conditions the answer, the intercultural questioning can only break this circle thanks to the principle of dissatisfaction of the critique. A critical philosophy is the only one that can open a gap in the walls of the Western way of doing philosophy, and can make some exchange possible. This work of revision without conditions could be put into practice from the perspective of the so-called Third World, from the perspective of Latin America, and also from the Western perspective itself.

Critical philosophy is produced in the act of verifying the fundaments of philosophy. And it is there, in that probationary act, where one can create a space of exchange and of mutual contributions, where philosophy is no longer an instrument of the ideological globalization of the West to the detriment of other cultures, but the beginning of its own critique and of the critique of its prejudices, and where the recognition of its positive contribution to humanity is possible. Perhaps here, in the critique, at least for an instant, the primigenial *thaumadsein* of philosophy is reborn.[3]

Franz Wimmer is right in raising four questions about this point:

First question: "From the conceptual point of view, what reasons can one find for the treatment of the history of philosophy from an intercultural perspective?"

In responding, the conceptual point of view of the one questioned (his *Weltanschauung*, "ideology," "mythology," "field of values," does not matter what it is called) cannot be different from that assumed by the interrogator, because the hope is that the question will be understood. If the one questioned belongs to a culture different from the Western philosophical tradition, he will have to take a leap and situate himself within that tradition in order to understand the question, assume himself to be the interrogated and answer with certain signs and canons belonging to the West and foreign to his own culture. In order to respond, he has to alienate himself, at least partially from his own conceptual roots, in order to migrate to another space of comprehension. In this way, the exchange runs the risk of being marked by violence. The treatment of the history of philosophy, from this perspective, ceases to be intercultural, in order to convert itself into the history of the globalization of Western thought.

There exists another possibility, namely, that the question of exchange is raised from within a culture alien to Western philosophy; but then there arises a problem: how to translate the answer, as it needs to be westernized so that it could be understood "philosophically." Moreover it is possible to think that there exist *Weltanschauungen* in the light of which this kind of questioning is impossible.

When one wonders, then, how to value the different positions relative to the study of cultural exchange in philosophy, I think that this assessment should be made considering the investigator's attitude with respect to the following points: 1) identifying the exchanges—what brought them about, what need motivated them, what influences were exerted, and what remained in the end; 2) focusing on tensions—on cases or situations in which the exchange was accompanied by resistance; defining the reasons and the results of that conflictive period. These criteria have two assumptions and thus recognize their relativity: On the one hand, they are established from a Western perspective of philosophy, and on the other, consequently, they assume that the questions interfere with the answers.

Second question: "What possibilities do you see for overcoming the problems of translating (Übersetzens) fundamental philosophical concepts from the non-European cultural context to the context of contemporary European and Anglo-American philosophy?"

Today, the Anglo-American and Eurocentric currents of thought and forms of life predominate in philosophy and almost totally in daily life. In this context, the problem of translation is not primordially a technological, linguistic, or conceptual problem. Rather, it is a question of a political nature, that is, that which depends on the relation of forces: On one of the parties' capacity to impose something, and on the other, the need to assimilate it. Very frequently, the processes of exchange are produced for utilitarian reasons. A proof of this is the incorporation of foreign words in the English language, for example. But even in this sense, the inverse process is more overwhelming. Today one recognizes a phenomenon of the Anglicization of other languages, especially through technical vocabulary. Global philosophy can borrow ideas and words if it needs them, and if it can fit them in its own conceptual framework. To understand primitive myths, lines of kinship, codes of aggression or of self-defense, the theorist first elaborates one point of conceptual reference in which everything is subsumed, including the borrowed terminology . . . But could he do it in any other way, if his very resources for comprehension are constitutive for him like a second nature, to employ the stoic expression?

In the same way, the different readings of Marx's theoretical legacy reveal a Eurocentric predominance. The political force visible in certain Third-World movements which were doctrinally linked to Marxism did not originate from the doctrine, but from their own historical conditions, from their unlivable world; although certain intercultural syntheses or the world geopolitical phenomenon dominant until the end of the 1980s cannot be excluded. The theory imparted a creative direction to the movement, at least in the period that Sartre called groups in fusion, that is to say, during the war but not afterwards, when institutional inertia was imposed.

A model of what creative and fruitful philosophical intercultural relations could be like is the one offered by the history of contemporary art: synthetic exchange with the Orient, with primitive African sculpture, with American indigenism. When artistic ties are unleashed, something new, something that does not prohibit *thaumadsein* arises.

Third question: "Which are the institutional and political particularities, and the traditionalist conditionings, that are right now determinant in the practice of philosophical research of your cultural environment?"

In America there are countries like Argentina, Costa Rica, and Uruguay, whose cultural environment generally responds to the European. Actually, Europe or the modern Anglo-American civilization impose themselves as the identificatory models, at times even stronger than the countries' pasts themselves. This past, however, has seen a marked European presence and a breaking off with the aborigine cultures or their annihilation, in other words a disencounter of two cultures.

In Costa Rica the presence of the indigenous people is limited to small isolated groups, almost extinct, and because of this, inhibited from influencing the everyday, cultural, or institutional life. Measures have been taken (without much success) in order to protect them against the corrupting influence of the white (alcoholism) and work is done in order to rescue their culture and languages. The solitude imposes a law: There are aboriginal languages that are now spoken only by a handful of people.

The English builders of the railway that linked the center of the country to the Caribbean shore brought in Jamaican workers of African origin. These people now inhabit a part of the Costa Rican Atlantic shore; they speak an English dialect and incarnate more than anyone else the stereotypes of the black tropics. The cultural exchange with them is poor. Rather, their intercultural models are in the North American horizon. Or, they accept the predominant tendencies in the Costa Rican society, which generally are not autochthonous.

In other words, the intercultural phenomena, with aborigines or blacks of a minority culture, reproduce, in a concrete society and on a small scale, the general phenomenon of intercultural relations. These contradictions are very serious in countries with an indigenous majority, such as Guatemala or Peru, and should attract the attention of the philosophical researcher.

In Costa Rica conditions of this kind do not exist. The philosophy is doctrinally prolific and global, that is to say that the philosophical conditioning originates from Western philosophy itself. Not to be excluded here are many other factors that influence the investigator: his social status, the discourses that he comes across, his wishes and his rationalizations, his processes of moral disculpation . . .

Wimmer's fourth question: "According to you, what are the contributions of the traditional philosophies of your culture for the confirmation of a contemporary vision of the world and of man? In view of the emergence of a global culture, in what way can such contributions be fruitful?"

I must return to the topic of critical philosophy. Whichever way one looks at it, in view of a global culture, apart from opposing one's values, it is necessary to confront that culture with criticism, attack its roots, assault its self-gratifying intimacy.

It might be desirable that in philosophical thought something similar to that in gastronomy happened. There are nations that preserve certain sacred spaces free from desecration such as those of their culinary preferences. It is known that the regional Italian table, for example, has shielded itself from the heavy artillery of a cosmopolitan gastronomy (which goes from hamburgers and hot dogs to the so-called international cuisine). Could there be something like the rights of taste in philosophy erected in bastions in the face of globalization?

Many things tend to conform the image of man and of the contemporary world. There are too many things that compromise this vision. The image of man is, in some extreme cases, simple, reduced to ideologies of power like a machine obedient to the behavioral engineering; or in other extremes, complex, almost unapproachable, monstrous, made of pieces, baroque, and condemned to death through its own work of destruction.

Certainly man is what one makes of him. So it is sound to put in methodic crisis the assumptions, the prejudices, the sacred pretension of his acts. The best way of contributing to contemporary culture, that is unfortunately becoming more and more globalizing, is to revise at all times its foundations, and the foundations of its self-deception. To this the critical perspective of the Western, Eurocentrist global philosophy, which is what the present discourse has adopted (as there is no other way of doing so), or the philosophies alien to Europe that enter in contact critically with her can contribute, procreating, not bastard sons, but sons of the future man.

The global, technological, technocratizing society does not leave much space for philosophy, which sees itself reduced, in its eyes, to a rhetoric and inefficient speculation. The West creates the conditions of abolition of its own philosophy. The West today is self-sufficient with other resources less conceptual and more productive, teleologically speaking. Philosophy, including global philosophy, must wrest from the technocratism and from the ideologies of power its own space of survival and a legitimacy that should not consist ever in turning itself into the handmaid of power. This is possible to do from within, in intercultural connections and as a critique of the foundations of power, violence and self-complacency. This critique should precede the philosophy of philosophy from the intercultural perspective, in order to overcome its conditionings.

There is no meeting of the two worlds in the field of philosophy. In fact, in America which has been forged for five hundred years, there converge, fuse or enter into conflict, not two, but various worlds: black, Indian, Spanish, Christian, pagan . . . The official emblem of this commemoration is all-inclusive; above the fifth centenary there hovers a crown that marks the center of hegemony. This is not all false nor is it all true. The West, through Spain, has imposed itself on America as a horizon of historical possibility; and the American philosophy has to start from this fact to critically construct its identity.

Notes

1. The philosopher Zdenek Kourím convened various Latin American authors to write about the Latin American philosophy on the occasion of the V Centenary in the Prague philosophical magazine *Filosofický časopis*. The present text appears in Czech under the title of "Filosofie po peti stech letech" (974-83), and closely follows the first part of my article "Kritik der Globalphilosophie," in F. Wimmer (ed.), *Vier Fragen Zur Philosophie in Afrika, Asien und Lateinamerika*. See also "El autoengaño o crítica de la ética global," in *Revista de filosofía de la Univ. de Costa Rica*.

2. Albertina Saravia Enríquez, in "El delito de Julián Tzul," explains that the Guatemalan Indian Julián Tzul was judged and condemned by a jury of European origin. His crime was to defend himself from the threats of a sorcerer, whom he killed in an instant of terror. The sorcerer had harmed his family using black magic and had threatened him with the same animistic resources. Hispanic justice was incapable of understanding the conduct of Tzul in view of the evil arts of magic deeply rooted in the Quiché cultural environment.

3. For further reading on the antecedents of European culture, see Dieter Wyss' *Strukturen der Moral*.

Works Cited

Herra, Rafael Ángel. "El autoengaño o la crítica de la ética global." *Revista de filosofía de la Universidad de Costa Rica* 31.74 (1993): 11-16.

Husserl. E. *Die Krisis der europäischen Wissenschaften und die transzendentale Phänomenologie*. La Haya: W. Biemel, 1962.

Kapler, C. *Monstres, démons et merveilles a la fin du Moyen Âge*. Paris: Payot, 1980.

Kouřím, Zdeněk. "Filosofie po pěti stech letech." *Filosoficky casopis* 40.6 (1992): 974-83.

Saravia, Enríquez Albertina. "El delito de Julián Tzul." *Cultura en Guatemala* 5.2 (1984): 53-101.

Wimmer, F. ed. *Vier Fragen zur Philosophie in Afrika, Asien und Lateinamerika*. Vienna: Passagen Verlag, 1988.

Wyss, Dieter. *Strukturen der Moral: Untersuchungen zur Anthropologie und Genealogiemoralischer Verhaltensweisen*. Goettingen: Vandenhoeck and Ruprecht, 1968.

◆ 15.

Cultural Topologies

Daniel Altamiranda and Hernán Thomas

(*translated by Jean Graham-Jones*)

From right to left

We look at things from our vantage point here in the South. And, as seen from the South, the universe organizes itself from right to left.

To our right, an original, originating world unfolds itself, a generator of objects and histories, of customs and realities—the European world. To our left, like the other column in double-entry bookkeeping, a fantasy. Perhaps it is nothing more than an empty column. As a consequence, we find ourselves positioned in a kind of disconnection between a world that theoretically belongs to us (the one we belong to)—the European world—and a world that theoretically does not exist.

> It is my understanding that Mexicans, who in reality see the world from the other side [i.e., the North], tend to a potentiality that leads them toward their right, that is, the mestizo world that lives on within them. In our case, here in Buenos Aires, mestizaje has practically no meaning, and when it does, it takes on a flood-like nature. This was produced by migrations to our capital at the end of the 19th and throughout the 20th century, but it does not appear to be the source of our present situation—even though it probably must be examined as a distinguishing characteristic.

Perhaps this second world exists as a theoretical entity but does not itself have access, in practice, to real existence. It is a fantasy. And that American [i.e. Latin American but also, implicitly, Native American] fantasy, which we all apparently share, conditions our perception of everything. That is because our World is created in and between *two processes of idealization*:

1. the process of idealizing Europe (i.e., what we are not but believe ourselves to be)
2. the process of idealizing America (i.e., what we do not possess but wish to become).

As we all know, the result of any duality can be nothing but tension.

Local(e) Logic

From deep down within our initial acknowledgment of this condition, a sort of logic begins to function, a logic that establishes, with terrifying ingenuity, possible and not possible sites. According to this set-up, *the East exists, but for us it is the West. An incisive paradox* (Incisive because it calls attention to something, and even more so because it does this rather like a wound might work to gain an organ's attention). Whenever we think about the Argentine Republic, whenever we wish to speak openly of our country's northwestern region, the area appears to us as if it were the East, rather like the effect of a specular vision. *A kind of chiasmus is delineated at the Equator.* It's where the universe is flipped upside down because, although we are the "West," Mother West is in the East. This, nevertheless, does not happen to, say, the Mexicans because they possess that other Northern dimension, translated to their local territory. We in the South experience the inverse.

Rounding Out Reality

Huge Gaps

An important question arises at this point in our discussion, a question that has to do with the construction of meaning—how meaning rounds out reality.

In order to round out reality, it is necessary to connect disparate elements, but, in our daily lives, it seems preferable and possibly even more comfortable for us to operate with basic categories that function like, shall we say, potential working packages. We think in conceptual sets that aren't closed nor entirely unfolded. Like black holes. We know they exist . . . They're out there somewhere . . . As long as we are able to get by with other categories, categories that we do unfold, we allow ourselves to live tranquilly, we're able to work (on) and generate objects and actions. In our own particular (that is, Argentinean) case, the category of what is European is sharply defined; we also have a clearly characterized category for all that is (Latin) American; and, finally, we possess a category of what is considered Argentinean (one of whose characteristics is a certain game of indefinition between a maximum commitment to being subcharacterized as European, and some element of a definition, by coincidence, of being considered American). We used to possess other functioning categories that were maintained by our intellectuals up until the 1980s, categories such as the one reified in socialist countries that offered the possibility of the East. Of course, there are still groups that justify themselves based upon this same set of categories. These cultural models continue to be evoked in informal chats over cups of coffee and during serious debates and political discussions. Another category that continues to function is the (North) American model, which has been unexpectedly fertile perhaps due to the absence of the other model's specter. At least until now, we've clearly seen it as something different, and it's possible that generations to come won't regard it as something different but rather as an instance of integration. Finally, we have a certain notion of the Orient, somewhat diffuse and beyond our grasp: laundries, techno-scrap iron, Sumo wrestling, Geishas, clones . . .

In and among these, there are other packages; nearly empty, nearly hollow, they are like labels in our mental space. Without exploring it too much, the first example that comes to mind is Africa. Africa not only does not exist within our local knowledge; it doesn't even exist tangentially as a relation.

It's certainly true that at one point in Argentina's history, the African element existed, and that, as a social component, it was eliminated because of several factors. However, that elimination cut even deeper than socially. I have confirmed this with my students at the University, when I've shown them an advertisement for a North American journal dedicated to African studies. My students' reactions demonstrated that this was the first time it had occurred to them that they might devote themselves to the study of African literature. Not only do we not read any African literature, and frankly that's not because it isn't accessible—a good part of African literature is written in European languages (French, English, or Portuguese), the problem is that it hasn't even occurred to Argentine students that they might devote themselves to reading these texts.

Perhaps we could document a permanent erasure of the African connection on some unconscious level. We all know that an African universe exists, but we never take the time to think about it; we don't contemplate it at all. It comes upon us by chance, like in an adventure film or a Hollywood remake of *Tarzan*; we occasionally hear about some African writer winning the Nobel Prize; we know of the problems in South Africa with apartheid; we've heard of Mandela, and we sing along on *Biko*; we think that they're developing nations or, in the worst of cases, that they've already been totally destroyed; we have some idea that they're postcolonial. *But it never occurs to us to think that we too are postcolonial.* Maybe because our own post- or neocolonizing process happened a bit earlier in time, or maybe because we'd prefer to believe that it did. How is it possible that it's never even occurred to us to develop an understanding of the African world *in comparison to* our own?

The experience of the postcolonial in Africa, as distinguished from our own experience, does not constitute a spatial but rather a temporal rupture. We continue to perceive Africa as a recent colony and, when moved to think about our own colonial past, we experience it as remote. Perhaps because, as Argentines, we were never a colony; we ceased being a colony before we ever became Argentinean.

We

The Vision of Spanish Pronouns Demands Separate Consideration

To who does this "we" (nosotros) refer when we utter the word? Ultimately, its specific content becomes increasingly defined as the text unfolds. Even so, it's a good idea to make a preliminary clarification: *nosotros* possesses a temporal axis as well as a spatial axis.

Inscribed within the temporal dimension are narratives (the fruits of anachronic interpretations that should some day be processed as such). And we, *of necessity*, either identify or break with some of these narratives: the mytheme of the *Black Legend* or its counterpart, the Golden Legend; the debate over cultural inheritance; the question of the national that would allow for the interpretation of the colonial as a (proto)national structure, etc.

In Spanish, "America" possesses an inclusive, omni-comprehensive meaning; in English, it has a restrictive meaning, referring specifically to citizens of the United States. Thus there's something rather centrifugal in the Spanish-American meaning as well as something cohesive, given the U.S. presence. And that's where Hispanic identity can be

recovered, when we're faced with the risk of not being
America, of being nothing at all.

What we've just said merits at the very least a concrete example:
The debate regarding dependency theory appeared, in its moment,
as a response to a particular chronologistic hypothesis that was being
developed in the North. Theories such as Rostow's posited a guide
for the North, a temporal guide with specific slots for stages of
development into which the rest of the world's countries were
deposited. Our own domestic discourse, which inspired so many
alliances in the 1970s, was oriented more than anything toward a
chronological cocktail based on a foreign theory. That is, it was
directed toward a reading, not in the least bit ingenuous, of a process
of time-based accumulation and away from any analysis and
construction of critical categories.

Recognizing the Imaginary

When held up to the light, what we're proposing here is something
different: the recognition of the imaginary within which we work, and
the acknowledgment of how we activate and deactivate the various
zones of ideas that make up this imaginary. Once we've accepted this
process, the diagnosis of our situation is much more serious than we
might have predicted. This has to do with not only the (missing)
parallel with Africa, where, in effect, there has been a temporal
distortion, but also other parallels with Mexico or Venezuela, where,
despite the fact that their historical processes were more or less similar
to ours, they're not even taken as points of comparison.

When we teach history to our children, we make an intensely
marked cut that predetermines a very clear descending order: First, we
study the context of insertion, European History, which is the history
of a continent, the history of multiple cultures, a history-puzzle. But
when we study our national Argentinean history, differentiation
disappears. Instead, a single unifying metaphor is postulated: All
roads, no matter how diverse, lead to one national Self. Of course, it's
clear to all that a selection of roads is itself constructed within this very
same movement: Some roads lead us toward our goal while others do
not. In the process, we leave out mountains of things. What have we
retained, in the long run, of the history of the nineteenth and twentieth
centuries? English, French, and North American influences and
phenomena that we do not conceive of as categorical influences.
Immigration would be one example. In this case, we do not think in
terms of a functional nation but rather in terms of a group of
individuals. We remove ourselves from the level of state structures to
the level of individuation.

Nor do we have any awareness of Portugal as functioning in a unified manner, of having had an imperial American headquarters. That fact, which appears only marginally in our textbooks, is not a part of our perception.

Shall we put into practice a parallel articulation regarding the topic of Africans? No one questions that Africans did not arrive in America of their own volition, neither as individuals nor as communities; rather, they made the trip, physically in British or Portuguese boats, and ideologically through Spain and England. In other words, it seems impossible to think that this was natural and that the historical process had to be necessarily that way.

Despite the fact that fewer and fewer people adhere to the possibility of seeing everything, the principle continues to live on with inexplicable vitality.

The teaching of geography in Argentina responds to the same criterion that was sketched out above regarding the teaching of history. There are multiple lines, all the possible lines are stated (remembering that, once again, these are only those lines conceived of as "all the possible" lines, and that behind this situation hides the powerful fantasy that we can even apprehend totality as such), and these lines come together in one imaginary triangle that points back at us: Imbued with such a logic, we're able to think of the ancient Greeks as our immediate ancestors. It's probable that, following this same line of logic, there exists a notion of a messianic, self-confident and hypostasized people, a people with a destiny. Said vision is constitutive of our educational system. When all this began to develop during the previous century (to be more precise, in the 1880s), it had some meaning, in particular because of the struggle over federal powers—the confrontation between centralized and decentralized power—or because of such problems as the affirmation of a national border or sovereignty over Patagonia. Yet, even though said issues are no longer problematic, the old myths remain vigorously alive.

As far as geography is concerned, it's significant that the specific geographies of Asia and Africa are studied together as part of world geography. This spirit, of concentrating first on the most external and universal in order to arrive later at the most internal and specific, is what initially connected Africa and Asia with planetary geography. Then, slowly, the focus turned to America and only after that was Argentina placed within a context.

This way of organizing thematic cuts transforms the idea of near-and-far and the notion of inhabited space. Obviously, within our Argentine imaginary, Africa is farther away than Europe. Added to that idea is the fact that our worldview depends on cartographic projections that necessarily portray an experienced and not objective view. Based on the way planispheres lay out the Southern zone, it would appear that Argentina had more territory and therefore must be perceived as different from Central America, which, in turn, appears somewhat diminished in size, or Spain, which also appears much smaller. These are the projections by way of which we project ourselves.

In earlier times, it wasn't surprising to hear of the development of an Indian frontier or of a Southern border at the Samborombón River (only 200 kilometers away from our nation's capital), and to think of each one as the *edge of civilization*. After so much of this sort of theorizing, too many lies begin to accumulate. On one side, the national border identified as the border of civilization; and on the other, civilization with respect to market relations that, obviously, cannot be understood without the Indian. And *beyond* the frontier-border, the Southern colonies such as Trelew.

Not only are there elements that deserve to be explained in these thematic cuts, there are others that do not merit even the slightest explanation.

We and the Others

Before moving on to the theory of "Otherness," let's consider "us." The Spanish *nosotros* is a compound, and its Romance language equivalents (the French *nous*, the Italian *noi*) are units that do not incorporate the notion of *otros* (others), the comparison.

It is also present in Catalonian: noialtres.

We are "nos los otros," the others' others. Perhaps by accident, the Spanish language has retained something that is a kind of nuclear stone in our thinking.

Following on this conditioning imposed by linguistic observation, it's worth noting that theories of otherness have grown out of, and merit forced discussion in, countries where this very phenomenon does not exist. Countries like France or the United States have developed the notion of otherness, or alterity. For us, this notion does not even stand out today as a guiding element of our thinking unless it has been incorporated into our way of thinking as a theoretical import. So it is still an Other that belongs to others.

A thought coming from an outside second party becomes indispensable to forging the idea of Otherness. "Other" fundamentally implies difference. On the other hand, the vision of a third party would presuppose synthesis, a common element.

And by cultural tradition, we are a people of commonalities rather than differences.

If one were to rummage around in history's most despicable aspects, it would not be difficult to document difference historically as a series of internal disputes. Nevertheless, even under such conditions, and even including the question of ethnic confrontations (reiterated *ad libitum* in various latitudes), even there it isn't obvious: Why doesn't the same conflict occur at the domestic Argentinean level? The unaware observer might conclude that modalities of antagonism don't even register among local subcommunities. There must be a strange and unique cultural emulsion that makes our *nosotros* look like a type of different link between the French *nous* and *autre*.

In the word *nosotros* itself and the world views that this word supplies, the key element that we pointed out earlier becomes a presence: *the word "nosotros" presupposes that we behave like others, that we conceive of ourselves as others, that we are not an entity in and of ourselves.* This not being-in/of-oneself allows for a margin of possibility of convenient and peaceful coexistence/complicity. In reality, when we find ourselves in a situation of identifying with the other, the process becomes complex for us. Who is our other?

Because *within ourselves (nosotros), there is also something like a with-others (con-otros).*

The Other, Identified

Anyone who appears as the other of this "our-selves" (*nosotros*) is regional and clearly identified as "local." The other, at times, is Peruvian, Brazilian, "cabecita negra"[1] or gringo. Anyone who identifies himself as his (own)self is the other. Anyone who has an identity per se. Anyone who's not hybrid (*sintético*). Anyone who's not cosmopolitan.

Political Parties

And, to take the lines of derivation to their extreme, this attitude could be related to the character of Argentinean political parties, which, in general, are associations of synthesis, some of which have had fluctuating success in the sphere of interests and acceptance on the part of majority groups. Anyone seeking an accurate, reliable ideological identification will end up, in some way, sanctioned by the electorate.

A clear identity is penalized as suspicious. Anyone who maintains such an identity is suspect of some ulterior motive, of being a marginal figure, as if other public figures did not share a unique purpose. Because our *we (nosotros)* is *innocent. By having no identity, it is generous. It belongs to everyone.*

Difference and Morals

It appears to be a great cloak of virtue, a cover (up). Differences, nevertheless, do exist, but they are left hanging by this "us" (*el nosotros*). As a matter of fact, forms of segregationism and racism function within our society, but these phenomena are never seen as problems within the scope of the community. No cases of whites coming to blows with blacks appear to have been registered on the public conscience. And if such an unusual situation were to occur, due to some strange fluke, and if it were to achieve any kind of generalized recognition, both parties would be condemned, the one brandishing the weapon as well as the one receiving the blows.

Said reaction would respect, then, the hidden maxims of typical social functioning, independent of the fact that many individuals may display a certain type of distance in relation to minority groups. *Our tolerance functions at a general level*, but in specific cases it materializes with the same mechanisms of prejudice that exist in many other societies. What do we do? We suspend differentiation at the general level. Not even the same subjects capable of making the occasional racist comment are capable of thinking of themselves as racists within the context of our society. It's likely, therefore, that hypocrisy is structural.

Who Constructed Space?

The average Argentine today experiences divisions of space much like a division or split of the other. For example, because of an-other's decision, many know about the Yalta issue and the fact that the world is divided—or was divided, if you will—into East and West. For us, there is a division located at the Andean mountain range, but it too is understood as a sort of resolution by an-other. It is not, in any way, the same experience of limits that a European might have after fighting for centuries to establish a humanly created border.

In our case, wherever a border has been created by humans, an-other constructed it (a British arbitration decision, the Perito Moreno, a Vatican mediator), and in every other circumstance, the delimitation has come from nature.

Evidently, this is not the notion of limits at which an indigenous American might arrive either.

It's possible that the explanation of this phenomenon is connected to the strategy of colonization, which was—among the various adjectives proposed—differentiated. Colonization made a clean *sweep* through these Pampas we have inherited. This strategy resembles somewhat the initiative that the English took with their early Northern colonies: They hurled themselves forward, they pushed, they swept; then, with an open field, they generated something specific, *sui generis*. In those distant territories, there was no standard of integration.

> *Moreover, that space doesn't even emerge as if it had been constructed by oneself. It's a tension that holds a promise, that makes one end up trying, over and over again, to find one's identity across a gap, a void that history has left for us.*

In our case, there was no standard of integration either, and that has remained with us like a sore or a grief, suffered particularly by our intellectuals, in the form of a fantasy about a truly American world. Stated in its quintessential formulation, it means we don't have something that we would like to have, and, because we don't have it, we're not even able to know exactly what it is. That is why we are always idealizing, always postulating a WORLD category, without anything definite ever being created.

Irreverent proof of this can been found in statements made by *porteños*[2] when they attempt to define and delimit who they are: "We have all four seasons"; "We have the widest river"; "We have the longest boulevard." They always define themselves with a "we have" and never with a "we are." *It's a given space*, a space that has nothing to do with social constructions.

Optimism/pessimism

A topological factor that does not form any part of our Argentinean vision is the bio-oceanic element, present in the way territory was appropriated by cultural centers in the United States.

Few Latin American countries are bi-oceanic, and those that are, such as the Caribbean countries, do not experience their bi-oceanicity as a process of development. The United States' arrival to the Pacific marked the nation's identity, not only because it constituted a precise objective but also because it connoted a complete development. Argentina, on the other hand, has no sense of completion. On the contrary, one could speak here of an after-the-fact resignation (or, to put it another way, of a retrospective indignation) on the part of revisionists for Argentina's having lost the Banda Oriental (Uruguay), for having lost Paraguay, for having lost Patagonia to the Chileans. In that sense, we can restate the subjective significance of the notions of optimism and pessimism. The latter notion, formulated as the risk of losing something one has, is more prevalent in the local Argentine mentality; the involuntary contrast, a certain optimistic vision, is seen in the legacy of North American migrants. If an "I can make anything" attitude seems appropriate to the North, here it meets with an "I'd better make do with what I have because I could lose it."

The 1880s Generation

But, wait, it wasn't always that way here. The distribution of optimism and pessimism we have described seems logical today because this is an age of losses, yet optimism once reigned, within the coordinates of what has been recognized as the "80's generation." For that generation, it was a qualitative (modernizing), not quantitative (expanding), historical process.

. Certainly, they lived this optimism through an extremely selective judgment. If we think of the various products of the 1880s generation and take, as a paradigmatic case, the development of the train system, we cannot help but notice the spatial distribution that was established. It wasn't that these men thought about developing the occupied territory in its totality and generating a balanced order. The criteria they worked with were not those that might seem reasonable in light of our knowledge today but rather others.

Quadrants

They sliced up the country. Argentina was subdivided into quadrants, and the parts that received the greatest infrastructure were the Central-Southern and the Central-Northern regions. The Western zones either developed on their own, thanks to the initiative of local interests, or they did not develop at all. The legacy of these processes: Patagonia became a kind of reservation of nothing, a national territory—or patrimony—for the "future." In contrast, over the course of a century, the axis of Buenos Aires-Rosario-Córdoba became the national axis.

> At this point in our exposition and national history, the theory of the Atlantic littoral becomes more than problematic. We first have to determine if our real "littoral," defined in terms of a principle of development, is not the northern border. If that were true, we could see how the Alfonsín government's proposal of moving the capital[3] repeated that same plan (which no longer prevails) of developing the littoral. We

*would then have to rethink in what sense does the "Southern"
objective continue to be relevant.*

The question of outside interests justifying domestic orientations
arises once again with the subject of Argentina's ports and its
structure of *funneling* products through these ports to the rest of the
country. Under this same formulation, even some of the physical
limits of the rail system appear in reality to be logistical—extending
the system into a forested region in order to obtain wood for railroad
ties (which is what happened with the Quebracho forests in the Chaco
region), or in order to obtain firewood (as in the case of San Luis) for
example. Our railroads only go that far. Their builders did not seek to
extend the system from coast to coast, as their North American
counterparts did; nor do the railroads operate as a system of internal
relations: the nation's entire internal flow comes together from a
starting point of contact with the outside world (e.g., Buenos Aires). *It
is in this outside world where domestic identity is to be found: yet
another curious projection.* Curious more than anything when
considered in relation to the constitution of a "we" (*nosotros*), in a
certain sense merely pronominal, with only scarce material support. *A
"we" (nosotros) of only occasional meaning.*

Geostrategy?

Once upon a time, within the context of inconsequential speculation,
we could justify a scandalous apothegm: deep down, *we are not an
imperialist country because we don't have the guts.* Our foreign
policy has always been protective and protectionist, rather than
aggressive. Once again, hold on to what we have . . . The image of the
viceroyalty and our losses.

We have no idea what Bolivians think of the viceroyalty. Do they
think of the Argentinean territory as their own loss? And, following
that same line of questioning, how do Uruguayans see it? Because it's
true that Buenos Aires was the capital of the viceroyalty, but only after
it was created administratively. Peruvians, with as much right as we
have, could lament the loss of this vast territory that once depended on
Lima. Is it because we're in Buenos Aires that we believe the rights to
these territories once belonged to us, only to be lost?

*That's how the Paraguayan Dr. Francia saw it in 1811, when
he proposed that they did not wish to replace the Spanish
mother-nation (Cádiz and its assembly) with another
American metropolis (Buenos Aires and its assembly).
Whenever free trade through the port of Buenos Aires was
discussed, Francia reiterated his desire for free trade at the*

continental level, in particular the free navigation of the
rivers. A different vision of the other dwelt in his perspective, a
vision that, in part, extended to the Triple Alliance and the
subjugation of the López's.[4]

We are left with the last of the metropolis, Buenos Aires, and it is
merely because of that situation, because of origins and inheritance,
that we believe we have any rights over anyone else.

Continental Regionalization

Planetary trends, nevertheless, appear to point in other directions, ones
that do not facilitate the construction of a "we" (nosotros).
"Globalization". . . "Latin American integration." We experience
today's situation concretely as if it were an-other's history: Spain's
1992 repositioning with respect to the European economic
community is a Spanish problem; the integration of Mexico into the
North American Free Trade Agreement is a Mexican problem;
Mercosur is our problem. Any apparently viable means for
integration is at a subcontinental level.

The Atlantic Question

The Atlantic, transformed for Western eyes into a symbol of union, is
in our immediate reality a distancing agent, far beyond the reach of
aero navigation and telecommunications.

It was only during Columbus's first voyage that the Atlantic
meant proximity. From that moment on, it has signified distance. The
only "we" (nosotros) that we can recover, in the sense of unity, was
seen in that first trip: a first kiss that turned into a long romance with a
tragic destiny but also a comedy of intrigue mixed with passages from
an epistolary history, replete with misunderstandings. In pursuit of the
metaphor, almost all the plot action that has followed has concerned
itself with securing the shipments: the phatic function.

Notes

1. "Cabecita negra" is a despective term used in Buenos Aires for rural migrants
from the country's interior. [Translator's Note].

2. "Porteño" literally means port-dweller; in this case, it refers to the
inhabitants of Buenos Aires. [Translator's Note].

3. The authors refer here to President Raúl Alfonsín's 1986 attempt to
decentralize the federal government by proposing to move the national capital to the
Patagonian city of Viedma. The project was never realized. [Translator's Note].

4. The references are to subsequent Paraguayan leaders and their ultimate loss to the three allied countries of Argentina, Brazil, and federalist Uruguay during the struggles of 1865-1870. [Translator's Note].

◆ **Afterword**

Postmodernity in the Periphery is Not What You Think

Horacio Machín

The interdisciplinary essays included in this volume of *Hispanic Issues* focus on the question of whether or not postmodernity is a way to chart contemporary cultural change in Latin America. Coming from the humanities and the social sciences, these essays show how a Latin American creative social imagination and cultural politics can add new depth to cultural analysis and theory.

The volume consists of Emil Volek's "Introduction" and fifteen essays grouped in four parts. Part I deals with theoretical concerns on Latin American modernity and modernization. Part II focuses on identity and the challenges of postmodernity and globalization. Part III includes cross-cultural approaches to Latin American local/global phenomena in societies, politics and arts, and explores strategies of cultural resistance. Part IV is a collection of various "classic" texts representative of Latin American new cultural agenda and of the discourses in which these texts come across. Part III is, perhaps, the volume's more specific contribution to Latin American cultural studies.

Parts I and II share an internal coherence of goals and meanings and can be read as a unity. José Joaquín Brunner (sociology of culture) focuses on traditionalism and modernity in Latin America; Jesús Martín-Barbero (theory of culture and communication) deals with theoretical concerns regarding Latin American modernity and communication theory; Fernando Aínsa (writer and literary essayist) considers the issue of identity and the challenges of postmodernity and globalization; Jorge Larraín's (social and cultural theory) focuses on the theoretical nexus between postmodernism and Latin American identity; and José Joaquín Brunner explores Latin American dramatization of identity.

In Part III the respective essays of Mario Roberto Morales, Armando Silva, Osvaldo Pelleteri, Raúl Bueno, and Abelardo Castillo use different lenses, scales, and disciplinary approaches (cultural anthropology, urbanism, philosophy, theater, and literary and cultural theory) for a mapping of Latin American Late Modernity. These polysemical essays constitute stimulating cross-cultural approaches. In addition, Morales's "Autochthonous Cultures and Global Market" and "Silva's Post-Cities and Politics: New Urban Movements in Two Americas" articulate an innovative Latin American cultural studies approach compatible with the local/global paradigm prevalent from the 1990s to the present. Finally, Part IV is a dossier of "some Classic Texts from the 1990s" written by Mempo Giardinelli, Nelly Richards, Rafael Ángel Herra, Daniel Altamiranda, and Hernán Thomas. According to Volek, these texts are called "classic" only because "they are likely better known in the American academy" ("Introduction").

My own reading of the first three parts of this volume highlights two related modalities that might be called *cartographic* and *strategic*. The *cartographic* essays (chapters 1-3; 5-8) have a cognitive interest in using theoretical concepts for representing contemporary social transformation and cultural change in Latin America. The *strategic* essays (chapters 4, 9-11) have a stronger interest in cultural politics as well as in strategies of resistance to global processes. To some extent one might say that all essays in this volume are both cartographic and strategic, even if the former more than the latter use theoretical concepts for cultural analysis. My own classification only stresses a different emphasis in their interpretations.

Postmodern discourse is a grid that helps us to organize our thinking about complex social realities. The inclusion in this volume of materials dealing with the debates around Latin American Postmodernity seems to arise both from a desire to arrive at a readable cross-cultural interpretation of a very complex field of study and from a belief that while postmodern perspectives illuminate new features of contemporary Latin-America culture, the claim concerning a new rupture in society and history is exaggerated.

In some way or other, these essays deal with the living experience of the 1980s, when Latin America first faced the social dilemma of either opting for neoliberal modernization (and with it, accepting the exclusion of wide sectors of the population) or privileging social integration and running the risk of being relegated to the margins of economic development. The question that arose in the 1980s was how to conceive democracy when its classical basis—national integration—was diluted through state cuts, neoliberal modernization, external debt, transnational development, and new global processes. For the liberal, Marxist and Christian Latin American intellectual traditions, order is based on a certain idea of community that is incompatible with neoliberal social exclusion. Such exclusion cannot be legitimated by these traditions, even if it is democratically allowed by the very social sectors that are excluded. The debates around Latin American Postmodernity after the 1980s are connected, in some way or another, with this social dilemma. Those debates articulate postmodern cultural demands—"new subject positions" (Laclau)—with an imagined order: a Latin American democratic civil society (Martín-Barbero, Brunner, García Canclini, Monsiváis, Sarlo, and Ortiz, among others). Thus, for these "new" cultural interpreters, a Latin American democratic order cannot appear unless beliefs and values are changed in civil society, i.e., at the social movements and grassroots level and beyond the nation-state.

The rise of postmodern theories after the 1980s is expressive of a shift to a politics of discourse. Thus, weaved throughout Latin American Postmodernity discourse are observations of the ways in which theory is shaped by culture. On the negative side, theory performs a reifying function and replicates the problematic features of contemporary culture and identity in a world characterized by the experience of fragmentation and difference. On the positive side, the hegemony of signification requires one to think of power and resistance in cultural terms, that is, in terms of the power and the subversion of discourse. An important risk of this politics of discourse is to miss the realities of power as a constituent element of identity formation and relations of difference. It is fair to say that in this volume the realities of power are neither neglected nor do they receive much attention. Such is the case, for instance, with Fernando Aínsa's "Challenges of Posmodertnity and Globalization: Multiple of Fragmented Identity?" In this cosmopolitan essay the globalization issue is rather an opportunity for exploring a creative identity politics beyond the nation-state than a crisis in contemporary social life. If one accepts the idea that globalization helps to propel societies beyond the modern, then this notion either competes with or is complementary to the notion of Postmodernity.[1]

At this juncture in world history, cultural nationalism fades in significance as a coherent, organizing principle for any kind of thought or practical business. According to Eric Hobsbawn (1990), world history:

Can no longer be contained within the limits of "nations" and "nations states" as these used to be defined, either politically, or economically, or culturally, or even linguistically. It will see "nation-states" and "nations" or ethnic/linguistic groups primarily as retreating before, resisting, and adapting to, being absorbed or dislocated by, the new supranational restructuring of the globe. Nations and nationalism will be present in this history, but in subordinate, and often rather minor roles. (182)

In Latin America it has been difficult to think difference and identity without falling back on the enigmas of nationalism and essentialism. The situation characterized by Hobsbawan leaves any essay dealing with cultural nationalism in Latin America vulnerable on two fronts: 1) they are prone to the charge that the organization of knowledge centered around the conception of the nation-state belongs to an earlier phase of cognitive mapping; and 2) they are uncomfortably aware of how Latin American cultural nationalism is indebted to Eurocentric ideologies. In any case, the essays in this volume allow us to reflect on the related issues of difference and identity in Latin America, beyond the enigmas of nationalism and essentialism.

While in the second half of the 1980s, emergent Latin American theories of culture (Martín-Barbero 1987, García Canclini 1987, Ortiz 1988, and others) were obliged to grapple simultaneously with several aspects of Latin American Modernity's incompleteness and displacements, at present there is no longer the sense that Latin American Modernity has been entirely left behind. In "Modernity and Postmodernity in the Periphery," Martín-Barbero sums this perception: "This is a Postmodernity that instead of coming to replace comes to reorganize the relationship between Modernity and tradition" (36).

In "Traditionalism and Modernity in Latin American Culture," Brunner considers the impact of media culture. For him, recent Latin American culture does not express an order (nation, state, class, religion, tradition, etc.) but "the contradictory and heterogeneous processes of constitution of a late Modernity" (4). Brunner opposes some privileged constructs of the heirs of the *lettered city* (Angel Rama, Octavio Paz, Pablo Neruda, Gabriel García Márquez) and in his second essay included in this volume, "Latin American Identity—Dramatized," he rejects the *Macondo* writers' (1960s) Latin American ethnocentric approaches and their fundamentalism. This rejection of traditional forms of legitimation—shared by some of this volume's essays, such as, for instance, Mempo Giardinelli's "Variations on Postmodernity, or, What Does the Latin American Postboom Mean?" and Mario Roberto Morales's "Autochthonous Cultures and Global Markets"—seems to be a sort of literary reductionism.

While Latin American Modernity in the 1960s was still a project to be constructed, in the 1980s many cultural essayists complained that it had already been achieved (Martín-Barbero 1987, García Canclini 1987, Ortiz 1988, Brunner 1988, among others). For them, Latin American Modernity is no longer related to a promise of modernization (a project to be realized in the future) but to a discourse of the present "that is relatively open and problematically possible" (García Canclini 1989). Renato Ortiz (2000) says:

> In this new context, in conflict with local traditions, there is a new preoccupation with globalization, seen as something more than national identity, conceived as a world modernity. . . . In Latin America, identity is no longer simply equated with the nation-state. Indeed it is now possible to be modern without been national. (258-59)

In "Communications: Decentering Modernity," Martín-Barbero explores the transformation of Latin American national identities in light of recent transformations in the culture industries. He associates this process with the rise of a communicative rationality and with an increasingly globally interconnected market society. Martín-Barbero notes that these interconnections are producing changes within nations and are bringing into question the link between identity and place. Thus the space of the nation and the nature of identity are being reconfigured by new communicative possibilities within the dynamics of a global market. Martín-Barbero does not celebrate this postmodern process nor does he assume that Latin Americans can ignore or even elude them: "transformations of Modernity demand that we consider communications not only as a matter of markets and technologies but also as a decisive space in the construction of democracy" (45). The essays in this volume highlight the potential for a democratic cultural politics and underscore postmodern concerns with cultural identity and everyday experience in Latin America. While traditional politics is perceived as being increasingly constrained, transnational "democratic civil society" is perceived as an open possibility for any qualitative (cultural and/or political) transformation. Postmodernity, in one of its many senses, also refers to an intensification of cultural contacts. Narrating the international circumstances in which this volume arose, Volek ("Introduction") says that the project acquired the mission of "bridging the growing gap between two academies." According to Volek the aims of the project were: 1) to explore the postmodern debate from Latin American perspectives; 2) to develop an interpretative cultural approach "not to be confused with the Cultural Studies"; 3) to investigate Latin American issues in which "modern and premodern aspects continue to occupy an important place"; and 4) to bridge the "growing gap" between Latin American and American academies, which, according to Volek, are "on different tracks."

It seems evident in some of the essays in this volume that a tension exists between their particular Latin American perspectives and the cultural studies approaches common in the postmodern American academy. In fact, I would say that the rejection of the latter kind of cultural studies in the respective essays of Martín-Barbero and Larraín has to do with their affinity with the British cultural studies intellectual tradition, while Morales and Silva have an intellectual affinity with the emergent Latin American cultural studies paradigm common from the 1990s to the present.[2]

The earliest practitioners in the field of British cultural studies (Richard Hoggart, E.P. Thompson, Raymond Williams) were all working, in their different ways, with an idealized conception of community as an empowering and socially cohesive force. For instance, the cultural critic Raymond Williams laments "our divided time" and seeks to "define the theory of culture as the study of relationships between elements in a whole way of life."[3] In addition, he proposes to constitute "an alternative tradition" in which community may be imagined again (1989). In our postmodern "new time" (Stuart Hall), such investment in holistic communities has generally given way to discourse privileging various forms of mobility and exchange.[4] For instance, such is the case with Edward Said's "traveling theory" (1983)[5] and Zigmunt Bauman's reflections on "democratic community" (2001). In my opinion, some of this volume's important essays (Martín-Barbero, Larraín, and Morales, among others) constitute a post-William, sense of community ("alternative tradition") overlapping with a reflection on Latin American Late Modernity.

Martín-Barbero thinks of a notion of community "in which it would be possible to recreate forms of civil deliberation and coexistence, renewing identities and ways of symbolizing conflicts and agreements from the opacity of today's hybridizations and reappropiations" (54). Focusing on Latin American Modernity as a terrain of domination and resistance, his important essays suggest a model of media culture that enhances identities, builds participation, and promotes a democratic civil society: "the transformations of Modernity demand that we consider communication not only as a matter of market and technologies but as a decisive space in the construction of democracy" (45).

In "Postmodernism and Latin American Identity," Jorge Larraín examines the two contradictory ways in which postmodern discourse relates itself to the identity issue and emphasizes discourse as the center of culture and social life. Following Raymond Williams's differentiation between two senses of culture, Larraín distinguishes between postmodern discourse and the feelings, orientations, and social practices of people. On this issue he states:

> Although there is little doubt that the changes occurring in Late Modernity are very momentous and deeply affect individuals, I do not believe that they really get to the point of producing decentered subjects with dislocated identities. (96)

The question that arises from the essays published in this volume is whether or not a combination of the best resources of Modernity theories, along with some new postmodern perspectives on globalization and identity, provide the most useful tool for doing cultural criticism in today's Latin American context. While this question remains open for discussion, a possible answer to it is related to how close these essays are connected to the intellectual tradition of British cultural studies, whose practitioners contextualized its inquires with current sociopolitical struggles and events while portraying a promise of cultural change. Some of this volume's important essays (Martín-Barbero, Brunner, Larraín, Morales, Silva) intersect with a re-vision of the project developed by the Birmingham Center for Contemporary Cultural Studies in the United Kindom—after the 1980s[6]—and imply a rereading and/or a cultural translation of that revised project in response to contemporary Latin American conditions and challenges. I would also add that while all of this volume's essays portray a promise of cultural change (with a low profile), the above-mentioned ones also keep alive a post-Williams social sense of culture, mainly, as a "need to think and feel in common terms" (Williams 1958).

The relationship of this volume's essays with Latin American cultural studies as practiced in the postmodern American academy is not an easy one.[7] For instance, Morales's and Silva's essays have an explicit cultural studies approach. In "Autochthonous Cultures and Global Markets," Morales says:

> The analysis of intercultural relationships in Guatemala implies, from the transdisciplinary perspective of Latin American Cultural Studies, first, identifying the spaces in which the traditional cultures meet the transnational culture industry and, second, describing the transculturalization and hybridization processes that take place in that encounter. (124)

Together with Silva's innovative cultural studies approach, one sees not only a rearticulation of Latin American dominant modes of understanding culture, national ethnicity, and urban space and of representing history, but also the suggestion of a need to disrupt the notion of cultural studies as a theory and practice moving in a unidirectional way from advanced capitalist centers. Focusing on identity as a matter of cultural negotiation, Morales's essay revises the links between Latin American modernity, traditionalism, ethnicity, and nationalism in sectors less integrated to the work market. He also stresses the Guatemalan indigenous people's ability to negotiate their cultural identity within an international market and symbolic space of "participative and democratic interethnic negotiation" (152). Democratic "negotiation" (a key word in Morales's essay) involves not only the representation of an interethnic democratic community but also a sense "of place" in relation to particular and provisional rather than to necessary communities.

The essays in this collective volume suggest that in the contemporary (global/local) culture Latin America is not "fundamentally different" after all. In this sense they contribute to a better understanding of difference and identity in Latin America and situate critical discourse within the discourses of the world's metropolitan centers, something that has long been denied to Latin American cultural studies. As a result, Latin American peripheral (Post)Modernity and theories of culture cease to appear as simple repositories of literature to be processed by hegemonic academic centers in the U.S. and Europe. In contrast with cultural studies practices in the postmodern American academy, these essays do not assume the pedagogical task of transforming popular culture into a site of political analysis. Rather, they focus on a symbolic (and/or social) way of intervening in the production of an active multicultural citizenship and on the revitalization of a democratic public life.[8] They ultimately reject the postmodern notion of a lack of community and speak of Latin America not as a unified entity but as a contingent democratic community.

In conclusion, all this volume's essays converge on at least one of the following points: 1) an interdisciplinary (and/or multidisciplinary) perspective intersecting the humanities and the social sciences; 2) a selective use of postmodern arguments without supposing that Latin America's peripheral modernity has been entirely left behind; 3) an opposition, more or less explicit, to the *Latin Americanism* of the cultural studies practiced in the postmodern American academy, and 4) a democratic cultural politics beyond the limits of the nation-state. In these essays there is a tension between the professional goal of developing methodologies for the interpretation of cultural texts and the public goal of advancing the aims of a progressive cultural politics. In *Latin America Writes Back*: *Postmodernity in the Periphery*, this tension is (still) a critical one and works as a creative stimulus for a democratic cultural politics.

Notes

1. See, for instance, also published in *Hispanic Issues*: Amaryll Chandy, ed. *Latin American Identity and Construction of Difference* (1994); Anthony L. Geist and José B. Monleón, *Modernism and Its Margins* (1999); and Mercedes Durán Cogan and Antonio Gómez Moriana, eds., *National Identities and Sociopolitical Changes in Latin America* (2001).

2. In addition to ones published in *Hispanic Issues*, see, for instance; García Canclini (1999), Moraña, ed. (2000), Moreiras (2000), De la Campa (1999) Beverley and Oviedo, ed. (1993), Yúdice, Franco, and Flores, eds. (1992), Herlinghaus and Walter, ed. (1994), *Nuevo Texto Crítico* 6-7 (1990 and 1991), and *Latin American Perspectives* 27 (2000).

3. William, 1961: 46.

4. See Kuan-Hsing Chen, "The Formation of a Diasporic Intellectual: An Interview with Stuart Hall, in David Morley and Kuan-Hsing Chen," *Stuart Hall. Critical Dialogues in Cultural Studies* (1996): 484-503.

5. Said, 1983.

6. According to Stuart Hall (1996), British cultural studies in the 1990s see Williams's work differently and engages it critically rather than celebratively: "If you need British cultural studies it is because good work is still being done there, you don't need it as the 'origin' of anything. If you want to reconstruct the genealogy, there are texts there which are necessary to work through. . . . I am not suggesting that all the links are broken; but British cultural studies in the 1990s is very significantly different from British cultural studies in the 1970s. It is overwhelmingly preoccupied now with new questions, such as national culture, ethnicity and identities." For the positions of Hall on identity, ethnicity and globalization, see Stuart Hall in King (1997), pp. 19-68.

7. See, for instance, García Canclini (1999; Moraña, ed. (2000), De la Campa (1999), 1-30, 149-73.

8. On symbolic democracy and Latin American cultural studies shifting paradigm, see Machín (2000).

Works Cited

Bauman, Zygmunt. *Community. Seeking Safety in an Insecure World*. Cambridge: Polity Press, 2001.

Beverley, John, and José Oviedo, eds. *boundary* 2 20.3 *The Postmodernism Debate in Latin America*. Durham: Duke UP, 1993.

Chanady, Amaryll, ed. *Latin American Identity and the Construction of Difference*. Minneapolis: Hispanic Issues/U of Minnesota P, 1994.

De la Campa, Román. *Latin Americanism*. Minneapolis-London: U of Minnesota P. 1999.

García Canclini, Néstor. *Culturas Híbridas. Estrategias para entrar y salir de la posmodernidad*. México: Grijalbo, 1990.

_____. *La globalización imaginada*. México: Paidós, 1999.

_____. "Los estudios culturales: elaboración intelectual del intercambio América Latina-Estados Unidos." *Papeles de Montevideo*, 1 (1997): pp. 45-58.

Hall, Stuart. "Cultural Studies and the Politics of Internationalization. An Interview with Stuart Hall by Kuan-Hsing Cheng," in Morley, David and Kuan-Hsing

Cheng, *Stuart Hall. Critical Dialogues in Cultural Studies*. London and New York: Routledge, 1996, 392-408.

_____. "Cultural Studies and its Theoretical Legacies" in Grossberg, Lawrence, Gary Nelson, and Paula Treichler, eds. *Cultural Studies*. New York: Routledge, 1992, 277-86.

_____. "The local and the Global: Globalization and Ethnicity," in King, Richard, ed. *Culture, Globalization and the World System*, 1997, 19-39.

Herlinghaus, Herman, and Monika Walter, eds. *Posmodernidad en la periferia, Enfoques latinoamericanos de la nueva teoría cultural*. Berlin: Langer Verlag, 1994.

Hobsbawm, Eric. *Nations and Nationalism since 1780: Programme, Myth, Reality*. Cambridge: Cambridge UP, 1990.

King, Richard ed. *Culture, Globalization and the World System*. Minneapolis: U of Minnesota P, 1997.

Machín, Horacio. "Intérpretes culturales y democracia simbólica," in Mabel Moraña, *Nuevas perspectivas desde/sobre América Latina. El desafío de los estudios culturales*. Editorial Cuarto Propio, Chile, and Instituto Internacional de Literatura Latinoamericana, Pittsburgh: U of Pittsburgh, 2000, 35-350.

Machín Horacio, and Nicholas Spadaccini. Afterword. "Latin American Identities and Globalization," in Mercedes F. Durán Cogan and Antonio Gómez Moriana, eds., *National Identities and Sociopolitical Change in Latin America*. Hispanic Issues v. 23. New York and London: Routledge, 2001, 434-44.

Martín-Barbero, Jesús, *De los medios a las mediaciones*. Mexico: G. Gilli, 1987.

Moraña, Mabel. *Nuevas perspectivas desde/sobre América Latina. El desafío de los estudios culturales*. Editorial Cuarto Propio, Chile, and Instituto Internacional de Literatura Latinoamericana, Pittsburgh: University of Pittsburgh, 2000.

Morley, David, and Kuan-Hsing Cheng. *Stuart Hall. Critical Dialogues in Cultural Studies*. London and New York: Routledge, 1996.

Ortiz, Renato. *A moderna tradição Brasileira*. São Paulo: Brasilense, 1988.

_____. "From Incomplete Modernity to World Modernity," in *Daedalus, Journal of the American Academy of Arts and Sciences*, Winter 2000: 249-60.

Said, Edward. *The World, the Text, and the Critic*. Cambridge: Harvard, UP. 1983.

Williams, Raymond. *The Long Revolution*. New York: Columbia UP. 1961.

_____. *The Country and the City*. London: Chatto and Windus, 1973.

_____. *Politics and Letters: Interviews with New Left Review*. London: New Left Books, 1979.

_____. *Keywords. A Vocabulary of Culture and Society*; rev. ed. New York: Oxford UP. 1983.

_____. *The Politics of Modernism. Against the New Conformists*. London and New York: Verso, 1989.

Yúdice, George, Jean Franco, and Juan Flores, eds. *On Edge. The Crisis of Contemporary Latin American Culture*. Minneapolis and London: U of Minnesota P, 1992.

◆ **Contributors**

Fernando Ainsa is an Uruguayan writer and literary critic. PhD in Law and Social Sciences (1965). Since 1972 he worked in UNESCO; since 1991 he directed the editorial department of Ediciones UNESCO in Paris. Author of essays, *Necesidad de la utopía* (Buenos Aires: Tupac Ed., 1990), *De la edad de oro a El Dorado* (México: FCE, 1992), *Historia, mito, utopía y ficción de la Ciudad de los Césares* (Madrid: Alianza Universidad, 1992), *La Reconstruction de l'utopie* (París: Ed. Arcantères/UNESCO, 1997); literary criticism, *Las trampas de Onetti* (Montevideo: Alfa, 1970), *Tiempo reconquistado* (Geminis, 1977), *Los buscadores de la utopía* (Caracas: Monte Avila, 1977), *Identidad cultural de Iberoamérica en su narrativa* (Madrid: Gredos, 1986), *Nuevas fronteras de la narrativa uruguaya (1960-1993)* (Montevideo: Trilce, 1993); and novels, *El testigo* (Alfa, 1964), *Concierto asombroso* (Alfa, 1968), *De papa en adelante* (Monte Avila, 1970), *El paraíso de la reina María Julia* (Montevideo: Fin de Siglo, 1997). His work has been translated into more than twenty languages.

Daniel Altamiranda is an Argentinian literary critic. PhD from Arizona State University and Universidad de Buenos Aires. Professor of Modern Literature in the Instituto de Enseñanza Superior no. 1 of Buenos Aires. Adjunct Professor at the Universidad de Buenos Aires, Visiting Professor at Arizona State University. Literary theory, contemporary Latin American Literature and Golden Age Drama publications, including edition of the comedy *Basta callar*, de Pedro Calderón de la Barca (Kassel: Reichenberger, 1995), *Paralogías*: *Una lectura del mito del encuentro entre España y América* (Buenos Aires: Ediciones del Valle, 1996, with Hernán Thomas), a selection of critical studies about Latin American Literature *Spanish American Literature*: *A Collection of Essays* (Hamden, Conn.: Garland, 1998), 5 vols., and *Teorías literarias* (Buenos Aires: Editorial Docencia, 2001), 2 vols.

José Joaquín Brunner is a Chilean sociologist and student of contemporary culture. In the 1990's he served as Minister Secretary of the Government. From 1980 and 1988 he was Dean of the College of Latin American Social Sciences (FLACSO) in Santiago, Chile. His outstanding publications include *Un espejo trizado*: *Ensayos sobre cultura y políticas culturales* (Santiago: FLACSO, 1988), *América Latina*: *Cultura y modernidad* (México: Grijalbo, 1992), *Bienvenidos a la modernidad* (Santiago: Planeta, 1994), and most notably *Cartografías de la modernidad* (Santiago: Dolmen Ed., 1994) and *Globalización cultural y posmodernidad* (Mexico: FCE, 1998).

Raúl Bueno is a Peruvian critic and poet. Professor of Hispanic Literature at Dartmouth College (New Hampshire), and emeritus from San Marcos (1996). Heads journal *Revista de crítica literaria latinoamericana*. Published *Metodología del análisis semiótico* (Lima, 1980, in collaboration with D. Blanco), *Poesía hispanoamericana de vanguardia*: *Procedimientos de interpretación textual* (Lima, 1985) and *Escribir en Hispanoamérica Ensayos sobre teoría y crítica literarias* (Lima/Pittsburgh, 1991). Current research includes metaphors of culture in Latin America and effects of vanguardism in Latin America.

Abelardo Castillo is an Argentinian novelist, short story writer, playwright and essayist. Born in San Pedro (province of Buenos Aires). Member of Consejo de Presidencia de la Asamblea Permanente por los Derechos Humanos. Founder and head of important Argentinian literary journals: *El grillo de papel* (1959-1960), *El escarabajo de oro* (1961-1974) and *El ornitorrinco* (1977-1986). His publications include novels, *La casa de ceniza* (Buenos Aires: Estuario, 1967, Emecé, 1994), *El que tiene sed* (Emecé, 1985), *Crónica de un iniciado* (Emecé, 1991, Premio Club de los Trece 1992); short stories *Las otras puertas* (Premio Casa de las Américas, 1961), *Cuentos crueles* (J. Alvarez, 1966), *Las panteras y el templo* (Sudamericana, 1976), *Las maquinarias de la noche* (Emecé, 1992); theater, *El otro Judas* (1961), *Israfel* (1964); and essays, *Las palabras y los días* (Emecé, 1988) and *Ser escritor* (Perfil, 1997). Numerous awards include national award Premio Nacional Esteban Echeverría (1993) for his narrative writings.

Mempo Giardinelli is an Argentinian novelist, short story writer and essayist. Born in Resistencia, Chaco. Lived in exile in Mexico between 1976-1985. In Buenos Aires he founded and directed the journal *Puro cuento* (1986-1992). Currently mantains dual residency in Chaco and in Buenos Aires. He has published novels, *La revolución en bicicleta* (Barcelona: Pomaire, 1980), *El cielo con las manos* (Hanover, New Hampshire: Ed. del Norte, 1981), *¿Por qué prohibieron el circo?* (México: Oasis, 1983), *Luna caliente* (Oasis, award-winning Premio Nacional de Novela 1983, in México; filmed), *Qué solos se quedan los muertos* (Buenos Aires: Sudamericana, 1985), *Santo Oficio de la Memoria* (Barcelona: Norma, 1991, Rómulo Gallegos Award in 1993), *El décimo infierno* (Buenos Aires: Planeta, 1999, transl. *The Tenth Circle*, Pittsburg: Latin American Literary Review Press, 2001); short stories, *Vidas ejemplares* (Ed. del Norte, 1982), *La entrevista* (Madrid: Almarabu, 1986), *Luli la viajera* (1988), *El castigo de Dios* (Buenos Aires: Tesis, 1993) and *Imposible equilibrio* (Buenos Aires: Planeta); essays, *El género negro* (México: UNAM, 1984), *Así se escribe un cuento* (Buenos Aires: Beas, 1992), and *El país de las maravillas: los argentinos en el fin del milenio* (Buenos Aires: Planeta, 1998).

Rafael Ángel Herra is a Costa Rican philosopher, poet, novelist and essayist. PhD from University Johannes Gutenberg of Maguncia. Also studied classic and Romance philology and comparative literature. He is Professor of Philosophy at Universidad de Costa Rica and numerary member of Costa Rican Language Academy. Since 1973 he has directed and edited the UCR's journal *Revista de Filosofía*. He was Visiting Profesor at the Universities of Bamberg y Giessen in Germany. Was director of School of Collective Communication Sciences at UCR. Presently he is ambassador of Costa Rica in Germany. His publications include essay, *Sartre y los prolegómenos a la antropología* (San José: Ed. Univ. de CR, 1968, 1983), *Violencia, tecnocratismo y vida cotidiana* (Ed. Costa Rica, 1984, 1991, translated into French and edited in Quebec), *El desorden del espíritu: Conversaciones con Amighetti* (Ed. Univ. de CR, 1987), *Lo monstruoso y lo bello* (Ed. Univ. de CR, 1988), *Las cosas de este mundo* (Ed. Univ. de CR, 1990), *¿Sobrevivirá el marxismo?* (Ed. Univ. de CR, 1991); novels, *La guerra prodigiosa* (Ed. Costa Rica, 1986), *El genio de la botella* (Ed. Univ. de CR, 1990), *Viaje al reino de los deseos* (Ed. Univ. de CR, 1992); short stories, *El soñador del penúltimo sueño* (Ed. Costa Rica, 1983), *Había una vez un tirano llamado Edipo* (Euned, 1983); and poetry, *Escribo para que existas* (Ed. Univ. de CR, 1993).

Jorge Larraín is a Chilean sociologist and student of contemporary cultural processes. Ph.D. from the University of Sussex, England. He was Professor of Social Theory, Department of Cultural Studies and Sociology, University of Birmingham (1977-1997) and Professor and researcher at Latin American Institute of Doctrine and Social Studies (ILADES) in Santiago de Chile (1995-1997). He is currently Chair of Sociology Department, Universidad Alberto Hurtado. He was the First Chair of Department of Cultural Studies, University of Birmingham (1988-1993). His outstanding publications include *The Concept of Ideology* (London: Hutchinson/U of Georgia, 1979), *Marxism and Ideology* (Macmillan, 1983), *A Reconstruction of Historical Materialism* (Allen & Unwin, 1986), *Theories of Development* (Cambridge: Polity Press, 1989), *Ideology and Cultural Identity: Modernity and the Third World Presence* (Polity Press, 1994), *Modernidad: Razón e identidad en América Latina* (Santiago: Andrés Bello, 1996, trnsl. *Identity and Modernity in Latin America*, Polity Press, 2000), and *Identidad chilena* (Santiago: LOM Ediciones, 2001).

Horacio Machín is Assistant Professor of Spanish American Literature and Culture at the University of Minnesota. His publications include several essays in the area of Latin American cultural studies and his present research spans a number of issues, including the changing concepts of nation and nationalism in the current process of globalization. His forthcoming volume (co-edited) is titled *Old Nations/New Nations: Hispanic America, a Comparative Perspective*.

Jesús Martín Barbero is a Spanish-Colombian student of communication and contemporary culture. Born in Avila, Spain. He has lived in Colombia since 1963. PhD in Philosophy, Lovaina, Belgium. Founded Department of Sciences of Communication, Universidad del Valle, Cali. Past-president of ALAIC (Latin American Association of Communication Researchers). His outstanding publications include *Comunicación masiva: Discurso y poder* (Quito: Ciespal, 1978), *Ensayos de teoría literaria* (Cali: Univ. del Valle, 1983), *De los medios a las mediaciones* (México: G. Gili, 1987, transl. *Communication, Culture and Hegemony: From the Media to Mediations*, London: SAGE Publ., 1993), *Procesos de comunicación y matrices de cultura* (G. Gili, 1988) and *Televisión y melodrama: Géneros y lecturas de la telenovela en Colombia* (Bogotá: Tercer Mundo, 1992), and conversations *Contemporaneidad latinoamericana y análisis cultural* (Frankkfurt am Main: Vervuert, 2000).

Mario Roberto Morales is a Guatemalan writer, critic, and journalist. Lived in exile in the 1980s, later was professor of Latin American literature at the University of Northern Iowa. Ph.D. from Pittsburg. Currently resides in Guatemala. His publications include essays, *La ideología y la lírica de la lucha armada* (Guatemala: Ed. Univ. de Guatemala, 1994) and *La articulación de las diferencias, o el síndrome de Maximón. Los discursos literarios y políticos del debate interétnico en Guatemala* (Guatemala: FLACSO, 1998); prize-winning novels *Obraje* (1971) and *Los demonios salvajes* (1977, 1993), novel *El esplendor de la pirámide* (1986, 1993), novel-testimonio *Señores bajo los árboles* (Guatemala: Artemis, 1994, Transl. *Face of the Earth, Heart of the Sky*, Tempe: Bilingual Press, 2000), political memoir *Los que se fueron por la libre* (1998), and a "virtual novel for an interactive reader" *El angel de la retaguardia* (1997). Recently edited *Stoll-Menchú: La invención de la memoria* (Guatemala: Consucultura, 2001).

Osvaldo Pelletieri is an Argentinian student of theater and director. PhD in Philosophy and Letters, Universidad de Buenos Aires. He is director of Argentinian and Latin American Art History Institute, College of Philosophy and Letters, Universidad de Buenos Aires and researcher for CONICET. He is founder and director, GETEA (Argentinian Theater Studies Group); director journal *Teatro XXI*. He has been Visiting Professor at the Universities of Montreal, Valencia, Trieste, UNAM and the Universidad de la República (Uruguay). His numerous publications focus on literature theory and criticism and Argentinian and Latin American theater, including *Cien años de teatro argentino, 1886-1990* (Buenos Aires: Galerna, 1990), *Teatro argentino contemporáneo: 1980-1990* (Galerna, 1994), and *Una historia interrumpida: Teatro argentino moderno, 1949-1976* (Galerna, 1997). Has directed plays written by national and international authors, including: *Don Chicho* (Pepino el 88 Award for Best Director, 1979-1980), *El movimiento continuo* and *El hombrecito* (nominated for ACE award for best director, 1992-1993).

Nelly Richards is a Chilean art critic. She is editor of journal Revista de crítica cultural (Santiago, 1990-) and director of Certificate of Cultural Critique, Universidad Arcis, Santiago de Chile, 1997-1999, supported by Rockefeller Foundation. She was part of the artistic movement against Pinochet's dictatorship. Her publications include *La estratificación de los márgenes* (Santiago: F. Zegers, 1989), *Masculino/femenino: Prácticas de la diferenecia y cultura democrática* (F. Zegers, 1993), *La insubordinación de los signos: Cambio político, transformaciones culturales y poéticas de la crisis* (Cuarto Propio, 1994), *Art from Latin America: La cita transcultural* (Sydney: Museum of Cont. Art, 1996), and Residuos y metáforas: *Ensayos de* *crítica cultural sobre el Chile de la transición* (Santiago: Cuarto Propio, 1998).

Armando Silva is a Colombian semiologist and student of urbanism. PhD, University of California. He studied philosophy, semiotics, literature, and psychoanalysis in Colombia, Spain, Italy, France and the United States. He is director of Institute of Studies in Communication, Universidad Nacional de Colombia. His publications include *Imaginarios Urbanos: Bogotá y São Paulo: Cultura y comunicación urbana en América Latina* (Bogotá: Tercer Mundo, 1992, four consecutive editions), *Proyectar la comunicación* (Tercer Mundo, 1997), *The Family Photo Album* (electronic edition, University of California, 1996).

Hernán Thomas is an Argentinian historian of technology. PhD in Political Science and Technology, Universidad Estadual de Campinas, Brasil. He is currently Professor in Social Sciences Department, Universidad Nacional de Luján, Argentina. His research areas include sociology, history of technology and politics of technological innovation. His publications include *Paralogías* (1996, with D. Altamiranda), *Sur-desarrollo: Producción de tecnología en países subdesarrollados* (Buenos Aires: Centro Editor de América Latina, 1995).

◆ Index

Compiled by Heidi Ann García and Barbara D. Riess